THE ATLAS OF JEWISH HISTORY

THE ATLAS OF JEWISH HISTORY

Completely Revised and Updated

Martin Gilbert
Fellow of Merton College, Oxford

Cartography by ARTHUR BANKS, TERRY BICKNELL and TIM ASPDEN

WILLIAM MORROW AND COMPANY, INC.
NEW YORK

Gilbert, Martin. 1936-
    The atlas of Jewish history / Martin Gilbert.
        p.   cm.
    Published in Great Britain as: Jewish history atlas / Martin Gilbert. 4th ed. London : Weidenfeld and Nicolson, 1992.
    Includes bibliographical references.
    ISBN 0-688-12264-7
    1. Jews—History. 2. Historical geography—Maps. 3. Israel—Historical geography—Maps. 4. Middle East—Historical geography—Maps. I. Gilbert, Martin, 1936– Jewish history atlas.
    II. Title.
G1030.G45 1993 ‹G&M›
911′.56—dc20   92-18050
                                                                                      CIP
                                                                                     MAP

Printed in the United States of America

First U.S. Edition

1 2 3 4 5 6 7 8 9 10

Dedicated to the memory of Terry Bicknell
cartographer and friend

Preface

This atlas traces the world-wide Jewish migrations from ancient
Mesopotamia to modern Israel. It seeks to follow the diverse—and sometimes
obscure—path of a far-ranging people, and to map their strange experiences
in good times and bad.

My original concern was to avoid undue emphasis upon the many horrific
aspects of Jewish history. I wished to portray with equal force the
construction, achievements and normalities of Jewish life through almost
four thousand years. In part I believe that I have succeeded; for there are many
maps of traders, philosophers, financiers, settlers and sages. But as my
research into Jewish history progressed, I was surprised, depressed, and to
some extent overwhelmed by the perpetual and irrational violence which
pursued the Jews in every century and to almost every corner of the globe.
If, therefore, persecution, expulsion, torture, humiliation, and mass murder
haunt these pages, it is because they also haunt the Jewish story.

But not all terrors are unmitigated; and I have felt a great relief in being
able also to map the other side of the coin—the Jewish revolts against
Roman, Chinese and Persian oppression—the often repeated pattern of mutual
self-help and communal charity, the self-defence leagues organized against
the Russian and Ukrainian pogroms, the brave if hopeless risings in ghetto
and concentration camp during the Nazi era, and the stubborn resistance to
Arab pressures by modern Israel.

If this Atlas can help to answer even a small portion of the questions which
Jews so often ask about themselves, or can tell Christians something more
about the varied experiences of their neighbours, it will have served a
purpose. In particular, I hope that the maps succeed in portraying the complex
comings and goings of many different sorts of Jews, and the extraordinary
diversity of the Jewish saga.

In this Atlas I have tried to look at the role of the Jews in their
different national settings, and show their reaction to persecution, whether by
dispersal, acceptance or defence. Both in resisting the continual pressure of
hostile societies and in braving the dangers of flight and exile, the Jewish people
have shown high courage and a keen capacity to rise again; "trampled into the

dust" as Cardinal Manning described it, "and yet never combining with the dust into which it is trampled."

For those who wish to follow up some of the themes covered by the maps, I have provided a short bibliography. In it I have included a few general books, together with a number of specialist works in which I found information for remote or neglected topics.

Many of my maps are intended to make certain obscure episodes in Jewish history better known, if only in outline. There are many equally fascinating problems on which no detailed research has yet been done; and the history of the Jews which most people know is primarily the history of those episodes on which books or monographs have been written. There are still many areas of darkness. But as I hope this Atlas shows, those aspects of Jewish history which can be mapped are full of unusual details and dramatic moments, ranging over every continent and every civilization, and adding a unique dimension to the story of mankind.

Twenty-two years have now passed since the first edition of this atlas. The final maps of this fourth edition show the main developments in Jewish history since then. These include the emigration of more than half a million Jews from the Soviet Union to Israel between 1970 and 1990 (map 122). This map also shows Operation Solomon, which, with Operation Moses (map 119), brought more than 25,000 Ethiopian Jews to Israel.

I have brought up to date the map showing the number of non-Jews who were honoured for saving Jewish lives in the Second World War (map 104), and the map showing the number of Jews worldwide: this shows the Jewish population of Israel reaching four million in 1991 (map 123).

Several of the earlier maps have been redrawn with extra material, including a map showing Blood Libel accusations in the Middle Ages and beyond, and two maps showing the scale of Jewish resistance during the Holocaust.

I am grateful in this new edition to the cartographic skills of Tim Aspden, and I should once more welcome any notice of errors, as well as suggestions for further maps.

MARTIN GILBERT
Merton College, Oxford

25 October 1991

You may say you have been oppressed and persecuted – that has been your power! You have been hammered into very fine steel, and that is why you have never been broken.

LLOYD GEORGE IN 1925

List of Maps

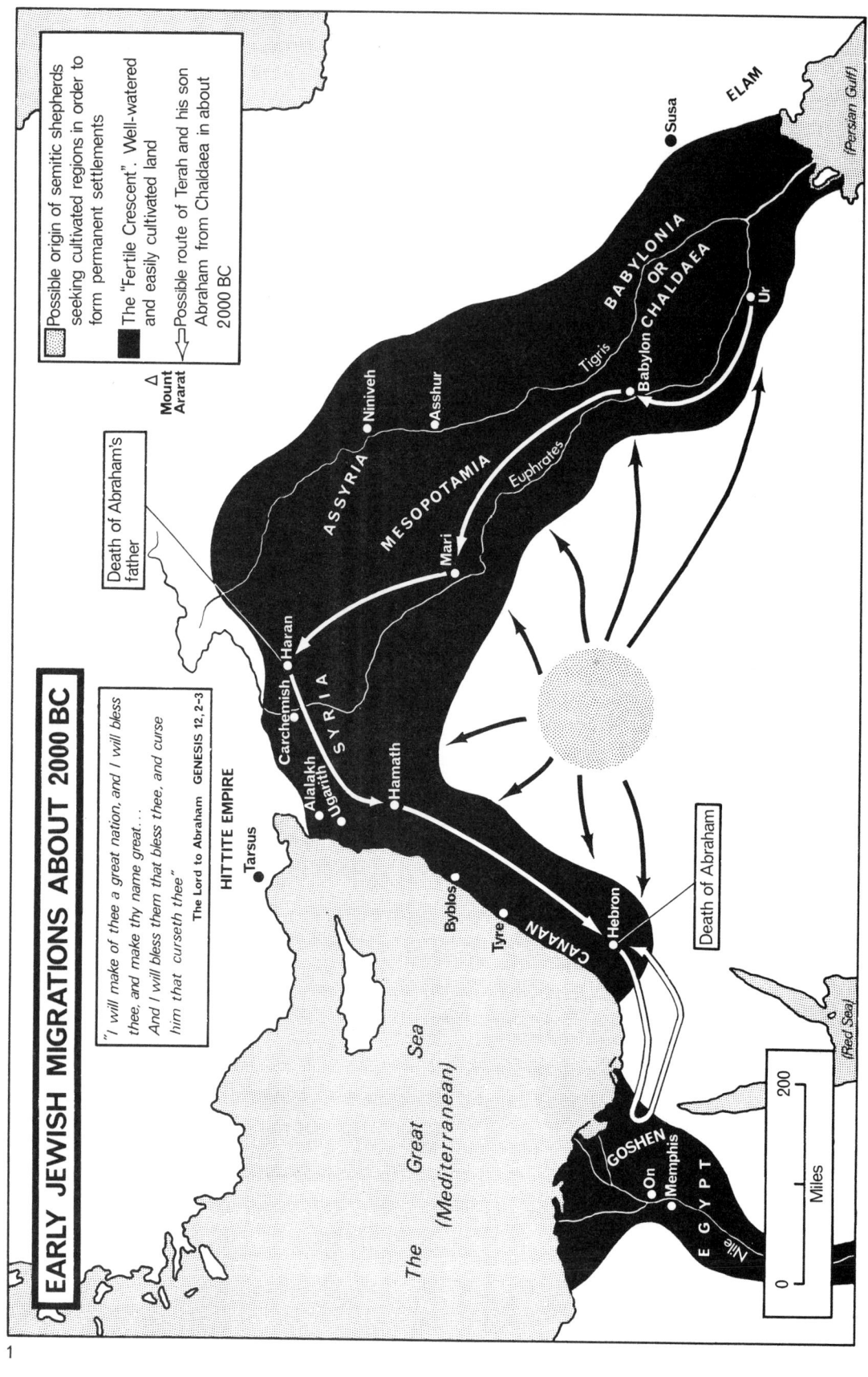

EARLY JEWISH MIGRATIONS ABOUT 2000 BC

"I will make of thee a great nation, and I will bless thee, and make thy name great...
And I will bless them that bless thee, and curse him that curseth thee"

The Lord to Abraham GENESIS 12, 2-3

Possible origin of semitic shepherds seeking cultivated regions in order to form permanent settlements

The "Fertile Crescent". Well-watered and easily cultivated land

Possible route of Terah and his son Abraham from Chaldaea in about 2000 BC

Death of Abraham's father

Death of Abraham

△ Mount Ararat

HITTITE EMPIRE

Tarsus

Carchemish

Haran

Alalakh
Ugarith

S Y R I A

Hamath

Byblos

Tyre

C A N A A N

Hebron

The Great Sea
(Mediterranean)

GOSHEN

On
Memphis

E G Y P T

Nile

(Red Sea)

Mari

MESOPOTAMIA

ASSYRIA

Nineveh

Asshur

Tigris

Euphrates

Babylon

BABYLONIA
OR
CHALDAEA

Ur

Susa

ELAM

(Persian Gulf)

Miles

0   200

1

FROM SLAVERY TO THE PROMISED LAND

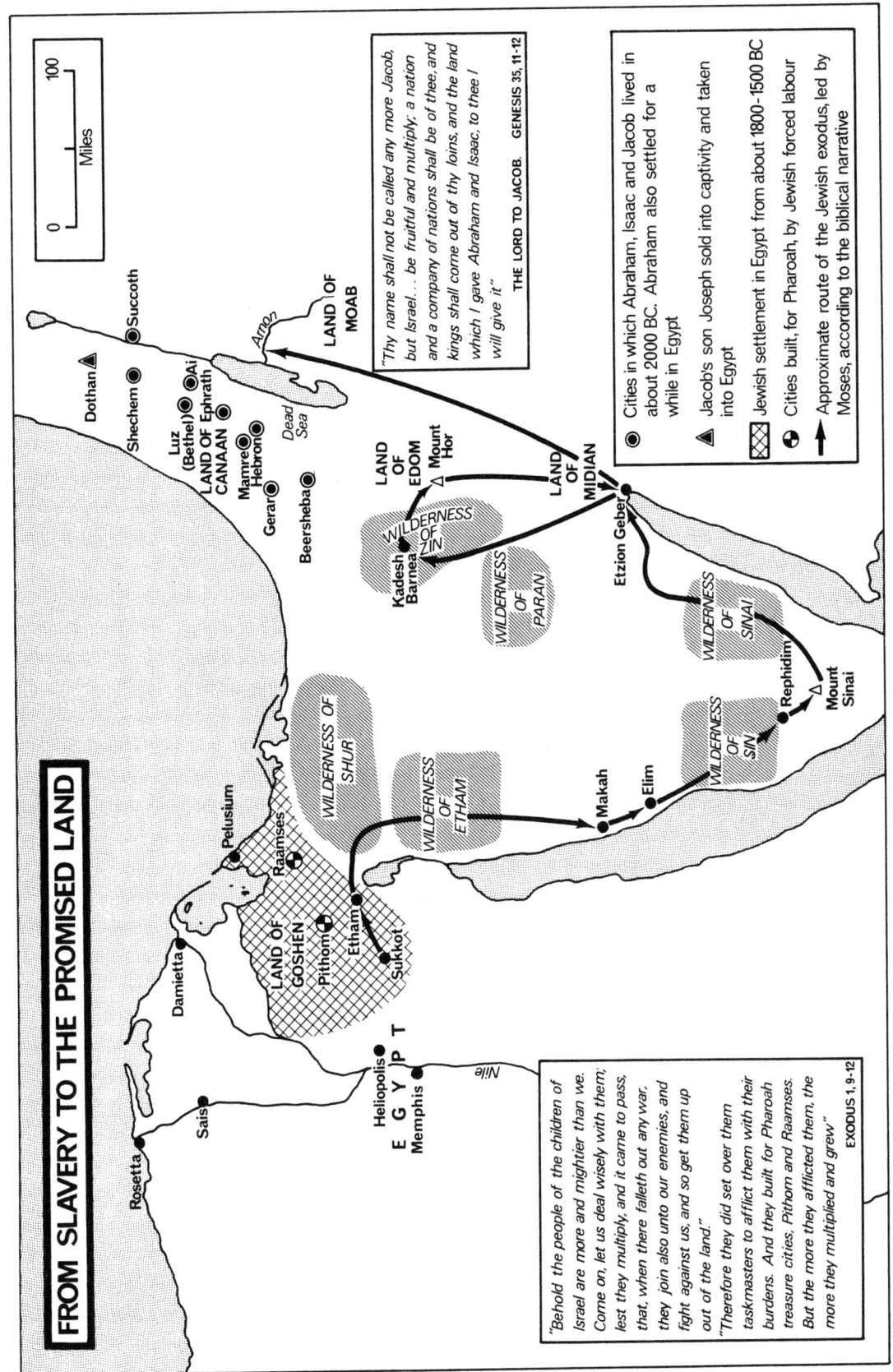

"Thy name shall not be called any more Jacob, but Israel . . . be fruitful and multiply; a nation and a company of nations shall be of thee, and kings shall come out of thy loins, and the land which I gave Abraham and Isaac, to thee I will give it."

THE LORD TO JACOB.   GENESIS 35, 11-12

◉ Cities in which Abraham, Isaac and Jacob lived in about 2000 BC. Abraham also settled for a while in Egypt

▲ Jacob's son Joseph sold into captivity and taken into Egypt

▨ Jewish settlement in Egypt from about 1800-1500 BC

◐ Cities built, for Pharoah, by Jewish forced labour

↑ Approximate route of the Jewish exodus, led by Moses, according to the biblical narrative

"Behold the people of the children of Israel are more and mightier than we. Come on, let us deal wisely with them; lest they multiply, and it come to pass, that, when there falleth out any war, they join also unto our enemies, and fight against us, and so get them up out of the land."

"Therefore they did set over them taskmasters to afflict them with their burdens. And they built for Pharoah treasure cities, Pithom and Raamses. But the more they afflicted them, the more they multiplied and grew."

EXODUS 1, 9-12

2

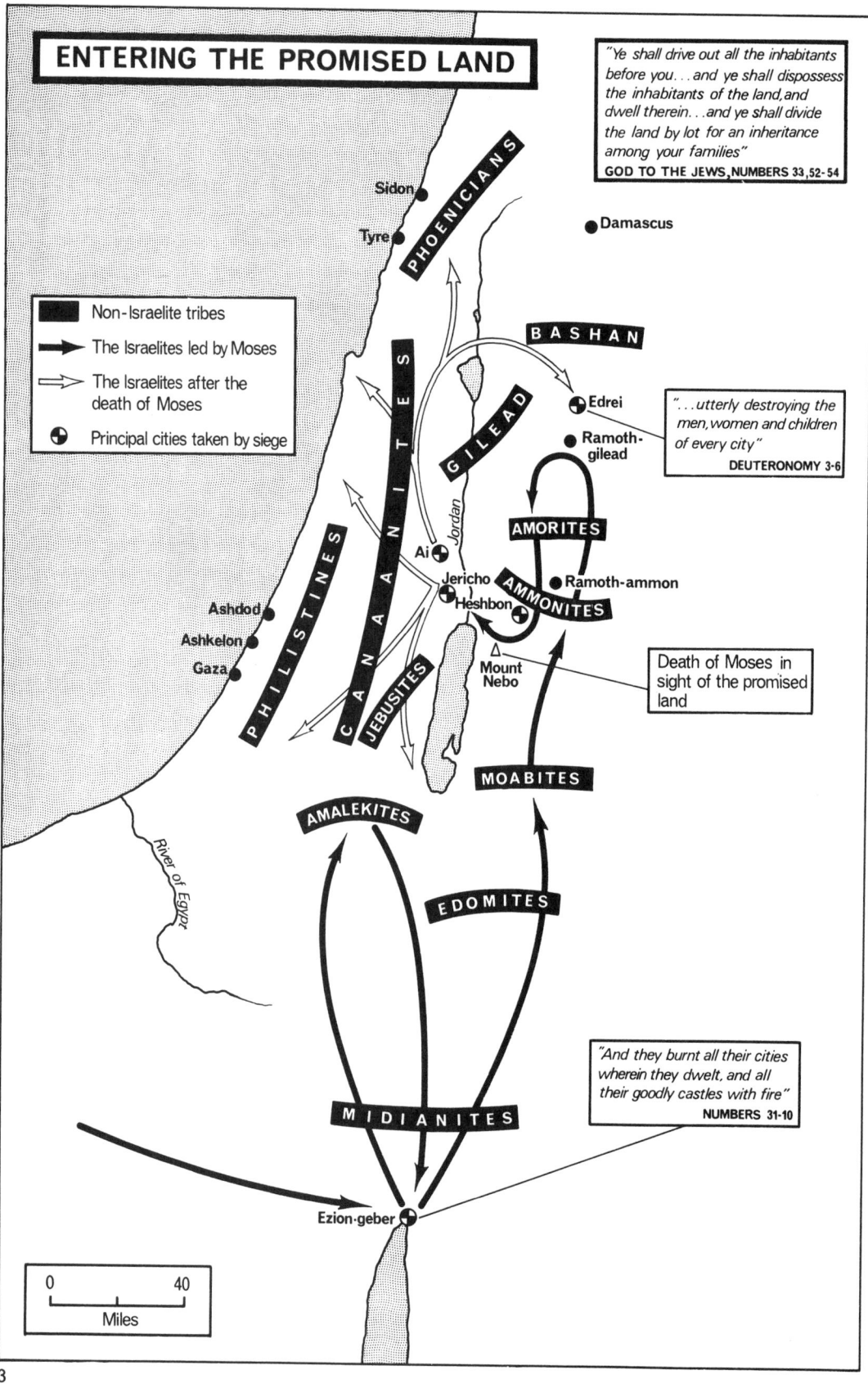

ENTERING THE PROMISED LAND

"Ye shall drive out all the inhabitants before you...and ye shall dispossess the inhabitants of the land, and dwell therein...and ye shall divide the land by lot for an inheritance among your families"
GOD TO THE JEWS, NUMBERS 33,52-54

Sidon

Tyre

PHOENICIANS

Damascus

Legend:
- Non-Israelite tribes
- The Israelites led by Moses
- The Israelites after the death of Moses
- Principal cities taken by siege

BASHAN

GILEAD

Edrei

Ramoth-gilead

AMORITES

"...utterly destroying the men, women and children of every city"
DEUTERONOMY 3-6

C A N A A N I T E S

Jordan

Ai

Jericho

Heshbon

AMMONITES

Ramoth-ammon

PHILISTINES

Ashdod

Ashkelon

Gaza

JEBUSITES

Mount Nebo

Death of Moses in sight of the promised land

MOABITES

AMALEKITES

EDOMITES

River of Egypt

"And they burnt all their cities wherein they dwelt, and all their goodly castles with fire"
NUMBERS 31-10

M I D I A N I T E S

Ezion-geber

0   40
Miles

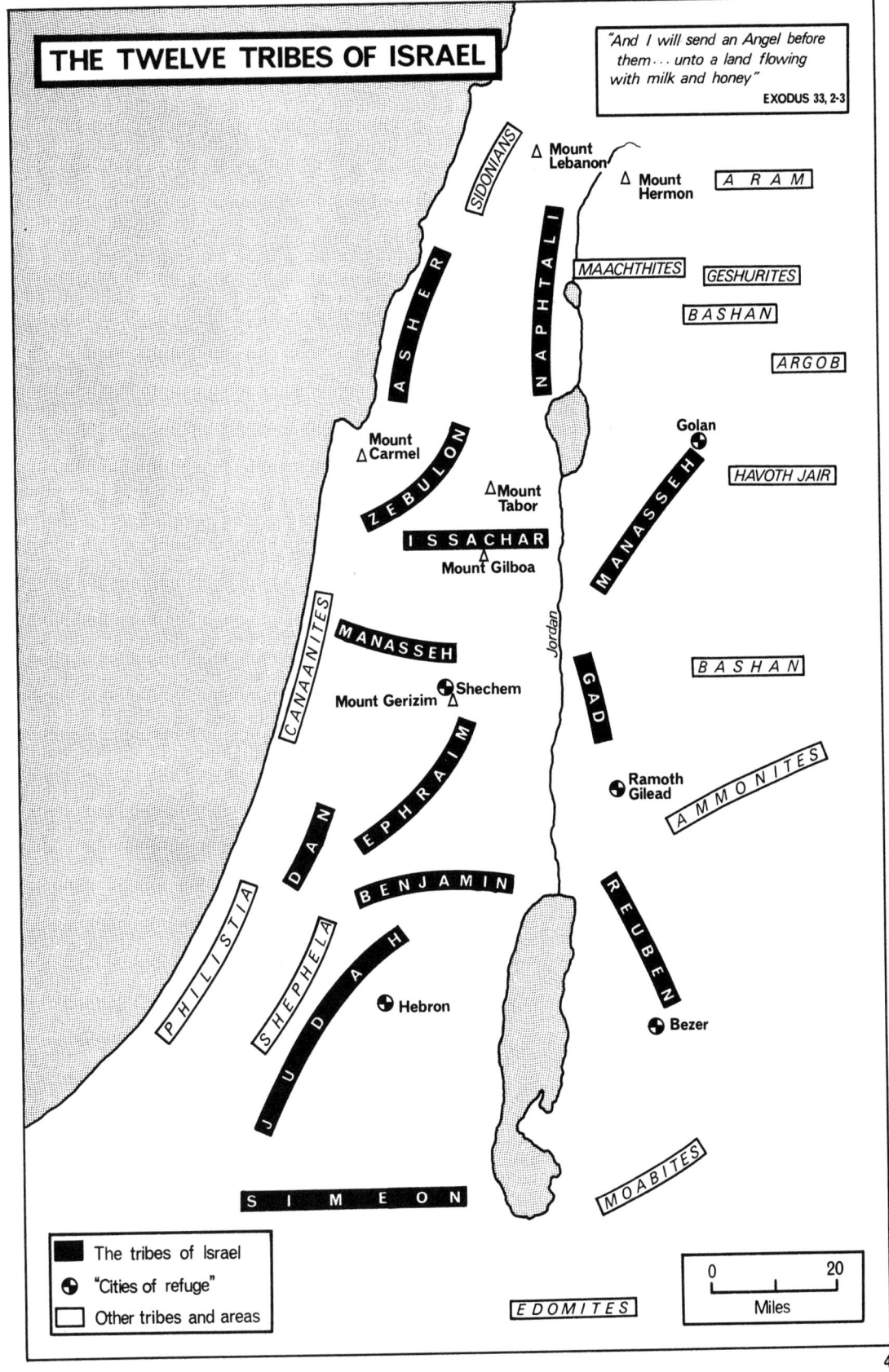

THE TWELVE TRIBES OF ISRAEL

"And I will send an Angel before them... unto a land flowing with milk and honey"

EXODUS 33, 2-3

△ Mount Lebanon
△ Mount Hermon
A R A M

SIDONIANS

MAACHTHITES
GESHURITES
B A S H A N
ARGOB

ASHER

NAPHTALI

Golan ✚
HAVOTH JAIR

Mount
△ Carmel

ZEBULON
△ Mount Tabor

ISSACHAR
△
Mount Gilboa

MANASSEH

Jordan

CANAANITES

MANASSEH

Mount Gerizim
✚ Shechem
△

B A S H A N

GAD

EPHRAIM

Ramoth ✚ Gilead

AMMONITES

DAN

BENJAMIN

REUBEN

PHILISTIA

SHEPHELA

J U D A H

✚ Hebron

✚ Bezer

S I M E O N

MOABITES

	The tribes of Israel
✚	"Cities of refuge"
	Other tribes and areas

0 ——— 20
Miles

E D O M I T E S

4

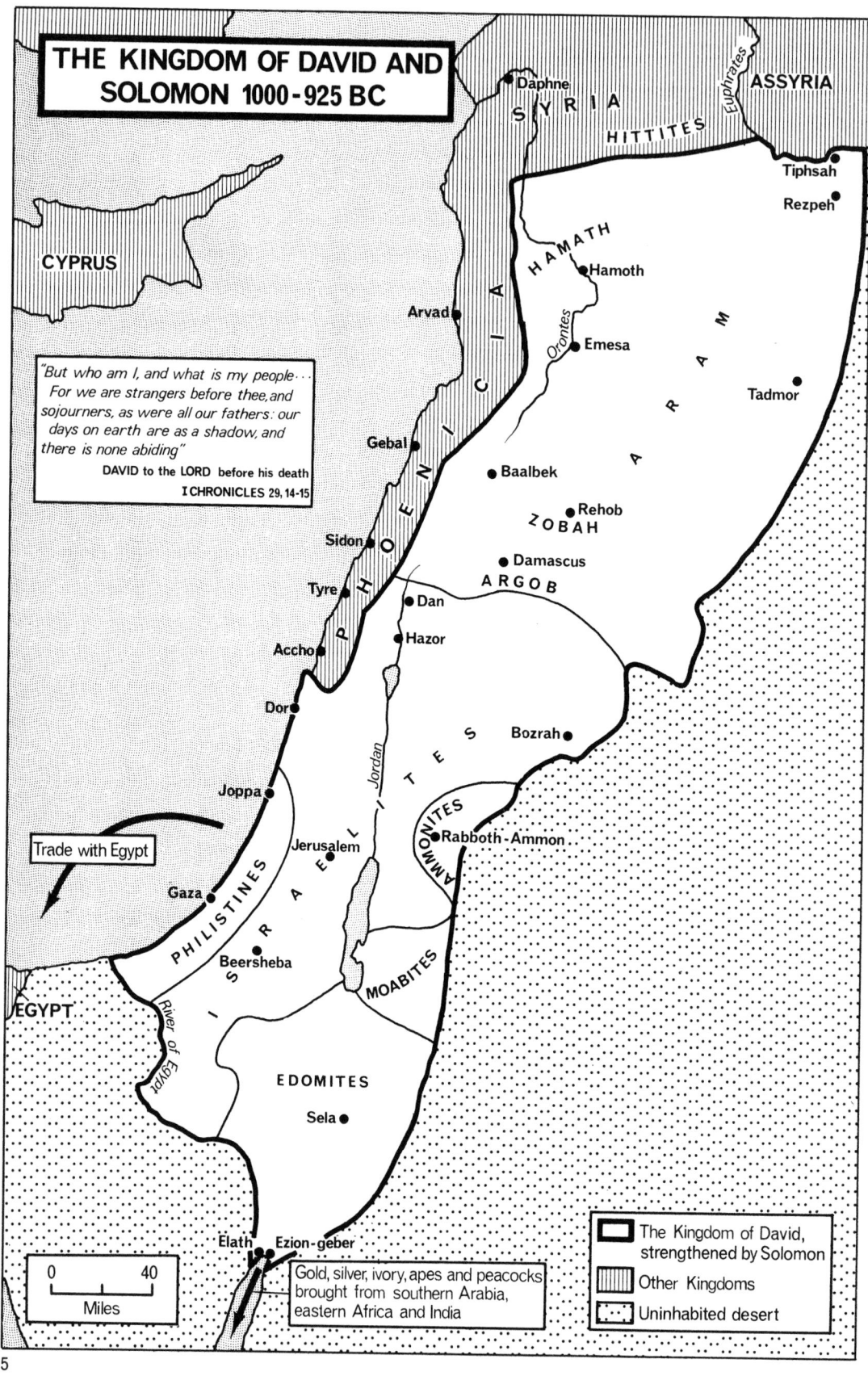

THE KINGDOM OF DAVID AND SOLOMON 1000-925 BC

SYRIA

Daphne

HITTITES

ASSYRIA

Euphrates

Tiphsah

Rezpeh

CYPRUS

H A M A T H

Hamoth

Arvad

Orontes

Emesa

Tadmor

A R A M

"But who am I, and what is my people...
For we are strangers before thee, and
sojourners, as were all our fathers: our
days on earth are as a shadow, and
there is none abiding"

DAVID to the LORD before his death
I CHRONICLES 29, 14-15

Gebal

Baalbek

Rehob

Z O B A H

Sidon

Damascus

Tyre

A R G O B

Dan

Accho

Hazor

Dor

Bozrah

Joppa

Trade with Egypt

Jerusalem

Jordan

AMMON

Rabboth-Ammon

Gaza

PHILISTINES

ISRAEL

Beersheba

MOABITES

EGYPT

River of Egypt

E D O M I T E S

Sela

PHOENICIA

HITTITES

Elath Ezion-geber

Gold, silver, ivory, apes and peacocks
brought from southern Arabia,
eastern Africa and India

0   40
Miles

The Kingdom of David,
strengthened by Solomon

Other Kingdoms

Uninhabited desert

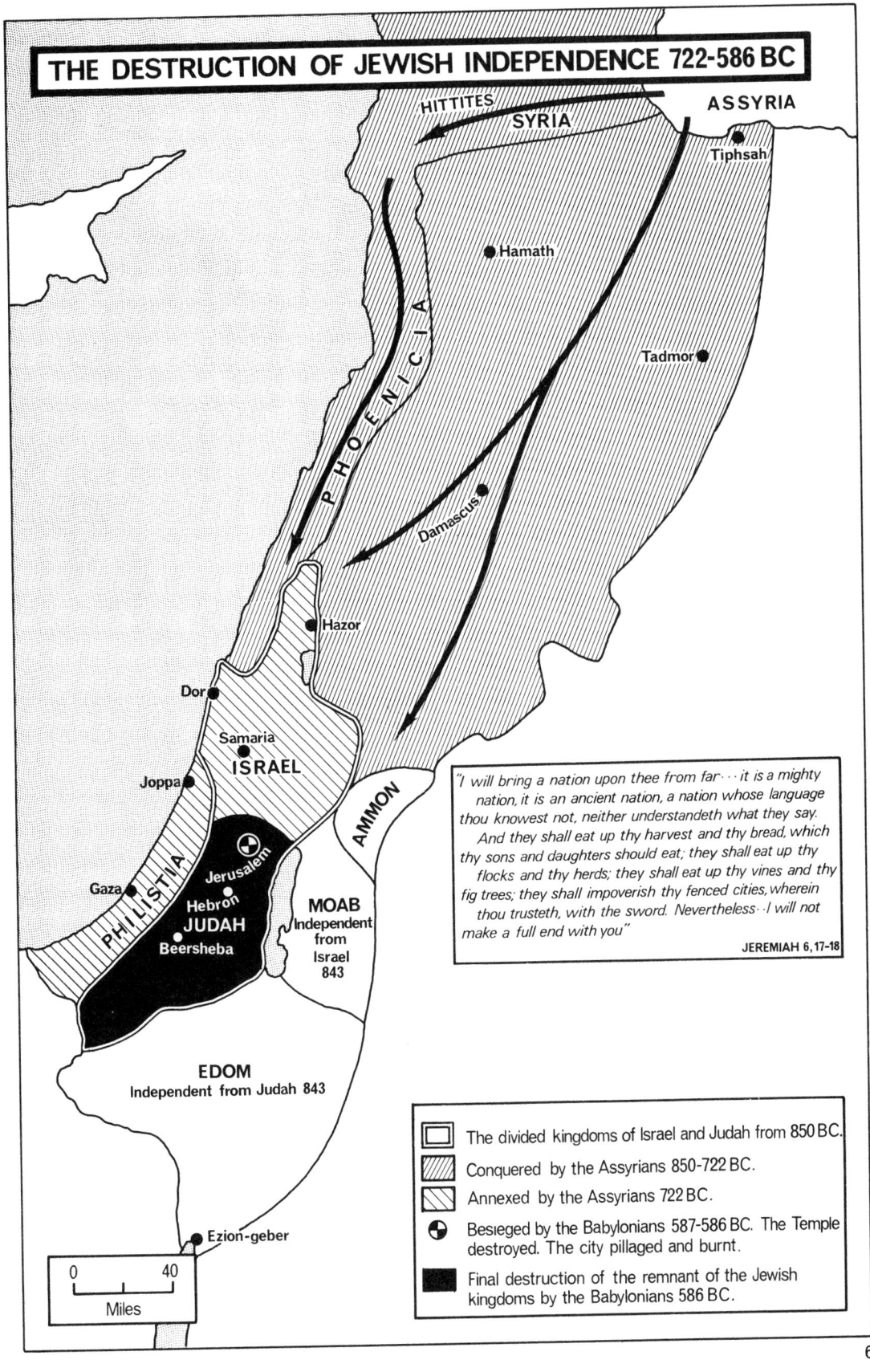

THE DESTRUCTION OF JEWISH INDEPENDENCE 722-586 BC

HITTITES

SYRIA

ASSYRIA

Tiphsah

Hamath

P H O E N I C I A

Tadmor

Damascus

Hazor

Dor

Samaria

ISRAEL

Joppa

AMMON

"I will bring a nation upon thee from far···it is a mighty
nation, it is an ancient nation, a nation whose language
thou knowest not, neither understandeth what they say.
And they shall eat up thy harvest and thy bread, which
thy sons and daughters should eat; they shall eat up thy
flocks and thy herds; they shall eat up thy vines and thy
fig trees; they shall impoverish thy fenced cities, wherein
thou trusteth, with the sword. Nevertheless···I will not
make a full end with you"

JEREMIAH 6, 17-18

Gaza

PHILISTIA

Jerusalem

Hebron

JUDAH

Beersheba

MOAB
Independent
from
Israel
843

EDOM
Independent from Judah 843

Ezion-geber

▢	The divided kingdoms of Israel and Judah from 850 BC.
▨	Conquered by the Assyrians 850-722 BC.
▨	Annexed by the Assyrians 722 BC.
✪	Besieged by the Babylonians 587-586 BC. The Temple destroyed. The city pillaged and burnt.
■	Final destruction of the remnant of the Jewish kingdoms by the Babylonians 586 BC.

0   40

Miles

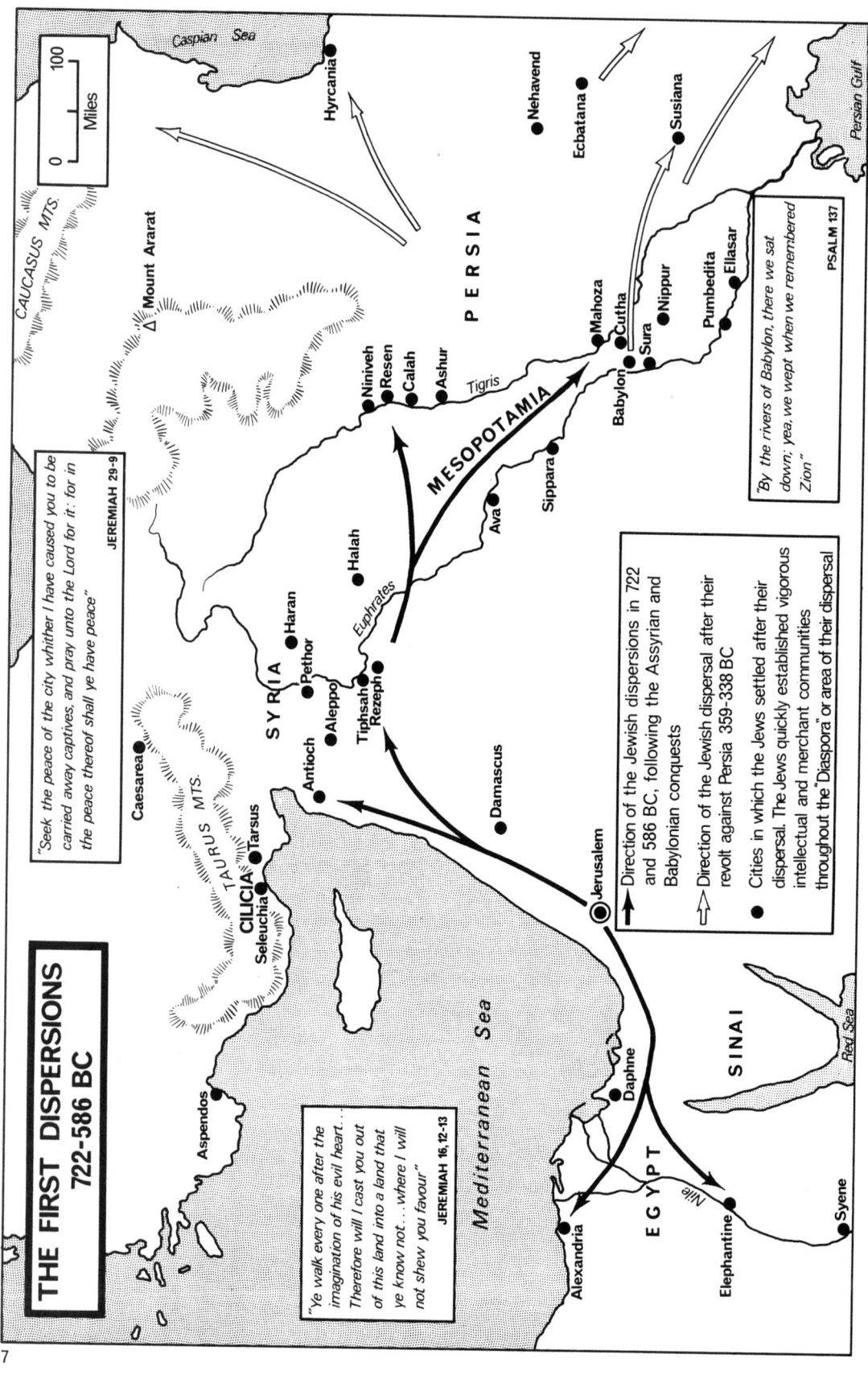

THE FIRST DISPERSIONS
722-586 BC

"Ye walk every one after the imagination of his evil heart... Therefore will I cast you out of this land into a land that ye know not...where I will not shew you favour"
JEREMIAH 16,12-13

"Seek the peace of the city whither I have caused you to be carried away captives, and pray unto the Lord for it: for in the peace thereof shall ye have peace"
JEREMIAH 29-9

"By the rivers of Babylon, there we sat down; yea, we wept when we remembered Zion"
PSALM 137

Direction of the Jewish dispersions in 722 and 586 BC, following the Assyrian and Babylonian conquests

Direction of the Jewish dispersal after their revolt against Persia 359-338 BC

Cities in which the Jews settled after their dispersal. The Jews quickly established vigorous intellectual and merchant communities throughout the "Diaspora" or area of their dispersal

Caspian Sea

CAUCASUS MTS.

Hyrcania

Mount Ararat

PERSIA

Nehavend

Ecbatana

Susiana

Persian Gulf

Niniveh
Resen
Calah
Ashur

Tigris

MESOPOTAMIA

Mahoza
Cutha
Babylon
Sura
Nippur
Pumbedita
Ellasar

Sippara

Ava

Halah

Euphrates

Haran
Pethor

SYRIA

Aleppo
Tiphsah
Rezeph

Antioch

Damascus

Caesarea

TAURUS MTS.

CILICIA
Tarsus
Seleuchia

Jerusalem

Aspendos

Mediterranean Sea

Daphne

SINAI

Red Sea

EGYPT

Nile

Alexandria

Elephantine

Syene

0   100
Miles

7

THE IMPERIAL POWERS 586–165 BC

THE BABYLONIAN EMPIRE 586–550 BC

"The virgin of Israel is fallen,
She shall no more rise;
She is cast down upon the ground,
There is none to raise her up."

AMOS 5–2

•Jerusalem

THE PERSIAN EMPIRE 550–333 BC

•Jerusalem

0   300
Miles

THE EMPIRE OF ALEXANDER THE GREAT 323 BC

•Jerusalem

THE PTOLEMAIC EMPIRE 270 BC

•Jerusalem

"Our inheritance is turned to strangers,
Our houses to aliens.
We are orphans and fatherless,
Our mothers are as widows.
Our necks are under persecution,
We labour, and have no rest."

LAMENTATIONS 5,2–5

■ Empires controlling Jerusalem after the Assyrian conquest. The Jews gradually settled throughout the territory of the imperial powers.

8

THE JEWS OF THE EASTERN MEDITERRANEAN BOTH BEFORE AND AFTER THE ARAB CONQUEST

0   20
Miles

For more than three thousand years Jews lived in the principal towns of the Eastern Mediterranean. The longest single overlordship of the area was that of Rome (677 years). Jewish rule in Judaea and Samaria in ancient times lasted a total of 641 years. Other rulers of the area included the Arabs (447 years), the Ottoman Turks (401 years) and the Crusaders (192 years)

Make war upon those who have been given scripture... until they pay the tribute readily, having been brought low
KORAN, SURA Nº 9, 29

ANTIOCH

In Roman times, a centre of Jewish settlement, whose Jews were granted equal citizenship rights with Greeks. In 600 AD, after attempts to forcible conversion, the Jews rebelled, and many were killed. In 1171 only 10 Jewish families still remained; in 1750 about 40; in 1894 about 80; in 1928 about 10

ALEPPO

Jews lived here from biblical times. In 1173 AD there were 1,500 Jews; in 1900 more than 10,000 forced to pay an annual poll tax

TRIPOLI

At the time of the Arab conquest, the Arab Governor established a garrison of Jewish troops to guard the town against Byzantine attack. Early in the 11th century Jews were persecuted, their synagogue turned into a mosque, and several houses destroyed. In the 16th century Jewish refugees from Spain settled and prospered. Early in the 17th century there were further persecutions and many Jews fled. In 1939 there were only four Jewish families left

BEIRUT

In 500 AD there was a flourishing Jewish community, but in 1173 Benjamin of Tudela found only 50 Jews. In 1889 there were 1,500 Jews out of a total population of 20,000, in 1913 5,000 out of 150,000

GAZA

Some Jews settled here in Talmudic times. In 1481 AD Meshullam of Volterra found 60 Jewish house-holders. From 1600-1799 the Jewish community flourished, but in 1799 it fled the city on the eve of Napoleon's arrival. Resettled in the 1880's, some 90 Jews were recorded in 1903

DAMASCUS

Contained some 10,000 Jewish inhabitants in Roman times, and over 3,000 when visited by Benjamin of Tudela in 1173 AD. In 1840 a ritual murder charge was brought against the Jews, and in 1880 they were falsely accused of taking part in a massacre of Christians. In 1901 there were eight synagogues, and as many as 20,000 Jews

RAFAH

A flourishing Jewish community lived here both before and after the Arab conquest, but in 1080 AD the Jews were driven out after nearly a thousand years of continuous settlement

⦿ Towns with Jewish inhabitants in Byzantine times, in which Jews were still living both before and after the Arab conquest in the seventh century AD

Antioch

Aleppo

Latakia

Baniyas

⦿ Hama

Masyaf

⦿ Homs

Tripoli

Jubail

⦿ Baalbek

Beirut

Sidon

⦿ Damascus

Tyre

Golan Heights

Naveh

Safed

Acre

Haifa Tiberias

Nazareth

SAMARIA

R. Jordan

Ajlun

Jaffa   Lod

Salt

Ramleh   Amman ⦿

JUDAEA   Jericho

Jerusalem

Hebron ⦿

Dead Sea

Gaza   Juttah

Rafah

⦿ Ayn-al-Yahudiyya

Punon ⦿

Mediterranean Sea

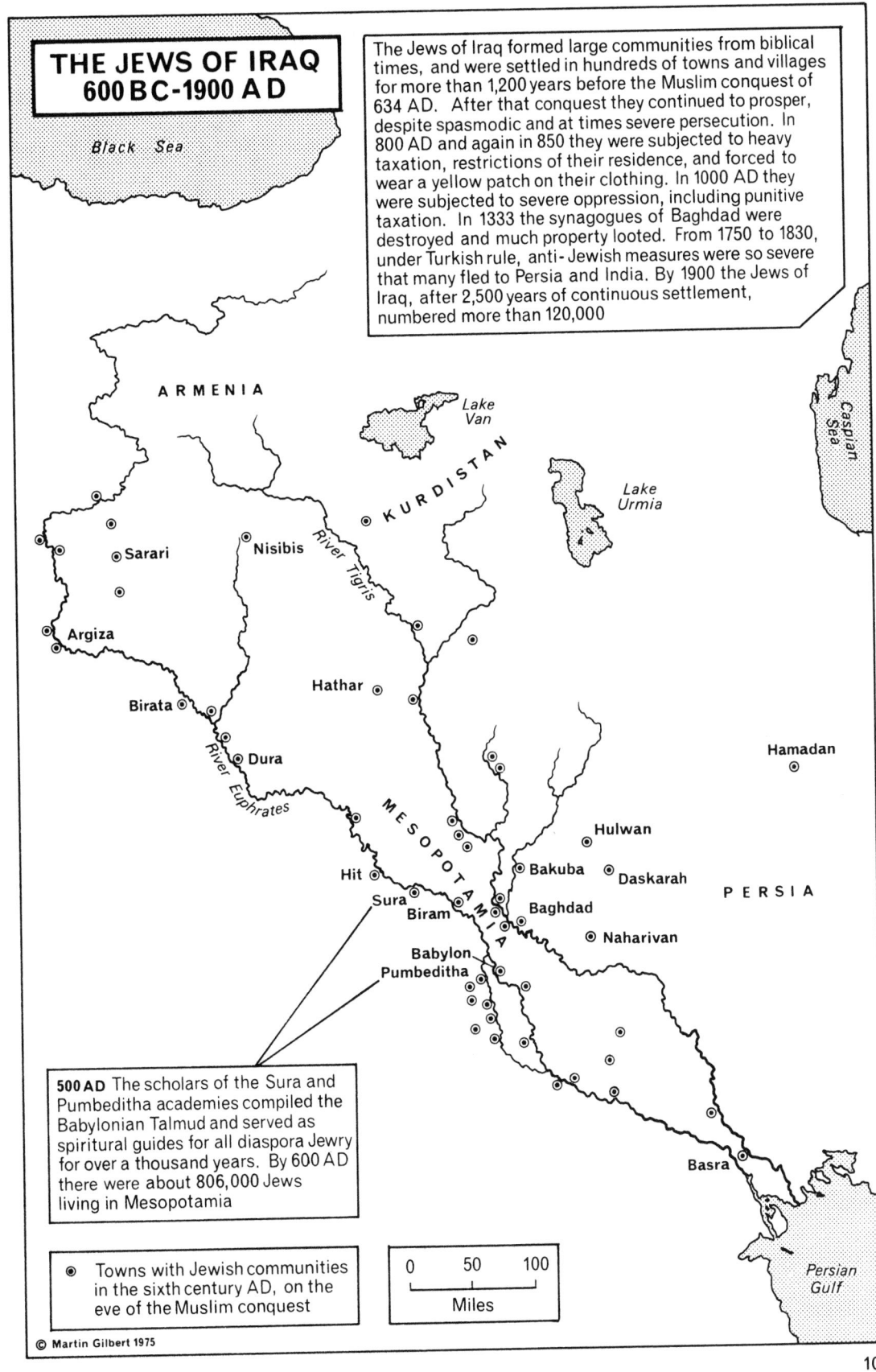

THE JEWS OF IRAQ 600 BC-1900 AD

Black Sea

The Jews of Iraq formed large communities from biblical times, and were settled in hundreds of towns and villages for more than 1,200 years before the Muslim conquest of 634 AD. After that conquest they continued to prosper, despite spasmodic and at times severe persecution. In 800 AD and again in 850 they were subjected to heavy taxation, restrictions of their residence, and forced to wear a yellow patch on their clothing. In 1000 AD they were subjected to severe oppression, including punitive taxation. In 1333 the synagogues of Baghdad were destroyed and much property looted. From 1750 to 1830, under Turkish rule, anti-Jewish measures were so severe that many fled to Persia and India. By 1900 the Jews of Iraq, after 2,500 years of continuous settlement, numbered more than 120,000

ARMENIA

Lake Van

Caspian Sea

KURDISTAN

Lake Urmia

Sarari

Nisibis

River Tigris

Argiza

Hathar

Birata

River Euphrates

Dura

Hamadan

MESOPOTAMIA

Hulwan

Hit

Bakuba   Daskarah

Sura

Biram

Baghdad

PERSIA

Babylon

Naharivan

Pumbeditha

500 AD The scholars of the Sura and Pumbeditha academies compiled the Babylonian Talmud and served as spiritual guides for all diaspora Jewry for over a thousand years. By 600 AD there were about 806,000 Jews living in Mesopotamia

Basra

⊙ Towns with Jewish communities in the sixth century AD, on the eve of the Muslim conquest

Persian Gulf

| 0 | 50 | 100 |

Miles

© Martin Gilbert 1975

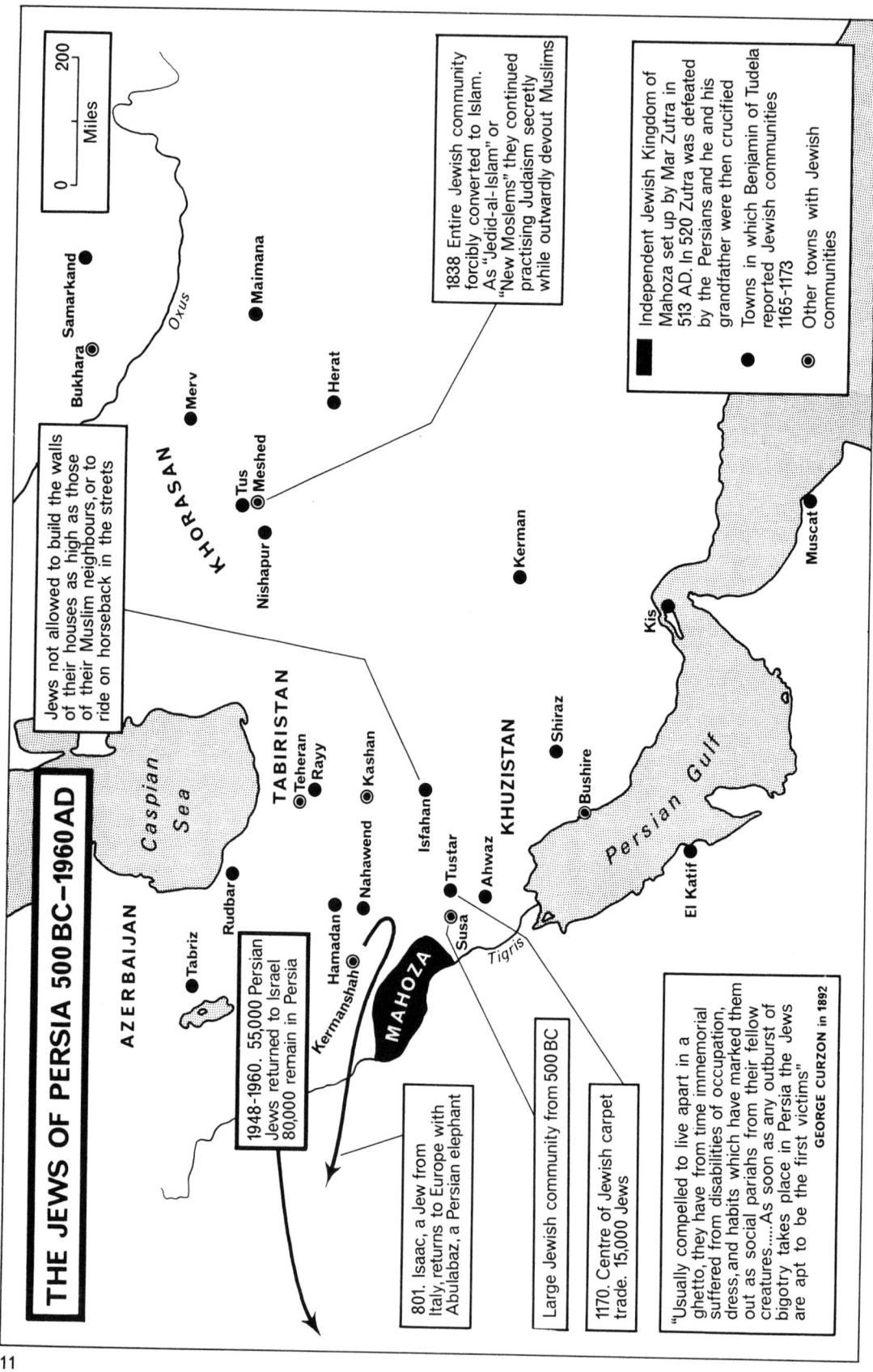

THE JEWS OF PERSIA 500 BC–1960 AD

Jews not allowed to build the walls of their houses as high as those of their Muslim neighbours, or to ride on horseback in the streets

1838 Entire Jewish community forcibly converted to Islam. As "Jedid-al-Islam" or "New Moslems" they continued practising Judaism secretly while outwardly devout Muslims

■ Independent Jewish Kingdom of Mahoza set up by Mar Zutra in 513 AD. In 520 Zutra was defeated by the Persians and he and his grandfather were then crucified

● Towns in which Benjamin of Tudela reported Jewish communities 1165-1173

◉ Other towns with Jewish communities

1948-1960. 55,000 Persian Jews returned to Israel 80,000 remain in Persia

801. Isaac, a Jew from Italy, returns to Europe with Abulabaz, a Persian elephant

Large Jewish community from 500 BC

1170. Centre of Jewish carpet trade. 15,000 Jews

"Usually compelled to live apart in a ghetto, they have from time immemorial suffered from disabilities of occupation, dress, and habits which have marked them out as social pariahs from their fellow creatures....As soon as any outburst of bigotry takes place in Persia the Jews are apt to be the first victims"
GEORGE CURZON in 1892

AZERBAIJAN
Caspian Sea
TABIRISTAN
KHORASAN
KHUZISTAN
MAHOZA
Persian Gulf

Tabriz
Rudbar
Kermanshah
Hamadan
Nahawend
Kashan
Teheran
Rayy
Isfahan
Tustar
Ahwaz
Susa
Tigris
Bushire
Shiraz
Kerman
Nishapur
Meshed
Tus
Herat
Maimana
Merv
Bukhara
Samarkand
Oxus
Kis
El Katif
Muscat

0   200
Miles

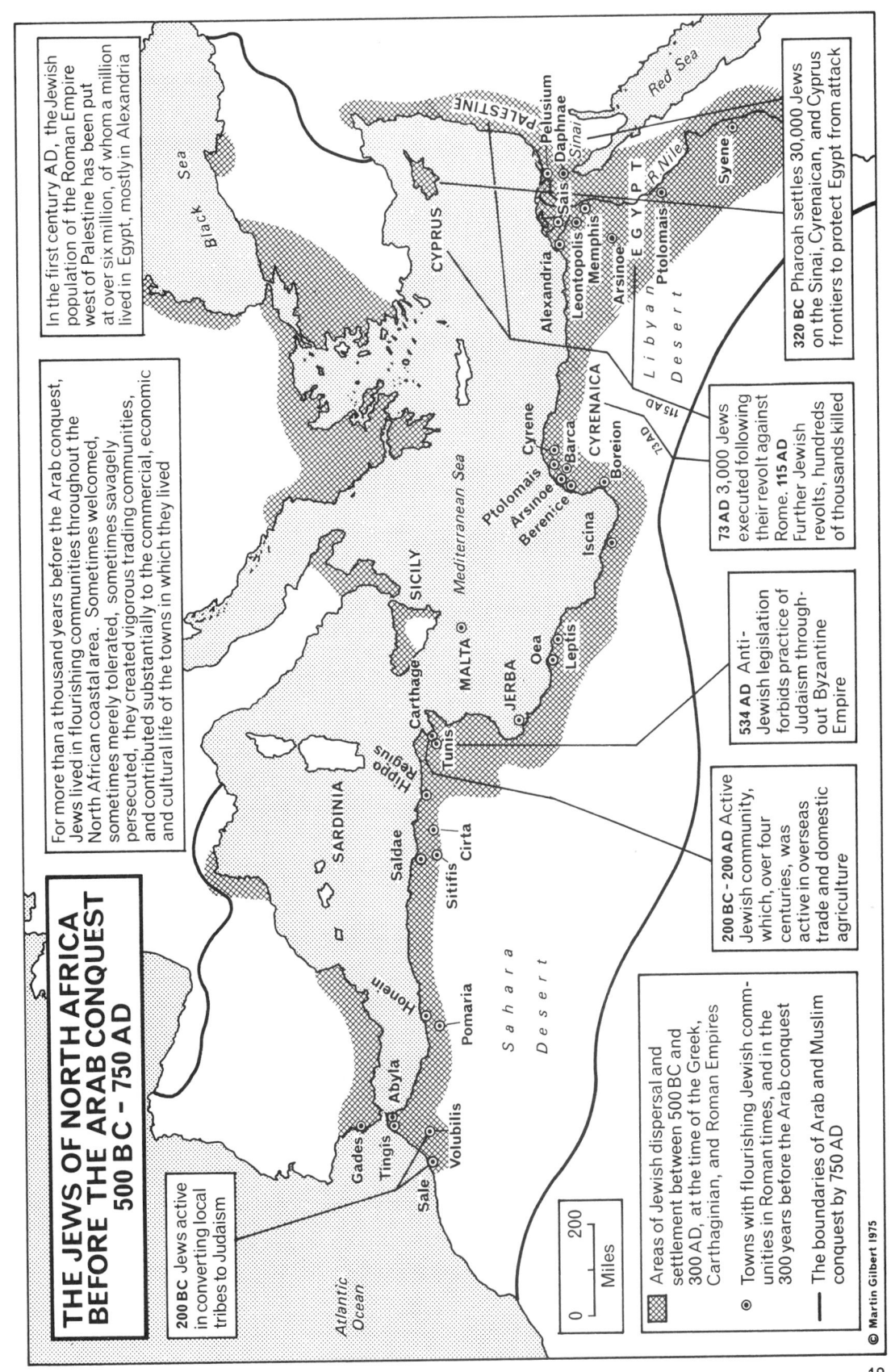

THE JEWS OF NORTH AFRICA
BEFORE THE ARAB CONQUEST
500 BC – 750 AD

200 BC Jews active in converting local tribes to Judaism

In the first century AD, the Jewish population of the Roman Empire west of Palestine has been put at over six million, of whom a million lived in Egypt, mostly in Alexandria

320 BC Pharoah settles 30,000 Jews on the Sinai, Cyrenaican, and Cyprus frontiers to protect Egypt from attack

For more than a thousand years before the Arab conquest, Jews lived in flourishing communities throughout the North African coastal area. Sometimes welcomed, sometimes merely tolerated, sometimes savagely persecuted, they created vigorous trading communities, and contributed substantially to the commercial, economic and cultural life of the towns in which they lived

73 AD 3,000 Jews executed following their revolt against Rome. **115 AD** Further Jewish revolts, hundreds of thousands killed

534 AD Anti-Jewish legislation forbids practice of Judaism through-out Byzantine Empire

200 BC - 200 AD Active Jewish community, which, over four centuries, was active in overseas trade and domestic agriculture

Areas of Jewish dispersal and settlement between 500 BC and 300 AD, at the time of the Greek, Carthaginian, and Roman Empires

⊙ Towns with flourishing Jewish communities in Roman times, and in the 300 years before the Arab conquest

— The boundaries of Arab and Muslim conquest by 750 AD

0   200
Miles

© Martin Gilbert 1975

Atlantic Ocean

Gades ⊙
Tingis ⊙ Abyla ⊙
Sale ⊙ Volubilis ⊙
Pomaria ⊙
Honein ⊙
Saldae ⊙
SARDINIA
Sitifis ⊙ Cirta ⊙
Hippo Regius ⊙
Tunis ⊙ Carthage ⊙
SICILY
MALTA ⊙
JERBA
Oea ⊙
Leptis ⊙

Sahara Desert

Mediterranean Sea

Black Sea

CYPRUS

PALESTINE

Alexandria ⊙ Sais ⊙ Daphnae ⊙ Pelusium
Leontopolis ⊙ Sinai
Memphis ⊙ R Nile
Arsinoe ⊙ E G Y P T
Ptolomais ⊙ Syene ⊙

Libyan Desert

Red Sea

CYRENAICA
Cyrene ⊙ Barca ⊙
Ptolomais ⊙ Boreion ⊙
Arsinoe ⊙
Berenice ⊙
Iscina ⊙

115 AD

73 AD

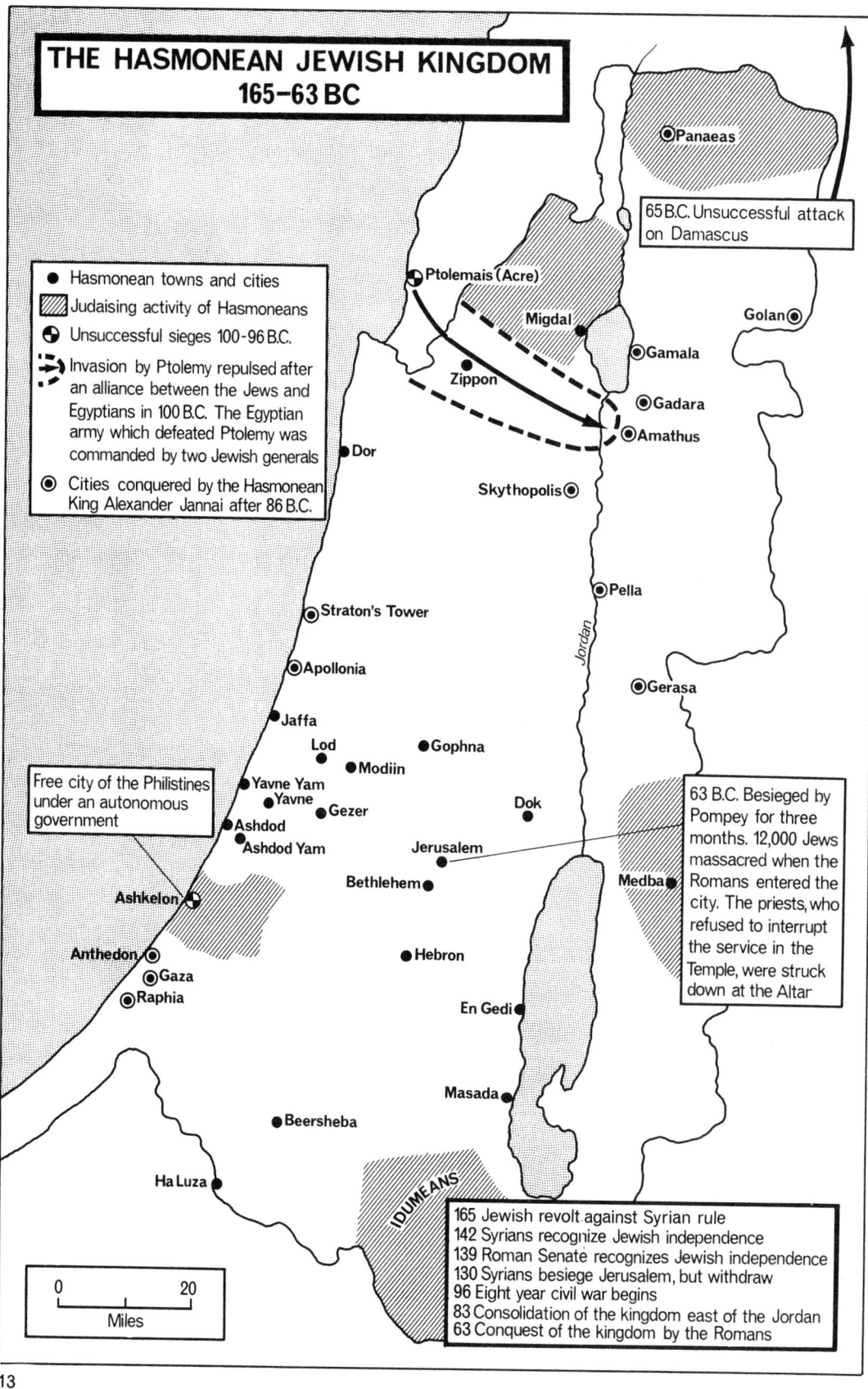

THE HASMONEAN JEWISH KINGDOM
165–63 BC

● Panaeas

65 B.C. Unsuccessful attack on Damascus

● Hasmonean towns and cities

▨ Judaising activity of Hasmoneans

◉ Unsuccessful sieges 100-96 B.C.

⇢ Invasion by Ptolemy repulsed after an alliance between the Jews and Egyptians in 100 B.C. The Egyptian army which defeated Ptolemy was commanded by two Jewish generals

◉ Cities conquered by the Hasmonean King Alexander Jannai after 86 B.C.

● Ptolemais (Acre)

Migdal

Golan ◉

◉ Gamala

Zippon

◉ Gadara

◉ Amathus

● Dor

Skythopolis ◉

● Pella

◉ Straton's Tower

◉ Gerasa

◉ Apollonia

● Jaffa

Lod

● Gophna

● Modiin

Dok

Free city of the Philistines under an autonomous government

● Yavne Yam
● Yavne
Gezer

● Ashdod
● Ashdod Yam

Jerusalem ●

63 B.C. Besieged by Pompey for three months. 12,000 Jews massacred when the Romans entered the city. The priests, who refused to interrupt the service in the Temple, were struck down at the Altar

Bethlehem ●

Medba ●

Ashkelon ✪

Anthedon ◉

● Hebron

◉ Gaza

◉ Raphia

En Gedi ●

Masada ●

● Beersheba

Ha Luza ●

IDUMEANS

165 Jewish revolt against Syrian rule
142 Syrians recognize Jewish independence
139 Roman Senate recognizes Jewish independence
130 Syrians besiege Jerusalem, but withdraw
96 Eight year civil war begins
83 Consolidation of the kingdom east of the Jordan
63 Conquest of the kingdom by the Romans

Jordan

0   20
Miles

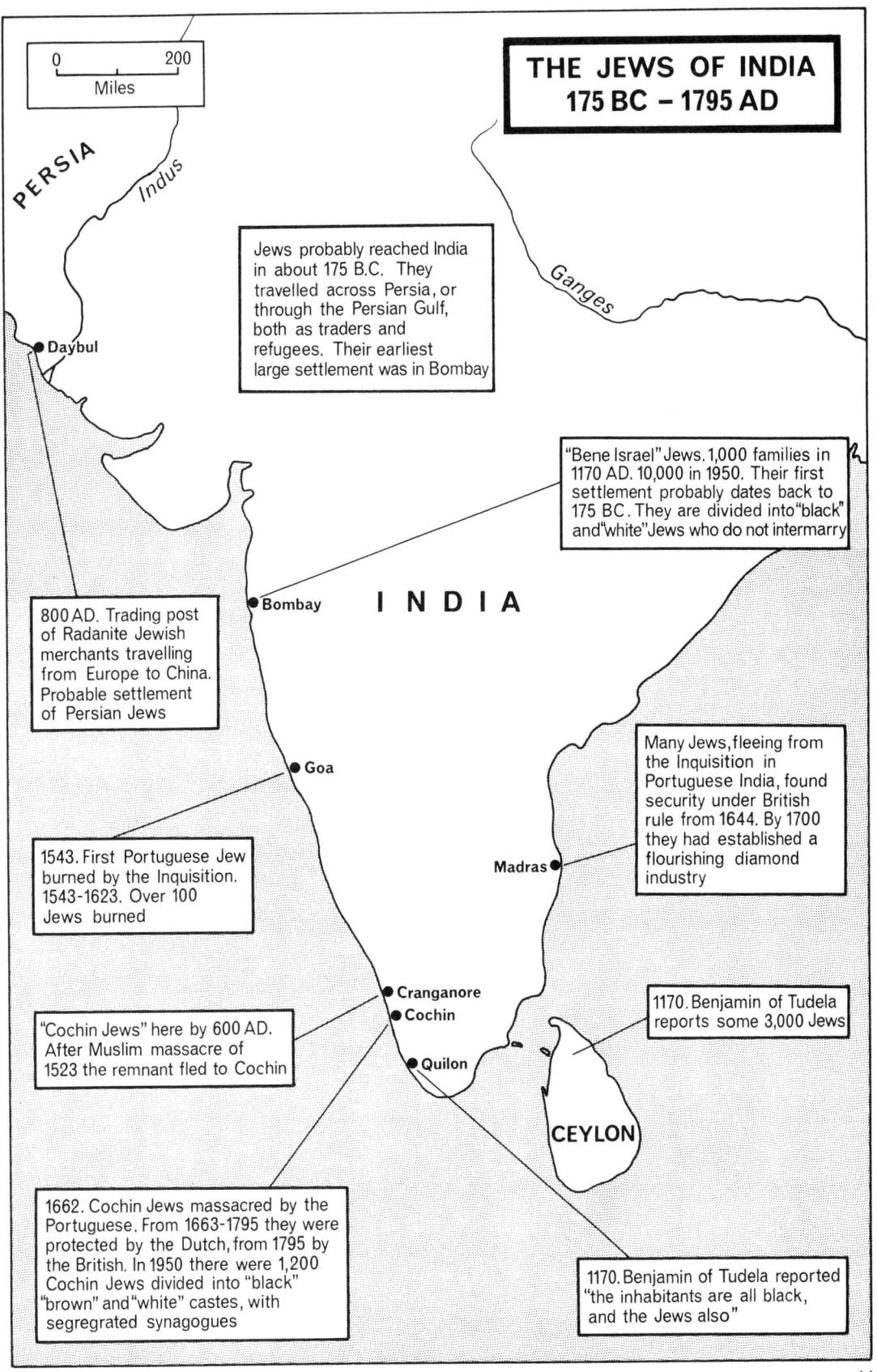

THE JEWS OF INDIA
175 BC – 1795 AD

0 _____ 200
Miles

PERSIA

Indus

Ganges

Jews probably reached India in about 175 B.C. They travelled across Persia, or through the Persian Gulf, both as traders and refugees. Their earliest large settlement was in Bombay

● Daybul

"Bene Israel" Jews. 1,000 families in 1170 AD. 10,000 in 1950. Their first settlement probably dates back to 175 BC. They are divided into "black" and "white" Jews who do not intermarry

800 AD. Trading post of Radanite Jewish merchants travelling from Europe to China. Probable settlement of Persian Jews

● Bombay

I N D I A

● Goa

Many Jews, fleeing from the Inquisition in Portuguese India, found security under British rule from 1644. By 1700 they had established a flourishing diamond industry

1543. First Portuguese Jew burned by the Inquisition. 1543-1623. Over 100 Jews burned

Madras ●

● Cranganore
● Cochin

1170. Benjamin of Tudela reports some 3,000 Jews

"Cochin Jews" here by 600 AD. After Muslim massacre of 1523 the remnant fled to Cochin

● Quilon

CEYLON

1662. Cochin Jews massacred by the Portuguese. From 1663-1795 they were protected by the Dutch, from 1795 by the British. In 1950 there were 1,200 Cochin Jews divided into "black" "brown" and "white" castes, with segregated synagogues

1170. Benjamin of Tudela reported "the inhabitants are all black, and the Jews also"

14

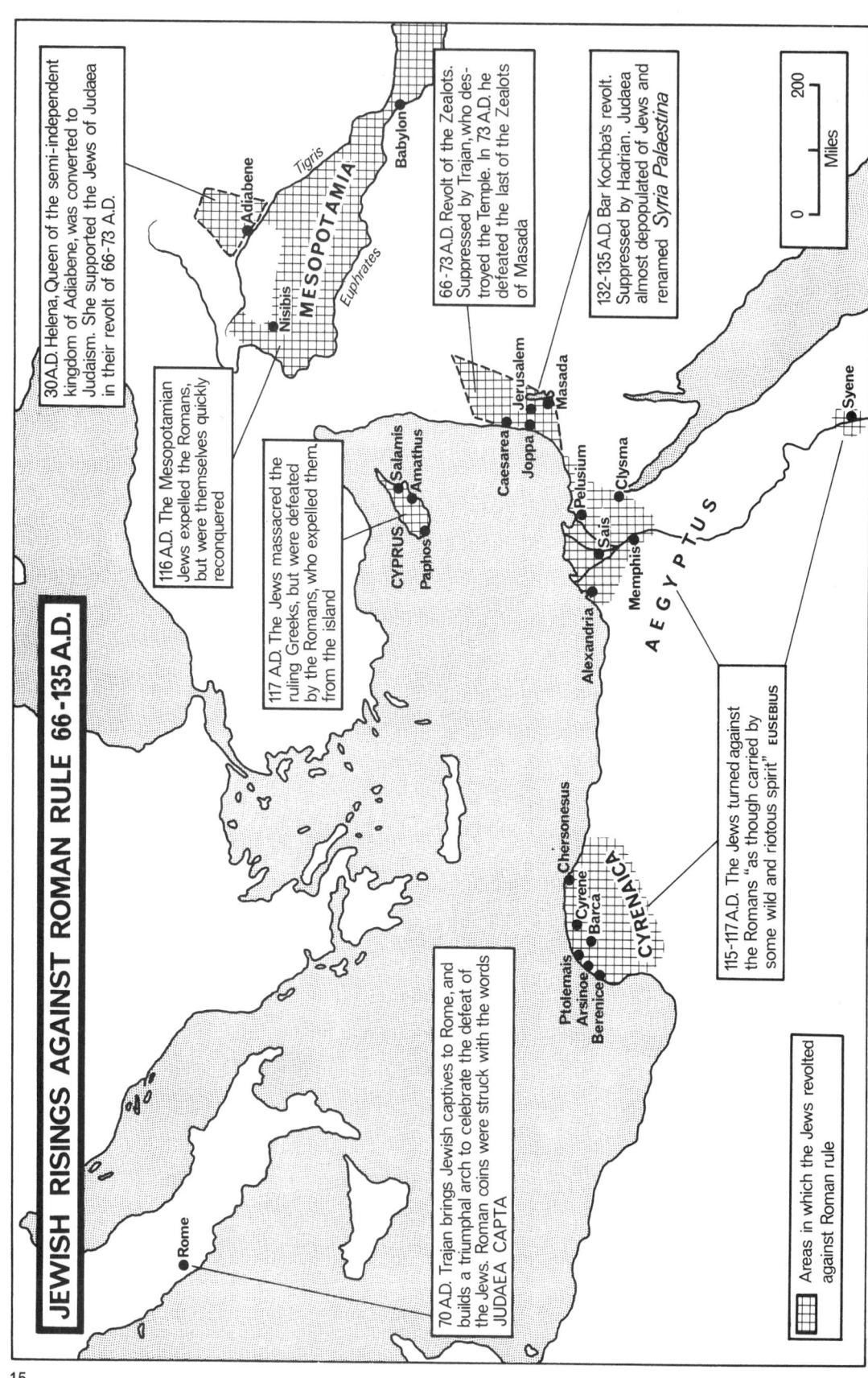

JEWISH RISINGS AGAINST ROMAN RULE 66-135 A.D.

30 A.D. Helena, Queen of the semi-independent kingdom of Adiabene, was converted to Judaism. She supported the Jews of Judaea in their revolt of 66-73 A.D.

116 A.D. The Mesopotamian Jews expelled the Romans, but were themselves quickly reconquered

117 A.D. The Jews massacred the ruling Greeks, but were defeated by the Romans, who expelled them from the island

66-73 A.D. Revolt of the Zealots. Suppressed by Trajan, who destroyed the Temple. In 73 A.D. he defeated the last of the Zealots of Masada

132-135 A.D. Bar Kochba's revolt. Suppressed by Hadrian. Judaea almost depopulated of Jews and renamed *Syria Palaestina*

115-117 A.D. The Jews turned against the Romans "as though carried by some wild and riotous spirit" EUSEBIUS

70 A.D. Trajan brings Jewish captives to Rome, and builds a triumphal arch to celebrate the defeat of the Jews. Roman coins were struck with the words JUDAEA CAPTA

Tigris

Euphrates

MESOPOTAMIA

Babylon

Adiabene

Nisibis

Jerusalem

Masada

Caesarea

Joppa

Salamis

Amathus

CYPRUS

Paphos

Pelusium

Clysma

Sais

Memphis

Alexandria

A E G Y P T U S

Svene

Chersonesus

Cyrene

Barca

CYRENAICA

Ptolemais

Arsinoe

Berenice

Rome

0   200

Miles

Areas in which the Jews revolted against Roman rule

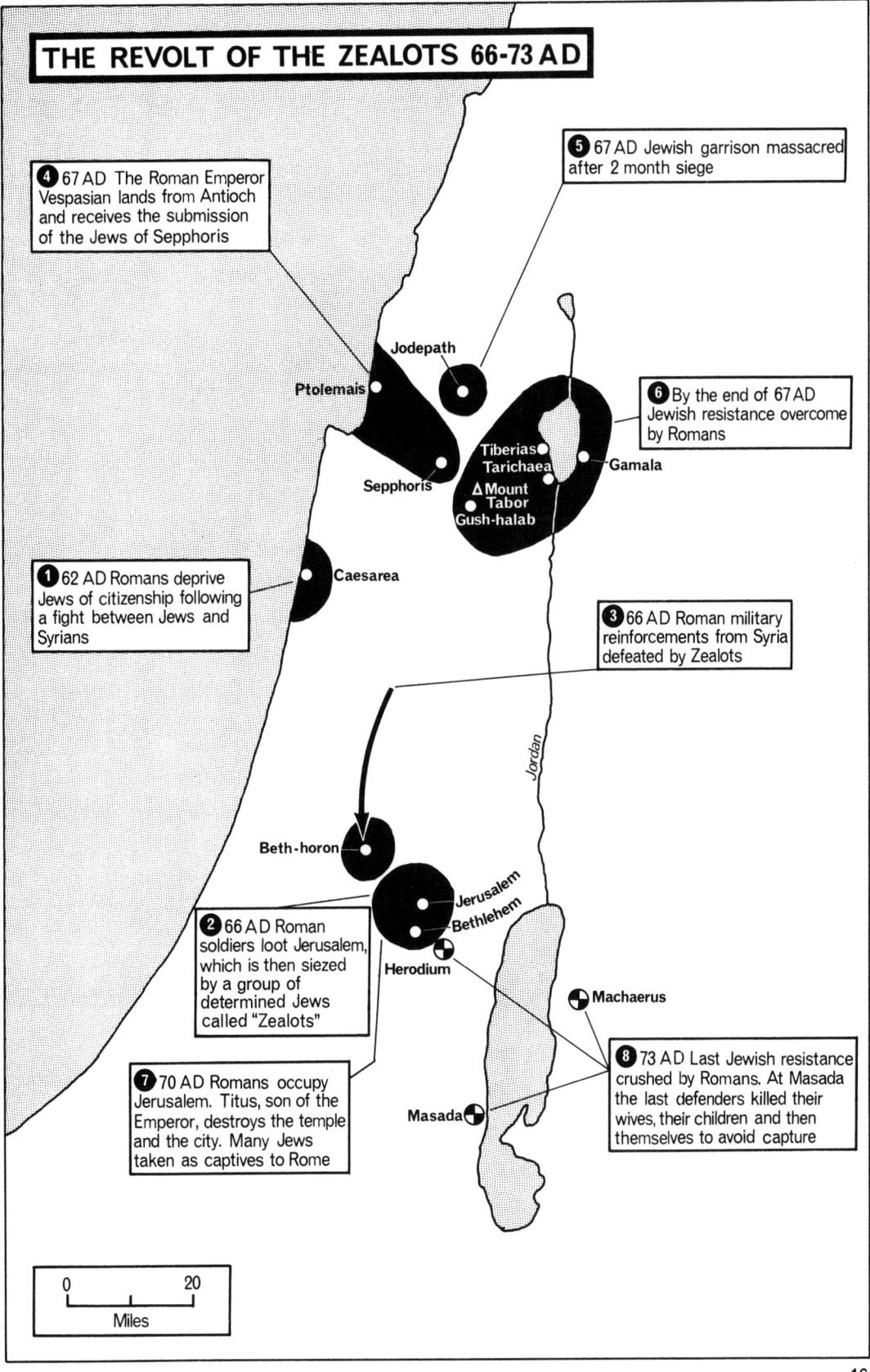

THE REVOLT OF THE ZEALOTS 66-73 AD

5 67 AD Jewish garrison massacred after 2 month siege

4 67 AD The Roman Emperor Vespasian lands from Antioch and receives the submission of the Jews of Sepphoris

6 By the end of 67 AD Jewish resistance overcome by Romans

Jodepath

Ptolemais

Tiberias
Tarichaea
△ Mount Tabor
Gush-halab
Gamala

Sepphoris

1 62 AD Romans deprive Jews of citizenship following a fight between Jews and Syrians

Caesarea

3 66 AD Roman military reinforcements from Syria defeated by Zealots

Jordan

Beth-horon

Jerusalem
Bethlehem

2 66 AD Roman soldiers loot Jerusalem, which is then siezed by a group of determined Jews called "Zealots"

Herodium

Machaerus

8 73 AD Last Jewish resistance crushed by Romans. At Masada the last defenders killed their wives, their children and then themselves to avoid capture

7 70 AD Romans occupy Jerusalem. Titus, son of the Emperor, destroys the temple and the city. Many Jews taken as captives to Rome

Masada

0   20
Miles

16

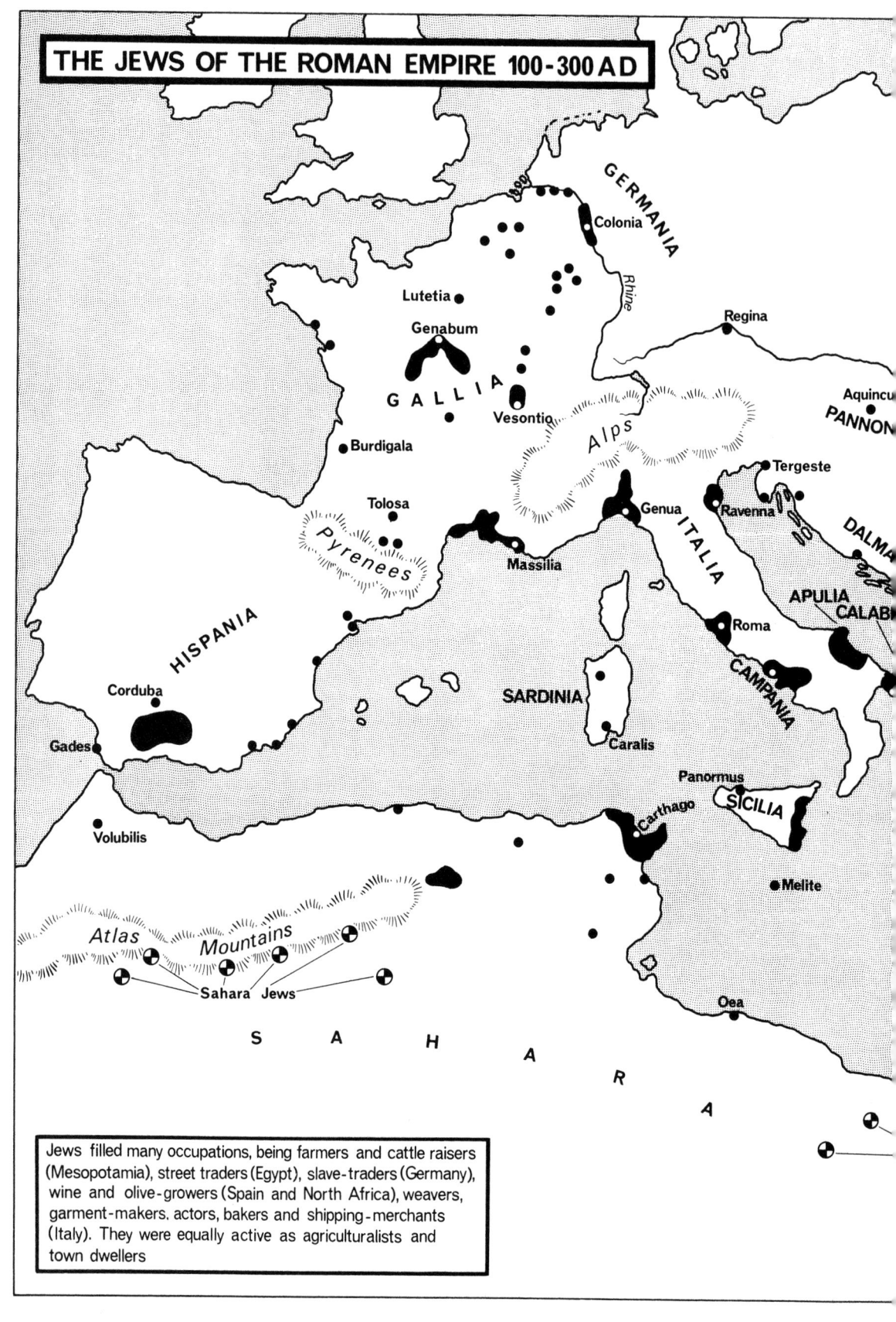

THE JEWS OF THE ROMAN EMPIRE 100-300 A D

GERMANIA

Colonia

Rhine

Regina

Lutetia

Genabum

Aquincu

GALLIA

PANNON

Vesontio

Alps

Tergeste

Burdigala

Genua

ITALIA

Ravenna

DALMA

Tolosa

Pyrenees

APULIA

Massilia

CALABI

Roma

CAMPANIA

HISPANIA

SARDINIA

Corduba

Caralis

Gades

Panormus

Carthago

SICILIA

Volubilis

Melite

Atlas

Mountains

Sahara Jews

Oea

S   A   H

A

R

A

Jews filled many occupations, being farmers and cattle raisers
(Mesopotamia), street traders (Egypt), slave-traders (Germany),
wine and olive-growers (Spain and North Africa), weavers,
garment-makers, actors, bakers and shipping-merchants
(Italy). They were equally active as agriculturalists and
town dwellers

By 300 A.D, the Jews had settled in every part of the Roman Empire except Britain. They were guaranteed freedom of religion and were allowed to practice Jewish law in disputes between Jews. They were exempt from military service.

There were probably at least three million Jews in 300 A.D, a million of whom lived west of Macedonia

0 — 200 Miles

Don

Tanais

Olbia

Phanagoria

Panticapaeum

Mountain Jews

Caucasus Mts.

Bursa

Danube

Serdica ● MOESIA

Byzantium

Prusa

Ancyra

Trapezus

Amisus

Melitene

Tigris

ASSYRIA

MESOPOTAMIA

PHRYGIA

Tarsus

Euphrates

Sura

Ephesus

CILICIA

Pumbedita
Babylon

Delos

LYCIA

CYPRUS

SYRIA

ACHAIA

MACEDONIA

● Damascus

Hierosolyma
(Jerusalem)

Cyrene

Berenice

Alexandria

Pelusium

Aelana

CYRENAICA

AEGYPTUS

The 40,000 Jews of Cyprus were expelled after rebelling against Roman rule in 115 AD

Cave-dwelling Jews

■ Areas of widespread Jewish settlement

● Towns with large Jewish communities

◉ Isolated Jewish communities established after the Roman conquest of Palestine and surviving to this day

17

THE PREACHING OF ST. PAUL 45-57 A.D.

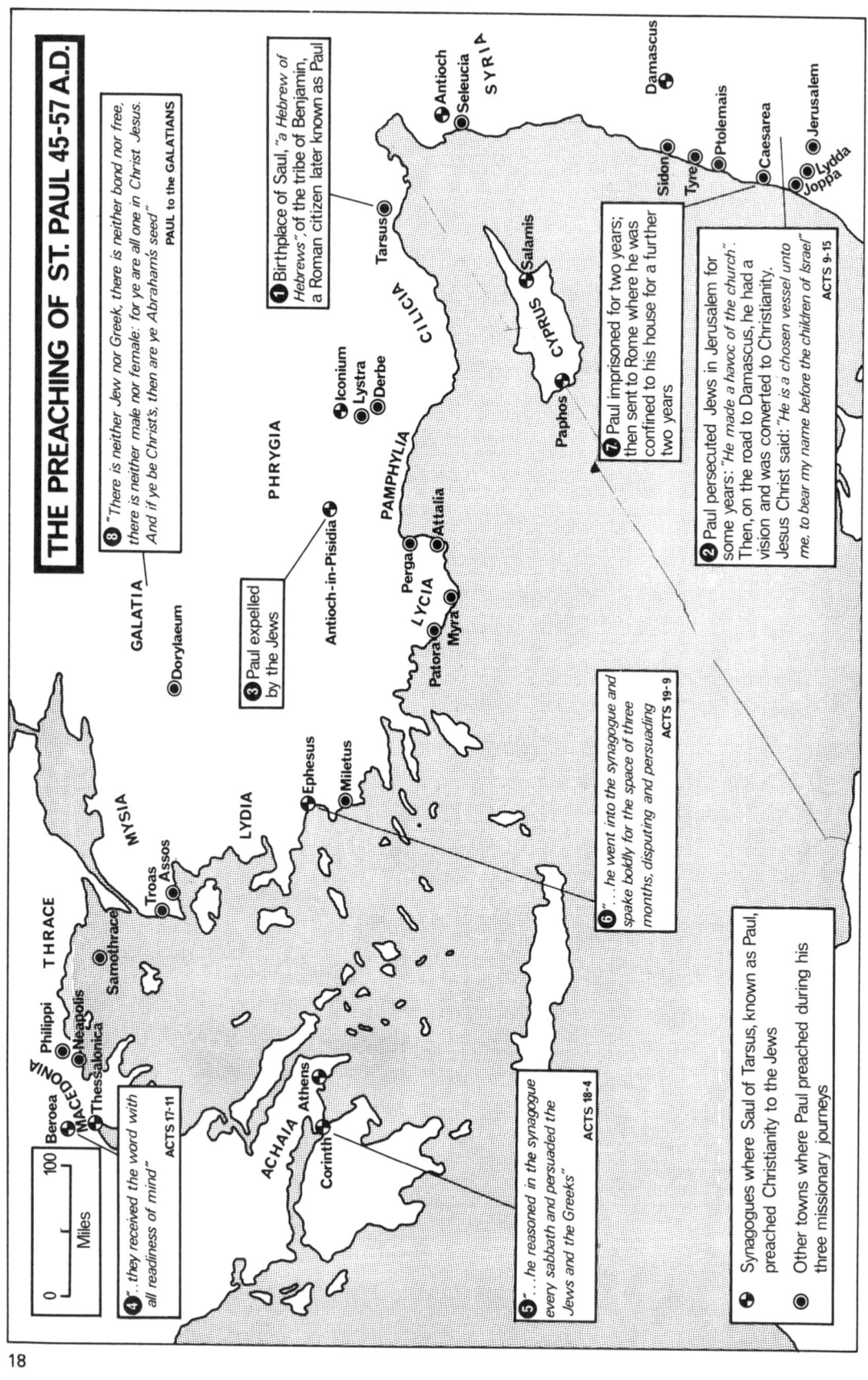

8 *"There is neither Jew nor Greek, there is neither bond nor free, there is neither male nor female: for ye are all one in Christ Jesus. And if ye be Christ's, then are ye Abraham's seed"*
PAUL to the GALATIANS

1 Birthplace of Saul, *"a Hebrew of Hebrews"*, of the tribe of Benjamin, a Roman citizen later known as Paul

2 Paul persecuted Jews in Jerusalem for some years: *"He made a havoc of the church"*. Then, on the road to Damascus, he had a vision and was converted to Christianity. Jesus Christ said: *"He is a chosen vessel unto me, to bear my name before the children of Israel"*
ACTS 9-15

3 Paul expelled by the Jews

7 Paul imprisoned for two years; then sent to Rome where he was confined to his house for a further two years

6 *"...he went into the synagogue and spake boldly for the space of three months, disputing and persuading"*
ACTS 19-9

4 *"...they received the word with all readiness of mind"*
ACTS 17-11

5 *"...he reasoned in the synagogue every sabbath and persuaded the Jews and the Greeks"*
ACTS 18-4

Synagogues where Saul of Tarsus, known as Paul, preached Christianity to the Jews

Other towns where Paul preached during his three missionary journeys

0 — 100
Miles

THRACE

MACEDONIA
Beroea
Philippi
Meapolis
Thessalonica
Samothrace

ACHAIA
Athens
Corinth

MYSIA
LYDIA
Troas
Assos
Ephesus
Miletus

GALATIA
Dorylaeum
PHRYGIA
Antioch-in-Pisidia
Iconium
Lystra
Derbe

PAMPHYLIA
Perga
Attalia
LYCIA
Patora
Myra

CILICIA
Tarsus

Antioch
Seleucia
SYRIA
Damascus

CYPRUS
Salamis
Paphos

Sidon
Tyre
Ptolemais
Caesarea
Lydda
Joppa
Jerusalem

18

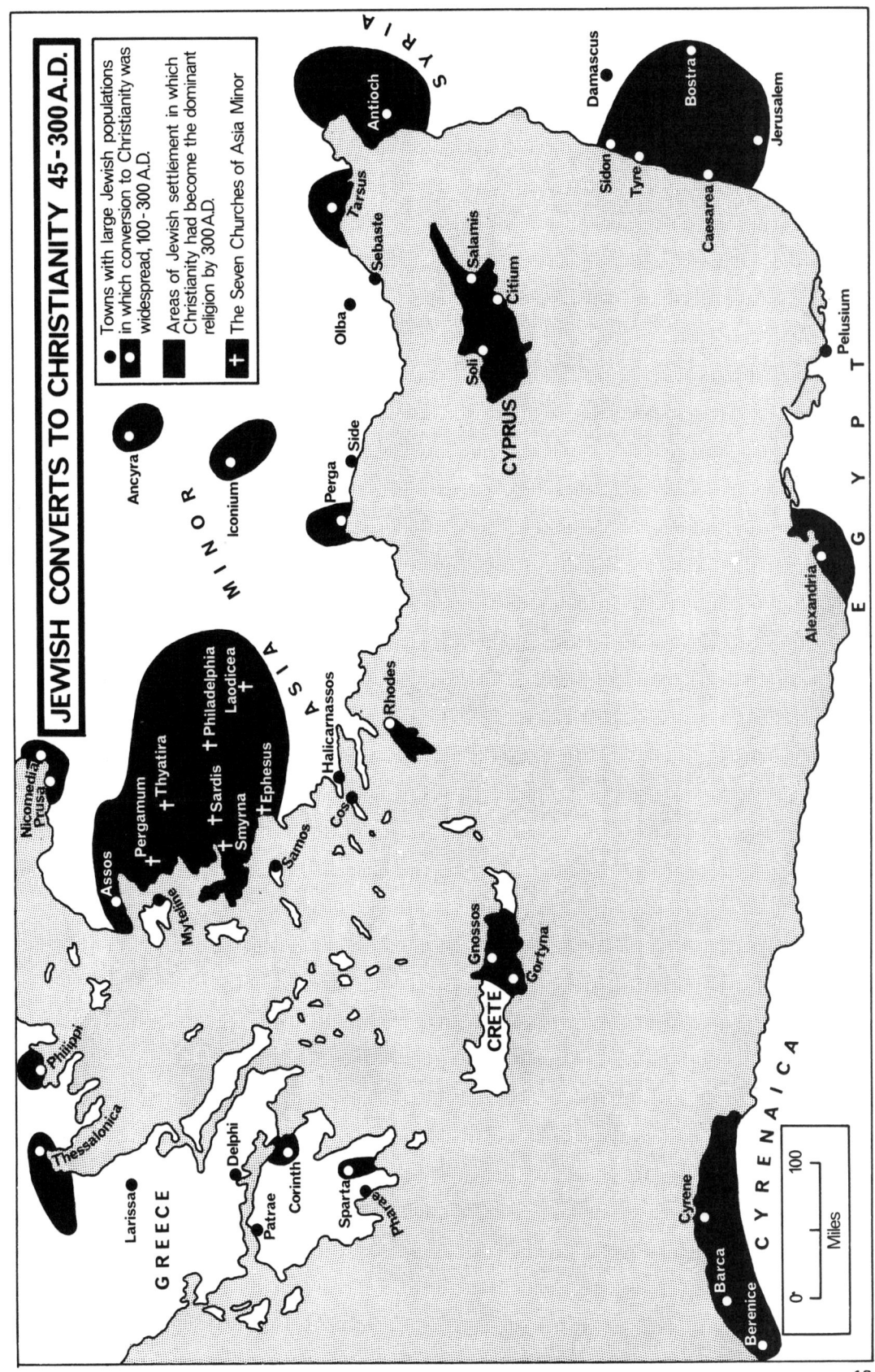

JEWISH CONVERTS TO CHRISTIANITY 45-300 A.D.

- ● Towns with large Jewish populations in which conversion to Christianity was widespread, 100 - 300 A.D.
- ● Areas of Jewish settlement in which Christianity had become the dominant religion by 300 A.D.
- ✝ The Seven Churches of Asia Minor

SYRIA

Antioch

Damascus

Bostra

Jerusalem

Tarsus

Sidon

Tyre

Sebaste

Caesarea

Olba

Salamis

Citium

Side

Soli

Perga

CYPRUS

Pelusium

EGYPT

ASIA MINOR

Ancyra

Iconium

Alexandria

Rhodes

Pergamum ✝ Thyatira

✝ Philadelphia

✝ Sardis Laodicea ✝

Smyrna ✝ Ephesus

Halicarnassos

Nicomedia
Prusa

Assos

Myteleme

Samos

Cos

Crossos

Gortyna

CRETE

Philippi

Thessalonica

Larissa

Delphi

Corinth

Patrae

Sparta

Pharae

GREECE

Cyrene

Barca

Berenice

CYRENAICA

0   100

Miles

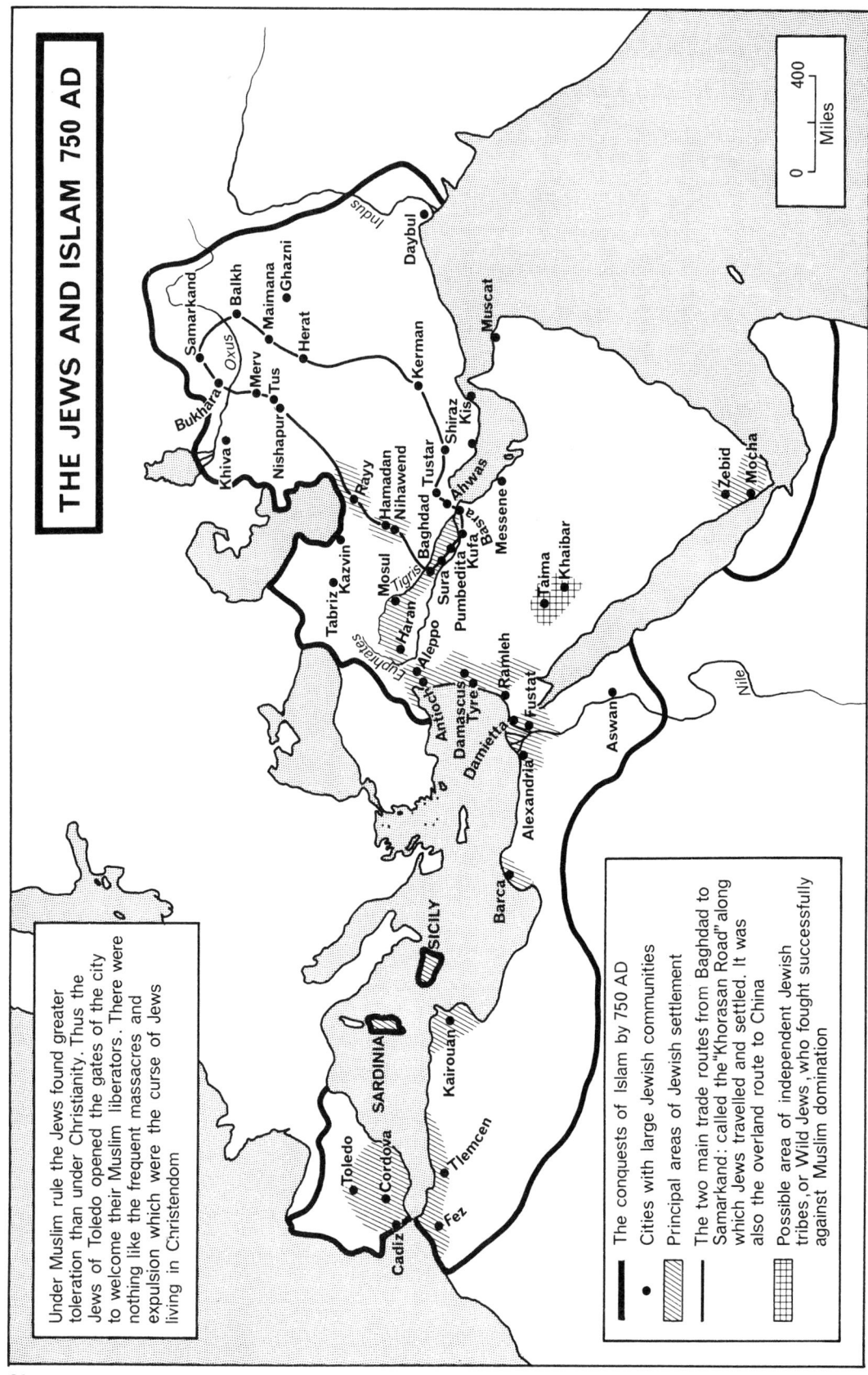

THE JEWS AND ISLAM 750 AD

Under Muslim rule the Jews found greater toleration than under Christianity. Thus the Jews of Toledo opened the gates of the city to welcome their Muslim liberators. There were nothing like the frequent massacres and expulsion which were the curse of Jews living in Christendom

400

0

Miles

Indus

Daybul

Ghazni

Balkh

Maimana

Samarkand

Muscat

Herat

Bukhara

Oxus

Merv

Kerman

Tus

Khiva

Nishapur

Shiraz

Kis

Rayy

Zebid

Hamadan

Baghdad

Tustar

Ahwas

Mocha

Nihawend

Kazvin

Basra

Tabriz

Mosul

Kufa

Messene

Tigris

Sura

Taima

Harah

Pumbedita

Khaibar

Aleppo

Euphrates

Ramleh

Antioch

Damascus

Fustat

Tyre

Damietta

Aswan

Alexandria

Nile

Barca

SICILY

SARDINIA

Kairouan

Tlemcen

Toledo

Cordova

Fez

Cadiz

The conquests of Islam by 750 AD

Cities with large Jewish communities

Principal areas of Jewish settlement

The two main trade routes from Baghdad to Samarkand: called the "Khorasan Road" along which Jews travelled and settled. It was also the overland route to China

Possible area of independent Jewish tribes, or Wild Jews, who fought successfully against Muslim domination

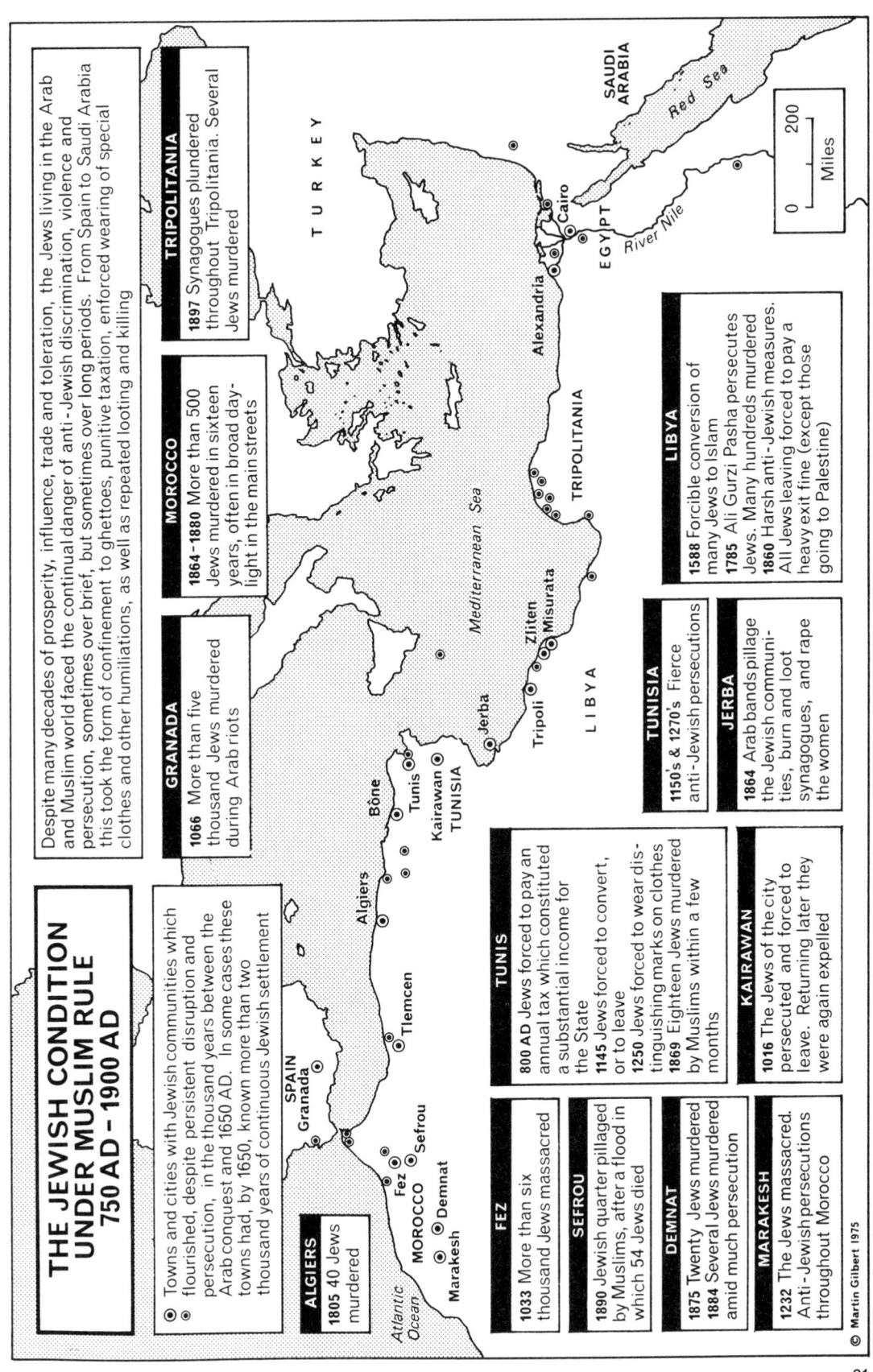

THE JEWISH CONDITION UNDER MUSLIM RULE 750 AD – 1900 AD

Despite many decades of prosperity, influence, trade and toleration, the Jews living in the Arab and Muslim world faced the continual danger of anti-Jewish discrimination, violence and persecution, sometimes over brief, but sometimes over long periods. From Spain to Saudi Arabia this took the form of confinement to ghettoes, punitive taxation, enforced wearing of special clothes and other humiliations, as well as repeated looting and killing

- Towns and cities with Jewish communities which flourished, despite persistent disruption and persecution, in the thousand years between the Arab conquest and 1650 AD. In some cases these towns had, by 1650, known more than two thousand years of continuous Jewish settlement

TRIPOLITANIA
1897 Synagogues plundered throughout Tripolitania. Several Jews murdered

MOROCCO
1864-1880 More than 500 Jews murdered in sixteen years, often in broad daylight in the main streets

GRANADA
1066 More than five thousand Jews murdered during Arab riots

LIBYA
1588 Forcible conversion of many Jews to Islam. 1785 Ali Gurzi Pasha persecutes Jews. Many hundreds murdered. 1860 Harsh anti-Jewish measures. All Jews leaving forced to pay a heavy exit fine (except those going to Palestine)

TUNISIA
1150's & 1270's Fierce anti-Jewish persecutions

JERBA
1864 Arab bands pillage the Jewish communities, burn and loot synagogues, and rape the women

TUNIS
800 AD Jews forced to pay an annual tax which constituted a substantial income for the State. 1145 Jews forced to convert, or to leave. 1250 Jews forced to wear distinguishing marks on clothes. 1869 Eighteen Jews murdered by Muslims within a few months

KAIRAWAN
1016 The Jews of the city persecuted and forced to leave. Returning later they were again expelled

ALGIERS
1805 40 Jews murdered

FEZ
1033 More than six thousand Jews massacred

SEFROU
1890 Jewish quarter pillaged by Muslims, after a flood in which 54 Jews died

DEMNAT
1875 Twenty Jews murdered. 1884 Several Jews murdered amid much persecution

MARAKESH
1232 The Jews massacred. Anti-Jewish persecutions throughout Morocco

Map labels: SAUDI ARABIA, Red Sea, TURKEY, EGYPT, River Nile, Cairo, Alexandria, Mediterranean Sea, Zliten, Misurata, Tripoli, LIBYA, TRIPOLITANIA, Jerba, Tripoli, Tunis, Kairawan TUNISIA, Bône, Algiers, Tlemcen, Fez, Sefrou, MOROCCO, Demnat, Marakesh, SPAIN, Granada, Atlantic Ocean

0 200 Miles

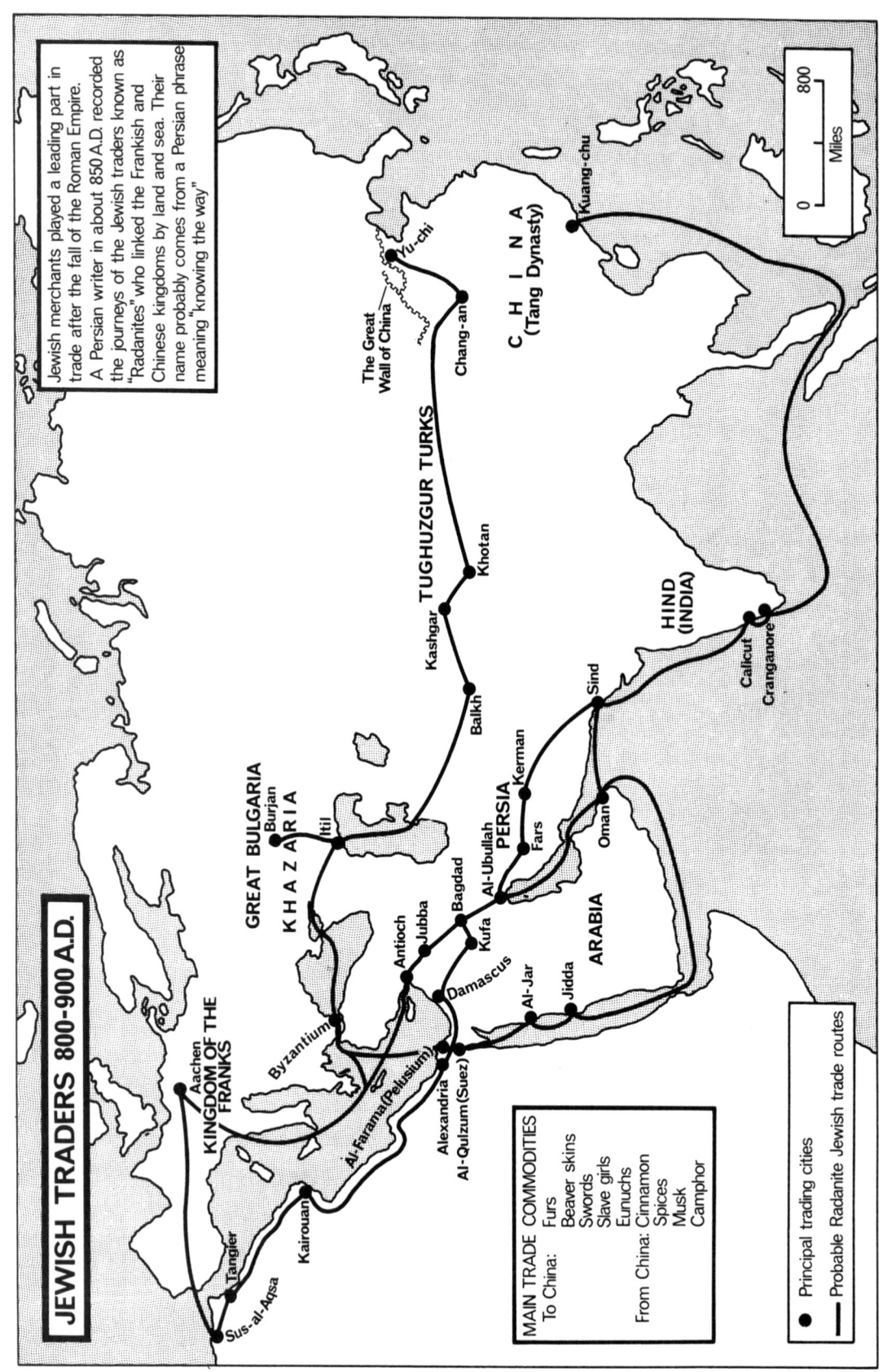

JEWISH TRADERS 800-900 A.D.

Jewish merchants played a leading part in trade after the fall of the Roman Empire. A Persian writer in about 850 A.D. recorded the journeys of the Jewish traders known as "Radanites" who linked the Frankish and Chinese kingdoms by land and sea. Their name probably comes from a Persian phrase meaning "knowing the way"

0 ____ 800

Miles

The Great Wall of China

Kuang-chu

Yu-chi

Chang-an

CHINA
(Tang Dynasty)

TUGHUZGUR TURKS

Khotan

Kashgar

Balkh

HIND
(INDIA)

GREAT BULGARIA

Burjan

KHAZARIA

Itil

Sind

Calicut
Cranganore

Kerman

PERSIA

Fars

Oman

Al-Ubullah

Bagdad

ARABIA

Antioch

Jubba

Kufa

Damascus

Al-Jar

Jidda

Byzantium

Al-Farama (Pelusium)

Alexandria

Al-Qulzum (Suez)

Aachen

KINGDOM OF THE FRANKS

Kairouan

Tangier

Sus-al-Aqsa

MAIN TRADE COMMODITIES
To China: Furs
Beaver skins
Swords
Slave girls
Eunuchs
From China: Cinnamon
Spices
Musk
Camphor

● Principal trading cities

—— Probable Radanite Jewish trade routes

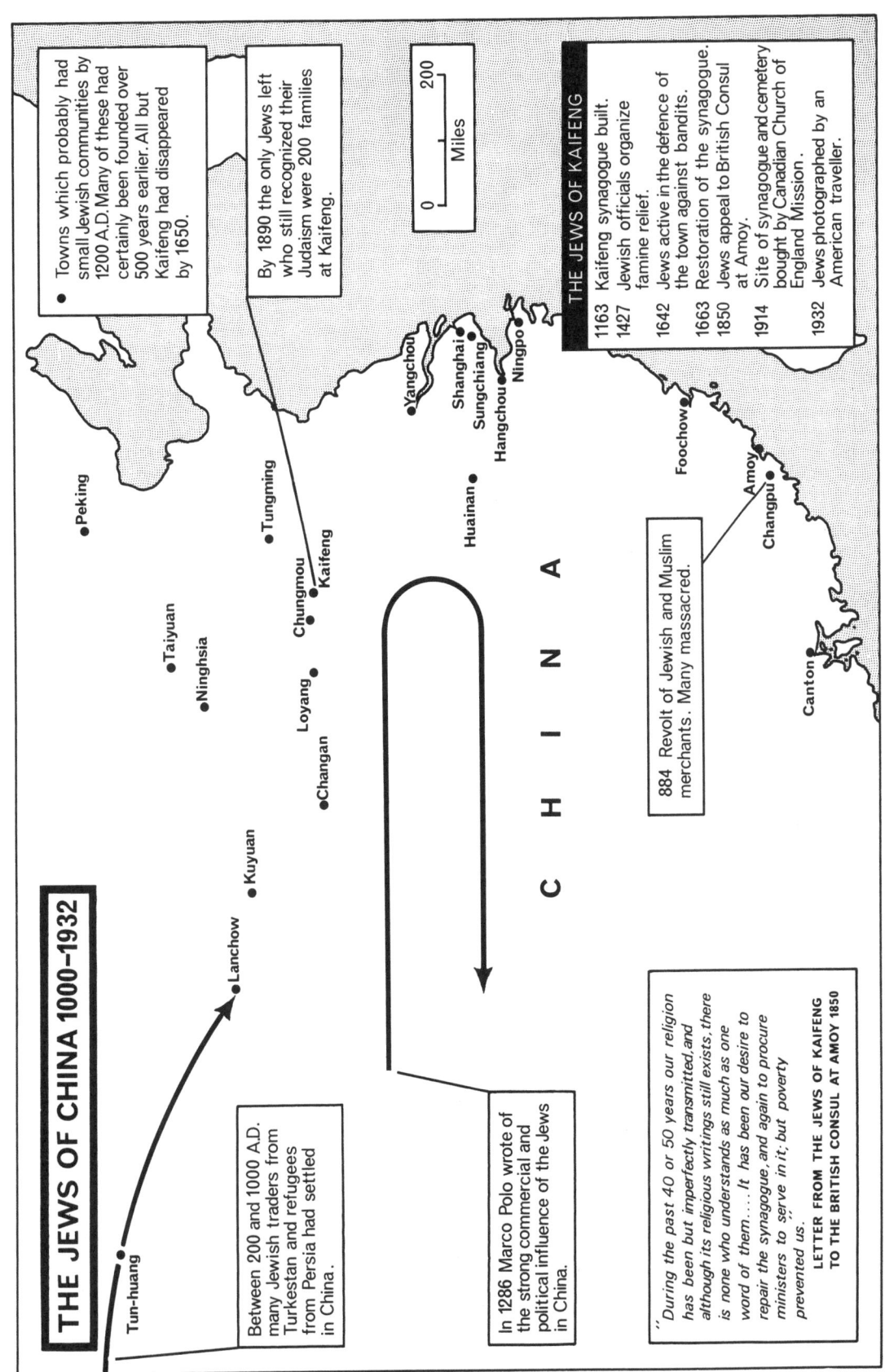

THE JEWS OF CHINA 1000–1932

Towns which probably had small Jewish communities by 1200 A.D. Many of these had certainly been founded over 500 years earlier. All but Kaifeng had disappeared by 1650.

By 1890 the only Jews left who still recognized their Judaism were 200 families at Kaifeng.

0   200
Miles

THE JEWS OF KAIFENG

1163	Kaifeng synagogue built.
1427	Jewish officials organize famine relief.
1642	Jews active in the defence of the town against bandits.
1663	Restoration of the synagogue.
1850	Jews appeal to British Consul at Amoy.
1914	Site of synagogue and cemetery bought by Canadian Church of England Mission.
1932	Jews photographed by an American traveller.

Between 200 and 1000 A.D. many Jewish traders from Turkestan and refugees from Persia had settled in China.

In 1286 Marco Polo wrote of the strong commercial and political influence of the Jews in China.

884 Revolt of Jewish and Muslim merchants. Many massacred.

"During the past 40 or 50 years our religion has been but imperfectly transmitted, and although its religious writings still exists, there is none who understands as much as one word of them.... It has been our desire to repair the synagogue, and again to procure ministers to serve in it; but poverty prevented us."

LETTER FROM THE JEWS OF KAIFENG TO THE BRITISH CONSUL AT AMOY 1850

C H I N A

Tun-huang

Lanchow

Kuyuan

Peking

Taiyuan

Ninghsia

Changan

Loyang

Chungmou

Kaifeng

Tungming

Huainan

Yangchou

Shanghai

Sungchiang

Hangchou

Ningpo

Foochow

Amoy

Changpu

Canton

23

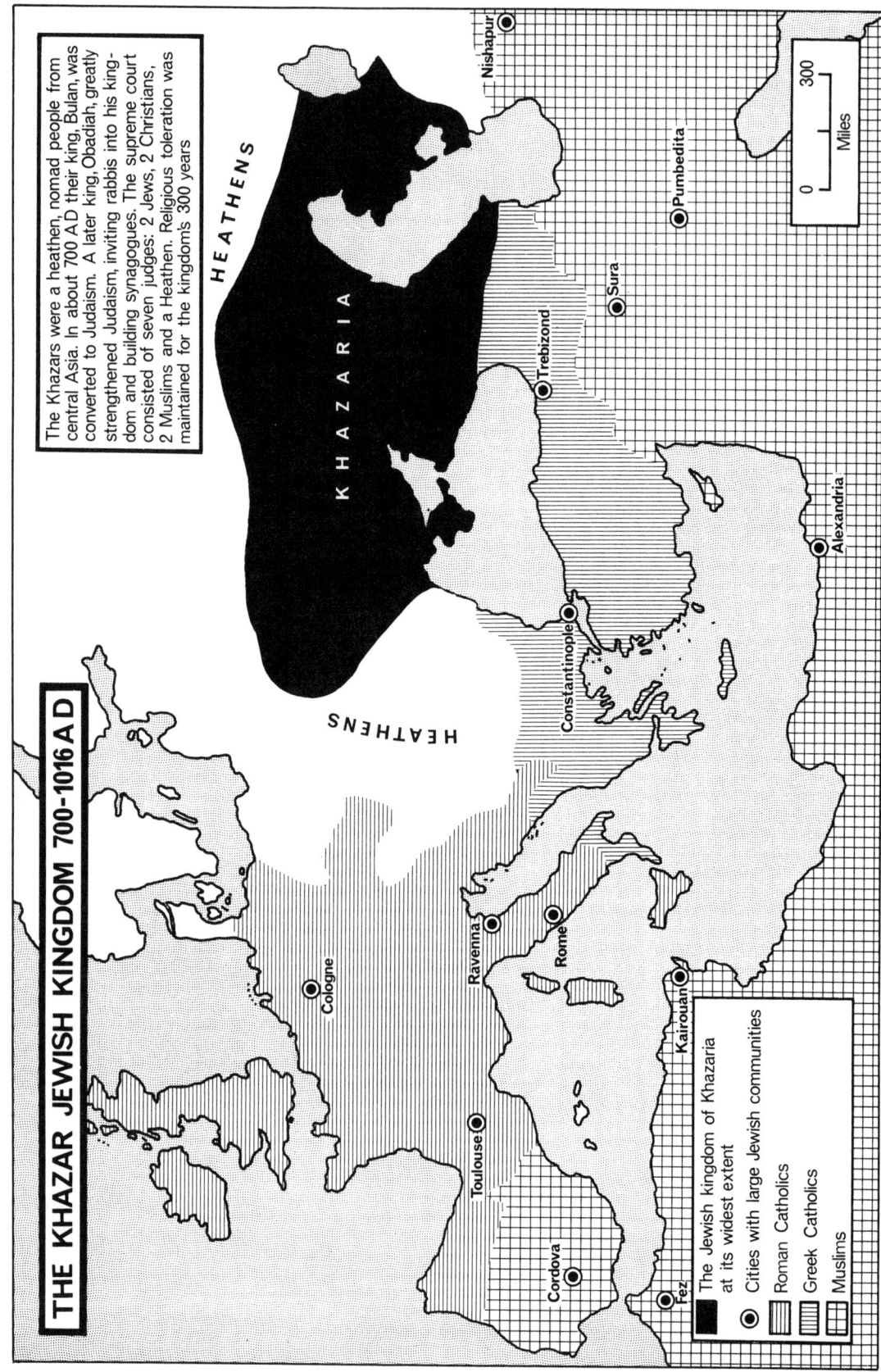

THE KHAZAR JEWISH KINGDOM 700-1016 AD

The Khazars were a heathen, nomad people from central Asia. In about 700 AD their king, Bulan, was converted to Judaism. A later king, Obadiah, greatly strengthened Judaism, inviting rabbis into his kingdom and building synagogues. The supreme court consisted of seven judges: 2 Jews, 2 Christians, 2 Muslims and a Heathen. Religious toleration was maintained for the kingdom's 300 years

HEATHENS

HEATHENS

KHAZARIA

Nishapur

Pumbedita

Sura

Trebizond

Alexandria

Constantinople

Cologne

Ravenna

Rome

Toulouse

Kairouan

Cordova

Fez

0   300
Miles

■ The Jewish kingdom of Khazaria at its widest extent

⊙ Cities with large Jewish communities

▤ Roman Catholics

▥ Greek Catholics

▦ Muslims

24

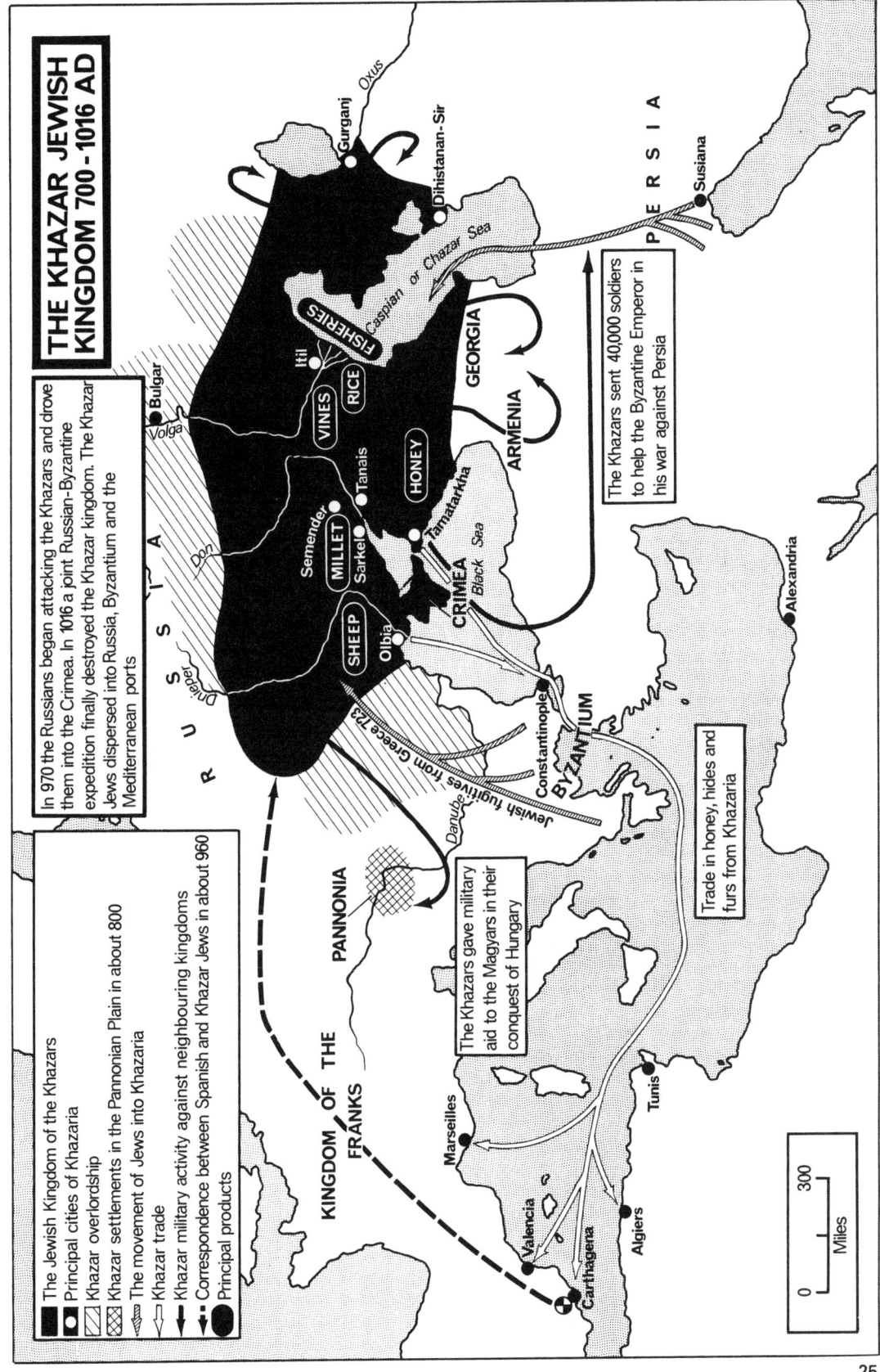

THE KHAZAR JEWISH KINGDOM 700 - 1016 AD

In 970 the Russians began attacking the Khazars and drove them into the Crimea. In 1016 a joint Russian-Byzantine expedition finally destroyed the Khazar kingdom. The Khazar Jews dispersed into Russia, Byzantium and the Mediterranean ports

The Khazars sent 40,000 soldiers to help the Byzantine Emperor in his war against Persia

Trade in honey, hides and furs from Khazaria

The Khazars gave military aid to the Magyars in their conquest of Hungary

Jewish fugitives from Greece 723

- ■ The Jewish Kingdom of the Khazars
- ○ Principal cities of Khazaria
- Khazar overlordship
- Khazar settlements in the Pannonian Plain in about 800
- The movement of Jews into Khazaria
- Khazar trade
- Khazar military activity against neighbouring kingdoms
- Correspondence between Spanish and Khazar Jews in about 960
- ● Principal products

PERSIA

Susiana

Oxus

Gurganj

Dihistanan- Sir

Caspian or Chazar Sea

Itil

FISHERIES

VINES

RICE

GEORGIA

ARMENIA

HONEY

Volga

Bulgar

Semender

MILLET

Tanais

Sarkel

Don

Tamatarkha

Black Sea

CRIMEA

SHEEP

Olbia

Dnieper

RUSSIA

Danube

Constantinople

BYZANTIUM

Alexandria

PANNONIA

KINGDOM OF THE FRANKS

Marseilles

Valencia

Carthagena

Algiers

Tunis

0   300

Miles

25

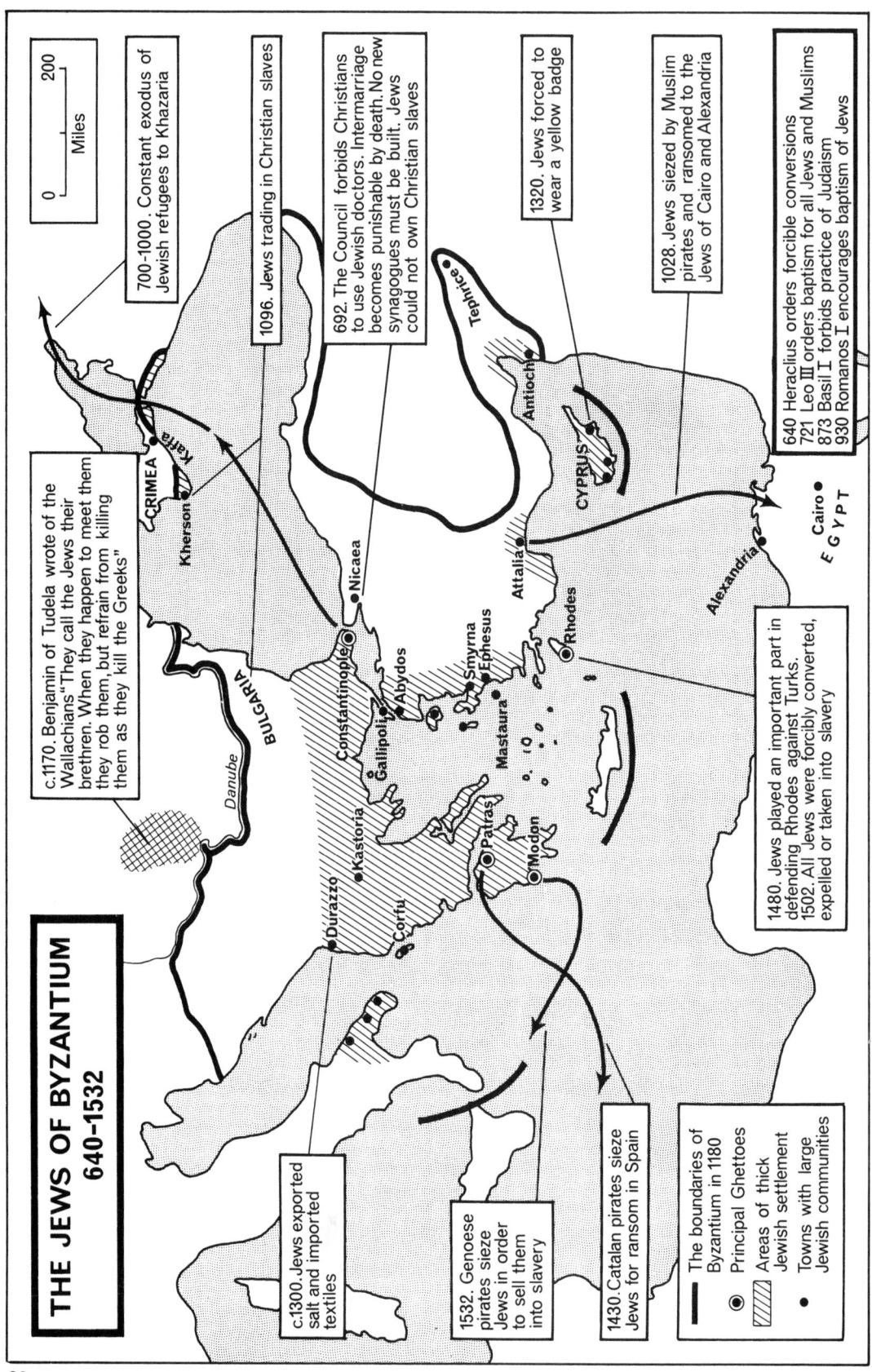

THE JEWS OF BYZANTIUM
640–1532

200

Miles

0

700-1000. Constant exodus of Jewish refugees to Khazaria

1096. Jews trading in Christian slaves

692. The Council forbids Christians to use Jewish doctors. Intermarriage becomes punishable by death. No new synagogues must be built. Jews could not own Christian slaves

1320. Jews forced to wear a yellow badge

1028. Jews siezed by Muslim pirates and ransomed to the Jews of Cairo and Alexandria

c.1170. Benjamin of Tudela wrote of the Wallachians "They call the Jews their brethren. When they happen to meet them they rob them, but refrain from killing them as they kill the Greeks"

640 Heraclius orders forcible conversions
721 Leo III orders baptism for all Jews and Muslims
873 Basil I forbids practice of Judaism
930 Romanos I encourages baptism of Jews

CRIMEA

Kaffa

Kherson

Tephrice

Antioch

CYPRUS

Nicaea

BULGARIA

Danube

Constantinople

Gallipoli

Abydos

Smyrna

Ephesus

Mastaura

Attalia

Rhodes

Alexandria

Cairo

E G Y P T

Kastoria

Patras

Durazzo

Corfu

Modon

1480. Jews played an important part in defending Rhodes against Turks.
1502. All Jews were forcibly converted, expelled or taken into slavery

c.1300. Jews exported salt and imported textiles

1532. Genoese pirates sieze Jews in order to sell them into slavery

1430. Catalan pirates sieze Jews for ransom in Spain

The boundaries of Byzantium in 1180

Principal Ghettoes

Areas of thick Jewish settlement

Towns with large Jewish communities

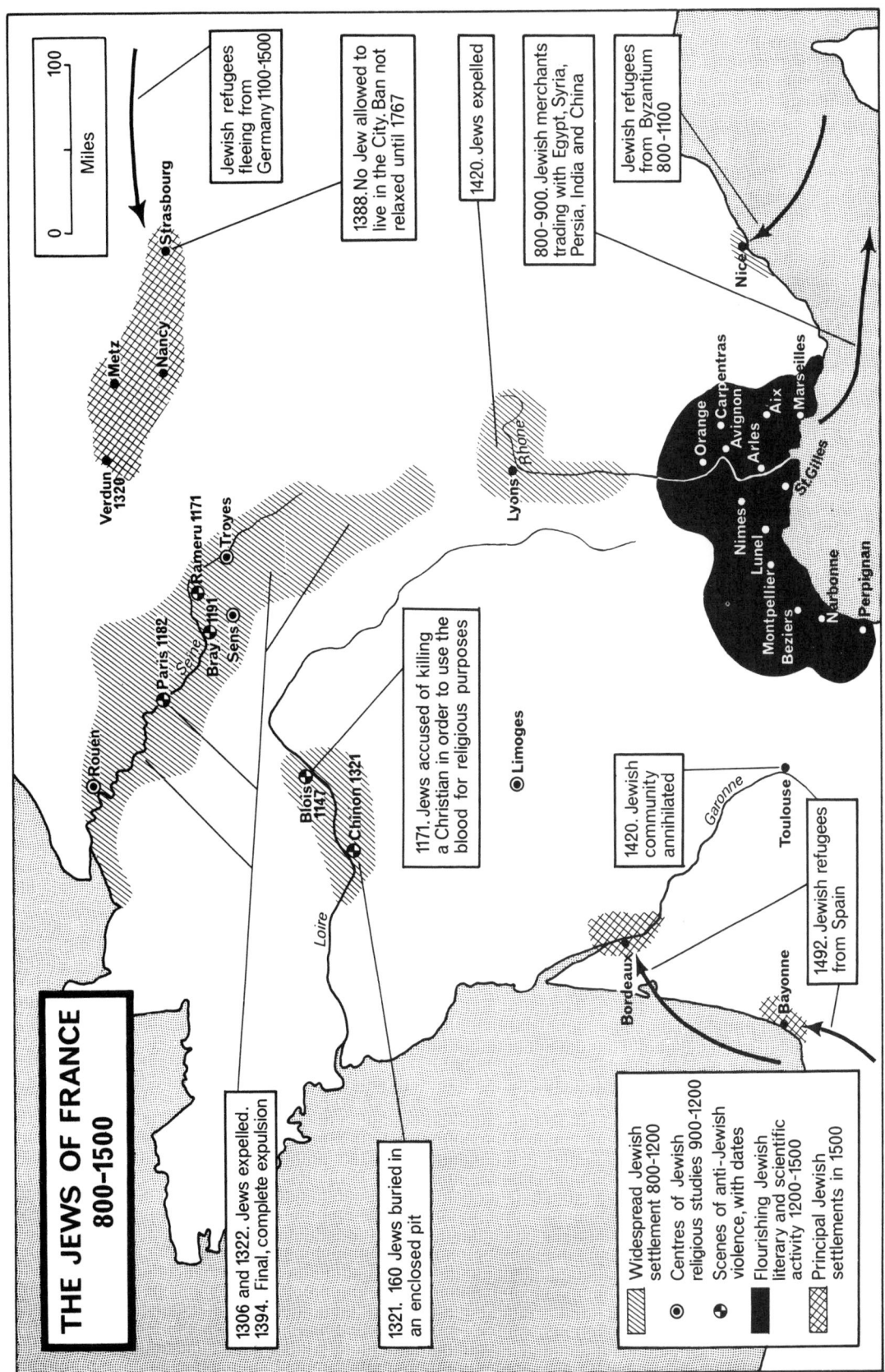

THE JEWS OF FRANCE 800-1500

Miles
0   100

Jewish refugees fleeing from Germany 1100-1500

1388. No Jew allowed to live in the City. Ban not relaxed until 1767

1420. Jews expelled

800-900. Jewish merchants trading with Egypt, Syria, Persia, India and China

Jewish refugees from Byzantium 800-1100

1306 and 1322. Jews expelled. 1394. Final, complete expulsion

1321. 160 Jews buried in an enclosed pit

1171. Jews accused of killing a Christian in order to use the blood for religious purposes

1420. Jewish community annihilated

1492. Jewish refugees from Spain

Verdun 1320
Metz
Nancy
Strasbourg
Rameru 1171
Troyes
Paris 1182
Seine
Bray 1191
Sens
Rouen
Blois 1147
Chinon 1321
Loire
Limoges
Lyons
Rhône
Orange
Carpentras
Avignon
Arles
Aix
Marseilles
St. Gilles
Nîmes
Lunel
Montpellier
Béziers
Narbonne
Perpignan
Nice
Garonne
Toulouse
Bordeaux
Bayonne

Widespread Jewish settlement 800-1200

Centres of Jewish religious studies 900-1200

Scenes of anti-Jewish violence, with dates

Flourishing Jewish literary and scientific activity 1200-1500

Principal Jewish settlements in 1500

27

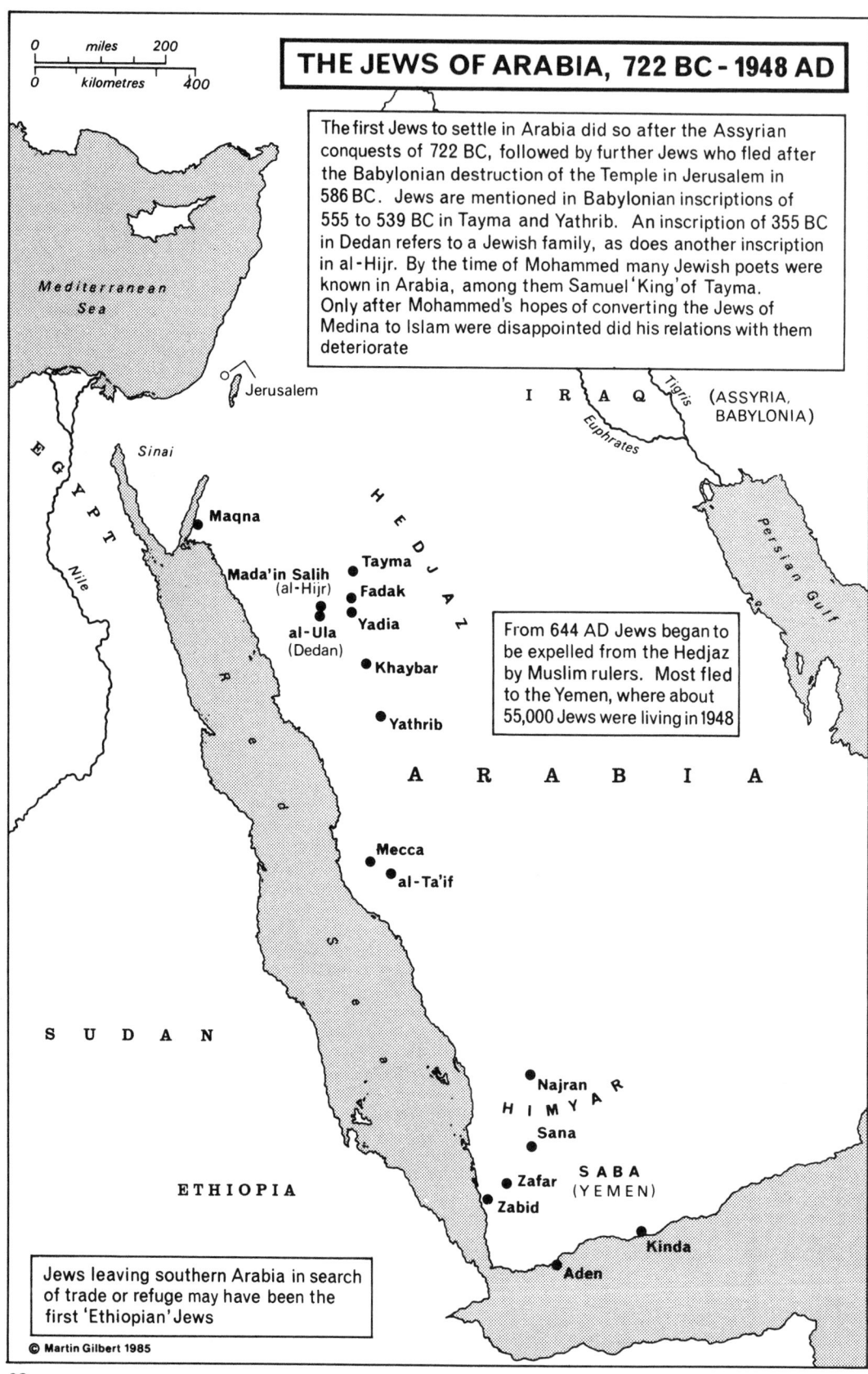

THE JEWS OF ARABIA, 722 BC - 1948 AD

The first Jews to settle in Arabia did so after the Assyrian conquests of 722 BC, followed by further Jews who fled after the Babylonian destruction of the Temple in Jerusalem in 586 BC. Jews are mentioned in Babylonian inscriptions of 555 to 539 BC in Tayma and Yathrib. An inscription of 355 BC in Dedan refers to a Jewish family, as does another inscription in al-Hijr. By the time of Mohammed many Jewish poets were known in Arabia, among them Samuel 'King' of Tayma.
Only after Mohammed's hopes of converting the Jews of Medina to Islam were disappointed did his relations with them deteriorate

Mediterranean Sea

Jerusalem

I R A Q   (ASSYRIA, BABYLONIA)

Tigris

Euphrates

Persian Gulf

E G Y P T

Sinai

Nile

H E D J A Z

Maqna

Mada'in Salih (al-Hijr)

Tayma

Fadak

Yadia

al-Ula (Dedan)

Khaybar

Yathrib

A R A B I A

From 644 AD Jews began to be expelled from the Hedjaz by Muslim rulers. Most fled to the Yemen, where about 55,000 Jews were living in 1948

Mecca

al-Ta'if

R   e   d   S   e   a

S U D A N

Najran

H I M Y A R

Sana

Zafar

S A B A (YEMEN)

ETHIOPIA

Zabid

Kinda

Aden

Jews leaving southern Arabia in search of trade or refuge may have been the first 'Ethiopian' Jews

© Martin Gilbert 1985

0   miles   200
0   kilometres   400

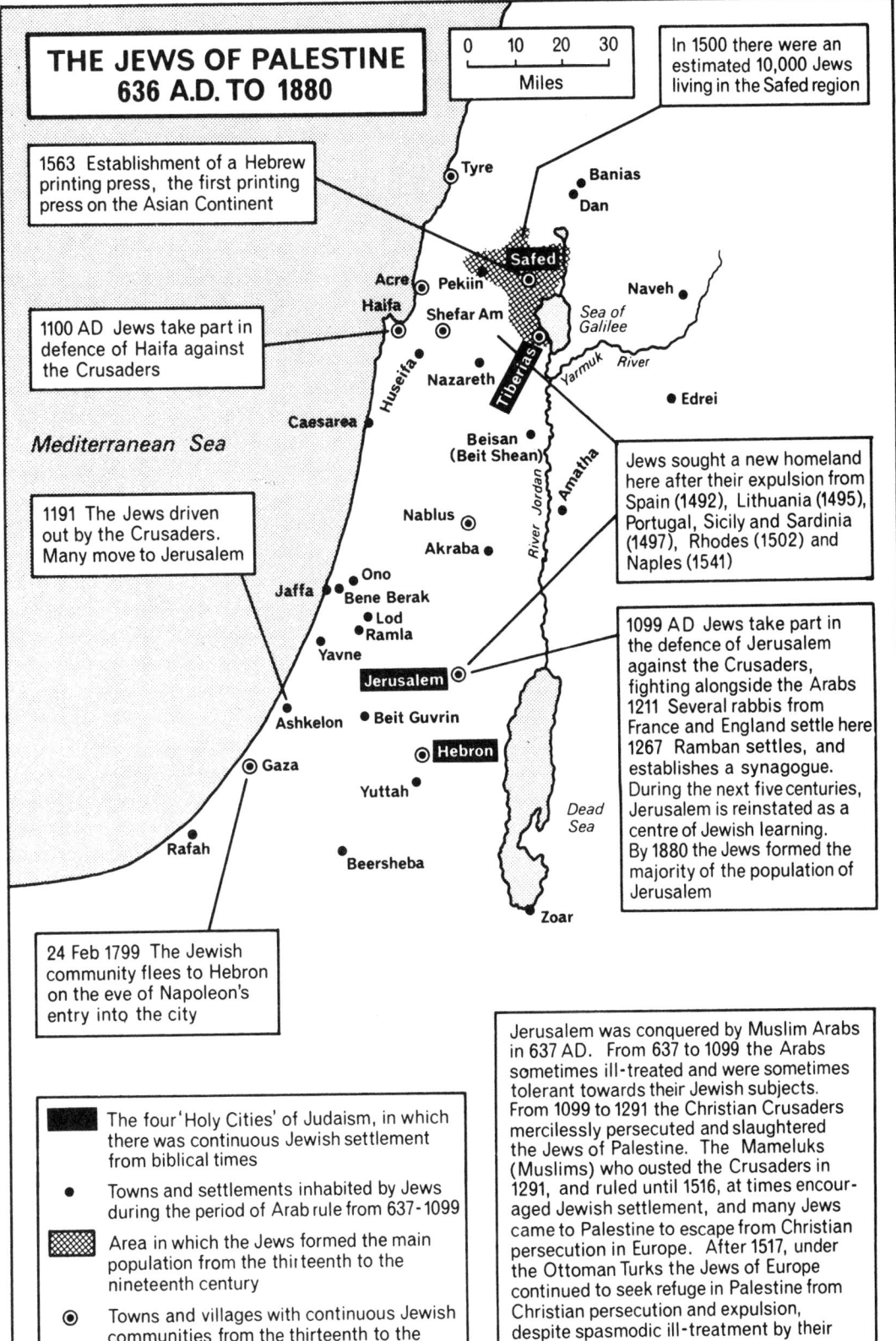

THE JEWS OF PALESTINE 636 A.D. TO 1880

0 10 20 30
Miles

In 1500 there were an estimated 10,000 Jews living in the Safed region

1563 Establishment of a Hebrew printing press, the first printing press on the Asian Continent

• Tyre

• Banias
  Dan

Safed

Acre • Pekiin

Naveh

Haifa

Shefar Am

Sea of Galilee

1100 AD Jews take part in defence of Haifa against the Crusaders

Huseifa

Nazareth

Tiberias

Yarmuk River

Caesarea

• Edrei

Mediterranean Sea

Beisan (Beit Shean)

Jews sought a new homeland here after their expulsion from Spain (1492), Lithuania (1495), Portugal, Sicily and Sardinia (1497), Rhodes (1502) and Naples (1541)

1191 The Jews driven out by the Crusaders. Many move to Jerusalem

Nablus

Akraba •

Ono

Jaffa • Bene Berak

• Lod

Ramla

Yavne

Jerusalem

Ashkelon • Beit Guvrin

Hebron

• Gaza

Yuttah

Dead Sea

Rafah

• Beersheba

Zoar

1099 AD Jews take part in the defence of Jerusalem against the Crusaders, fighting alongside the Arabs
1211 Several rabbis from France and England settle here
1267 Ramban settles, and establishes a synagogue. During the next five centuries, Jerusalem is reinstated as a centre of Jewish learning.
By 1880 the Jews formed the majority of the population of Jerusalem

24 Feb 1799 The Jewish community flees to Hebron on the eve of Napoleon's entry into the city

Jerusalem was conquered by Muslim Arabs in 637 AD. From 637 to 1099 the Arabs sometimes ill-treated and were sometimes tolerant towards their Jewish subjects. From 1099 to 1291 the Christian Crusaders mercilessly persecuted and slaughtered the Jews of Palestine. The Mameluks (Muslims) who ousted the Crusaders in 1291, and ruled until 1516, at times encouraged Jewish settlement, and many Jews came to Palestine to escape from Christian persecution in Europe. After 1517, under the Ottoman Turks the Jews of Europe continued to seek refuge in Palestine from Christian persecution and expulsion, despite spasmodic ill-treatment by their Muslim rulers

■ The four 'Holy Cities' of Judaism, in which there was continuous Jewish settlement from biblical times

• Towns and settlements inhabited by Jews during the period of Arab rule from 637-1099

▨ Area in which the Jews formed the main population from the thirteenth to the nineteenth century

⊙ Towns and villages with continuous Jewish communities from the thirteenth to the nineteenth century

© Martin Gilbert

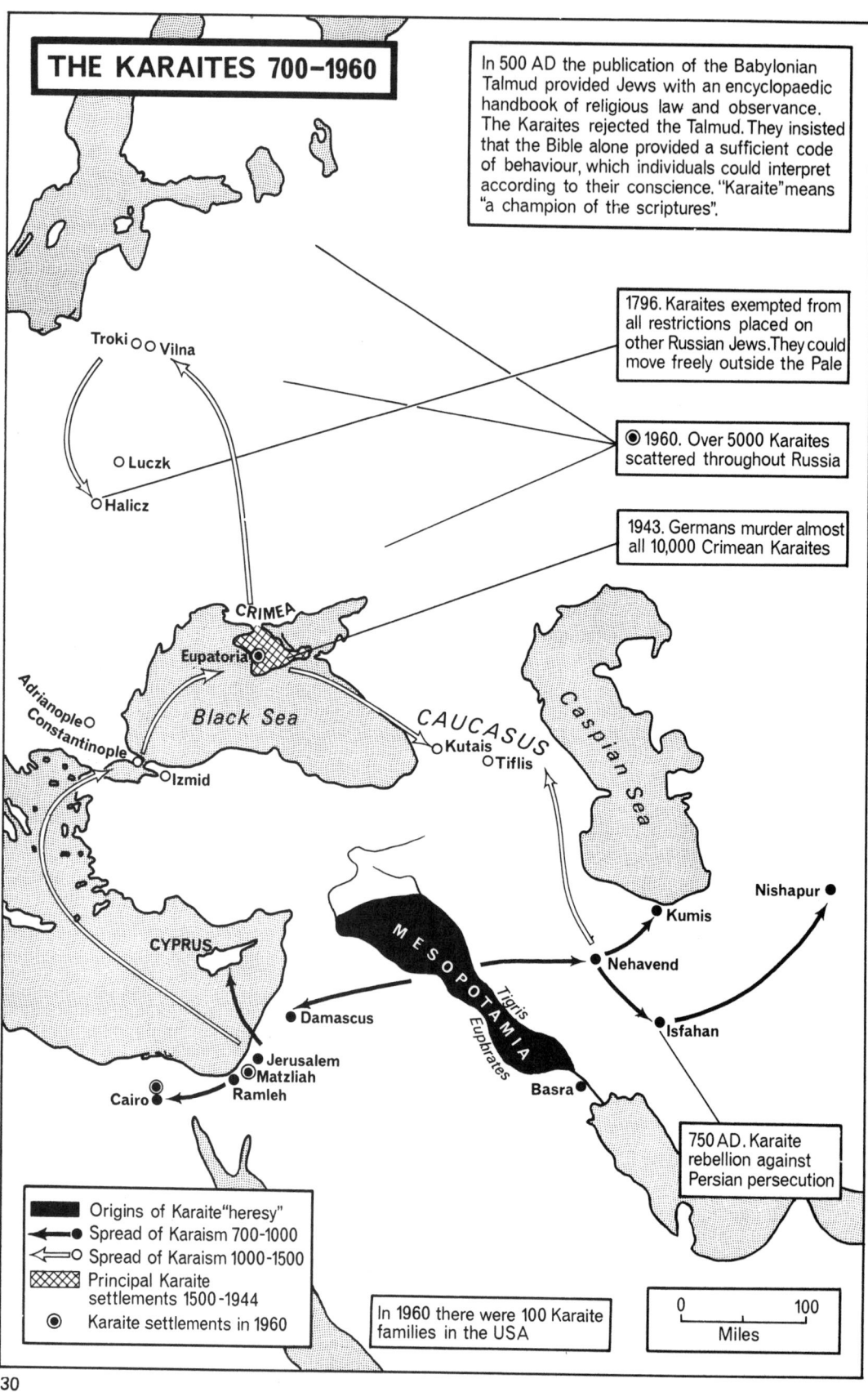

THE KARAITES 700–1960

In 500 AD the publication of the Babylonian Talmud provided Jews with an encyclopaedic handbook of religious law and observance. The Karaites rejected the Talmud. They insisted that the Bible alone provided a sufficient code of behaviour, which individuals could interpret according to their conscience. "Karaite" means "a champion of the scriptures".

1796. Karaites exempted from all restrictions placed on other Russian Jews. They could move freely outside the Pale

◉ 1960. Over 5000 Karaites scattered throughout Russia

1943. Germans murder almost all 10,000 Crimean Karaites

Troki ○ ○ Vilna

○ Luczk

○ Halicz

CRIMEA

Eupatoria ◉

Adrianople ○
Constantinople ○
○ Izmid

Black Sea

CAUCASUS

○ Kutais
○ Tiflis

Caspian Sea

Nishapur ●

CYPRUS

MESOPOTAMIA

Tigris
Euphrates

● Kumis

● Nehavend

● Isfahan

● Damascus

Jerusalem ●
◉ Matzliah
Ramleh

Cairo ◉ ●

Basra ●

750 AD. Karaite rebellion against Persian persecution

Legend:
- � Origins of Karaite "heresy"
- ←● Spread of Karaism 700–1000
- ⇐○ Spread of Karaism 1000–1500
- ▨ Principal Karaite settlements 1500–1944
- ◉ Karaite settlements in 1960

In 1960 there were 100 Karaite families in the USA

0 — 100
Miles

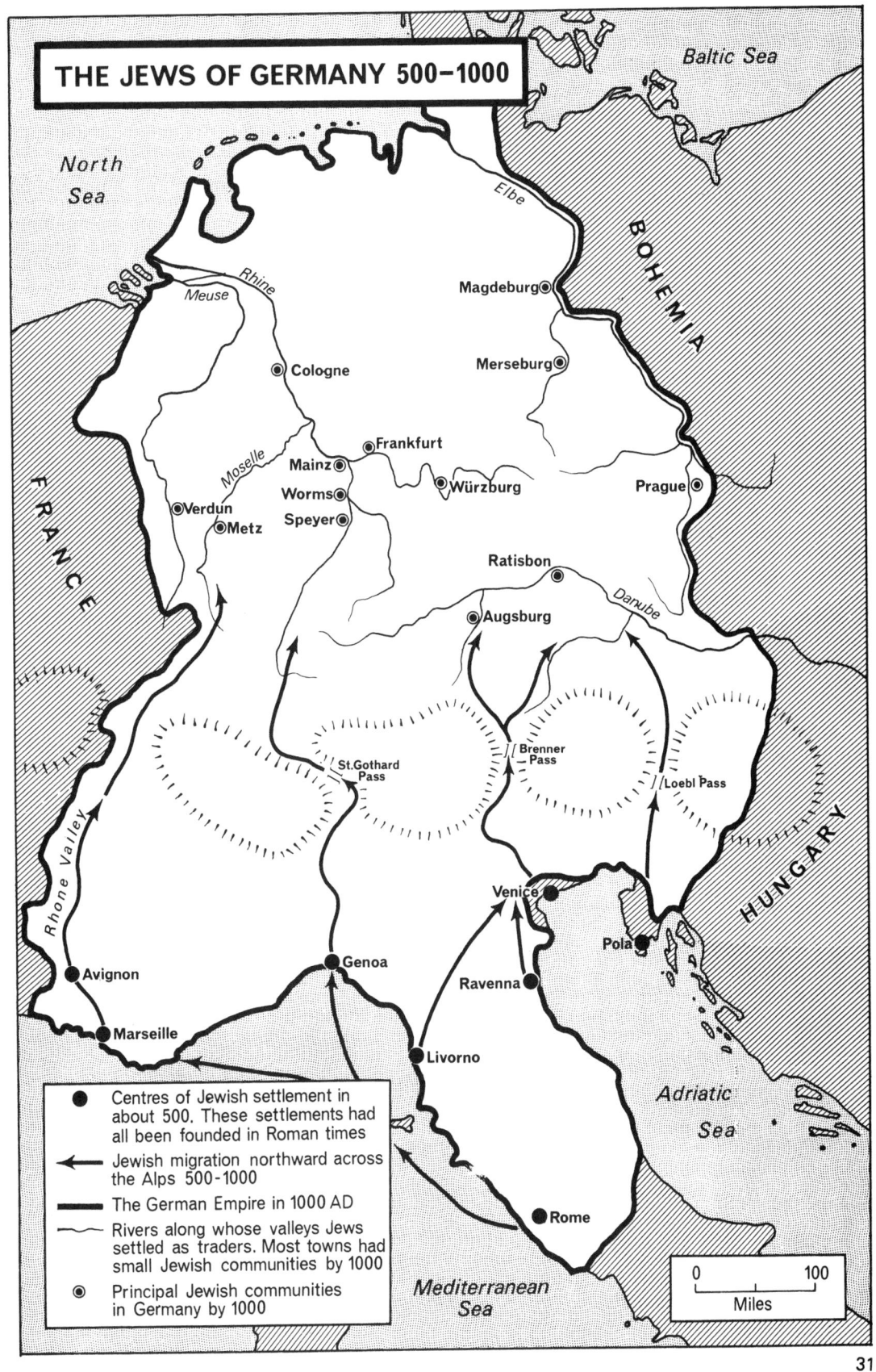

THE JEWS OF GERMANY 500–1000

Baltic Sea

North Sea

Elbe

BOHEMIA

Rhine

Meuse

● **Magdeburg** ◉

● **Merseburg** ◉

FRANCE

Moselle

◉ **Cologne**

◉ **Frankfurt**

Mainz ◉

◉ **Würzburg**

Worms ◉

◉**Verdun**

Speyer ◉

◉**Metz**

Prague ◉

Ratisbon ◉

Danube

◉ **Augsburg**

St.Gothard
Pass

]{**Brenner
Pass**

]{ **Loebl Pass**

HUNGARY

Rhone Valley

Venice ●

Pola ●

● **Avignon**

● **Genoa**

Ravenna ●

● **Marseille**

● **Livorno**

*Adriatic
Sea*

● **Rome**

●	Centres of Jewish settlement in about 500. These settlements had all been founded in Roman times
←	Jewish migration northward across the Alps 500-1000
▬	The German Empire in 1000 AD
~	Rivers along whose valleys Jews settled as traders. Most towns had small Jewish communities by 1000
◉	Principal Jewish communities in Germany by 1000

*Mediterranean
Sea*

0	100

Miles

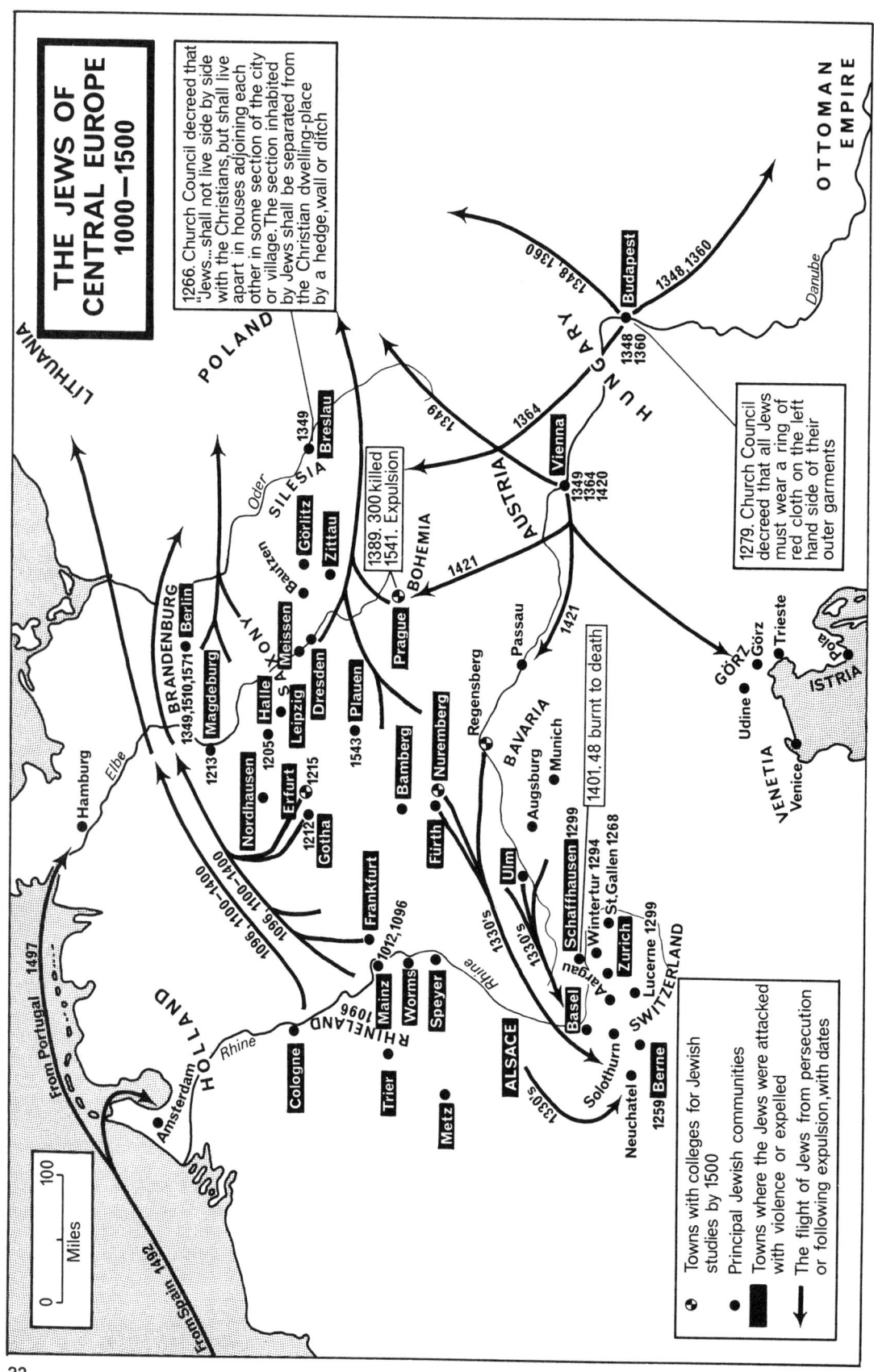

THE JEWS OF CENTRAL EUROPE 1000–1500

1266. Church Council decreed that "Jews...shall not live side by side with the Christians, but shall live apart in houses adjoining each other in some section of the city or village. The section inhabited by Jews shall be separated from the Christian dwelling-place by a hedge, wall or ditch

1279. Church Council decreed that all Jews must wear a ring of red cloth on the left hand side of their outer garments

LITHUANIA

POLAND

Oder

SILESIA   1349   Breslau

Görlitz

Bautzen   Zittau

BRANDENBURG   1349,1510,1571 ● Berlin

Magdeburg   1213

SAXONY   Meissen

Halle   Leipzig   Dresden

1205   1215   Plauen

Nordhausen   Erfurt   1543

1212   Gotha

Elbe

Hamburg

HOLLAND

Amsterdam

From Portugal 1497

From Spain 1492

Rhine

Cologne   RHINELAND 1096

Trier   Mainz   1012, 1096
Worms
Speyer

Metz

Frankfurt

Bamberg

Nuremberg

Fürth

1096, 1100–1400

Regensberg   Passau

BAVARIA   Munich

Augsburg

1330's   Ulm

1330's   Schaffhausen 1299
Wintertur 1294   St.Gallen 1268
Basel   Aargau   Zürich   Lucerne 1299

SWITZERLAND

1330's   Solothurn

Neuchatel   1259 Berne

1389. 300 killed
1541. Expulsion

BOHEMIA

Prague   1421

1349

AUSTRIA   1364   Vienna
1349
1364
1420

1421

1401, 48 burnt to death

GÖRZ   Görz
Udine   Trieste
VENETIA   ISTRIA
Venice

HUNGARY

Budapest   1348, 1360
1348
1360

Danube

OTTOMAN EMPIRE

Legend
- ☉ Towns with colleges for Jewish studies by 1500
- ● Principal Jewish communities
- ▬ Towns where the Jews were attacked with violence or expelled
- ↓ The flight of Jews from persecution or following expulsion, with dates

0   100
Miles

32

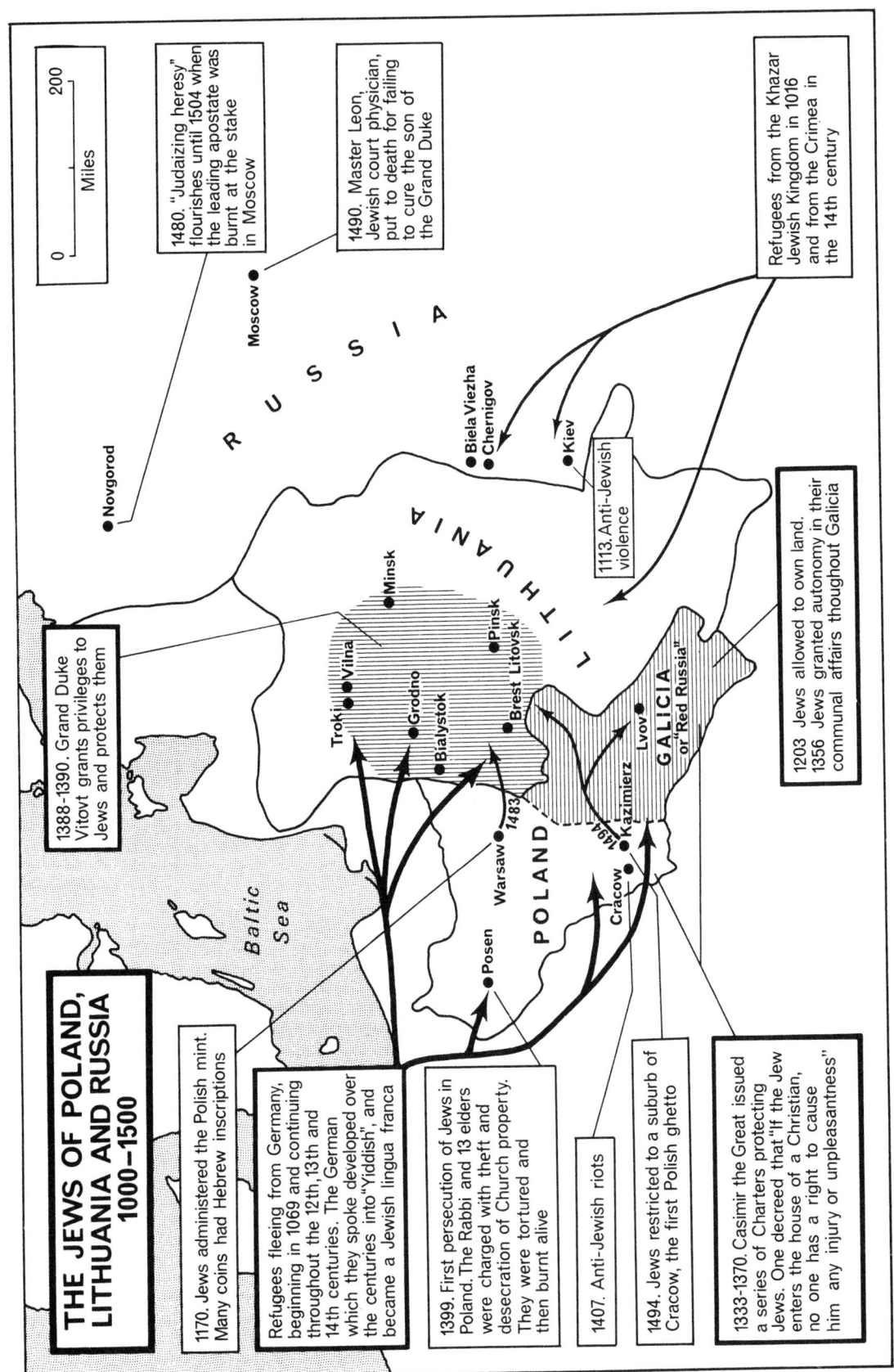

THE JEWS OF POLAND, LITHUANIA AND RUSSIA 1000–1500

0   200
Miles

1480. "Judaizing heresy" flourishes until 1504 when the leading apostate was burnt at the stake in Moscow

1490. Master Leon, Jewish court physician, put to death for failing to cure the son of the Grand Duke

Refugees from the Khazar Jewish Kingdom in 1016 and from the Crimea in the 14th century

1388-1390. Grand Duke Vitovt grants privileges to Jews and protects them

1113. Anti-Jewish violence

1203 Jews allowed to own land.
1356 Jews granted autonomy in their communal affairs throughout Galicia

1170. Jews administered the Polish mint. Many coins had Hebrew inscriptions

Refugees fleeing from Germany, beginning in 1069 and continuing throughout the 12th, 13th and 14th centuries. The German which they spoke developed over the centuries into "Yiddish", and became a Jewish lingua franca

1399. First persecution of Jews in Poland. The Rabbi and 13 elders were charged with theft and desecration of Church property. They were tortured and then burnt alive

1407. Anti-Jewish riots

1494. Jews restricted to a suburb of Cracow, the first Polish ghetto

1333-1370. Casimir the Great issued a series of Charters protecting Jews. One decreed that "If the Jew enters the house of a Christian, no one has a right to cause him any injury or unpleasantness"

RUSSIA

Moscow

Novgorod

Biela Viezha
Chernigov

Kiev

LITHUANIA

Minsk

Troki • Vilna

Grodno

Białystok

Pinsk

Brest Litovsk

Baltic Sea

Posen

Warsaw 1483

Kazimierz 1494

Lvov

GALICIA or "Red Russia"

POLAND

Cracow

33

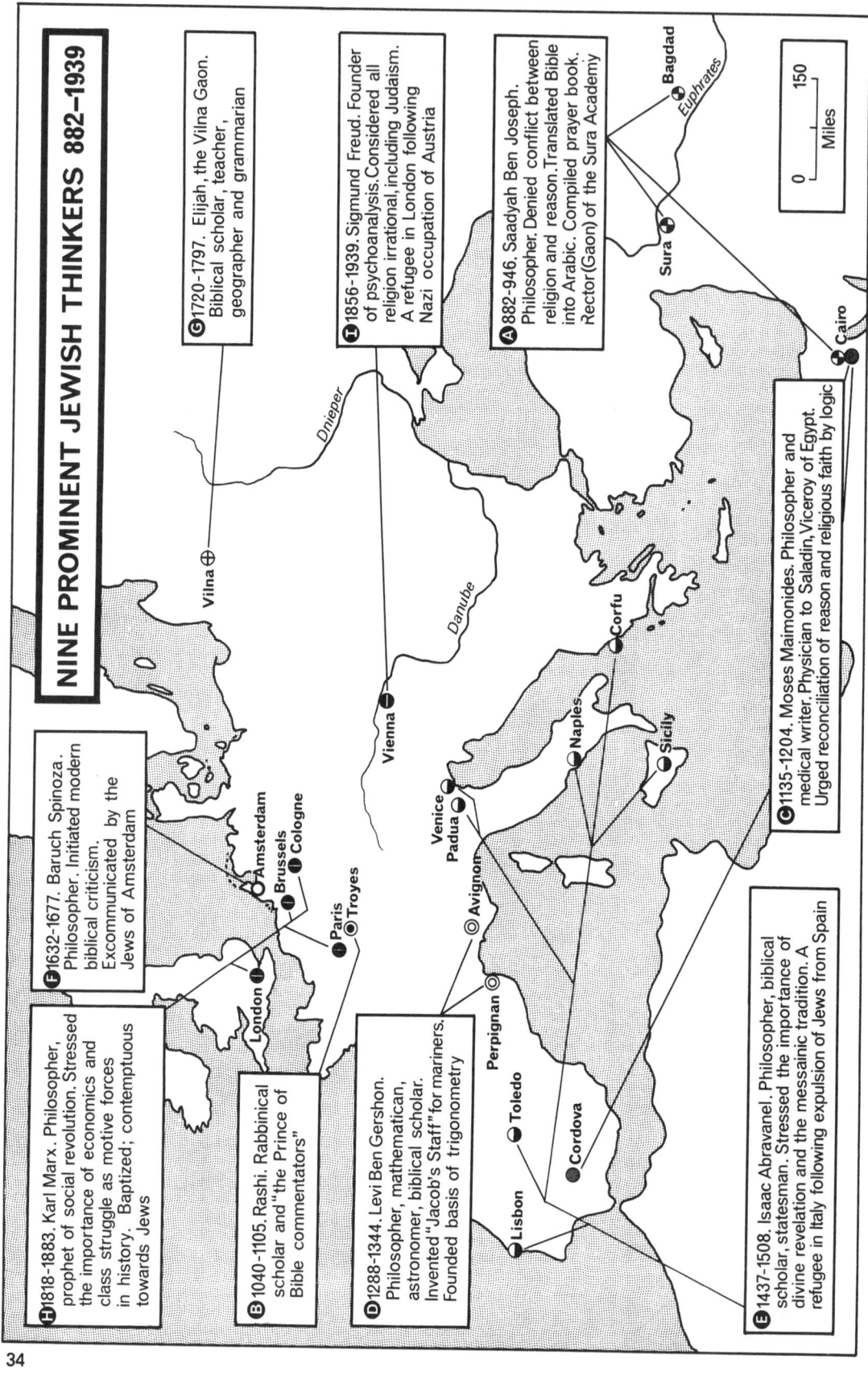

NINE PROMINENT JEWISH THINKERS 882–1939

F 1632-1677. Baruch Spinoza. Philosopher. Initiated modern biblical criticism. Excommunicated by the Jews of Amsterdam

H 1818-1883. Karl Marx. Philosopher, prophet of social revolution. Stressed the importance of economics and class struggle as motive forces in history. Baptized; contemptuous towards Jews

B 1040-1105. Rashi. Rabbinical scholar and "the Prince of Bible commentators"

D 1288-1344. Levi Ben Gershon. Philosopher, mathematician, astronomer, biblical scholar. Invented "Jacob's Staff" for mariners. Founded basis of trigonometry

G 1720-1797. Elijah, the Vilna Gaon. Biblical scholar, teacher, geographer and grammarian

H 1856-1939. Sigmund Freud. Founder of psychoanalysis. Considered all religion irrational, including Judaism. A refugee in London following Nazi occupation of Austria

A 882-946. Saadyah Ben Joseph. Philosopher. Denied conflict between religion and reason. Translated Bible into Arabic. Compiled prayer book. Rector (Gaon) of the Sura Academy

C 1135-1204. Moses Maimonides. Philosopher and medical writer. Physician to Saladin, Viceroy of Egypt. Urged reconciliation of reason and religious faith by logic

E 1437-1508. Isaac Abravanel. Philosopher, biblical scholar, statesman. Stressed the importance of divine revelation and the messainic tradition. A refugee in Italy following expulsion of Jews from Spain

0   150
Miles

Bagdad
Euphrates
Sura
Cairo
Dnieper
Vilna
Danube
Vienna
Corfu
Naples
Sicily
Venice
Padua
Avignon
Perpignan
Toledo
Cordova
Lisbon
Amsterdam
Brussels
Cologne
London
Paris
Troyes

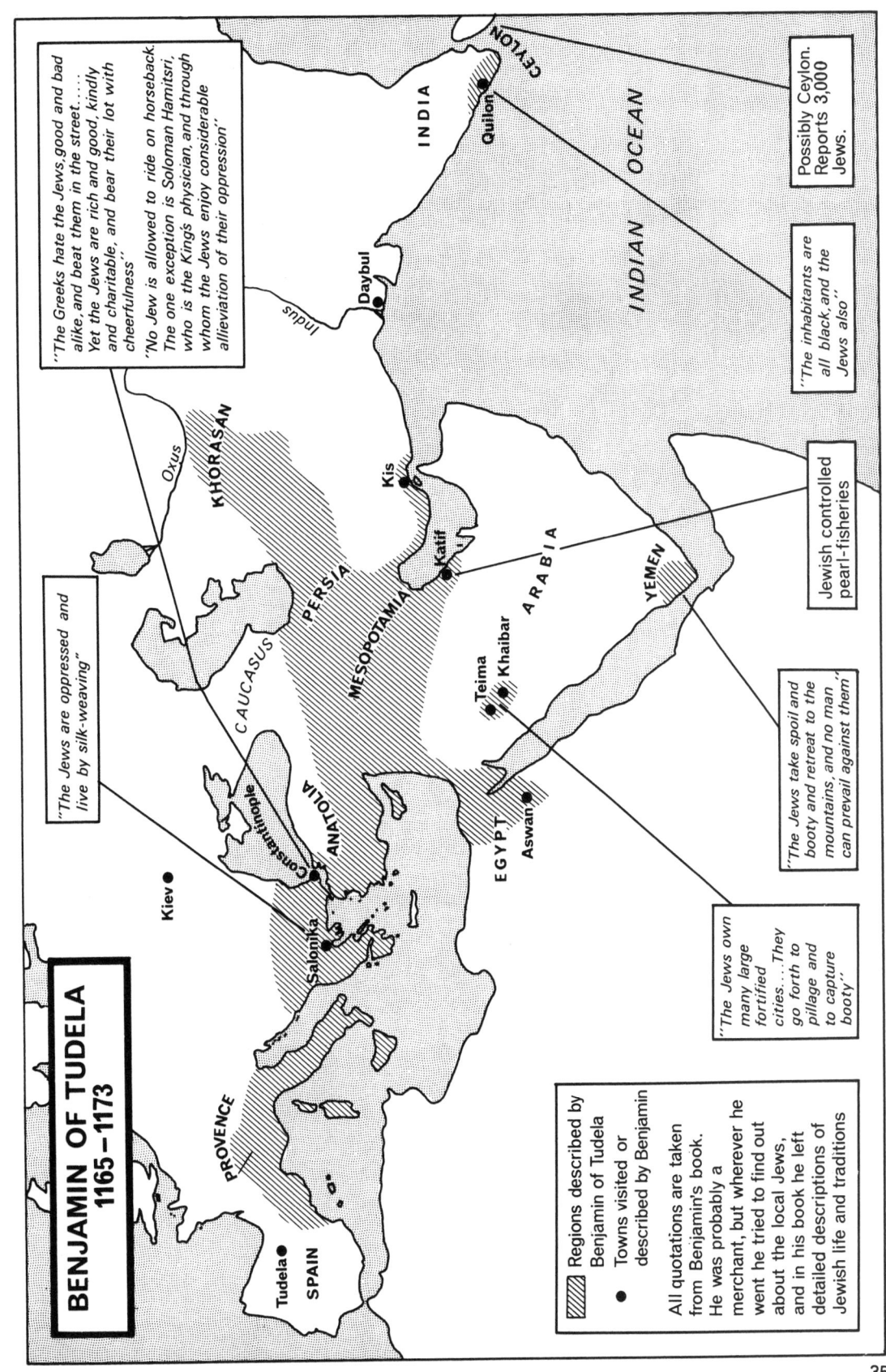

BENJAMIN OF TUDELA
1165 – 1173

"The Greeks hate the Jews, good and bad alike, and beat them in the street.... Yet the Jews are rich and good, kindly and charitable, and bear their lot with cheerfulness"

"No Jew is allowed to ride on horseback. The one exception is Soloman Hamitsri, who is the King's physician, and through whom the Jews enjoy considerable allieviation of their oppression"

"The inhabitants are all black, and the Jews also"

Possibly Ceylon. Reports 3,000 Jews.

"The Jews are oppressed and live by silk-weaving"

Jewish controlled pearl-fisheries

"The Jews take spoil and booty and retreat to the mountains, and no man can prevail against them"

"The Jews own many large fortified cities....They go forth to pillage and to capture booty"

INDIA

CEYLON

Quilon

Daybul

Indus

INDIAN OCEAN

KHORASAN

Oxus

Kis

Katif

PERSIA

ARABIA

YEMEN

Teima ● Khaibar

MESOPOTAMIA

CAUCASUS

ANATOLIA

Constantinople

EGYPT

Aswan

Kiev ●

Salonika

PROVENCE

Tudela ●
SPAIN

▨ Regions described by Benjamin of Tudela

● Towns visited or described by Benjamin

All quotations are taken from Benjamin's book. He was probably a merchant, but wherever he went he tried to find out about the local Jews, and in his book he left detailed descriptions of Jewish life and traditions

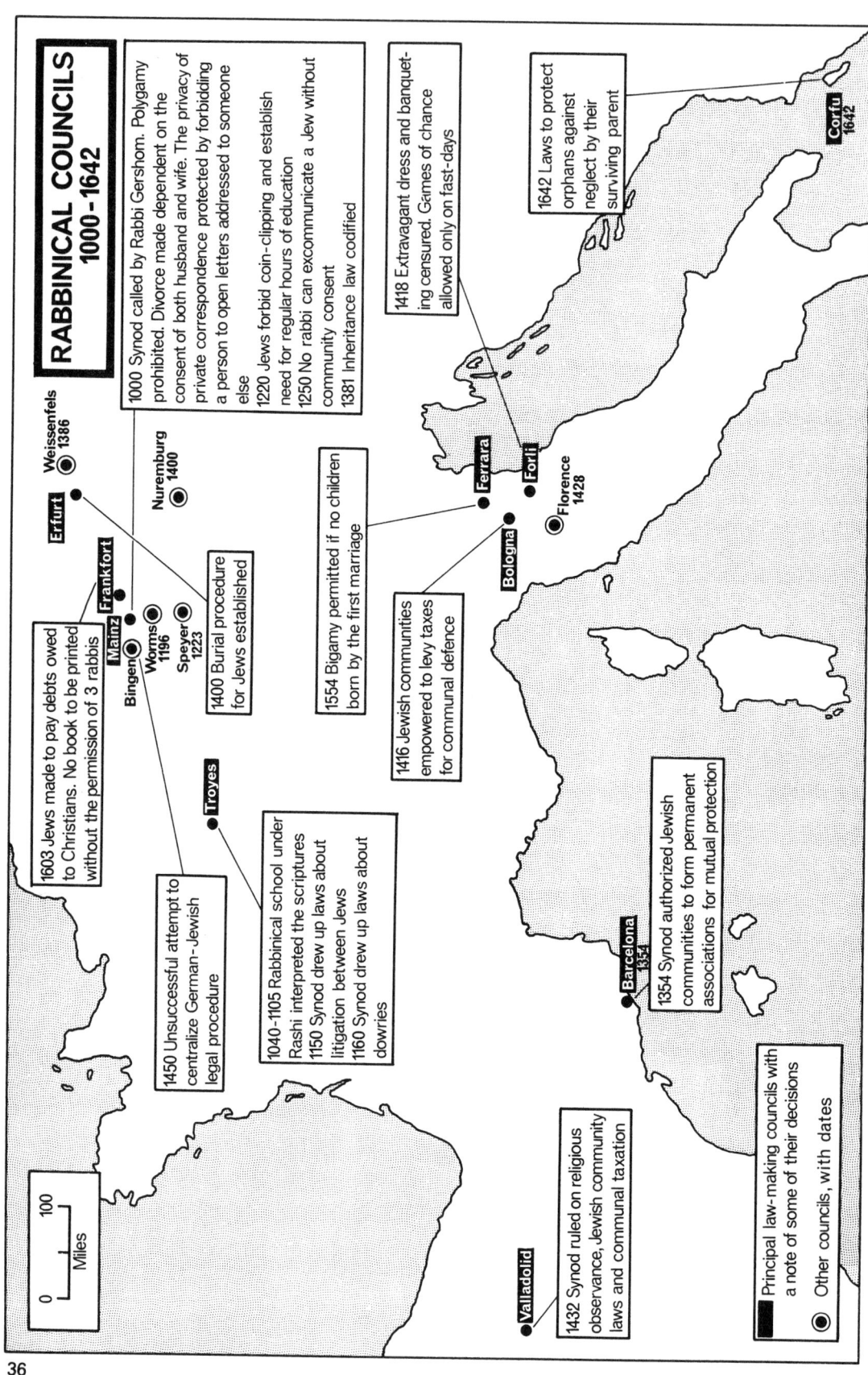

RABBINICAL COUNCILS 1000-1642

1000 Synod called by Rabbi Gershom. Polygamy prohibited. Divorce made dependent on the consent of both husband and wife. The privacy of private correspondence protected by forbidding a person to open letters addressed to someone else

1220 Jews forbid coin-clipping and establish need for regular hours of education

1250 No rabbi can excommunicate a Jew without community consent

1381 Inheritance law codified

1418 Extravagant dress and banqueting censured. Games of chance allowed only on fast-days

1642 Laws to protect orphans against neglect by their surviving parent

Corfu 1642

Weissenfels 1386

Erfurt

Nuremburg 1400

Frankfort

Mainz

Bingen

Worms 1196

Speyer 1223

1400 Burial procedure for Jews established

Ferrara

Forli

Florence 1428

Bologna

1554 Bigamy permitted if no children born by the first marriage

1416 Jewish communities empowered to levy taxes for communal defence

1603 Jews made to pay debts owed to Christians. No book to be printed without the permission of 3 rabbis

1450 Unsuccessful attempt to centralize German-Jewish legal procedure

Troyes

1040-1105 Rabbinical school under Rashi interpreted the scriptures
1150 Synod drew up laws about litigation between Jews
1160 Synod drew up laws about dowries

Barcelona 1354

1354 Synod authorized Jewish communities to form permanent associations for mutual protection

Valladolid

1432 Synod ruled on religious observance, Jewish community laws and communal taxation

0   100
Miles

◼ Principal law-making councils with a note of some of their decisions

⦿ Other councils, with dates

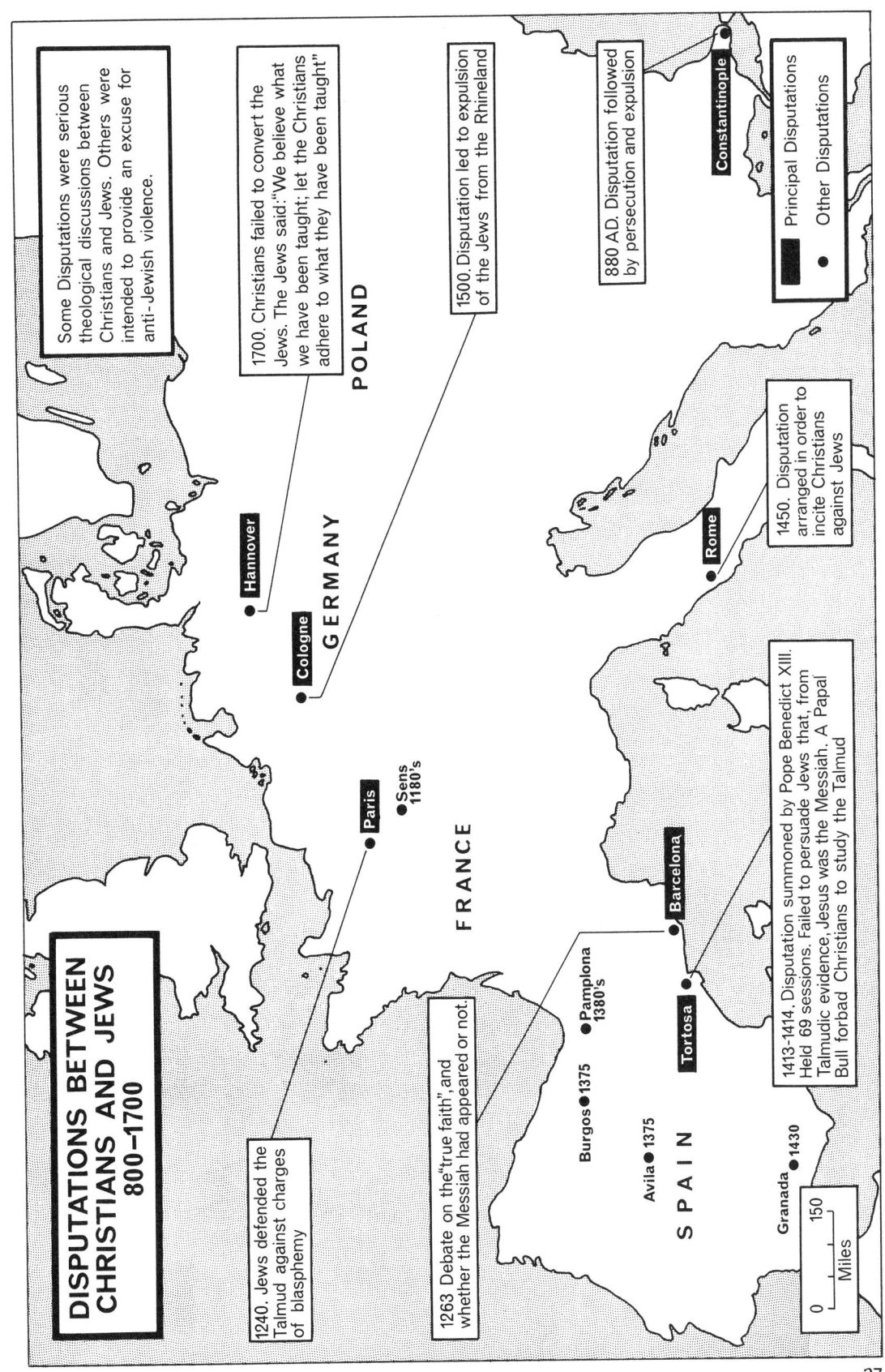

DISPUTATIONS BETWEEN CHRISTIANS AND JEWS 800–1700

Some Disputations were serious theological discussions between Christians and Jews. Others were intended to provide an excuse for anti-Jewish violence.

1700. Christians failed to convert the Jews. The Jews said: "We believe what we have been taught; let the Christians adhere to what they have been taught"

1500. Disputation led to expulsion of the Jews from the Rhineland

880 AD. Disputation followed by persecution and expulsion

■ Principal Disputations
● Other Disputations

1450. Disputation arranged in order to incite Christians against Jews

1240. Jews defended the Talmud against charges of blasphemy

1263 Debate on the "true faith", and whether the Messiah had appeared or not.

1413–1414. Disputation summoned by Pope Benedict XIII. Held 69 sessions. Failed to persuade Jews that, from Talmudic evidence, Jesus was the Messiah. A Papal Bull forbad Christians to study the Talmud

POLAND

GERMANY

■ Hannover
● Cologne

FRANCE

■ Paris
● Sens 1180's

SPAIN

Burgos ● 1375
● Pamplona 1380's
Avila ● 1375
■ Tortosa
■ Barcelona
Granada ● 1430

■ Constantinople

■ Rome

0   150
Miles

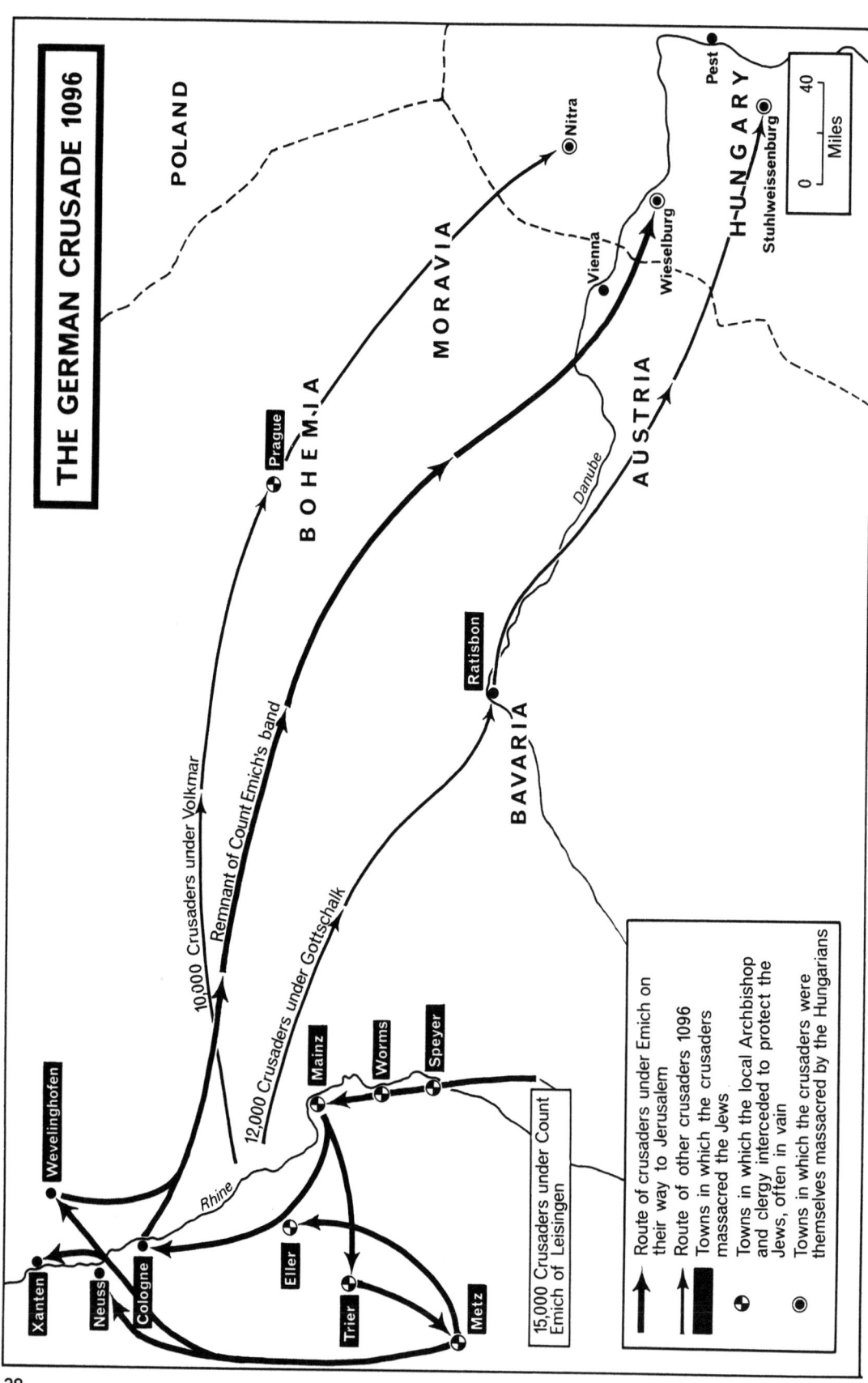

THE GERMAN CRUSADE 1096

POLAND

BOHEMIA
Prague

MORAVIA

10,000 Crusaders under Volkmar

Remnant of Count Emich's band

12,000 Crusaders under Gottschalk

Nitra

Vienna

Wieselburg

AUSTRIA

Danube

HUNGARY

Stuhlweissenburg

Pest

0   40
Miles

Ratisbon

BAVARIA

Rhine

Wevelinghofen

Xanten

Neuss

Cologne

Eller

Trier

Metz

Mainz

Worms

Speyer

15,000 Crusaders under Count
Emich of Leisingen

Route of crusaders under Emich on
their way to Jerusalem

Route of other crusaders 1096

Towns in which the crusaders
massacred the Jews

Towns in which the local Archbishop
and clergy interceded to protect the
Jews, often in vain

Towns in which the crusaders were
themselves massacred by the Hungarians

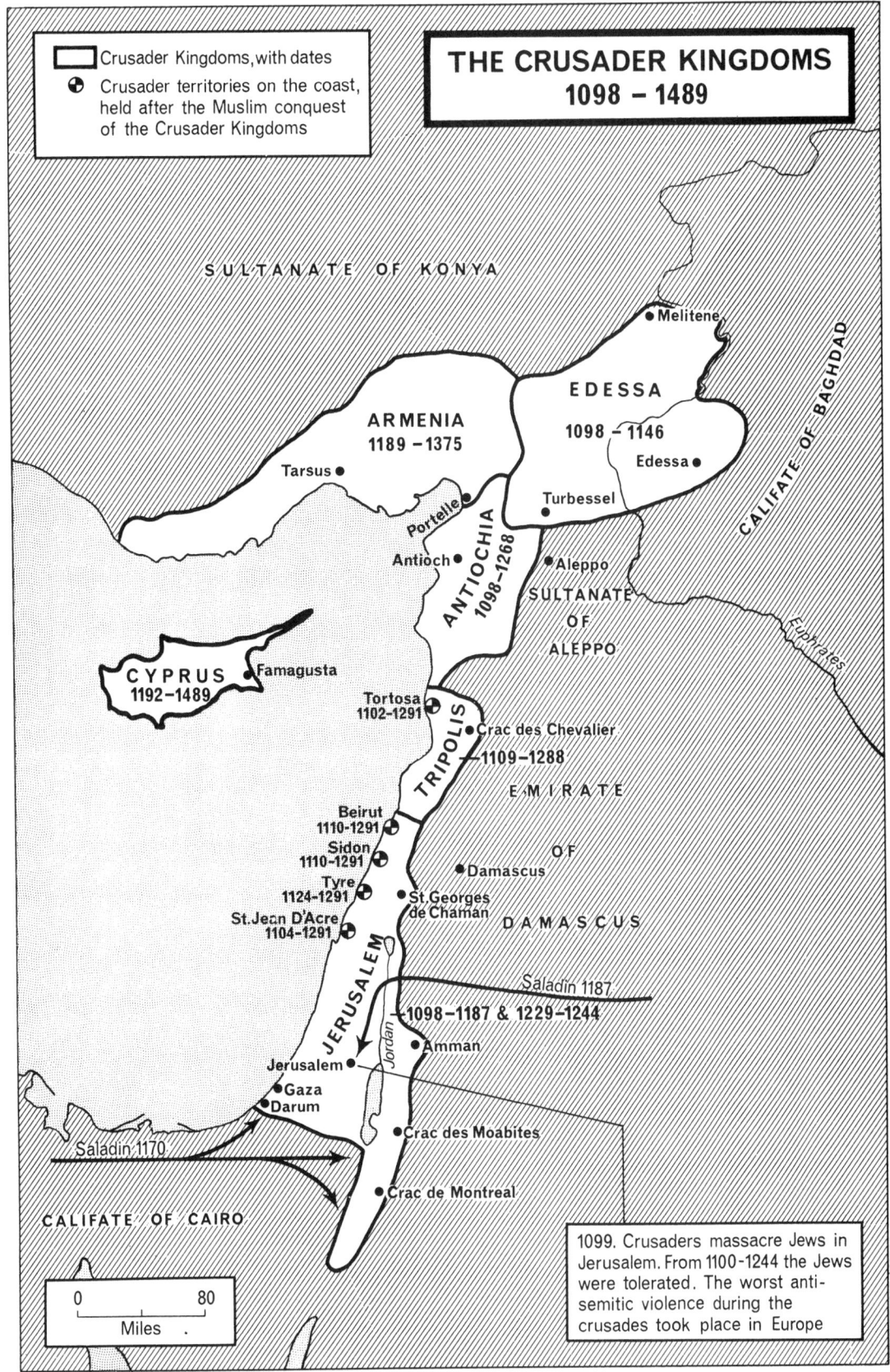

THE CRUSADER KINGDOMS
1098 – 1489

Crusader Kingdoms, with dates

Crusader territories on the coast, held after the Muslim conquest of the Crusader Kingdoms

SULTANATE OF KONYA

Melitene

EDESSA
1098 – 1146

Edessa

CALIFATE OF BAGHDAD

ARMENIA
1189 – 1375

Tarsus

Turbessel

Portelle

ANTIOCHIA
1098–1268

Antioch

Aleppo

SULTANATE
OF
ALEPPO

Euphrates

CYPRUS
1192 – 1489

Famagusta

Tortosa
1102–1291

Crac des Chevalier
1109–1288

TRIPOLIS

EMIRATE

Beirut
1110–1291

Sidon
1110–1291

OF

Tyre
1124–1291

Damascus

St.Jean D'Acre
1104–1291

St.Georges
de Chaman

DAMASCUS

JERUSALEM

Saladin 1187

1098–1187 & 1229–1244

Jordan

Amman

Jerusalem

Gaza

Darum

Crac des Moabites

Saladin 1170

Crac de Montreal

CALIFATE OF CAIRO

0   80
Miles

1099. Crusaders massacre Jews in Jerusalem. From 1100-1244 the Jews were tolerated. The worst anti-semitic violence during the crusades took place in Europe

39

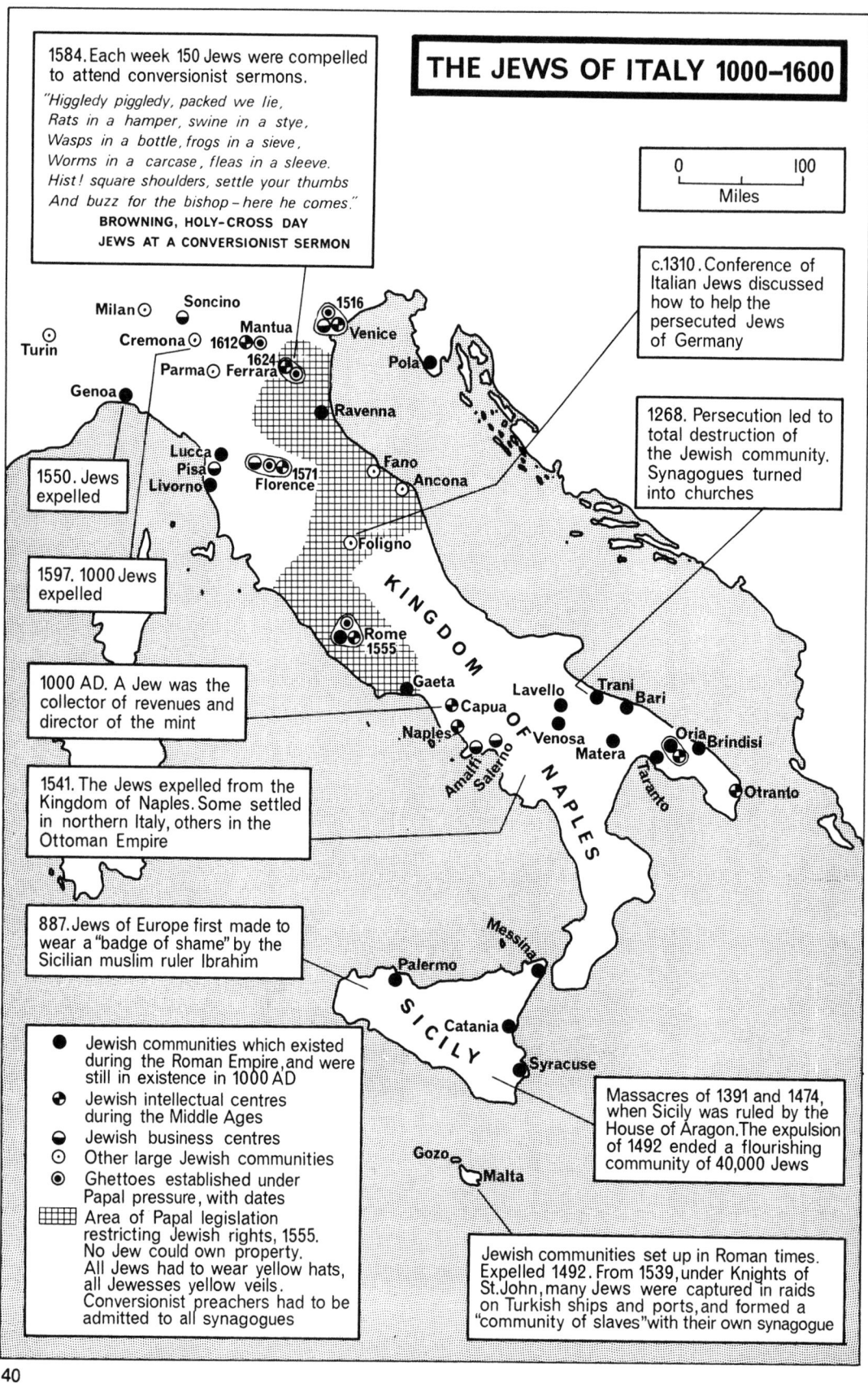

THE JEWS OF ITALY 1000–1600

1584. Each week 150 Jews were compelled to attend conversionist sermons.

"Higgledy piggledy, packed we lie,
Rats in a hamper, swine in a stye,
Wasps in a bottle, frogs in a sieve,
Worms in a carcase, fleas in a sleeve.
Hist! square shoulders, settle your thumbs
And buzz for the bishop – here he comes."
BROWNING, HOLY-CROSS DAY
JEWS AT A CONVERSIONIST SERMON

c.1310. Conference of Italian Jews discussed how to help the persecuted Jews of Germany

1268. Persecution led to total destruction of the Jewish community. Synagogues turned into churches

0 ————— 100
Miles

1550. Jews expelled

1597. 1000 Jews expelled

1000 AD. A Jew was the collector of revenues and director of the mint

1541. The Jews expelled from the Kingdom of Naples. Some settled in northern Italy, others in the Ottoman Empire

887. Jews of Europe first made to wear a "badge of shame" by the Sicilian muslim ruler Ibrahim

Turin
Milan
Soncino
Cremona
Mantua 1612
Parma Ferrara 1624
1516
Venice
Pola
Genoa
Ravenna
Lucca
Pisa
Livorno
Florence 1571
Fano
Ancona
Foligno

KINGDOM

Rome 1555

Gaeta
Capua
Naples
Amalfi
Salerno

OF

Lavello
Venosa
Matera
Taranto

Trani
Bari
Oria Brindisi
Otranto

NAPLES

Messina
Palermo
SICILY
Catania
Syracuse

Gozo
Malta

Massacres of 1391 and 1474, when Sicily was ruled by the House of Aragon. The expulsion of 1492 ended a flourishing community of 40,000 Jews

Jewish communities set up in Roman times. Expelled 1492. From 1539, under Knights of St. John, many Jews were captured in raids on Turkish ships and ports, and formed a "community of slaves" with their own synagogue

● Jewish communities which existed during the Roman Empire, and were still in existence in 1000 AD
◐ Jewish intellectual centres during the Middle Ages
◒ Jewish business centres
⊙ Other large Jewish communities
◎ Ghettoes established under Papal pressure, with dates
▦ Area of Papal legislation restricting Jewish rights, 1555. No Jew could own property. All Jews had to wear yellow hats, all Jewesses yellow veils. Conversionist preachers had to be admitted to all synagogues

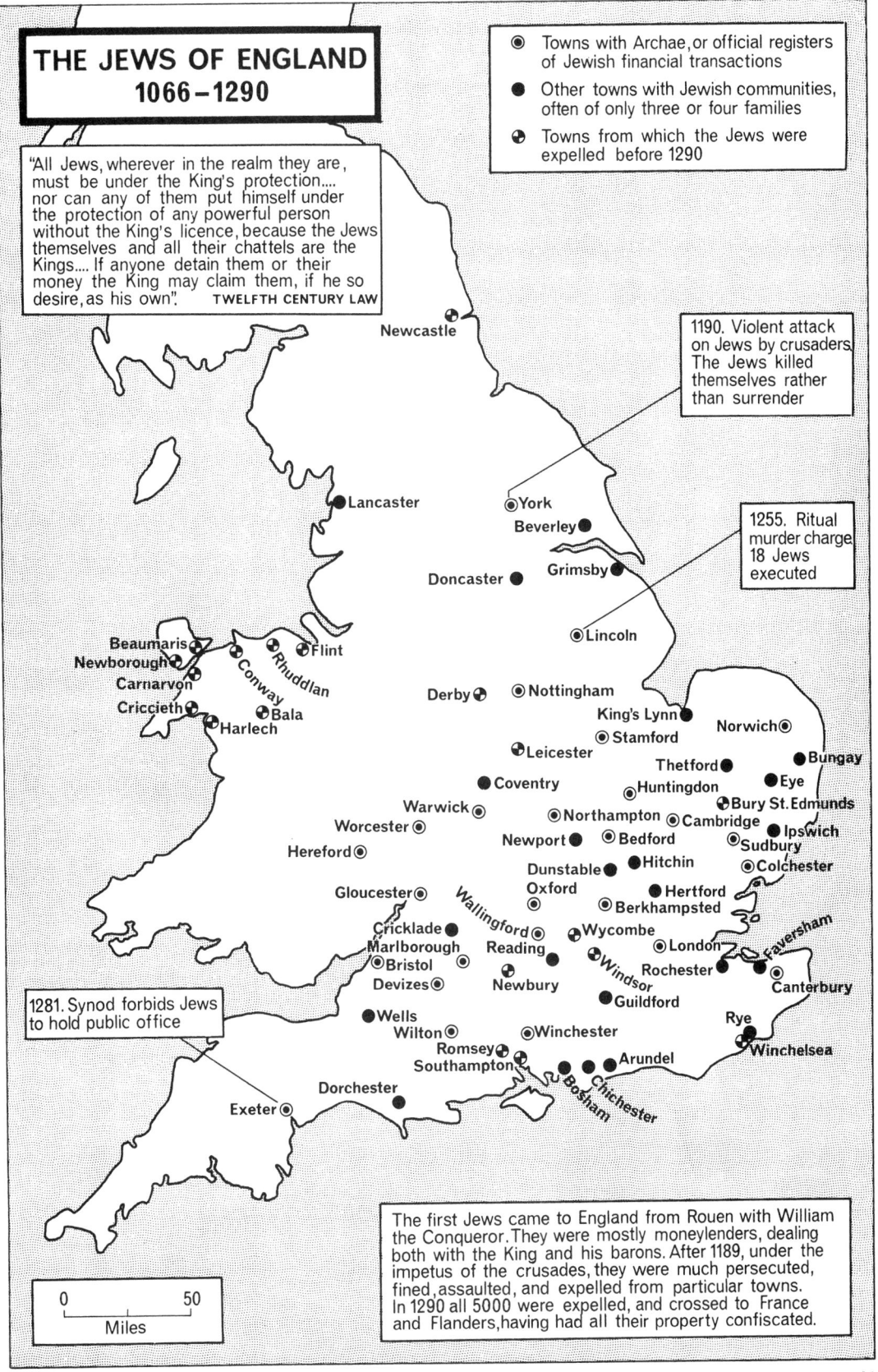

THE JEWS OF ENGLAND 1066-1290

"All Jews, wherever in the realm they are, must be under the King's protection.... nor can any of them put himself under the protection of any powerful person without the King's licence, because the Jews themselves and all their chattels are the Kings.... If anyone detain them or their money the King may claim them, if he so desire, as his own". **TWELFTH CENTURY LAW**

1190. Violent attack on Jews by crusaders. The Jews killed themselves rather than surrender

1255. Ritual murder charge 18 Jews executed

1281. Synod forbids Jews to hold public office

Newcastle

Lancaster

York
Beverley
Doncaster
Grimsby
Lincoln

Beaumaris
Newborough
Carnarvon
Criccieth
Harlech
Flint
Rhuddlan
Conway
Bala

Derby
Nottingham
King's Lynn
Norwich
Stamford
Leicester
Thetford
Bungay
Coventry
Eye
Huntingdon
Warwick
Bury St. Edmunds
Worcester
Northampton
Cambridge
Hereford
Newport
Bedford
Ipswich
Sudbury
Dunstable
Hitchin
Colchester
Gloucester
Oxford
Hertford
Cricklade
Wallingford
Berkhampsted
Marlborough
Reading
Wycombe
London
Bristol
Newbury
Windsor
Rochester
Devizes
Faversham
Guildford
Canterbury
Wells
Wilton
Winchester
Rye
Romsey
Arundel
Winchelsea
Southampton
Chichester
Bosham
Dorchester
Exeter

The first Jews came to England from Rouen with William the Conqueror. They were mostly moneylenders, dealing both with the King and his barons. After 1189, under the impetus of the crusades, they were much persecuted, fined, assaulted, and expelled from particular towns. In 1290 all 5000 were expelled, and crossed to France and Flanders, having had all their property confiscated.

0 50
Miles

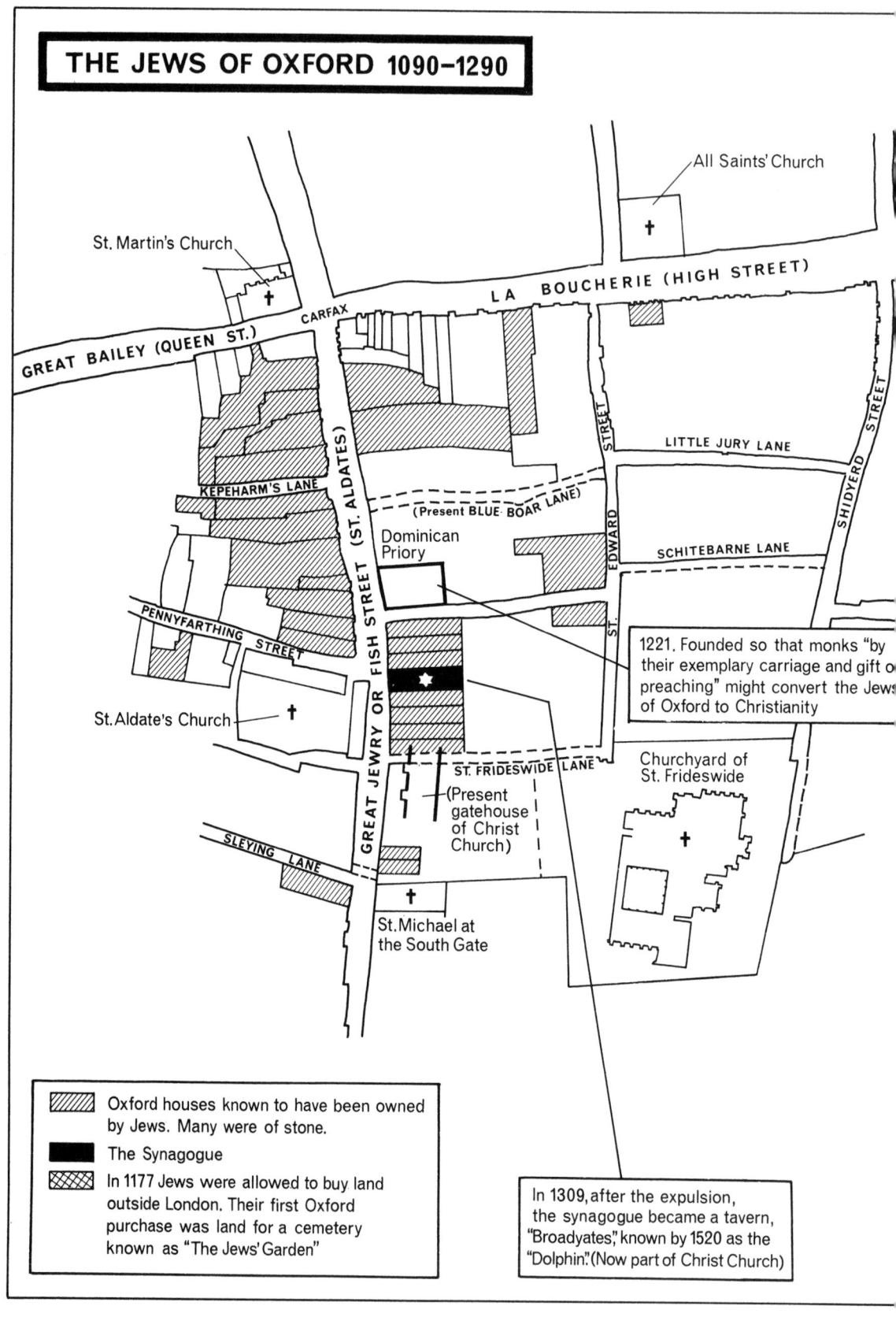

THE JEWS OF OXFORD 1090–1290

All Saints' Church

St. Martin's Church

LA BOUCHERIE (HIGH STREET)

GREAT BAILEY (QUEEN ST.)

CARFAX

LITTLE JURY LANE

KEPEHARM'S LANE

(Present BLUE BOAR LANE)

Dominican Priory

SCHITEBARNE LANE

PENNYFARTHING STREET

1221. Founded so that monks "by their exemplary carriage and gift of preaching" might convert the Jews of Oxford to Christianity

St. Aldate's Church

Churchyard of St. Frideswide

ST. FRIDESWIDE LANE

(Present gatehouse of Christ Church)

SLEYING LANE

St. Michael at the South Gate

GREAT JEWRY OR FISH STREET (ST. ALDATES)

SHIDYERD STREET

Oxford houses known to have been owned by Jews. Many were of stone.

The Synagogue

In 1177 Jews were allowed to buy land outside London. Their first Oxford purchase was land for a cemetery known as "The Jews' Garden"

In 1309, after the expulsion, the synagogue became a tavern, "Broadyates," known by 1520 as the "Dolphin." (Now part of Christ Church)

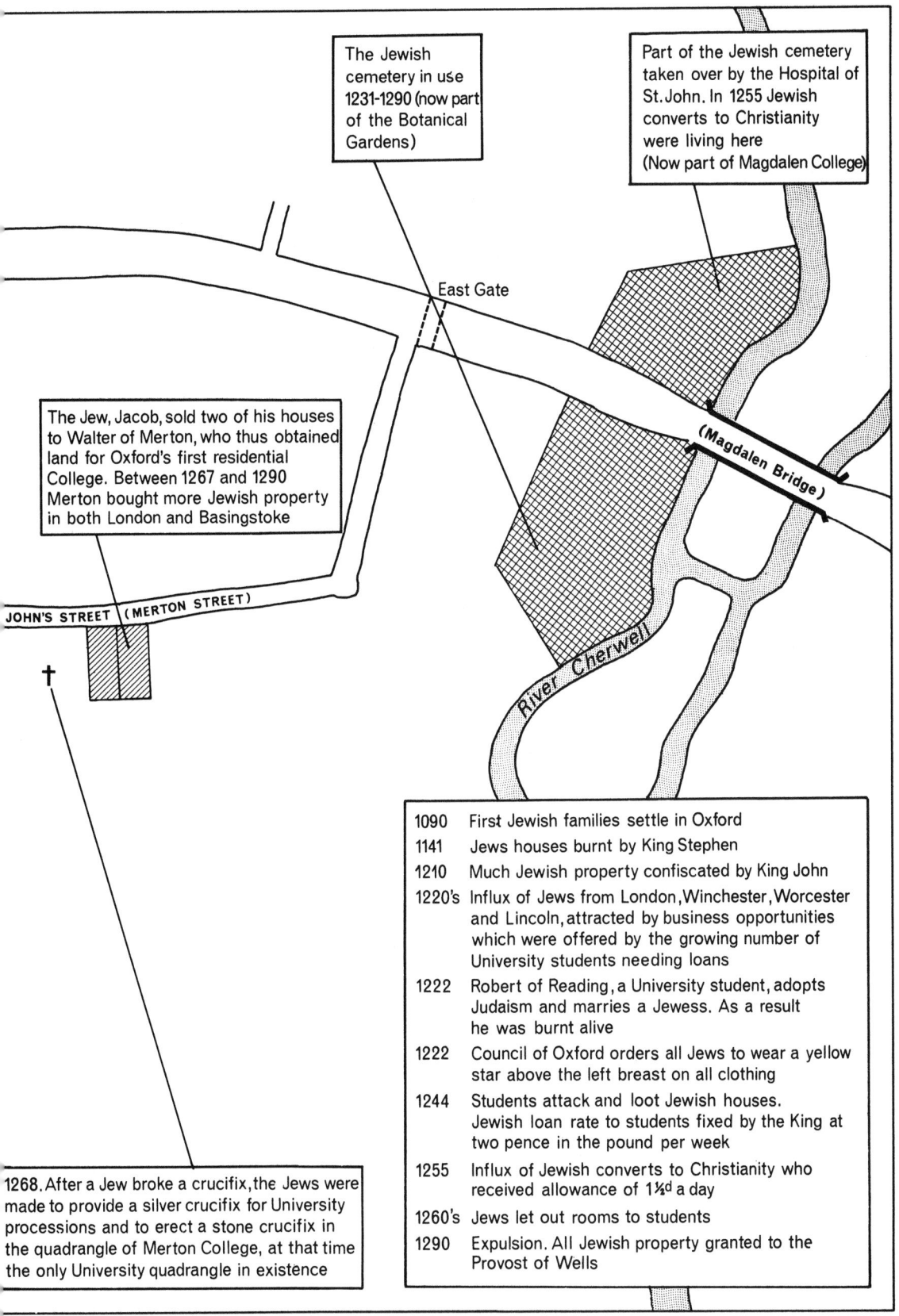

The Jewish cemetery in use 1231-1290 (now part of the Botanical Gardens)

Part of the Jewish cemetery taken over by the Hospital of St. John. In 1255 Jewish converts to Christianity were living here (Now part of Magdalen College)

East Gate

(Magdalen Bridge)

The Jew, Jacob, sold two of his houses to Walter of Merton, who thus obtained land for Oxford's first residential College. Between 1267 and 1290 Merton bought more Jewish property in both London and Basingstoke

JOHN'S STREET (MERTON STREET)

River Cherwell

1268. After a Jew broke a crucifix, the Jews were made to provide a silver crucifix for University processions and to erect a stone crucifix in the quadrangle of Merton College, at that time the only University quadrangle in existence

1090	First Jewish families settle in Oxford
1141	Jews houses burnt by King Stephen
1210	Much Jewish property confiscated by King John
1220's	Influx of Jews from London, Winchester, Worcester and Lincoln, attracted by business opportunities which were offered by the growing number of University students needing loans
1222	Robert of Reading, a University student, adopts Judaism and marries a Jewess. As a result he was burnt alive
1222	Council of Oxford orders all Jews to wear a yellow star above the left breast on all clothing
1244	Students attack and loot Jewish houses. Jewish loan rate to students fixed by the King at two pence in the pound per week
1255	Influx of Jewish converts to Christianity who received allowance of 1½d a day
1260's	Jews let out rooms to students
1290	Expulsion. All Jewish property granted to the Provost of Wells

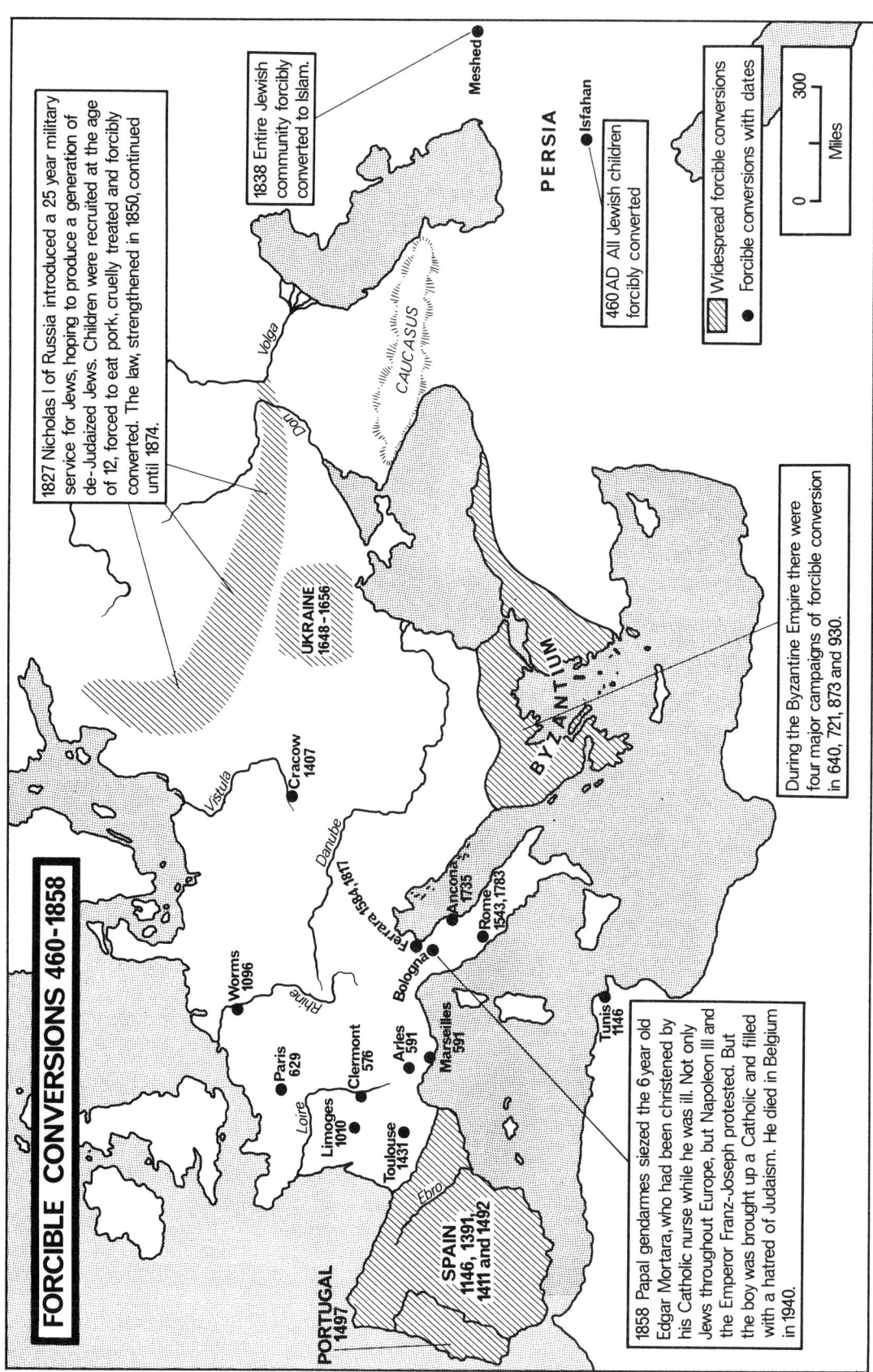

FORCIBLE CONVERSIONS 460-1858

1827 Nicholas I of Russia introduced a 25 year military service for Jews, hoping to produce a generation of de-Judaized Jews. Children were recruited at the age of 12, forced to eat pork, cruelly treated and forcibly converted. The law, strengthened in 1850, continued until 1874.

1838 Entire Jewish community forcibly converted to Islam.

460 AD All Jewish children forcibly converted

□ Widespread forcible conversions
● Forcible conversions with dates

0   300
Miles

During the Byzantine Empire there were four major campaigns of forcible conversion in 640, 721, 873 and 930.

1858 Papal gendarmes siezed the 6 year old Edgar Mortara, who had been christened by his Catholic nurse while he was ill. Not only Jews throughout Europe, but Napoleon III and the Emperor Franz-Joseph protested. But the boy was brought up a Catholic and filled with a hatred of Judaism. He died in Belgium in 1940.

PERSIA

●Meshed

●Isfahan

Volga

CAUCASUS

Don

UKRAINE
1648-1656

Vistula

Cracow
1407

Danube

Rhine

●Worms
1096

●Paris
629

●Clermont
576

Loire

Limoges
1010

●Toulouse
1431

●Arles
591

Marseilles
591

Ferrara 1584,1817

Bologna

Ancona
1735

Rome
1543,1783

BYZANTIUM

Ebro

SPAIN
1146, 1391,
1411 and 1492

PORTUGAL
1497

Tunis
1146

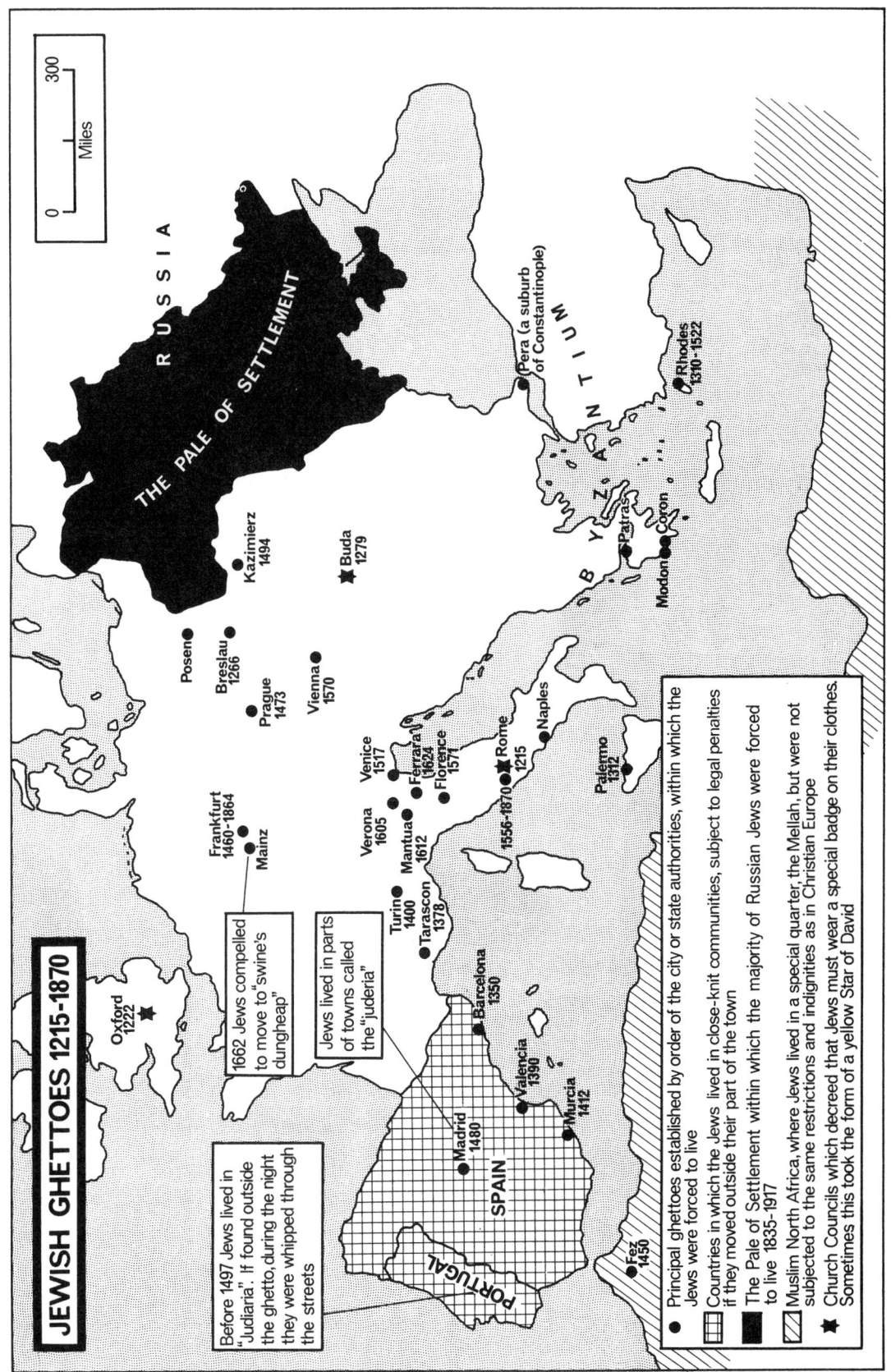

JEWISH GHETTOES 1215-1870

THE PALE OF SETTLEMENT

RUSSIA

Kazimierz 1494

Buda 1279

Posen

Breslau 1266

Prague 1473

Vienna 1570

Frankfurt 1460-1864

Mainz

Verona 1605

Venice 1517

Ferrara 1624

Florence 1571

Mantua 1612

Rome 1215

1556-1870

Naples

Turin 1400

Tarascon 1378

Palermo 1312

Barcelona 1350

Valencia 1390

Murcia 1412

Madrid 1480

SPAIN

PORTUGAL

Fez 1450

Oxford 1222

BYZANTIUM

Pera (a suburb of Constantinople)

Rhodes 1310-1522

Patras

Modon Coron

Before 1497 Jews lived in "Judiaria". If found outside the ghetto, during the night they were whipped through the streets

1662 Jews compelled to move to "swine's dungheap"

Jews lived in parts of towns called the "juderia"

Miles
0   300

● Principal ghettoes established by order of the city or state authorities, within which the Jews were forced to live

▦ Countries in which the Jews lived in close-knit communities, subject to legal penalties if they moved outside their part of the town

■ The Pale of Settlement within which the majority of Russian Jews were forced to live 1835-1917

▨ Muslim North Africa, where Jews lived in a special quarter, the Mellah, but were not subjected to the same restrictions and indignities as in Christian Europe

★ Church Councils which decreed that Jews must wear a special badge on their clothes. Sometimes this took the form of a yellow Star of David

44

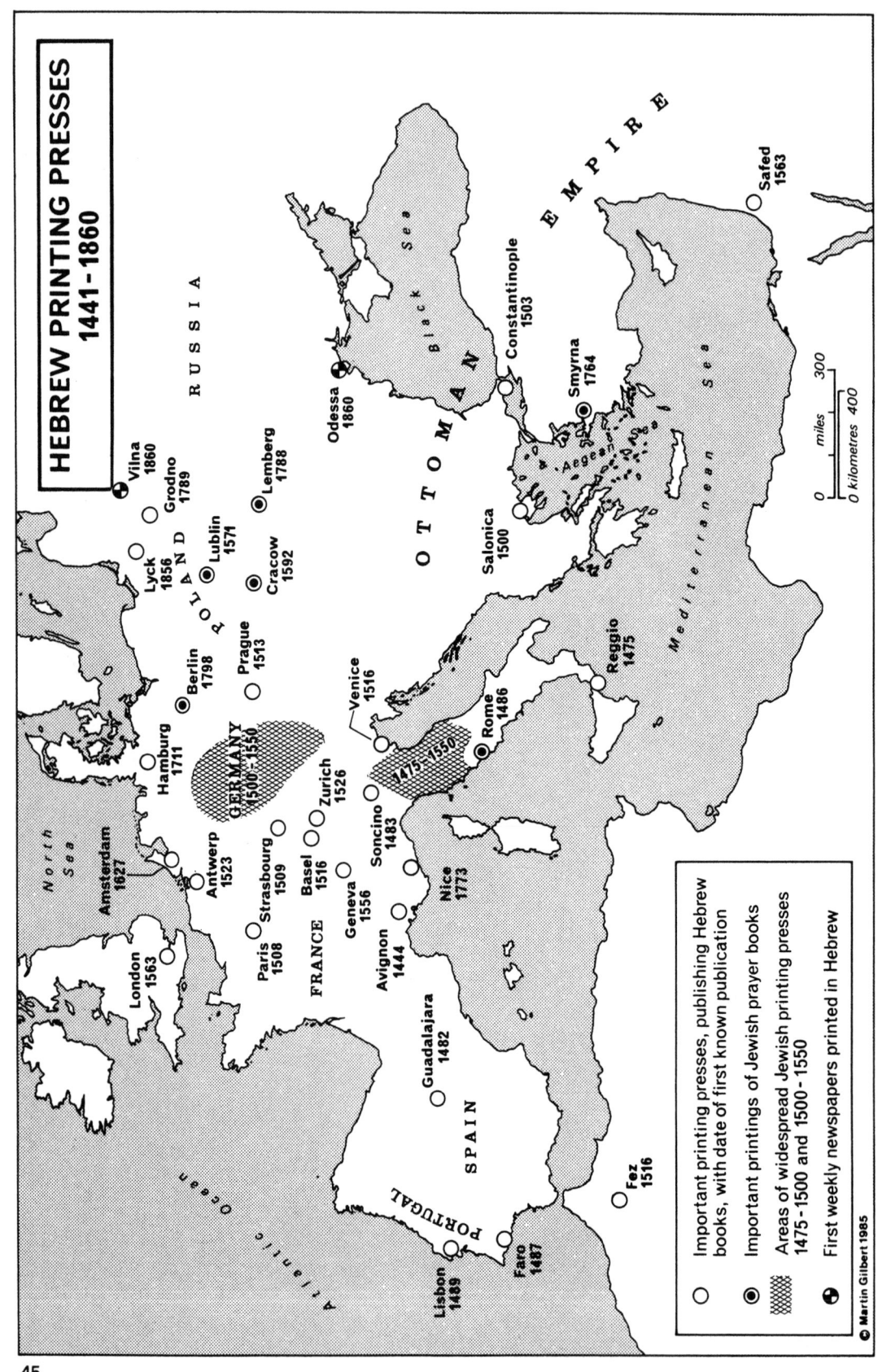

HEBREW PRINTING PRESSES 1441-1860

Safed 1563

EMPIRE

Constantinople 1503

Smyrna 1764

Black Sea

OTTOMAN

Odessa 1860

Salonica 1500

Aegean Sea

Mediterranean Sea

RUSSIA

Vilna 1860

Grodno 1789

Lemberg 1788

POLAND

Lyck 1856

Lublin 1571

Cracow 1592

Berlin 1798

Prague 1513

Venice 1516

Reggio 1475

Rome 1486

GERMANY 1500-1550

Hamburg 1711

Zurich 1526

1475-1550

Amsterdam 1627

Antwerp 1523

Strasbourg 1509

Basel 1516

Soncino 1483

Nice 1773

North Sea

Paris 1508

FRANCE

Geneva 1556

Avignon 1444

London 1563

Guadalajara 1482

SPAIN

Fez 1516

PORTUGAL

Lisbon 1489

Faro 1487

Atlantic Ocean

miles 300
0
0 kilometres 400

Important printing presses, publishing Hebrew books, with date of first known publication

Important printings of Jewish prayer books

Areas of widespread Jewish printing presses 1475-1500 and 1500-1550

First weekly newspapers printed in Hebrew

© Martin Gilbert 1985

45

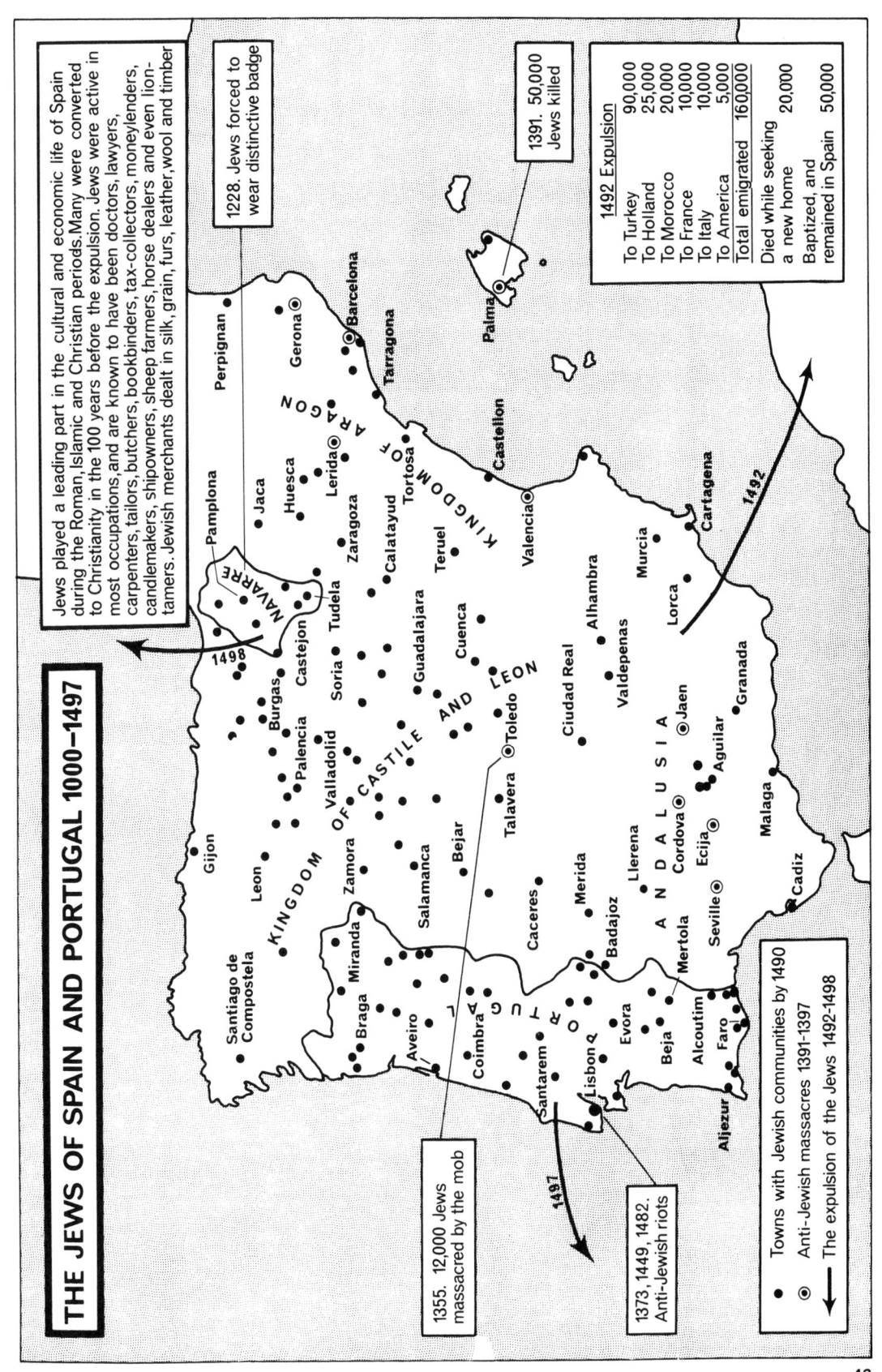

THE JEWS OF SPAIN AND PORTUGAL 1000–1497

Jews played a leading part in the cultural and economic life of Spain during the Roman, Islamic and Christian periods. Many were converted to Christianity in the 100 years before the expulsion. Jews were active in most occupations, and are known to have been doctors, lawyers, carpenters, tailors, butchers, bookbinders, tax-collectors, moneylenders, candlemakers, shipowners, sheep farmers, horse dealers and even lion-tamers. Jewish merchants dealt in silk, grain, furs, leather, wool and timber

1228. Jews forced to wear distinctive badge

1391. 50,000 Jews killed

1492 Expulsion	
To Turkey	90,000
To Holland	25,000
To Morocco	20,000
To France	10,000
To Italy	10,000
To America	5,000
Total emigrated	160,000
Died while seeking a new home	20,000
Baptized, and remained in Spain	50,000

1355. 12,000 Jews massacred by the mob

1373, 1449, 1482. Anti-Jewish riots

- Towns with Jewish communities by 1490
- ◉ Anti-Jewish massacres 1391-1397
- → The expulsion of the Jews 1492-1498

KINGDOM OF ARAGON

KINGDOM OF CASTILE AND LEON

NAVARRE

ANDALUSIA

PORTUGAL

Perpignan
Gerona
Barcelona
Tarragona
Castellon
Palma
Pamplona
Jaca
Huesca
Lerida
Tortosa
Zaragoza
Calatayud
Teruel
Valencia
Murcia
Cartagena
Lorca
Tudela
Castejon
Soria
Guadalajara
Cuenca
Alhambra
Burgas
Palencia
Valladolid
Toledo
Ciudad Real
Valdepenas
Granada
Jaen
Aguilar
Gijon
Leon
Zamora
Bejar
Talavera
Merida
Llerena
Cordova
Ecija
Malaga
Santiago de Compostela
Salamanca
Caceres
Badajoz
Seville
Cadiz
Braga
Miranda
Aveiro
Coimbra
Evora
Beja
Mertola
Alcoutim
Faro
Santarem
Lisbon
Aljezur

1498
1497
1492

46

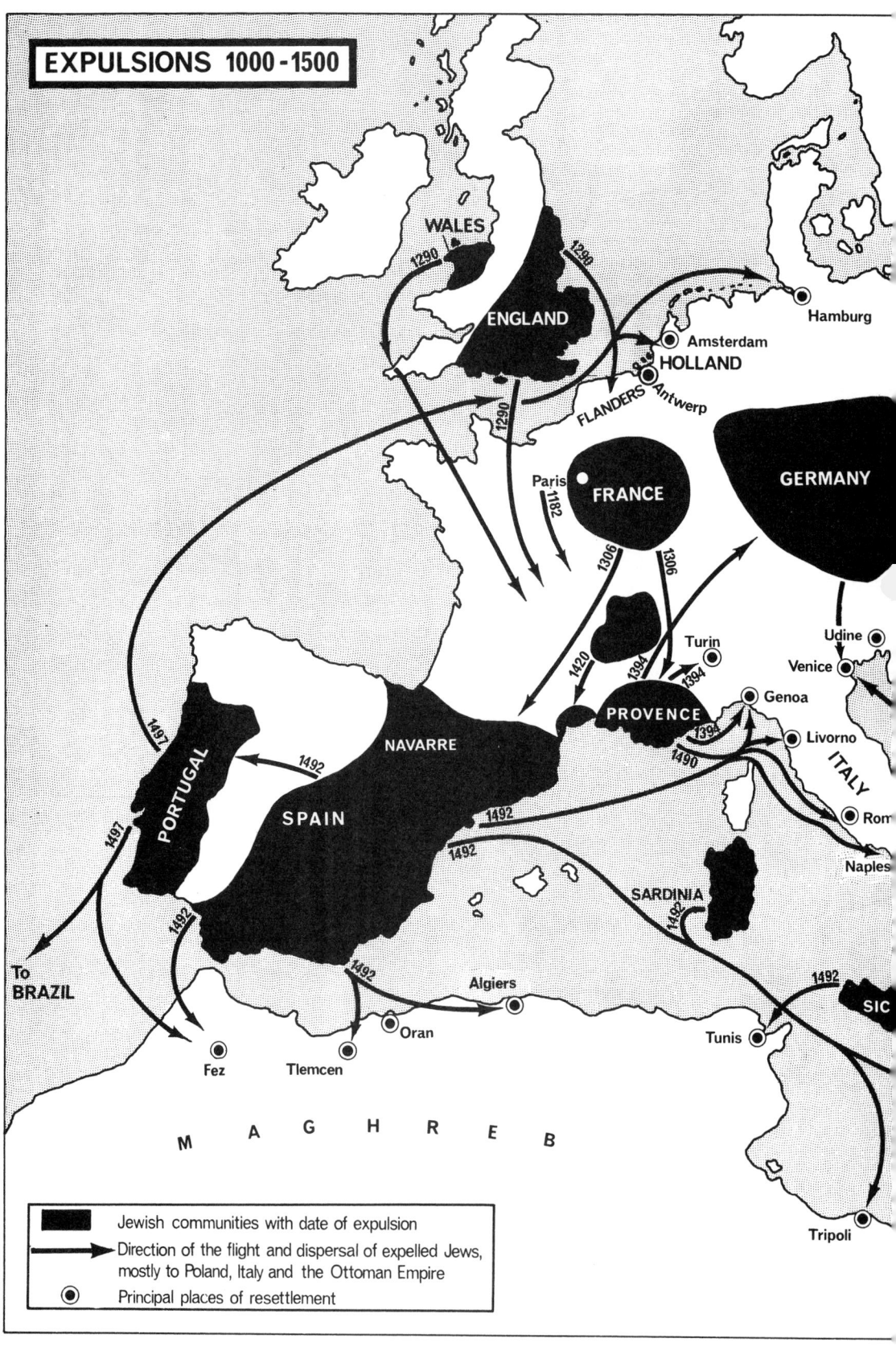

EXPULSIONS 1000-1500

WALES

1290 1290

ENGLAND

1290

Hamburg

Amsterdam

HOLLAND

FLANDERS Antwerp

GERMANY

Paris
1182

FRANCE

1306 1306

1420 1394 1394

Turin

Udine

Venice

Genoa

PROVENCE

1394

Livorno

1490

ITALY

PORTUGAL

1497

1492

NAVARRE

SPAIN

1492

1492

Rom

Naples

1497

1492

SARDINIA

1492

To
BRAZIL

1492

1492

Algiers

1492

SIC

Oran

Fez

Tlemcen

Tunis

Tripoli

M   A   G   H   R   E   B

Jewish communities with date of expulsion

Direction of the flight and dispersal of expelled Jews,
mostly to Poland, Italy and the Ottoman Empire

Principal places of resettlement

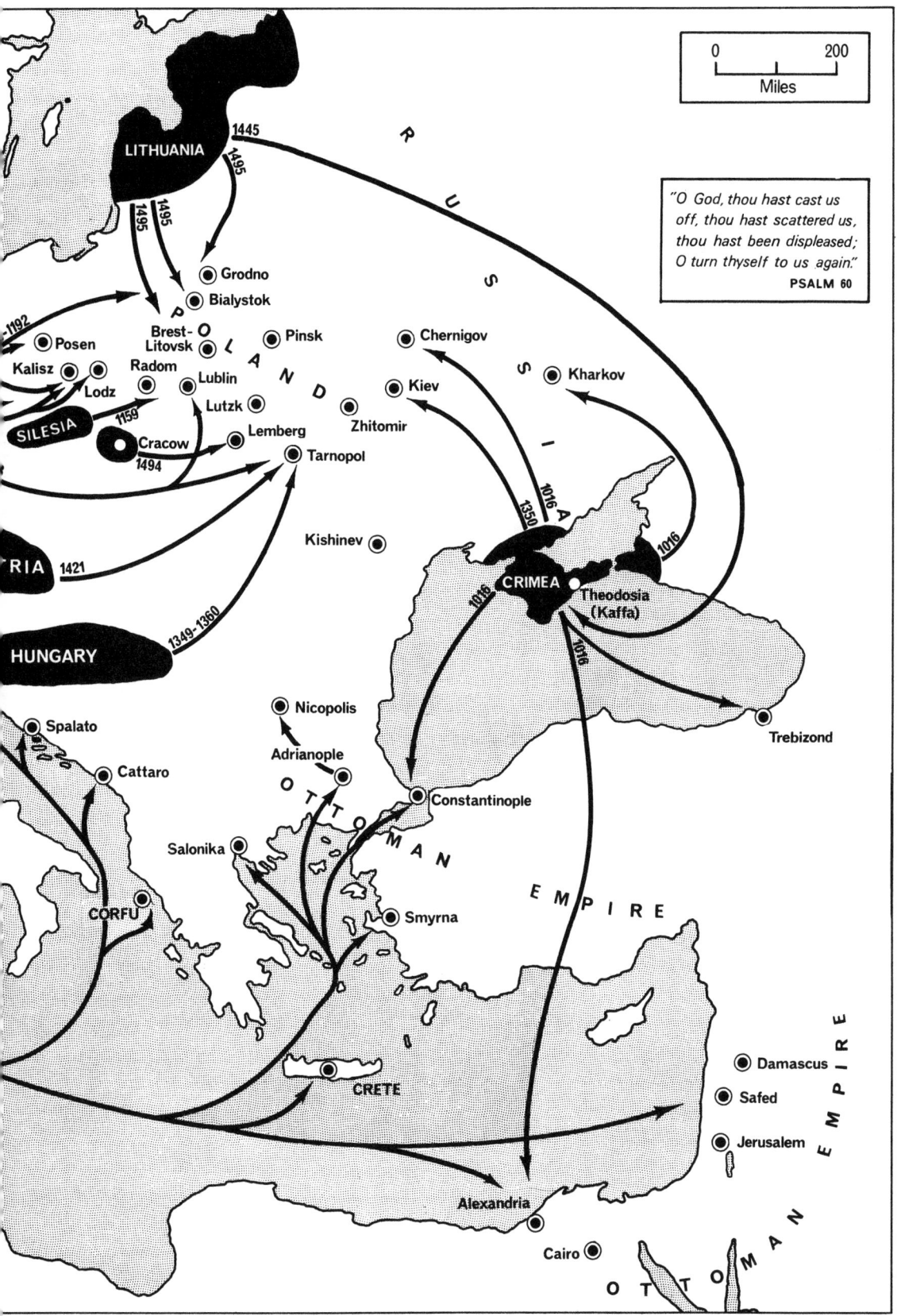

LITHUANIA

1445
1495
1495
1495

R U S S I A

0 — 200
Miles

"O God, thou hast cast us
off, thou hast scattered us,
thou hast been displeased;
O turn thyself to us again."
PSALM 60

◉ Grodno
◉ Bialystok

Brest-
Litovsk ◉
◉ Pinsk
◉ Chernigov
◉ Kharkov

1192
◉ Posen
Kalisz ◉ ◉
◉ Lodz
Radom ◉
◉ Lublin
◉ Kiev

SILESIA
1159
◉ Lutzk
◉ Zhitomir

◉ Cracow
◉ Lemberg
1494
◉ Tarnopol

RIA 1421
1350
1016
1016

◉ Kishinev

1016
CRIMEA
◉ Theodosia
(Kaffa)
1016

1349-1360
1016

HUNGARY

◉ Trebizond

◉ Nicopolis

◉ Spalato
Adrianople ◉

◉ Cattaro
O T T O
◉ Constantinople

Salonika ◉
M A N

CORFU ◉
E M P I R E

◉ Smyrna

◉ Damascus

CRETE ◉
◉ Safed

◉ Jerusalem

◉ Alexandria
O
T
T
O
M
A
N
Cairo ◉

E
M
P
I
R
E

O T T O M A N

47

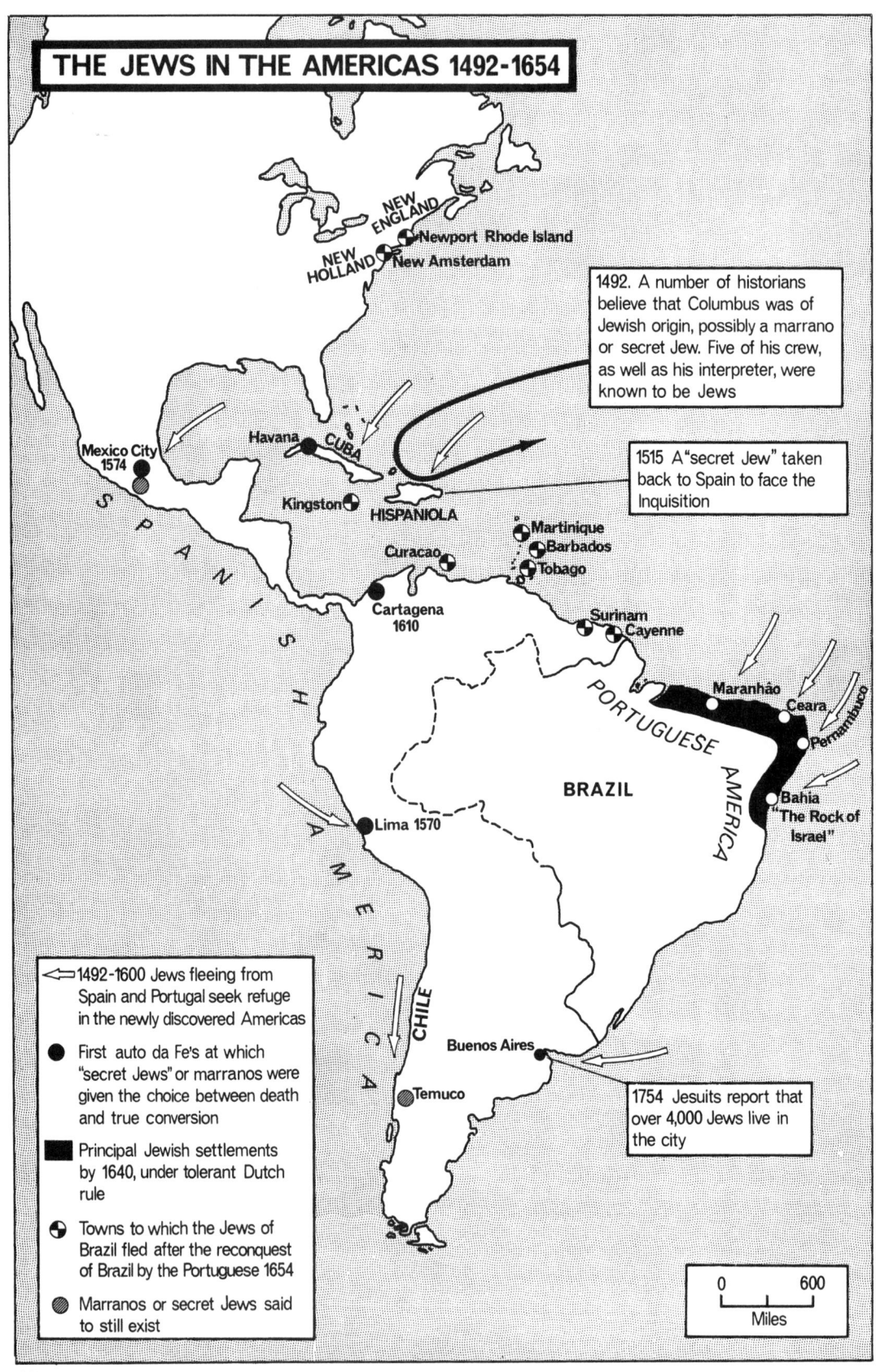

THE JEWS IN THE AMERICAS 1492-1654

NEW ENGLAND

NEW HOLLAND

Newport Rhode Island

New Amsterdam

1492. A number of historians believe that Columbus was of Jewish origin, possibly a marrano or secret Jew. Five of his crew, as well as his interpreter, were known to be Jews

Mexico City 1574

Havana CUBA

Kingston

HISPANIOLA

1515 A "secret Jew" taken back to Spain to face the Inquisition

Martinique

Barbados

Curacao

Tobago

Cartagena 1610

Surinam

Cayenne

S P A N I S H

A M E R I C A

PORTUGUESE

Maranhão

Ceara

Pernambuco

BRAZIL

AMERICA

Bahia "The Rock of Israel"

Lima 1570

CHILE

Buenos Aires

1754 Jesuits report that over 4,000 Jews live in the city

Temuco

1492-1600 Jews fleeing from Spain and Portugal seek refuge in the newly discovered Americas

First auto da Fe's at which "secret Jews" or marranos were given the choice between death and true conversion

Principal Jewish settlements by 1640, under tolerant Dutch rule

Towns to which the Jews of Brazil fled after the reconquest of Brazil by the Portuguese 1654

Marranos or secret Jews said to still exist

0   600
Miles

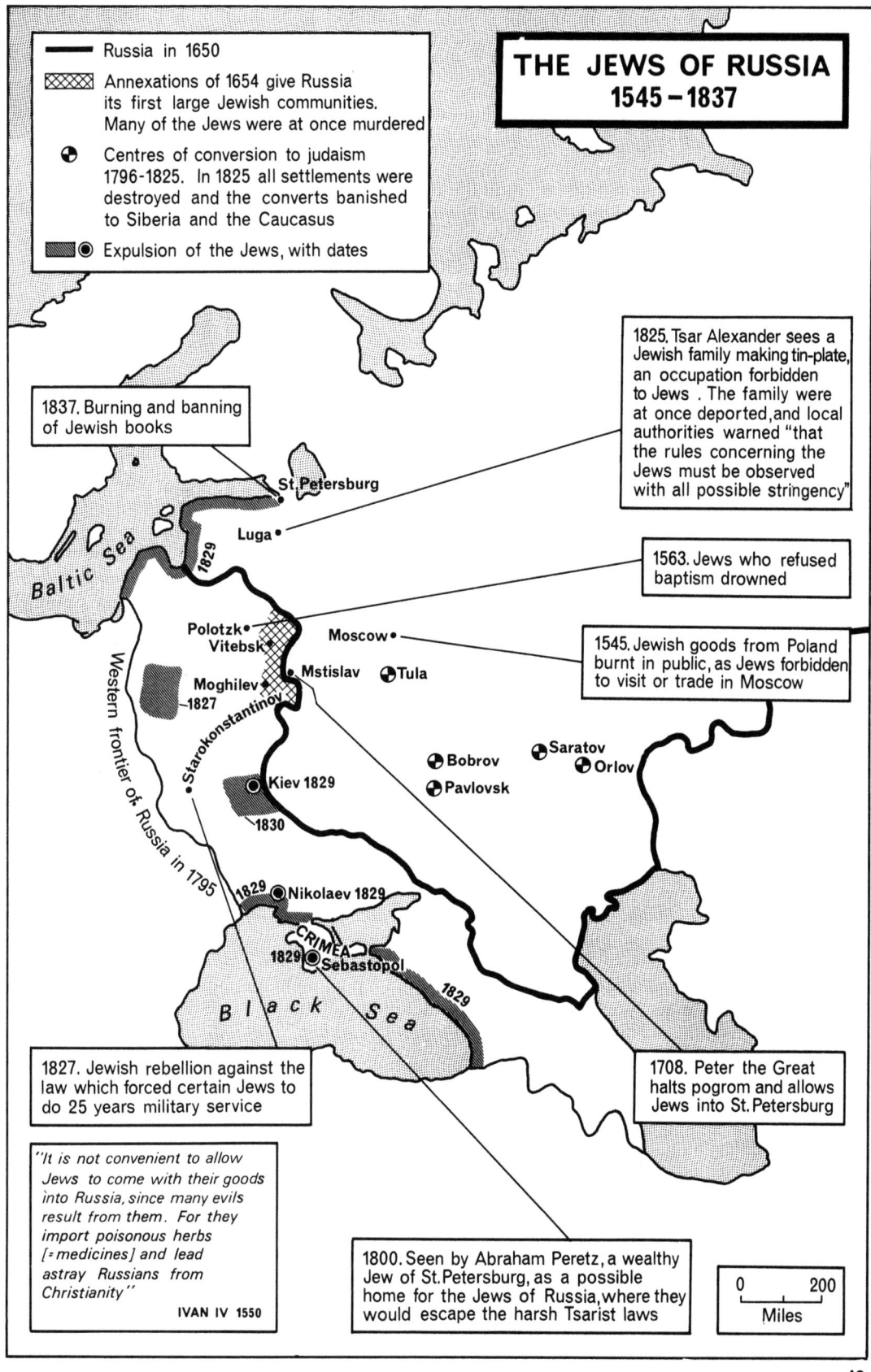

THE JEWS OF RUSSIA
1545–1837

Russia in 1650

Annexations of 1654 give Russia its first large Jewish communities. Many of the Jews were at once murdered

Centres of conversion to judaism 1796-1825. In 1825 all settlements were destroyed and the converts banished to Siberia and the Caucasus

Expulsion of the Jews, with dates

1837. Burning and banning of Jewish books

1825. Tsar Alexander sees a Jewish family making tin-plate, an occupation forbidden to Jews . The family were at once deported, and local authorities warned "that the rules concerning the Jews must be observed with all possible stringency"

1563. Jews who refused baptism drowned

1545. Jewish goods from Poland burnt in public, as Jews forbidden to visit or trade in Moscow

St.Petersburg

Luga

Baltic Sea

1829

Western frontier of Russia in 1795

Polotzk
Vitebsk
Moghilev
—1827
Starokonstantinov

Moscow

Mstislav   Tula

Bobrov   Saratov
Pavlovsk   Orlov

Kiev 1829

1830

1829   Nikolaev 1829

CRIMEA
1829   Sebastopol
1829

Black Sea

1827. Jewish rebellion against the law which forced certain Jews to do 25 years military service

1708. Peter the Great halts pogrom and allows Jews into St.Petersburg

"It is not convenient to allow Jews to come with their goods into Russia, since many evils result from them. For they import poisonous herbs [=medicines] and lead astray Russians from Christianity"

IVAN IV 1550

1800. Seen by Abraham Peretz, a wealthy Jew of St.Petersburg, as a possible home for the Jews of Russia, where they would escape the harsh Tsarist laws

0   200
Miles

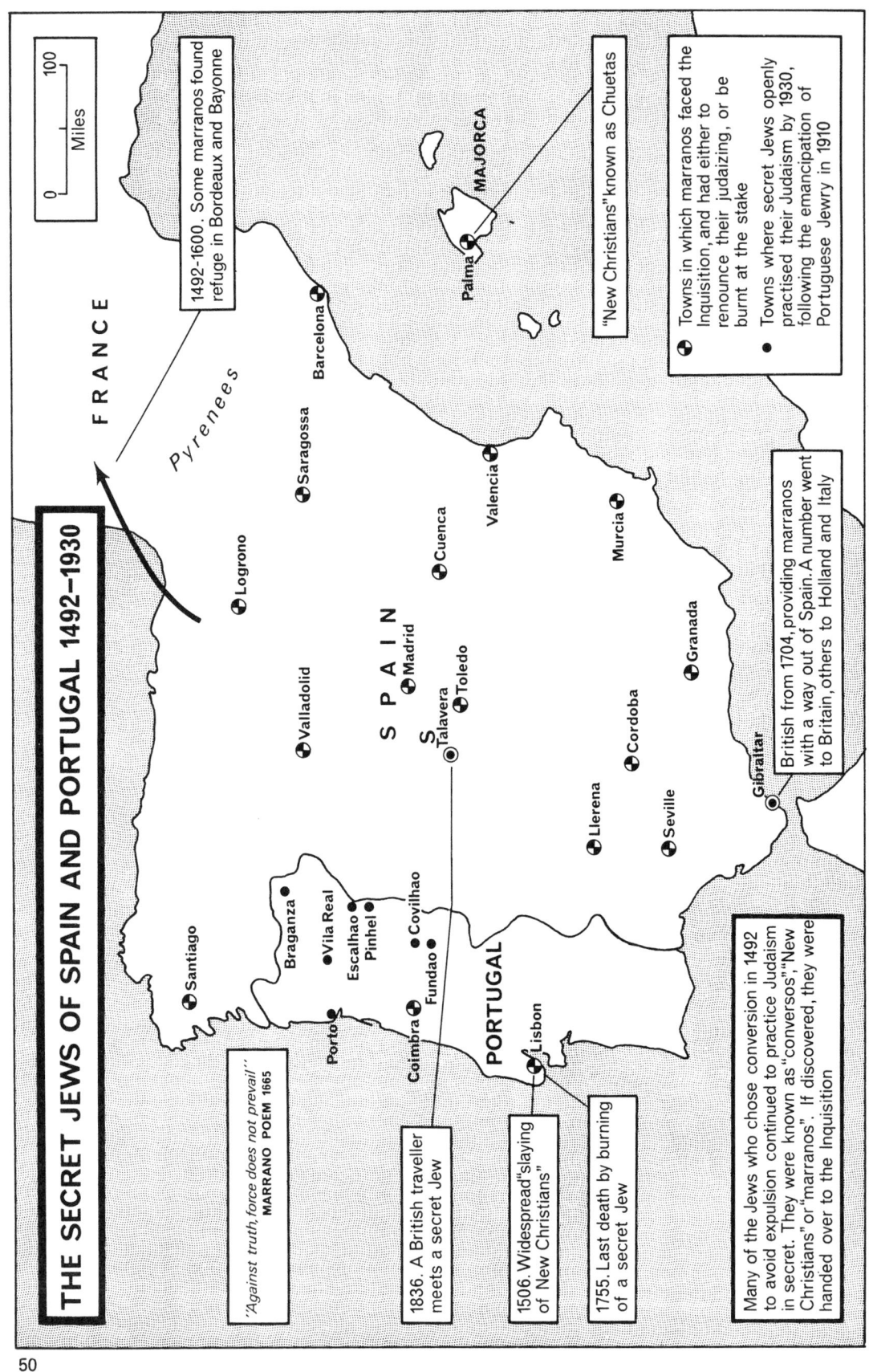

THE SECRET JEWS OF SPAIN AND PORTUGAL 1492–1930

"Against truth force does not prevail"
MARRANO POEM 1665

1492–1600. Some marranos found refuge in Bordeaux and Bayonne

"New Christians" known as Chuetas

⊕ Towns in which marranos faced the Inquisition, and had either to renounce their judaizing, or be burnt at the stake

● Towns where secret Jews openly practised their Judaism by 1930, following the emancipation of Portuguese Jewry in 1910

British from 1704, providing marranos with a way out of Spain. A number went to Britain, others to Holland and Italy

Many of the Jews who chose conversion in 1492 to avoid expulsion continued to practice Judaism in secret. They were known as "conversos","New Christians" or "marranos". If discovered, they were handed over to the Inquisition

1836. A British traveller meets a secret Jew

1506. Widespread "slaying of New Christians"

1755. Last death by burning of a secret Jew

FRANCE

Pyrenees

SPAIN

PORTUGAL

MAJORCA

⊕ Palma

⊕ Barcelona
⊕ Saragossa
⊕ Logrono
⊕ Cuenca
⊕ Valencia
⊕ Murcia
⊕ Madrid
⊕ Toledo
Ⓢ Talavera
⊕ Valladolid
⊕ Granada
⊕ Cordoba
⊕ Llerena
⊕ Seville
Ⓢ Gibraltar

⊕ Santiago
● Braganza
● Vila Real
Escalhao ●
Pinhel ●
● Covilhao
⊕ Coimbra
● Fundao
⊕ Porto
⊕ Lisbon

Miles
0   100

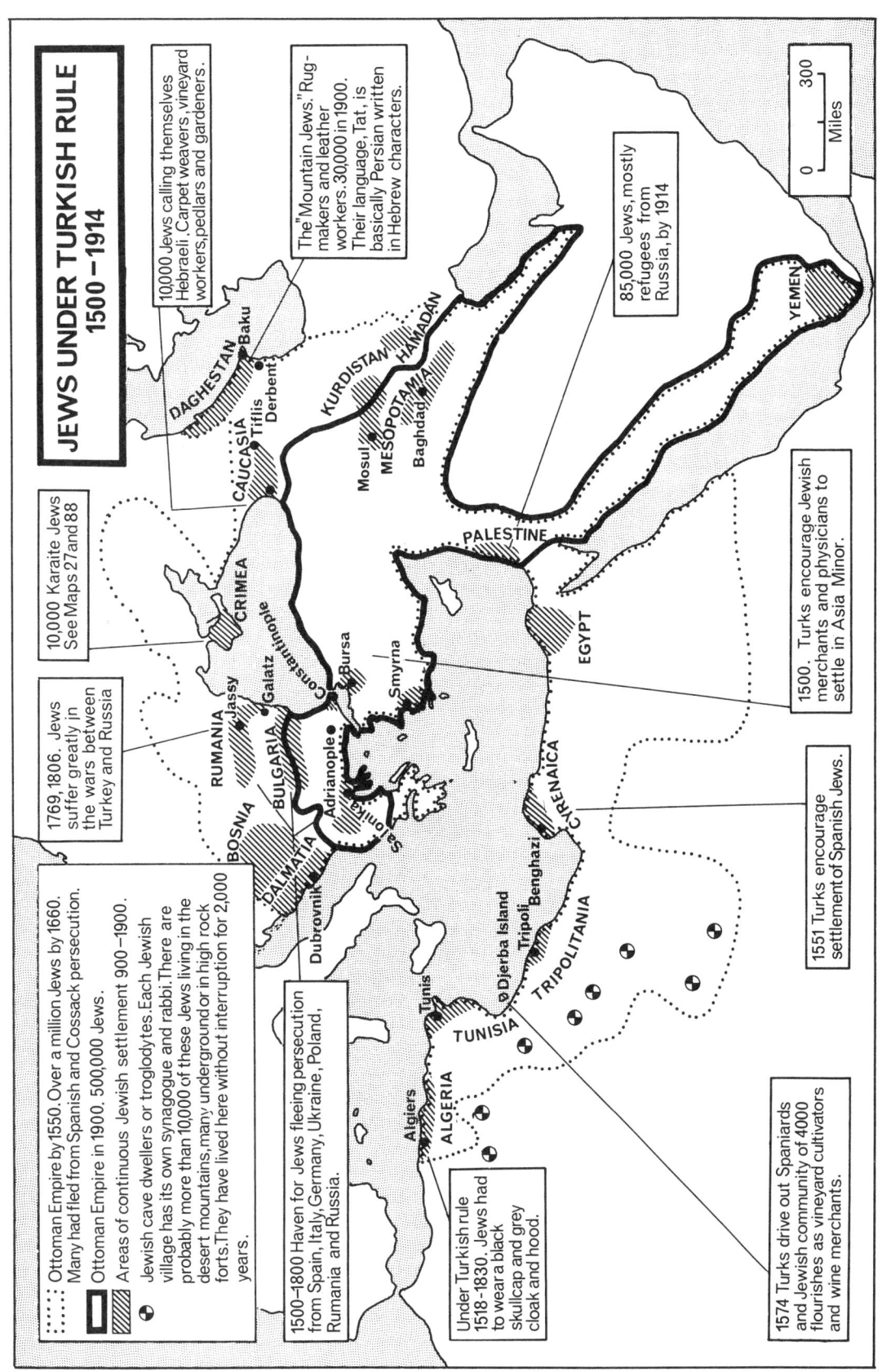

JEWS UNDER TURKISH RULE
1500 – 1914

10,000 Jews calling themselves Hebraeli. Carpet weavers, vineyard workers, pedlars and gardeners.

The "Mountain Jews." Rug-makers and leather workers. 30,000 in 1900. Their language, Tat, is basically Persian written in Hebrew characters.

85,000 Jews, mostly refugees from Russia, by 1914

YEMEN

DAGHESTAN

Baku

CAUCASIA

Tiflis

Derbent

KURDISTAN

HAMADAN

MESOPOTAMIA

Mosul

Baghdad

PALESTINE

1500. Turks encourage Jewish merchants and physicians to settle in Asia Minor.

10,000 Karaite Jews See Maps 27 and 88

CRIMEA

1769, 1806. Jews suffer greatly in the wars between Turkey and Russia

Galatz

Jassy

Constantinople

Bursa

Smyrna

EGYPT

Ottoman Empire by 1550. Over a million Jews by 1660. Many had fled from Spanish and Cossack persecution.

Ottoman Empire in 1900. 500,000 Jews.

Jewish cave dwellers or troglodytes. Each Jewish village has its own synagogue and rabbi. There are probably more than 10,000 of these Jews living in the desert mountains, many underground or in high rock forts. They have lived here without interruption for 2,000 years.

RUMANIA

BULGARIA

Adrianople

BOSNIA

Salonika

DALMATIA

Dubrovnik

CYRENAICA

Benghazi

1551 Turks encourage settlement of Spanish Jews.

1500–1800 Haven for Jews fleeing persecution from Spain, Italy, Germany, Ukraine, Poland, Rumania and Russia.

Under Turkish rule 1518-1830, Jews had to wear a black skullcap and grey cloak and hood.

Tunis

Djerba Island

Tripoli

TRIPOLITANIA

TUNISIA

Algiers

ALGERIA

1574 Turks drive out Spaniards and Jewish community of 4000 flourishes as vineyard cultivators and wine merchants.

300

0   Miles

Ottoman Empire by 1550...

Ottoman Empire in 1900...

Areas of continuous Jewish settlement 900–1900.

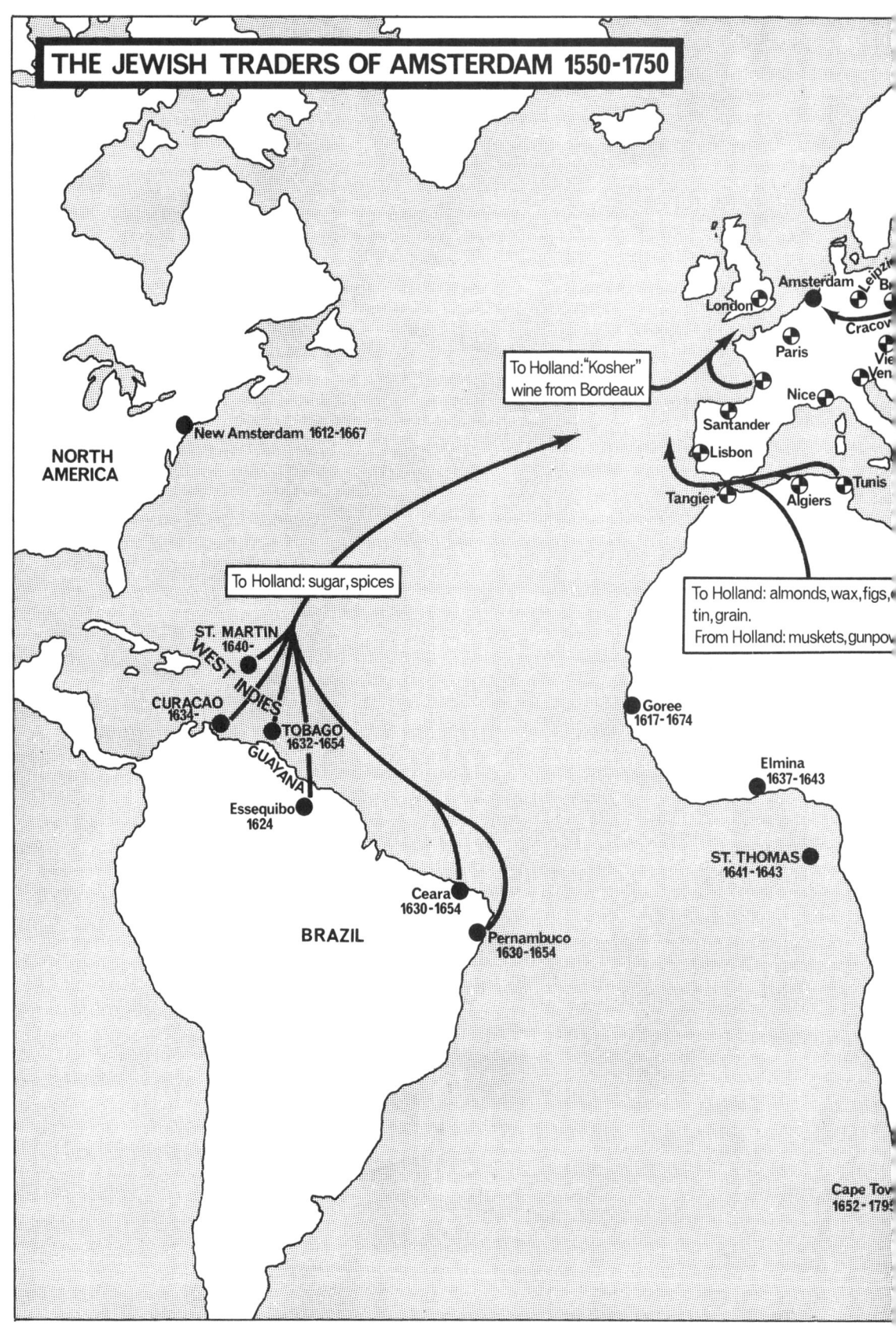

THE JEWISH TRADERS OF AMSTERDAM 1550-1750

To Holland:"Kosher" wine from Bordeaux

NORTH AMERICA

New Amsterdam 1612-1667

London

Amsterdam

Leipzig

Cracov

Paris

Vie

Ven

Nice

Santander

Lisbon

Tangier

Algiers

Tunis

To Holland: sugar, spices

To Holland: almonds, wax, figs, tin, grain.
From Holland: muskets, gunpov

ST. MARTIN 1640-

WEST INDIES

CURACAO 1634-

TOBAGO 1632-1654

GUAYANA

Essequibo 1624

Goree 1617-1674

Elmina 1637-1643

ST. THOMAS 1641-1643

Ceara 1630-1654

BRAZIL

Pernambuco 1630-1654

Cape Tov 1652-179

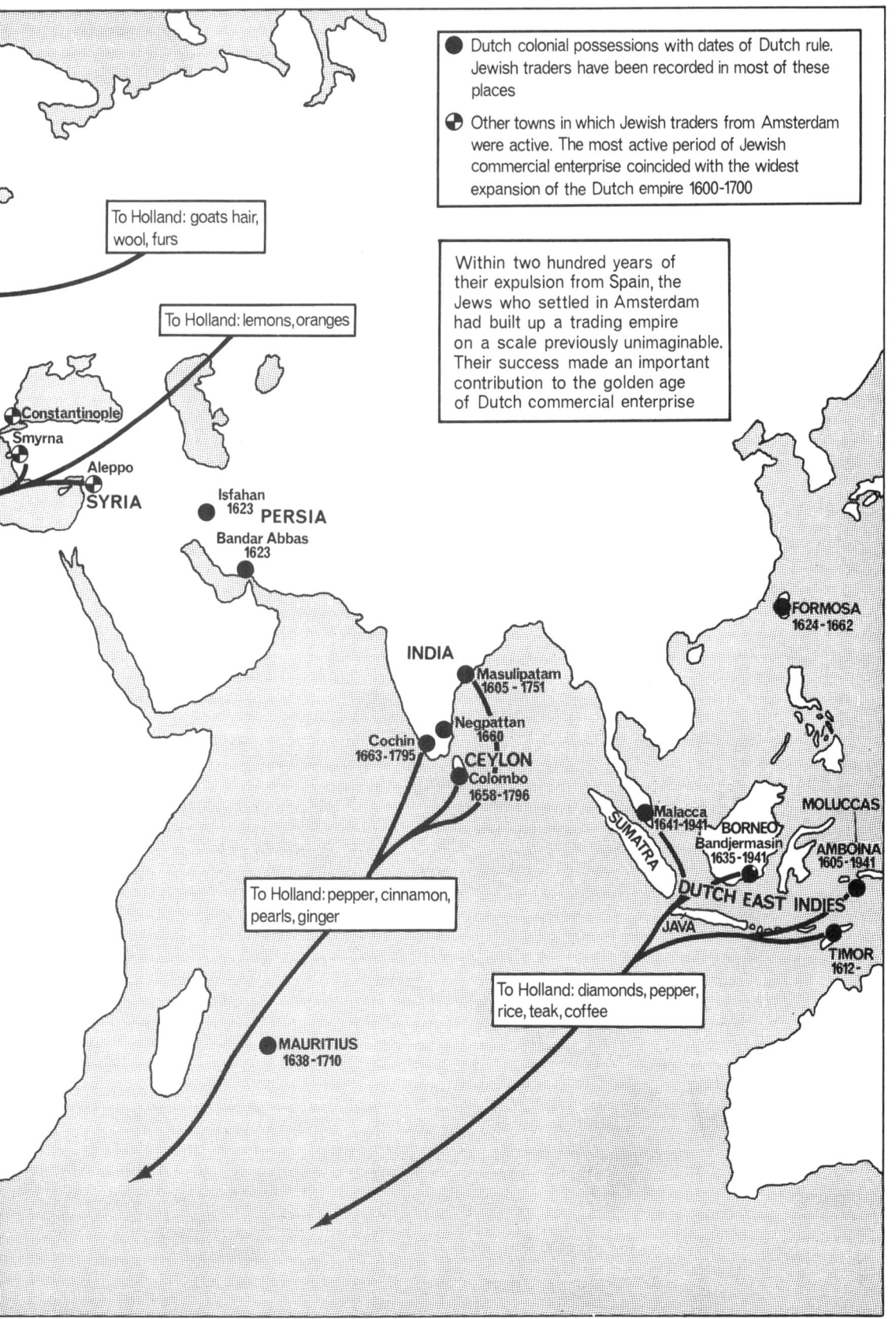

Dutch colonial possessions with dates of Dutch rule. Jewish traders have been recorded in most of these places

Other towns in which Jewish traders from Amsterdam were active. The most active period of Jewish commercial enterprise coincided with the widest expansion of the Dutch empire 1600-1700

Within two hundred years of their expulsion from Spain, the Jews who settled in Amsterdam had built up a trading empire on a scale previously unimaginable. Their success made an important contribution to the golden age of Dutch commercial enterprise

To Holland: goats hair, wool, furs

To Holland: lemons, oranges

Constantinople

Smyrna

Aleppo

SYRIA

Isfahan
1623

PERSIA

Bandar Abbas
1623

INDIA

Masulipatam
1605 - 1751

Cochin
1663-1795

Negpattan
1660

CEYLON

Colombo
1658-1796

FORMOSA
1624 - 1662

SUMATRA

Malacca
1641-1941

BORNEO

MOLUCCAS

Bandjermasin
1635-1941

AMBOINA
1605-1941

To Holland: pepper, cinnamon, pearls, ginger

DUTCH EAST INDIES

JAVA

TIMOR
1612-

To Holland: diamonds, pepper, rice, teak, coffee

MAURITIUS
1638-1710

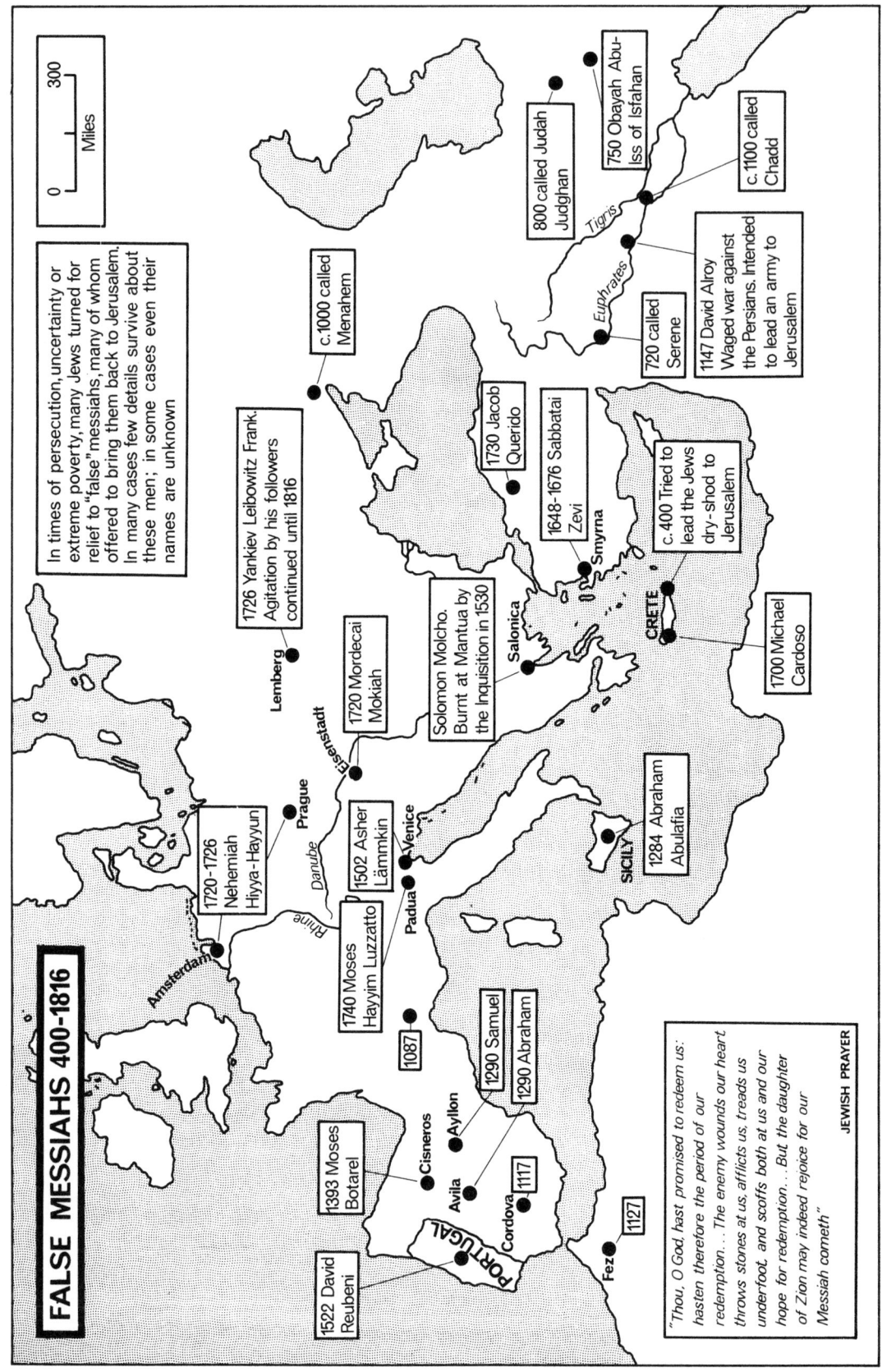

FALSE MESSIAHS 400-1816

In times of persecution, uncertainty or extreme poverty, many Jews turned for relief to "false" messiahs, many of whom offered to bring them back to Jerusalem. In many cases few details survive about these men; in some cases even their names are unknown

750 Obayah Abu-Iss of Isfahan

800 called Judah Judghan

c.1100 called Chadd

1147 David Alroy. Waged war against the Persians. Intended to lead an army to Jerusalem

720 called Serene

c.1000 called Menahem

1726 Yankiev Leibowitz Frank. Agitation by his followers continued until 1816

1730 Jacob Querido

1648-1676 Sabbatai Zevi

c. 400 Tried to lead the Jews dry-shod to Jerusalem

1700 Michael Cardoso

Solomon Molcho. Burnt at Mantua by the Inquisition in 1530

1720 Mordecai Mokiah

1720-1726 Nehemiah Hiyya-Hayyun

1502 Asher Lämmkin

1740 Moses Hayyim Luzzatto

1284 Abraham Abulafia

1393 Moses Botarel

1290 Samuel

1290 Abraham

1522 David Reubeni

Smyrna

Salonica

CRETE

SICILY

Eisenstadt

Prague

Venice

Padua

Lemberg

Amsterdam

Avila

Ayllon

Cisneros

Cordova

PORTUGAL

Fez

Danube

Rhine

Tigris

Euphrates

1087

1117

1127

"Thou, O God, hast promised to redeem us: hasten therefore the period of our redemption... The enemy wounds our heart, throws stones at us, afflicts us, treads us underfoot, and scoffs both at us and our hope for redemption... But the daughter of Zion may indeed rejoice for our Messiah cometh"

JEWISH PRAYER

0   300
Miles

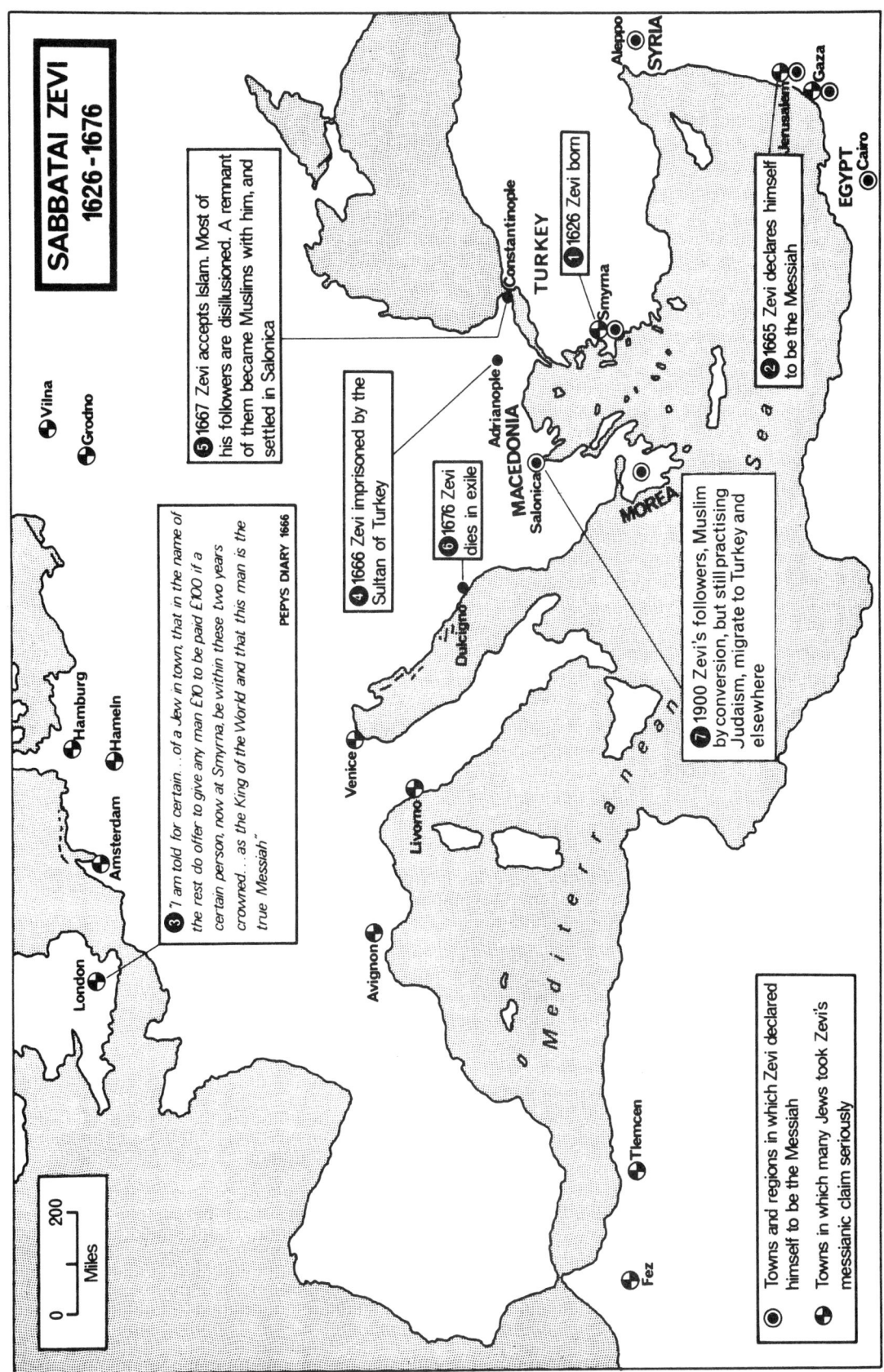

SABBATAI ZEVI
1626 - 1676

3 *"I am told for certain... of a Jew in town, that in the name of the rest do offer to give any man £10 to be paid £100 if a certain person, now at Smyrna, be within these two years crowned... as the King of the World and that this man is the true Messiah"*

PEPYS DIARY 1666

5 1667 Zevi accepts Islam. Most of his followers are disillusioned. A remnant of them became Muslims with him, and settled in Salonica

4 1666 Zevi imprisoned by the Sultan of Turkey

6 1676 Zevi dies in exile

7 1900 Zevi's followers, Muslim by conversion, but still practising Judaism, migrate to Turkey and elsewhere

1 1626 Zevi born

2 1665 Zevi declares himself to be the Messiah

- ◉ Towns and regions in which Zevi declared himself to be the Messiah
- ◗ Towns in which many Jews took Zevi's messianic claim seriously

Vilna
Grodno
Hamburg
Hameln
Amsterdam
London
Venice
Livorno
Avignon
Tlemcen
Fez
Constantinople
TURKEY
Smyrna
Adrianople
MACEDONIA
Salonica
MOREA
Dulcigno
Aleppo
SYRIA
Gaza
Jerusalem
Cairo
EGYPT

Mediterranean Sea

0   200
Miles

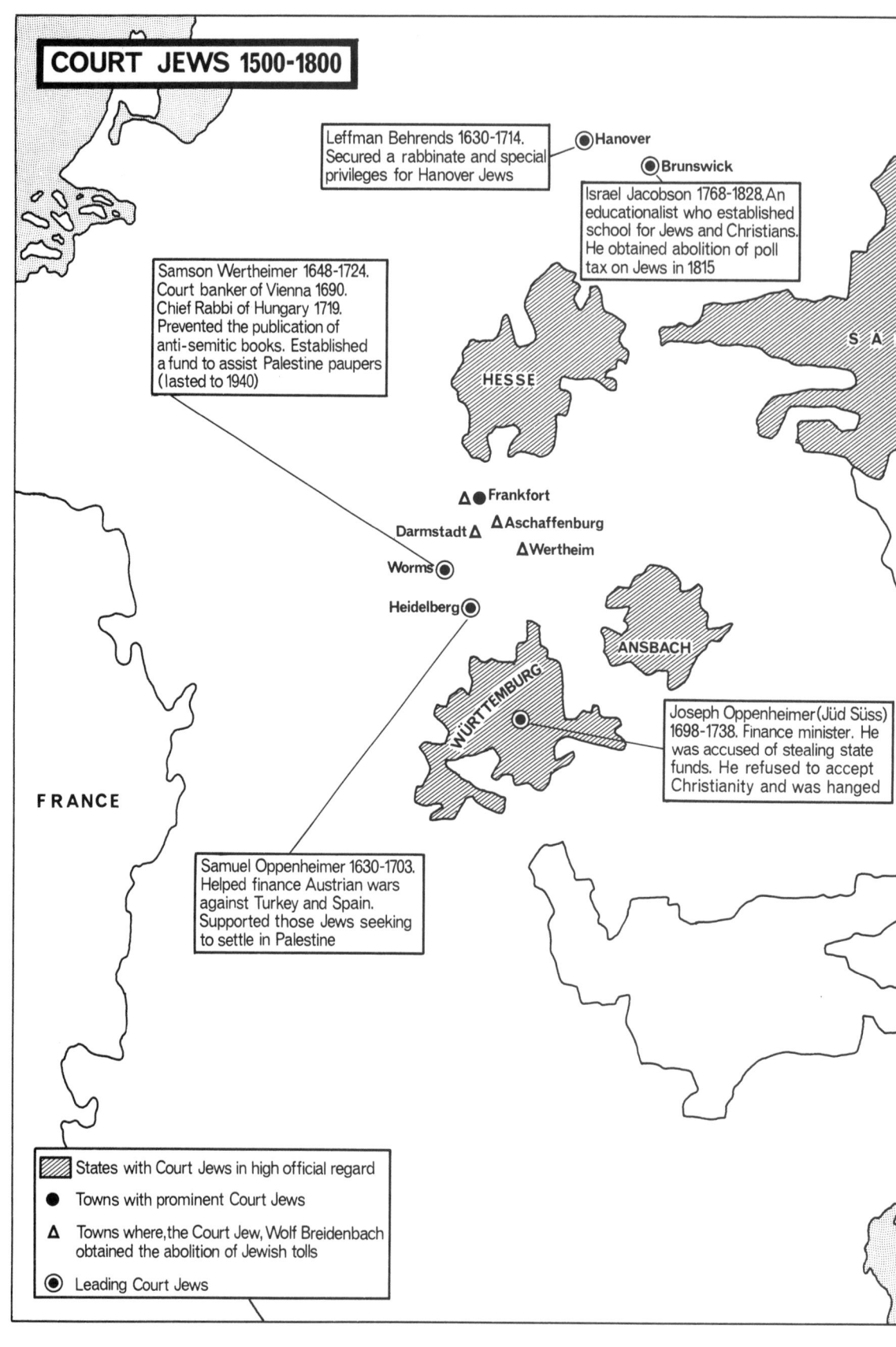

COURT JEWS 1500-1800

Leffman Behrends 1630-1714. Secured a rabbinate and special privileges for Hanover Jews

⊙ Hanover
⊙ Brunswick

Israel Jacobson 1768-1828. An educationalist who established school for Jews and Christians. He obtained abolition of poll tax on Jews in 1815

Samson Wertheimer 1648-1724. Court banker of Vienna 1690. Chief Rabbi of Hungary 1719. Prevented the publication of anti-semitic books. Established a fund to assist Palestine paupers (lasted to 1940)

HESSE

S · A · X

△ ● Frankfort
△ Aschaffenburg
Darmstadt △
△ Wertheim
Worms ⊙
Heidelberg ⊙

ANSBACH

WÜRTTEMBURG

Joseph Oppenheimer (Jüd Süss) 1698-1738. Finance minister. He was accused of stealing state funds. He refused to accept Christianity and was hanged

FRANCE

Samuel Oppenheimer 1630-1703. Helped finance Austrian wars against Turkey and Spain. Supported those Jews seeking to settle in Palestine

▨ States with Court Jews in high official regard

● Towns with prominent Court Jews

△ Towns where, the Court Jew, Wolf Breidenbach obtained the abolition of Jewish tolls

⊙ Leading Court Jews

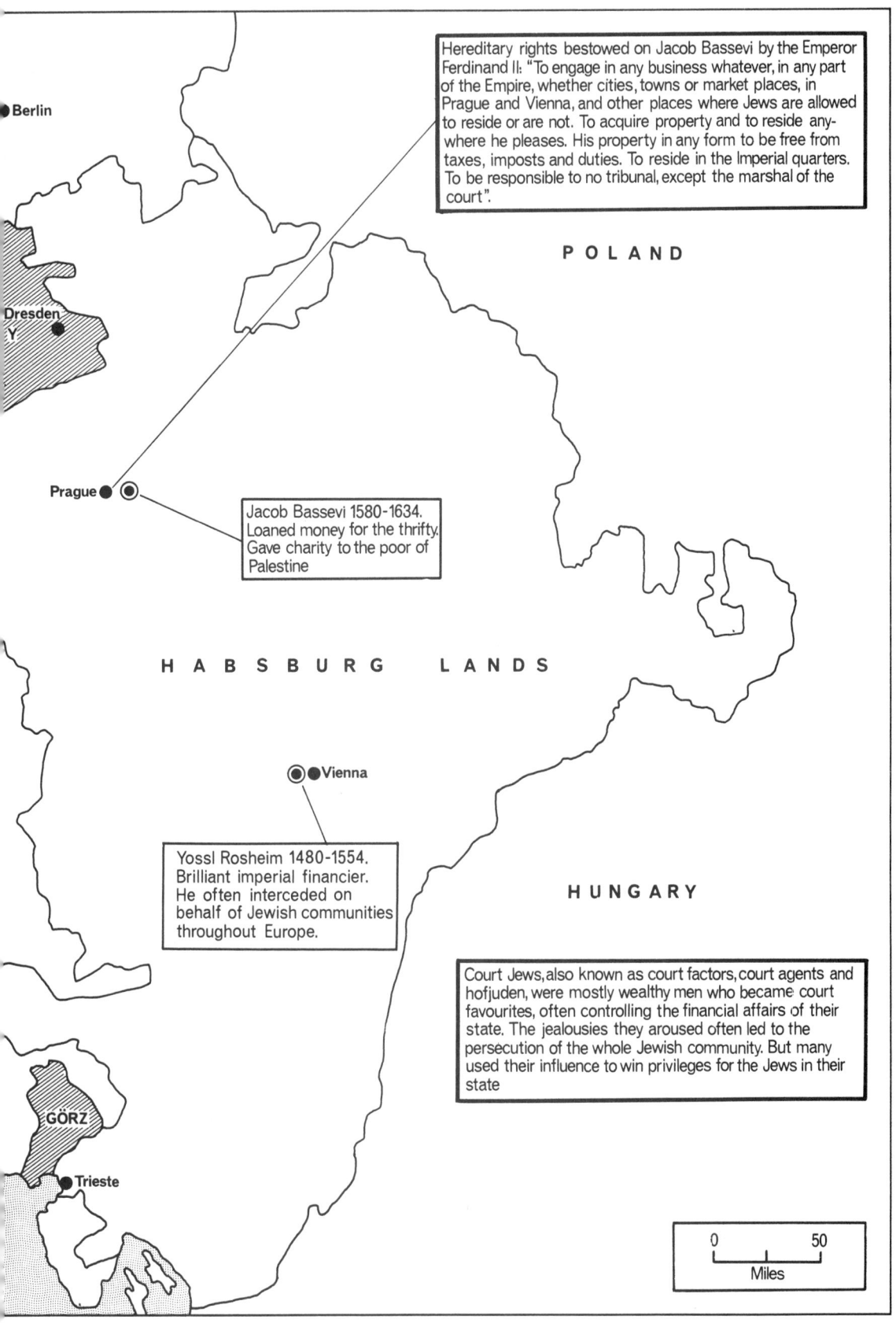

Berlin

Dresden
Y

Hereditary rights bestowed on Jacob Bassevi by the Emperor Ferdinand II: "To engage in any business whatever, in any part of the Empire, whether cities, towns or market places, in Prague and Vienna, and other places where Jews are allowed to reside or are not. To acquire property and to reside anywhere he pleases. His property in any form to be free from taxes, imposts and duties. To reside in the Imperial quarters. To be responsible to no tribunal, except the marshal of the court".

P O L A N D

Prague ● ◎

Jacob Bassevi 1580-1634. Loaned money for the thrifty. Gave charity to the poor of Palestine

H A B S B U R G   L A N D S

◎● Vienna

Yossl Rosheim 1480-1554. Brilliant imperial financier. He often interceded on behalf of Jewish communities throughout Europe.

H U N G A R Y

Court Jews, also known as court factors, court agents and hofjuden, were mostly wealthy men who became court favourites, often controlling the financial affairs of their state. The jealousies they aroused often led to the persecution of the whole Jewish community. But many used their influence to win privileges for the Jews in their state

GÖRZ

● Trieste

0   50
Miles

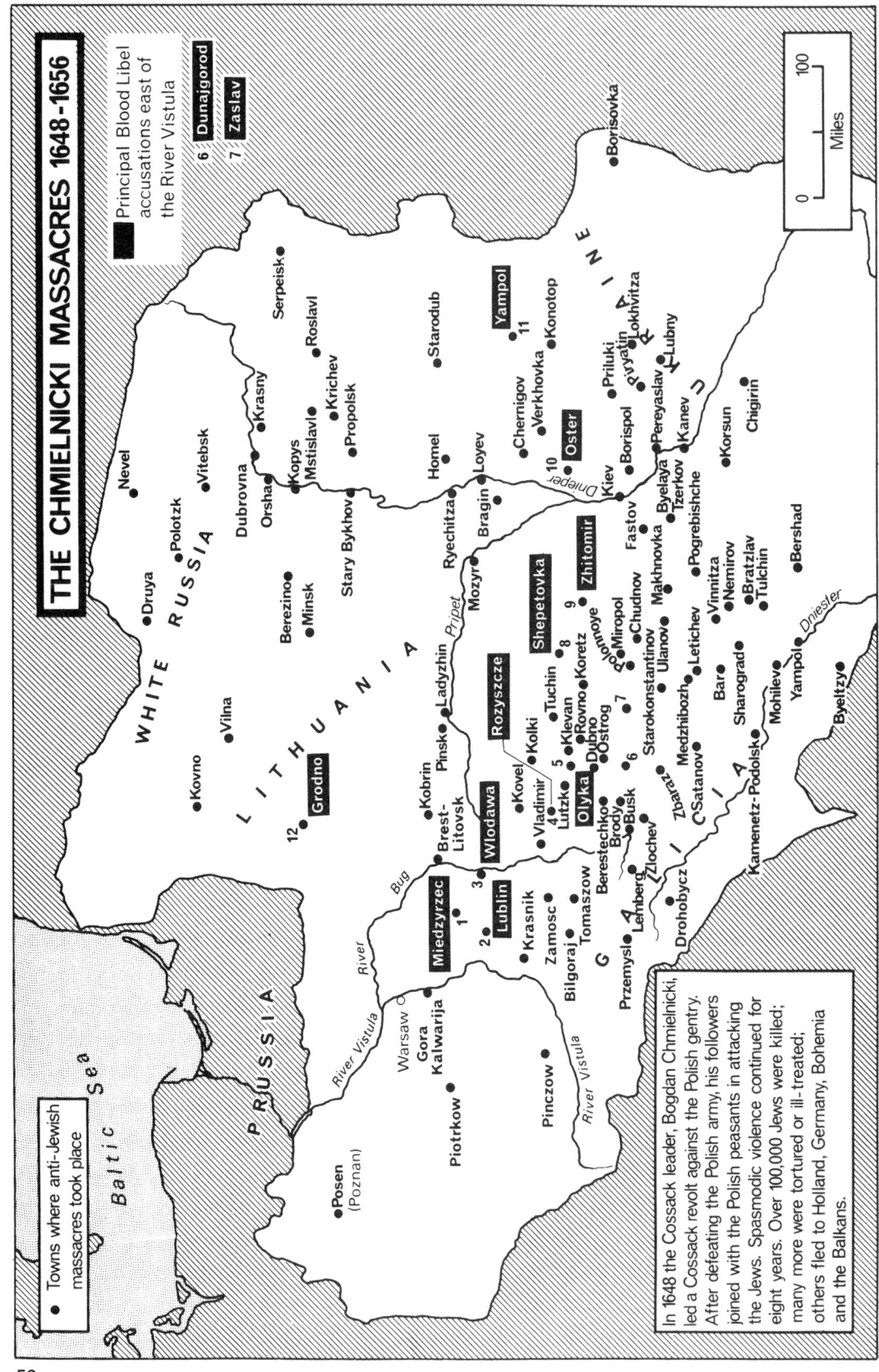

THE CHMIELNICKI MASSACRES 1648-1656

Principal Blood Libel
accusations east of
the River Vistula

6 Dumajgorod
7 Zaslav

• Towns where anti-Jewish
massacres took place

0 ___ 100
Miles

In 1648 the Cossack leader, Bogdan Chmielnicki,
led a Cossack revolt against the Polish gentry.
After defeating the Polish army, his followers
joined with the Polish peasants in attacking
the Jews. Spasmodic violence continued for
eight years. Over 100,000 Jews were killed;
many more were tortured or ill-treated;
others fled to Holland, Germany, Bohemia
and the Balkans.

Baltic Sea

PRUSSIA

WHITE RUSSIA

LITHUANIA

UKRAINE

Borisovka

Serpeisk
Roslavl
Starodub
Krasny
Krichev
Propolsk
Mstislavl
Kopys
Orsha
Dubrovna
Vitebsk
Polotzk
Druya
Nevel

Verkhovka
Chernigov
Yampol 11
Konotop
Lokhvitza
Lubny
Pryluki
Priluki
Pereyaslav
Kaniev
Chigirin
Korsun

Oster 10

Kiev
Borispol
Fastov
Byelaya
Tzerkov
Pogrebishche
Makhnovka
Chudnov
Pomnoye
Miropol
Bershad

Zhitomir 9

Shepetovka

Rozyszcze

Grodno 12

Berezino
Minsk
Stary Bykhov
Ladyzhin
Pinsk
Pripet
Mozyr
Bragin
Loyev
Rychitza
Hornel

Vitebsk
Vilna
Kovno

Kobrin
Brest-
Litovsk
Wlodawa

Kovel
Vladimir
Lutzke
Kolki
Kolki
Tuchin
Rovno
Klevan
Dubno
Ostrog
Olyka
Starokonstantinov
Ulanov
Letichev
Medzhibozh
Bar
Vinnitza
Nemirov
Bratzlav
Tulchin
Sharograd
Mohilev
Yampol
Byeltzy
Kamenetz-Podolsk
Zbaraz
CSatanov
Busk
Zlocher
Brody
Berestechko
Drohobycz
Lemberg
Przemysl

Dniester

Dnieper

Miedzyrzec
Lublin
Krasnik
Zamosc
Bilgoraj
Tomaszow

Piotrkow
Pinczow
Kalwarija
Gora
Warsaw
Posen
(Poznan)

River Vistula
River Vistula
Bug

1
2
3
4
5
6
7
8

56

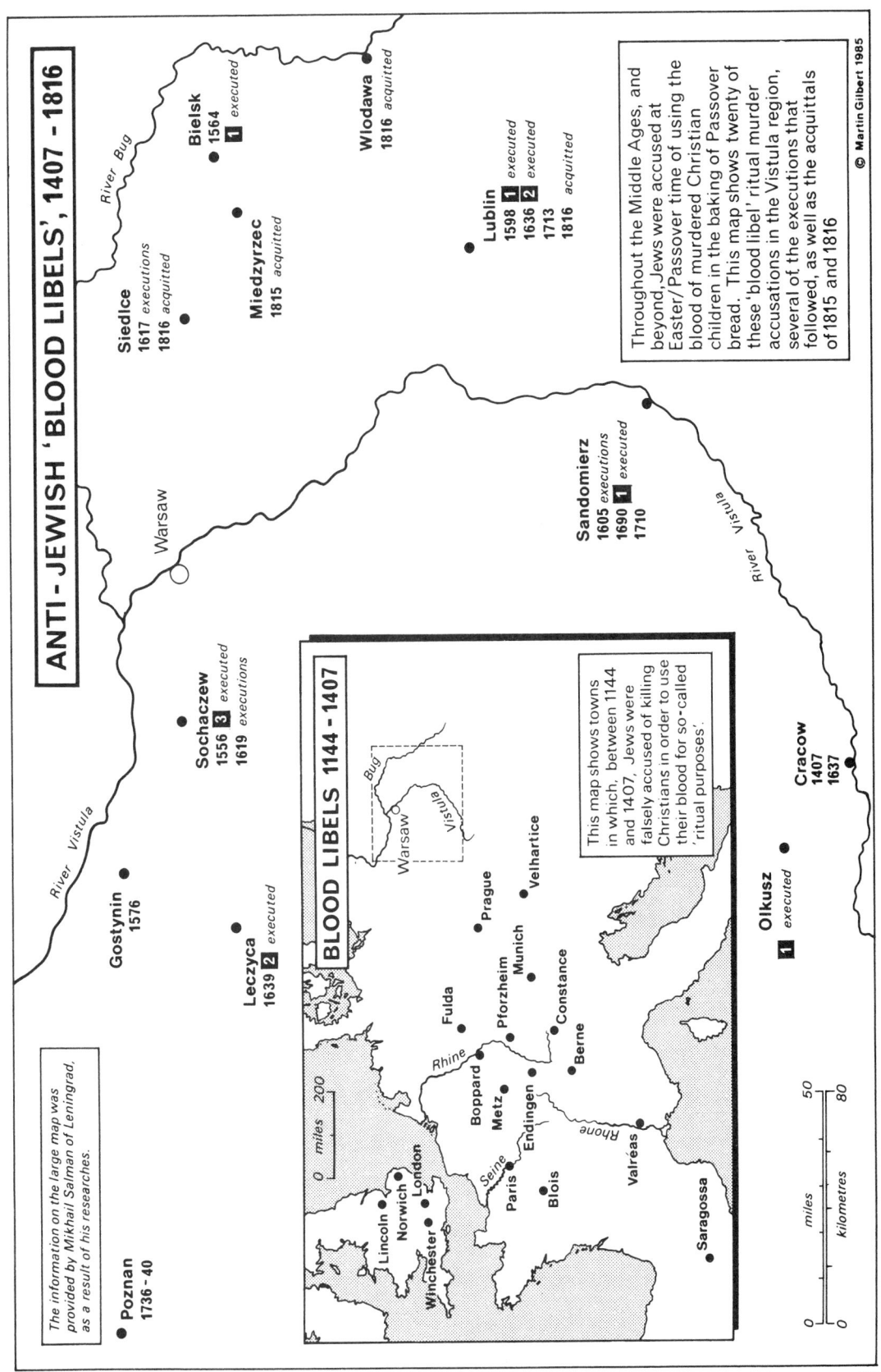

ANTI-JEWISH 'BLOOD LIBELS', 1407 – 1816

The information on the large map was provided by Mikhail Salman of Leningrad, as a result of his researches.

Poznan
1736 – 40

Gostynin
1576

River Vistula

Sochaczew
1556 **3** *executed*
1619 *executions*

Leczyca
1639 **2** *executed*

Siedlce
1617 *executions*
1816 *acquitted*

River Bug

Bielsk
1564 **1** *executed*

Wlodawa
1816 *acquitted*

Miedzyrzec
1815 *acquitted*

Warsaw

Lublin
1598 **1** *executed*
1636 **2** *executed*
1713
1816 *acquitted*

Sandomierz
1605 *executions*
1690 **1** *executed*
1710

River Vistula

Throughout the Middle Ages, and beyond, Jews were accused at Easter/Passover time of using the blood of murdered Christian children in the baking of Passover bread. This map shows twenty of these 'blood libel' ritual murder accusations in the Vistula region, several of the executions that followed, as well as the acquittals of 1815 and 1816

© Martin Gilbert 1985

BLOOD LIBELS 1144 – 1407

Bug

Vistula

Warsaw

Prague

Velhartice

Munich

Pforzheim

Constance

Berne

Rhine

Fulda

Boppard

Metz

Endingen

Paris

Blois

Seine

Rhône

Valréas

Lincoln

Norwich

London

Winchester

Saragossa

This map shows towns in which, between 1144 and 1407, Jews were falsely accused of killing Christians in order to use their blood for so-called 'ritual purposes'.

0 miles 200

Olkusz
1 *executed*

Cracow
1407
1637

0 miles 50
0 kilometres 80

57

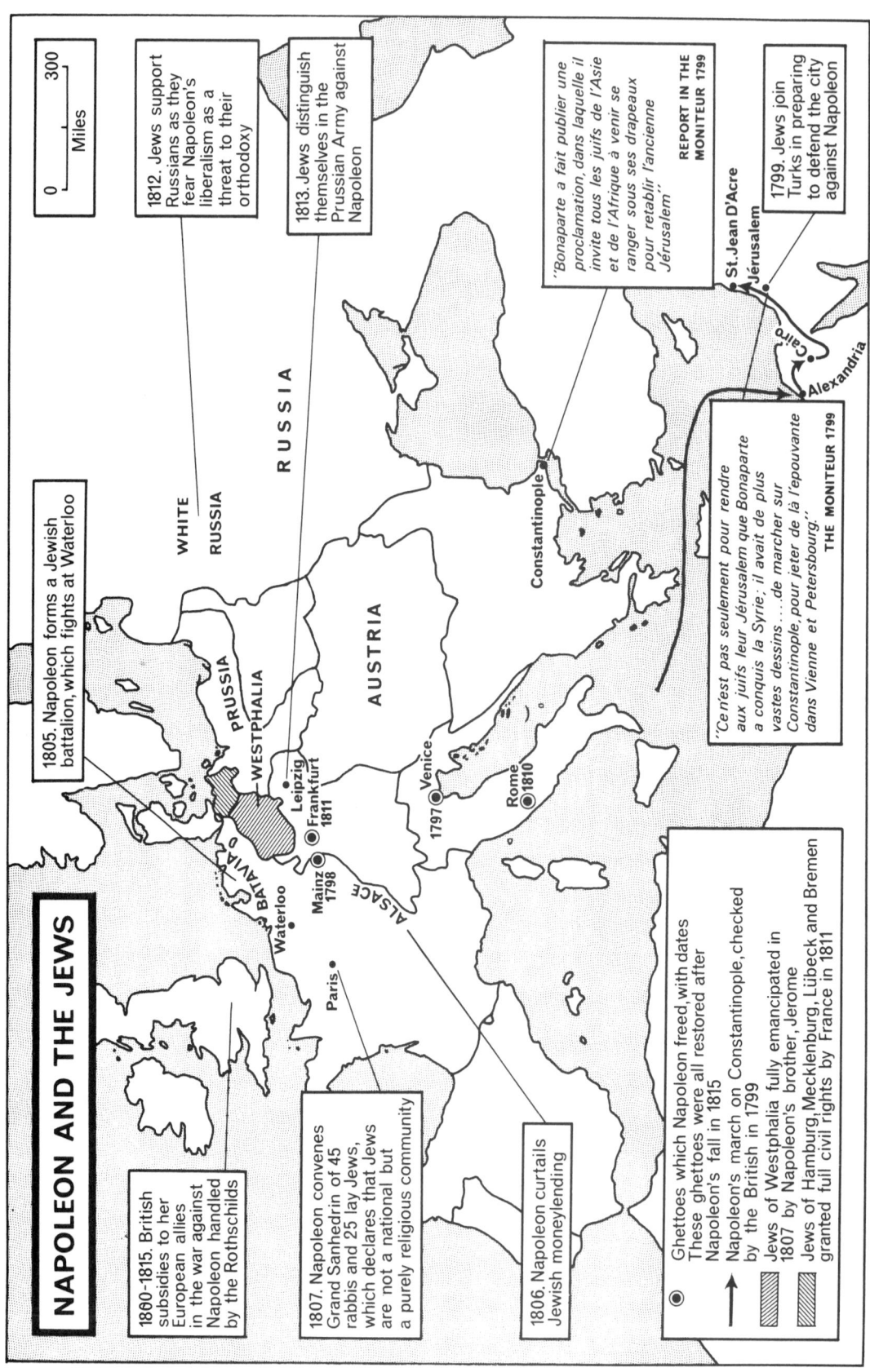

NAPOLEON AND THE JEWS

0 ——— 300
Miles

1812. Jews support Russians as they fear Napoleon's liberalism as a threat to their orthodoxy

1813. Jews distinguish themselves in the Prussian Army against Napoleon

"Bonaparte a fait publier une proclamation, dans laquelle il invite tous les juifs de l'Asie et de l'Afrique à venir se ranger sous ses drapeaux pour rétablir l'ancienne Jérusalem"

REPORT IN THE MONITEUR 1799

1799. Jews join Turks in preparing to defend the city against Napoleon

1805. Napoleon forms a Jewish battalion, which fights at Waterloo

WHITE RUSSIA

RUSSIA

St.Jean D'Acre
Jérusalem
Cairo
Alexandria

Constantinople

"Ce n'est pas seulement pour rendre aux juifs leur Jérusalem que Bonaparte a conquis la Syrie; il avait de plus vastes dessins....de marcher sur Constantinople, pour jeter de là l'épouvante dans Vienne et Petersbourg."

THE MONITEUR 1799

1860-1815. British subsidies to her European allies in the war against Napoleon handled by the Rothschilds

PRUSSIA
WESTPHALIA
AUSTRIA

Leipzig
Frankfurt 1811
Mainz 1798
ALSACE
BATAVIA
Waterloo
Paris

Venice
1797

Rome
1810

1807. Napoleon convenes Grand Sanhedrin of 45 rabbis and 25 lay Jews, which declares that Jews are not a national but a purely religious community

1806. Napoleon curtails Jewish moneylending

Ghettoes which Napoleon freed, with dates
These ghettoes were all restored after Napoleon's fall in 1815

Napoleon's march on Constantinople, checked by the British in 1799

Jews of Westphalia fully emancipated in 1807 by Napoleon's brother, Jerome

Jews of Hamburg, Mecklenburg, Lübeck and Bremen granted full civil rights by France in 1811

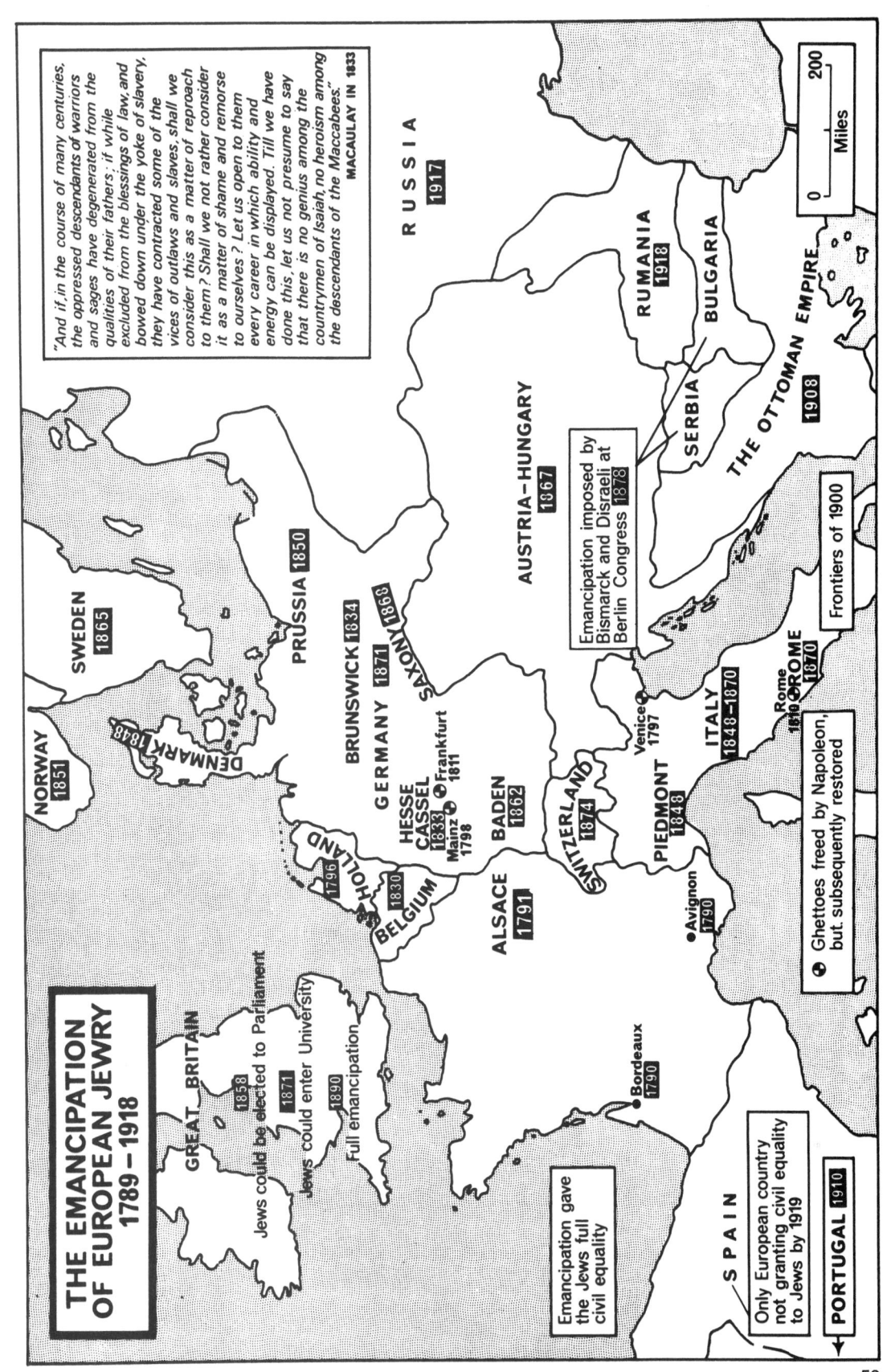

THE EMANCIPATION OF EUROPEAN JEWRY 1789–1918

"And if, in the course of many centuries, the oppressed descendants of warriors and sages have degenerated from the qualities of their fathers; if while excluded from the blessings of law, and bowed down under the yoke of slavery, they have contracted some of the vices of outlaws and slaves, shall we consider this as a matter of reproach to them? Shall we not rather consider it as a matter of shame and remorse to ourselves? Let us open to them every career in which ability and energy can be displayed. Till we have done this, let us not presume to say that there is no genius among the countrymen of Isaiah, no heroism among the descendants of the Maccabees."

MACAULAY IN 1833

GREAT BRITAIN

1858 Jews could be elected to Parliament
1871 Jews could enter University
1890 Full emancipation

Emancipation gave the Jews full civil equality

NORWAY 1851

SWEDEN 1865

DENMARK 1848

HOLLAND 1796

BELGIUM 1830

PRUSSIA 1850

BRUNSWICK 1834

GERMANY 1871

SAXONY 1868

HESSE CASSEL 1833

Frankfurt 1811

Mainz 1798

BADEN 1862

ALSACE 1791

SWITZERLAND 1874

Bordeaux 1790

Avignon 1790

PIEDMONT 1848

ITALY 1848–1870

Venice 1797

Rome 1810
ROME 1870

RUSSIA 1917

AUSTRIA–HUNGARY 1867

Emancipation imposed by Bismarck and Disraeli at Berlin Congress 1878

RUMANIA 1918

SERBIA

BULGARIA

THE OTTOMAN EMPIRE 1908

Frontiers of 1900

⊕ Ghettoes freed by Napoleon, but subsequently restored

S P A I N

Only European country not granting civil equality to Jews by 1919

PORTUGAL 1910

0   200
Miles

59

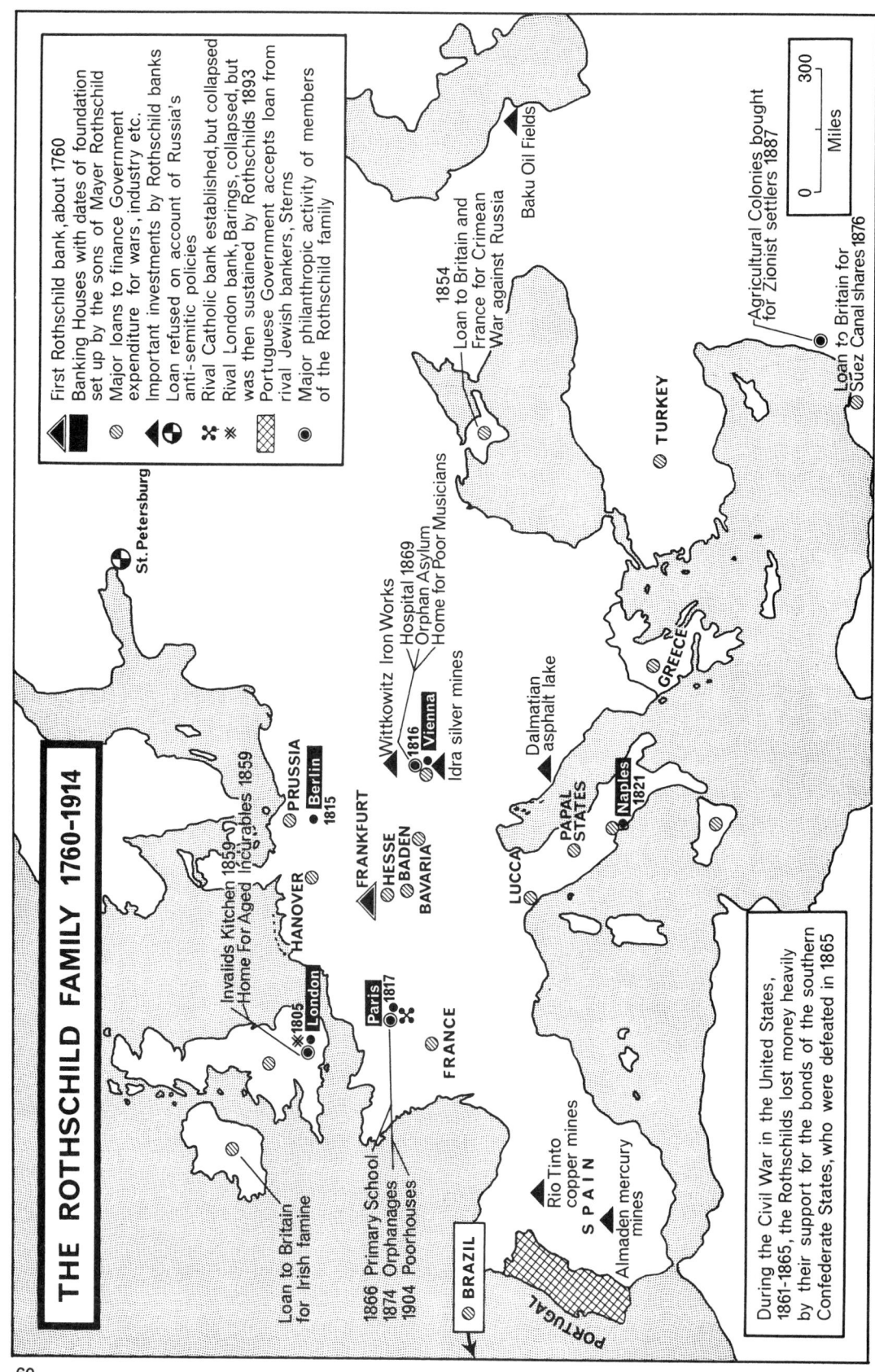

THE ROTHSCHILD FAMILY 1760-1914

Key / Legend:

- First Rothschild bank, about 1760
- Banking Houses with dates of foundation set up by the sons of Mayer Rothschild
- Major loans to finance Government expenditure for wars, industry etc.
- Important investments by Rothschild banks
- Loan refused on account of Russia's anti-semitic policies
- Rival Catholic bank established, but collapsed
- Rival London bank, Barings, collapsed, but was then sustained by Rothschilds 1893
- Portuguese Government accepts loan from rival Jewish bankers, Sterns
- Major philanthropic activity of members of the Rothschild family

Scale: 0 — 300 Miles

St. Petersburg

Baku Oil Fields

1854
Loan to Britain and France for Crimean War against Russia

TURKEY

Loan to Britain for Suez Canal shares 1876

Agricultural Colonies bought for Zionist settlers 1887

Invalids Kitchen 1859-91
Home For Aged Incurables 1859

PRUSSIA
● **Berlin**
1815

HANOVER

Wittkowitz Iron Works
Hospital 1869
Orphan Asylum
Home for Poor Musicians
1816
● **Vienna**
Idra silver mines

FRANKFURT
HESSE
BADEN
BAVARIA

Dalmatian asphalt lake

LUCCA

PAPAL STATES

Naples
1821

GREECE

Loan to Britain for Irish famine

1866 Primary School
1874 Orphanages
1904 Poorhouses

London
1805
●

Paris
1817
●

FRANCE

Rio Tinto copper mines

SPAIN

Almaden mercury mines

PORTUGAL

● **BRAZIL**

During the Civil War in the United States, 1861-1865, the Rothschilds lost money heavily by their support for the bonds of the southern Confederate States, who were defeated in 1865

60

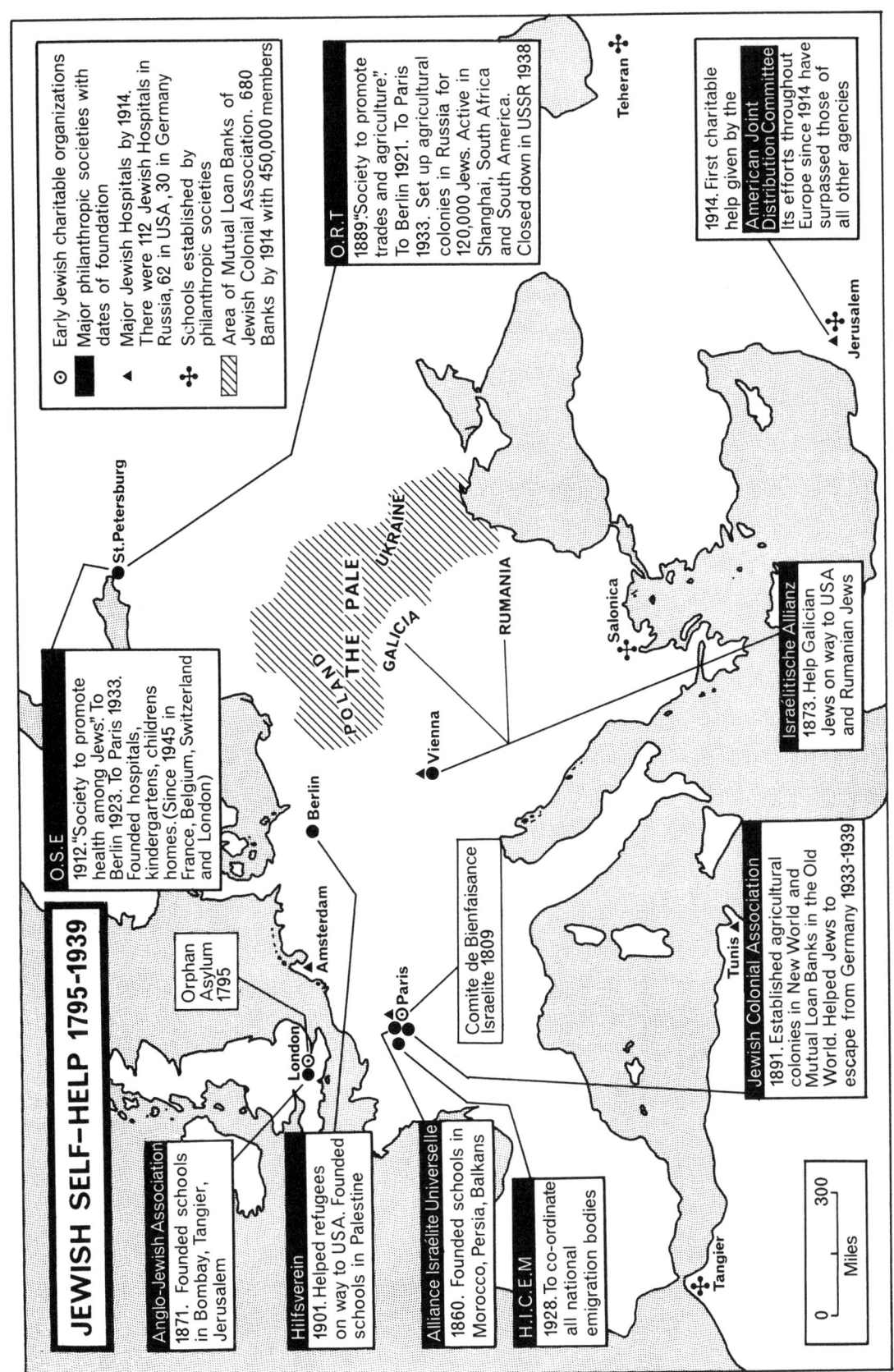

JEWISH SELF-HELP 1795-1939

Legend:
- ⊙ Early Jewish charitable organizations
- ■ Major philanthropic societies with dates of foundation
- ▲ Major Jewish Hospitals by 1914. There were 112 Jewish Hospitals in Russia, 62 in USA, 30 in Germany
- ✣ Schools established by philanthropic societies
- ▨ Area of Mutual Loan Banks of Jewish Colonial Association. 680 Banks by 1914 with 450,000 members

O.R.T
1889."Society to promote trades and agriculture". To Paris 1921. To Berlin 1933. Set up agricultural colonies in Russia for 120,000 Jews. Active in Shanghai, South Africa and South America. Closed down in USSR 1938

1914. First charitable help given by the American Joint Distribution Committee. Its efforts throughout Europe since 1914 have surpassed those of all other agencies

O.S.E
1912."Society to promote health among Jews". To Berlin 1923. To Paris 1933. Founded hospitals, kindergartens, childrens homes. (Since 1945 in France, Belgium, Switzerland and London)

Anglo-Jewish Association
1871. Founded schools in Bombay, Tangier, Jerusalem

Orphan Asylum 1795

Hilfsverein
1901. Helped refugees on way to USA. Founded schools in Palestine

Alliance Israélite Universelle
1860. Founded schools in Morocco, Persia, Balkans

H.I.C.E.M
1928. To co-ordinate all national emigration bodies

Comité de Bienfaisance Israélite 1809

Jewish Colonial Association
1891. Established agricultural colonies in New World and Mutual Loan Banks in the Old World. Helped Jews to escape from Germany 1933-1939

Israélitische Allianz
1873. Help Galician Jews on way to USA and Rumanian Jews

POLAND
THE PALE
UKRAINE
GALICIA
RUMANIA

St.Petersburg
Berlin
Amsterdam
London
Paris
Vienna
Salonica
Tunis
Tangier
Teheran
Jerusalem

0   300
Miles

61

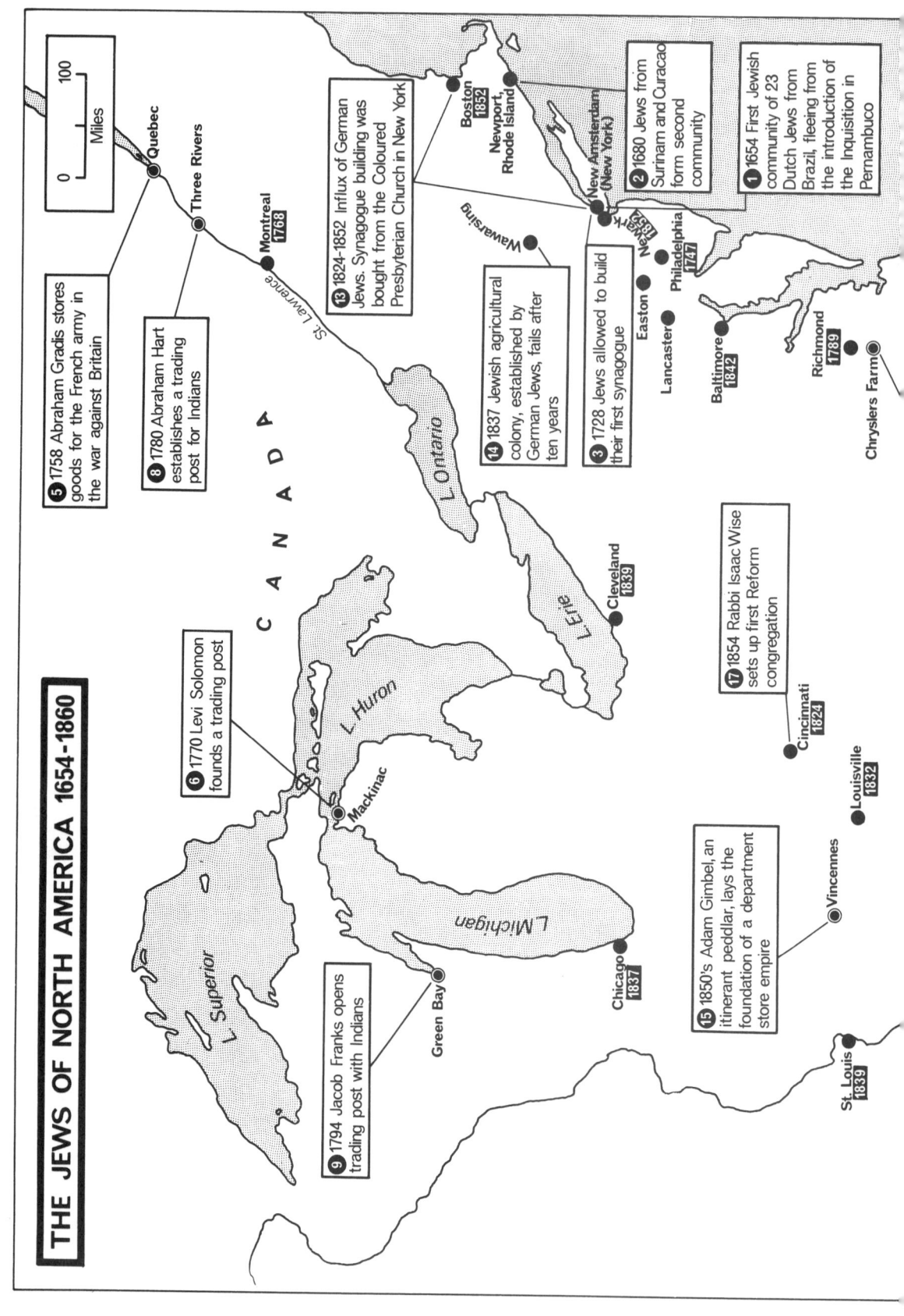

THE JEWS OF NORTH AMERICA 1654-1860

0 ___ 100
Miles

5 1758 Abraham Gradis stores goods for the French army in the war against Britain

8 1780 Abraham Hart establishes a trading post for Indians

6 1770 Levi Solomon founds a trading post

9 1794 Jacob Franks opens trading post with Indians

13 1824-1852 Influx of German Jews. Synagogue building was bought from the Coloured Presbyterian Church in New York

14 1837 Jewish agricultural colony, established by German Jews, fails after ten years

3 1728 Jews allowed to build their first synagogue

2 1680 Jews from Surinam and Curacao form second community

1 1654 First Jewish community of 23 Dutch Jews, fleeing from the introduction of the Inquisition in Pernambuco

17 1854 Rabbi Isaac Wise sets up first Reform congregation

15 1850's Adam Gimbel, an itinerant peddlar, lays the foundation of a department store empire

CANADA

St. Lawrence

Quebec

Three Rivers

Montreal 1768

L. Ontario

L. Erie

L. Huron

L. Michigan

L. Superior

Mackinac

Green Bay

Chicago 1837

Vincennes

St. Louis 1839

Louisville 1832

Cincinnati 1824

Cleveland 1839

Wawarsing

Boston 1852

Newport, Rhode Island

New Amsterdam (New York)

New York 1852

Easton

Lancaster

Philadelphia 1747

Baltimore 1842

Richmond 1789

Chryslers Farm

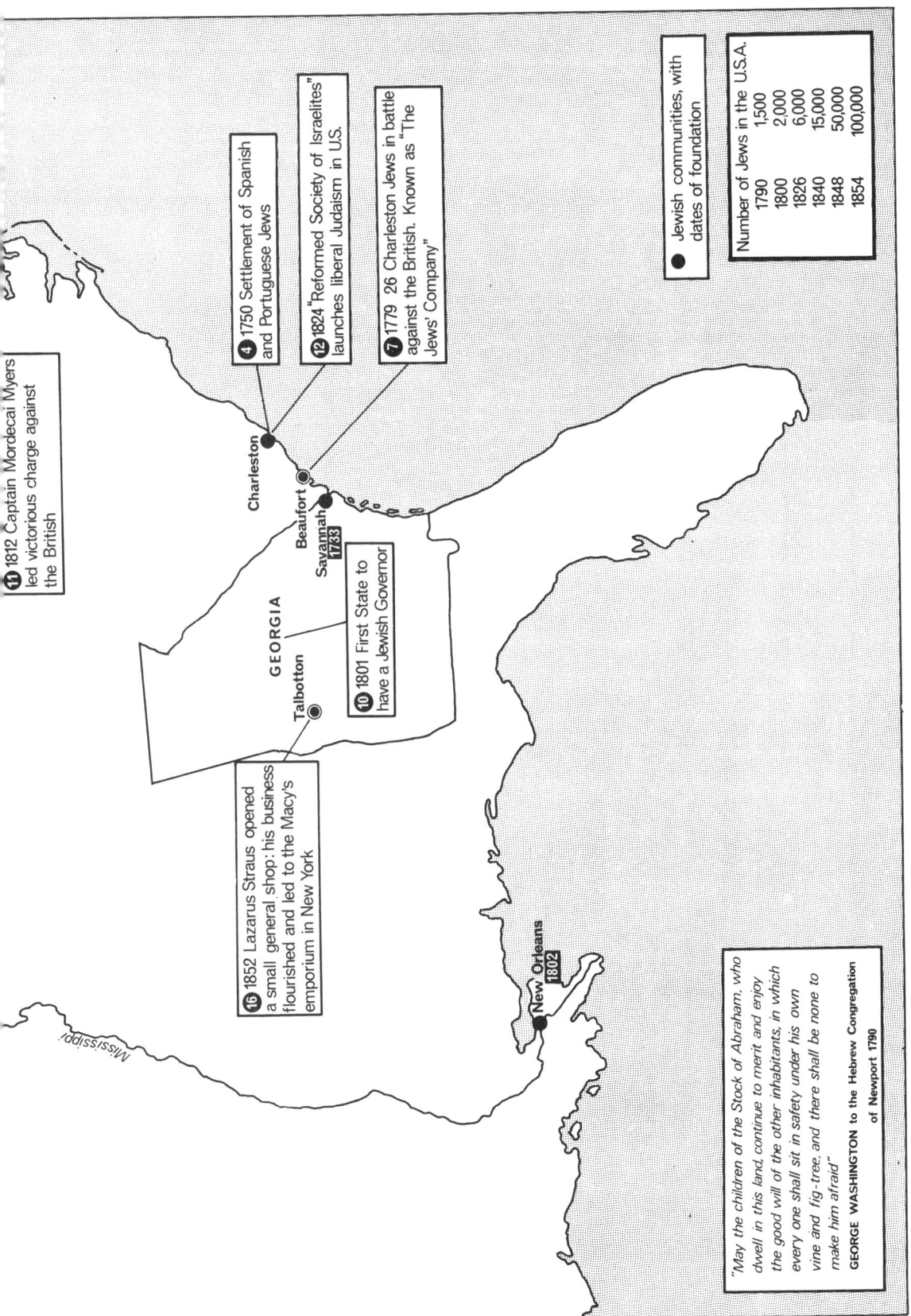

11 1812 Captain Mordecai Myers led victorious charge against the British

4 1750 Settlement of Spanish and Portuguese Jews

12 1824 "Reformed Society of Israelites" launches liberal Judaism in U.S.

7 1779 26 Charleston Jews in battle against the British. Known as "The Jews' Company"

10 1801 First State to have a Jewish Governor

16 1852 Lazarus Straus opened a small general shop: his business flourished and led to the Macy's emporium in New York

Charleston

Beaufort
Savannah 1733

GEORGIA

Talbotton

New Orleans 1802

Mississippi

● Jewish communities, with dates of foundation

Number of Jews in the U.S.A.
1790   1,500
1800   2,000
1826   6,000
1840   15,000
1848   50,000
1854   100,000

"May the children of the Stock of Abraham, who dwell in this land, continue to merit and enjoy the good will of the other inhabitants, in which every one shall sit in safety under his own vine and fig-tree, and there shall be none to make him afraid"
GEORGE WASHINGTON to the Hebrew Congregation of Newport 1790

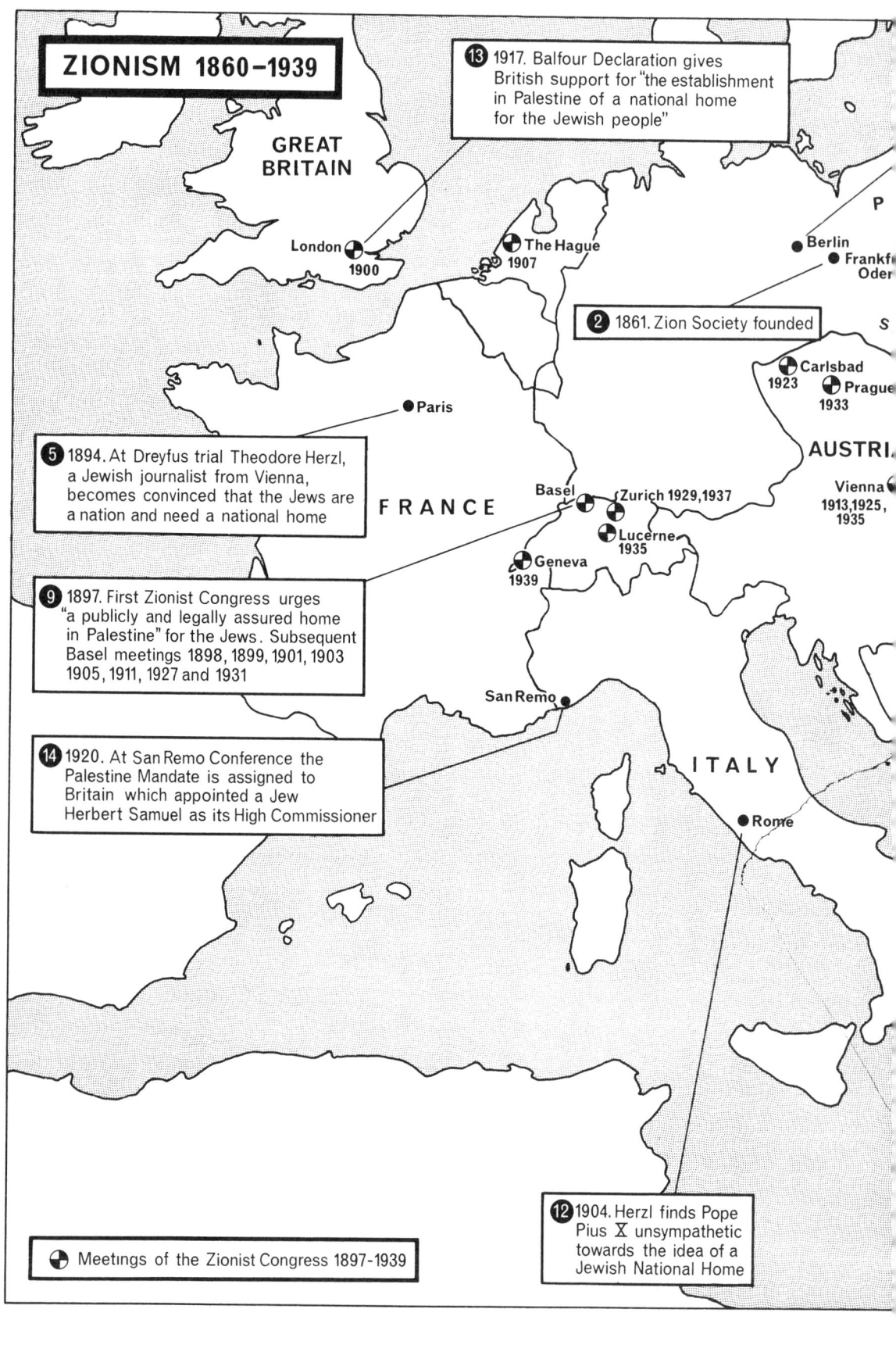

ZIONISM 1860-1939

13 1917. Balfour Declaration gives British support for "the establishment in Palestine of a national home for the Jewish people"

GREAT BRITAIN

London 1900

The Hague 1907

Berlin
Frankf
Oder

2 1861. Zion Society founded

Carlsbad 1923
Prague 1933

AUSTRI

Paris

Vienna 1913, 1925, 1935

5 1894. At Dreyfus trial Theodore Herzl, a Jewish journalist from Vienna, becomes convinced that the Jews are a nation and need a national home

FRANCE

Basel

Zurich 1929, 1937

Lucerne 1935

Geneva 1939

9 1897. First Zionist Congress urges "a publicly and legally assured home in Palestine" for the Jews. Subsequent Basel meetings 1898, 1899, 1901, 1903 1905, 1911, 1927 and 1931

San Remo

ITALY

14 1920. At San Remo Conference the Palestine Mandate is assigned to Britain which appointed a Jew Herbert Samuel as its High Commissioner

Rome

⊕ Meetings of the Zionist Congress 1897-1939

12 1904. Herzl finds Pope Pius X unsympathetic towards the idea of a Jewish National Home

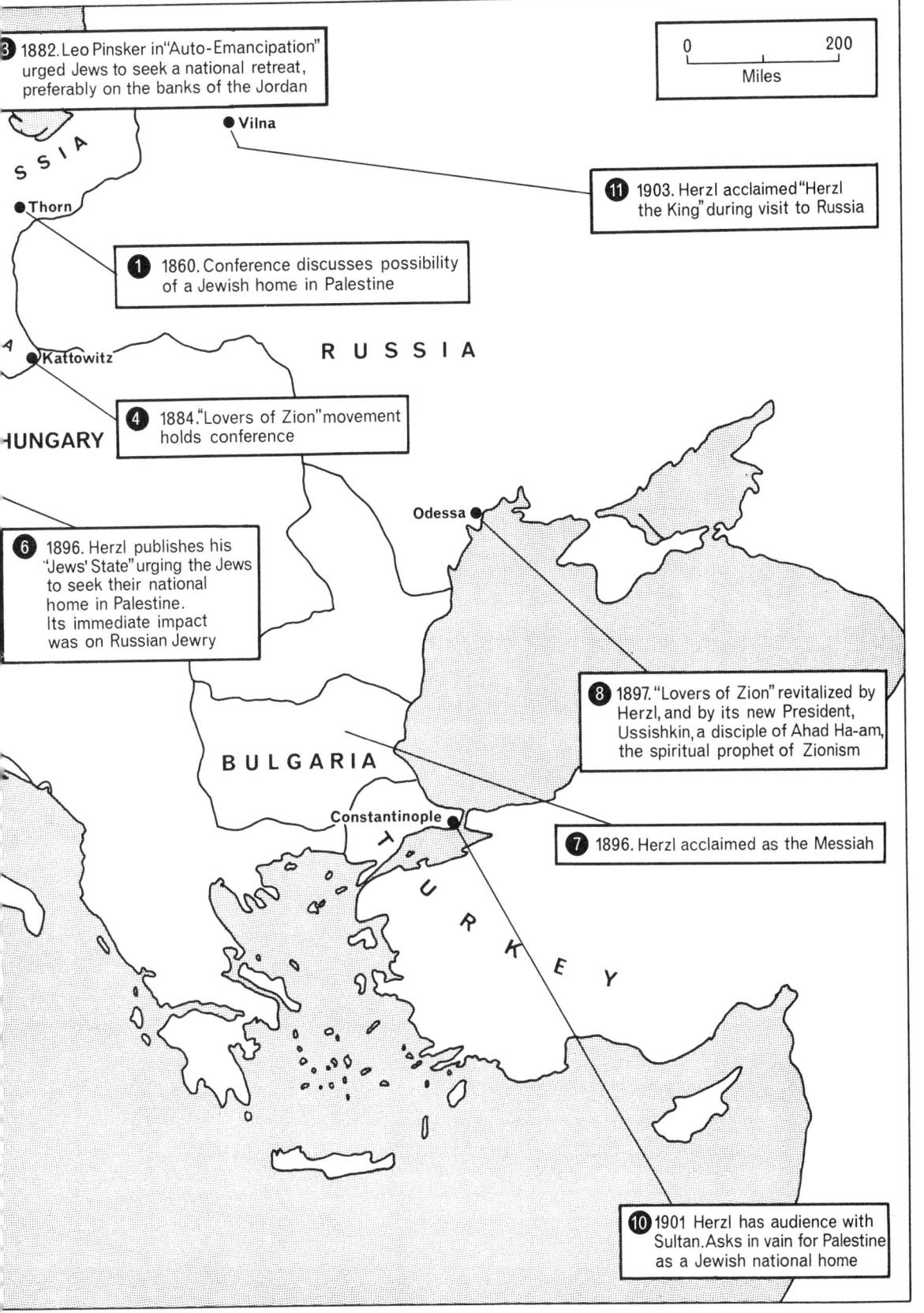

3 1882. Leo Pinsker in "Auto-Emancipation" urged Jews to seek a national retreat, preferably on the banks of the Jordan

• Vilna

11 1903. Herzl acclaimed "Herzl the King" during visit to Russia

S S I A

• Thorn

1 1860. Conference discusses possibility of a Jewish home in Palestine

R U S S I A

• Kattowitz

4 1884. "Lovers of Zion" movement holds conference

HUNGARY

Odessa •

6 1896. Herzl publishes his "Jews' State" urging the Jews to seek their national home in Palestine. Its immediate impact was on Russian Jewry

8 1897. "Lovers of Zion" revitalized by Herzl, and by its new President, Ussishkin, a disciple of Ahad Ha-am, the spiritual prophet of Zionism

B U L G A R I A

Constantinople •

7 1896. Herzl acclaimed as the Messiah

T U R K E Y

10 1901 Herzl has audience with Sultan. Asks in vain for Palestine as a Jewish national home

0   200
Miles

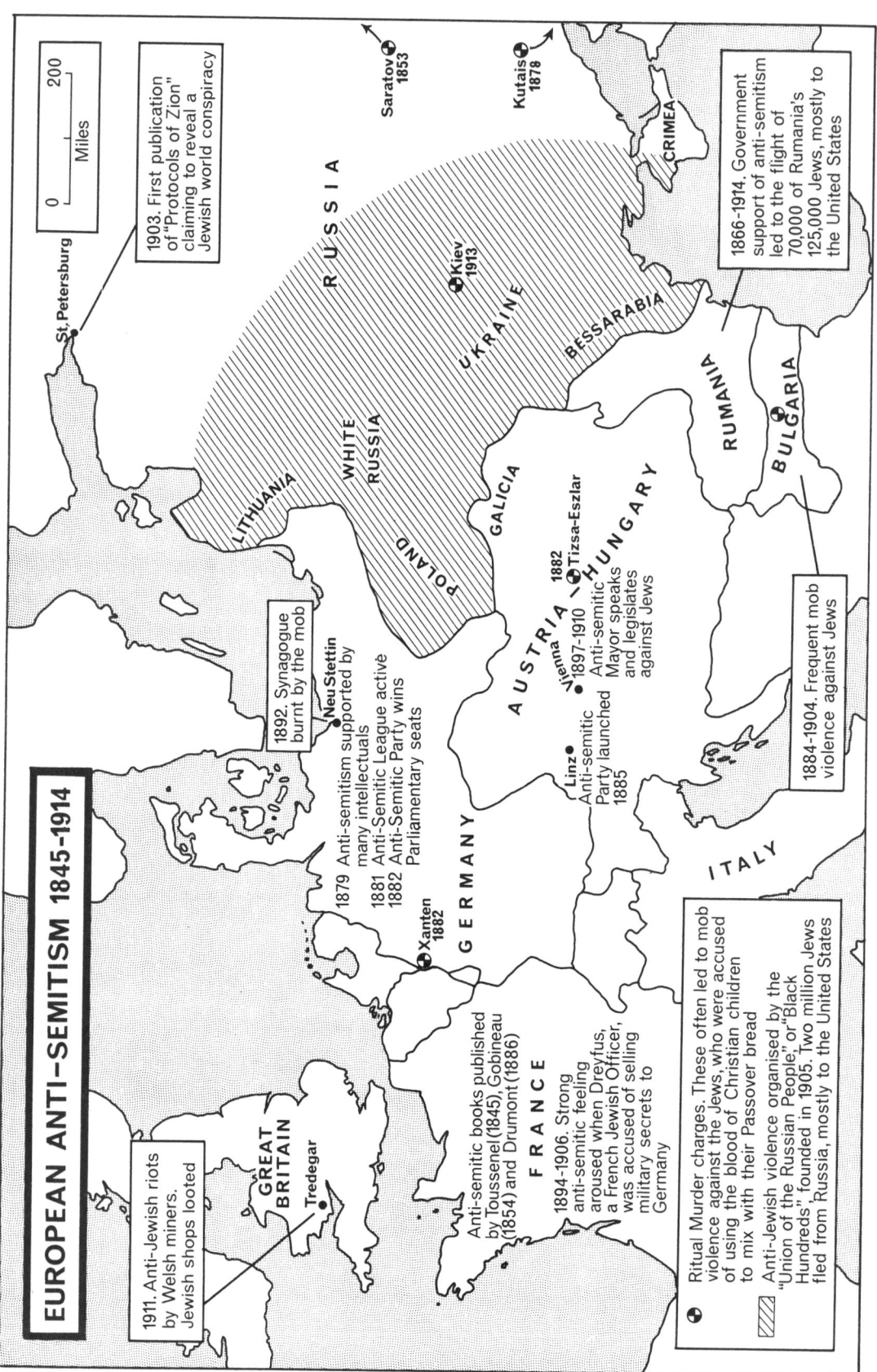

EUROPEAN ANTI-SEMITISM 1845-1914

0   200
Miles

1903. First publication of "Protocols of Zion" claiming to reveal a Jewish world conspiracy

Saratov 1853

Kutais 1878

CRIMEA

R U S S I A

Kiev 1913

UKRAINE

BESSARABIA

LITHUANIA

WHITE RUSSIA

POLAND

GALICIA

HUNGARY

Tizsa-Eszlar 1882

AUSTRIA 1882
Vienna 1897-1910
Anti-semitic Mayor speaks and legislates against Jews

RUMANIA

BULGARIA

1866-1914. Government support of anti-semitism led to the flight of 70,000 of Rumania's 125,000 Jews, mostly to the United States

St.Petersburg

1892. Synagogue burnt by the mob

Neu Stettin

1879 Anti-semitism supported by many intellectuals
1881 Anti-Semitic League active
1882 Anti-Semitic Party wins Parliamentary seats

Linz
Anti-semitic Party launched 1885

1884-1904. Frequent mob violence against Jews

ITALY

Xanten 1882

G E R M A N Y

Anti-semitic books published by Toussenel(1845), Gobineau (1854) and Drumont (1886)

F R A N C E

1894-1906. Strong anti-semitic feeling aroused when Dreyfus, a French Jewish Officer, was accused of selling military secrets to Germany

GREAT BRITAIN

Tredegar

1911. Anti-Jewish riots by Welsh miners. Jewish shops looted

Ritual Murder charges. These often led to mob violence against the Jews, who were accused of using the blood of Christian children to mix with their Passover bread

Anti-Jewish violence organised by the "Union of the Russian People," or "Black Hundreds" founded in 1905. Two million Jews fled from Russia, mostly to the United States

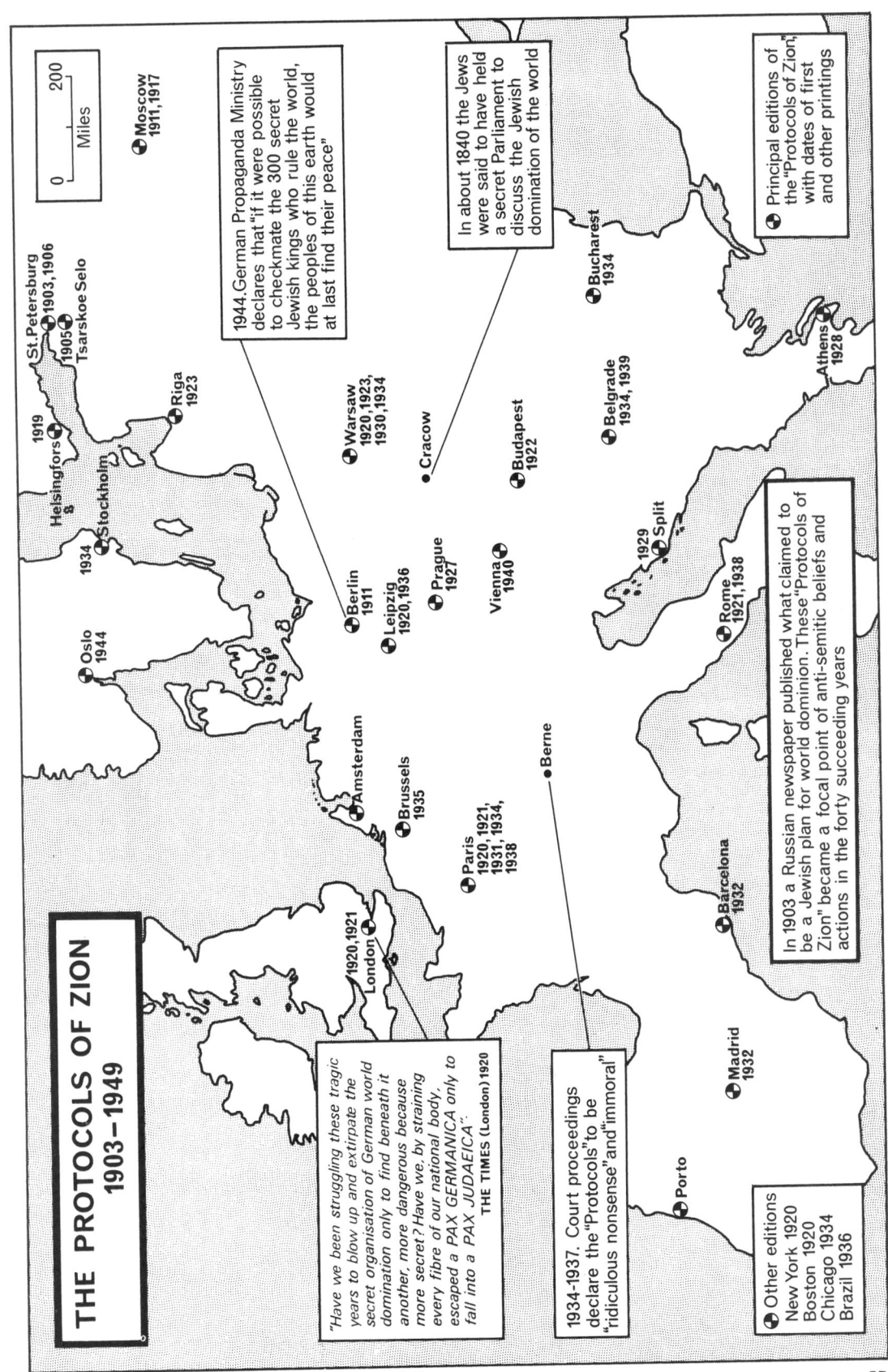

THE PROTOCOLS OF ZION
1903–1949

0 ___ 200
Miles

● Moscow
1911, 1917

St. Petersburg
● 1903, 1906
● 1905
Tsarskoe Selo

● 1919
Helsingfors

● Stockholm
1934

● Riga
1923

● Oslo
1944

● Berlin
1911

● Leipzig
1920, 1936

Amsterdam

● Brussels
1935

● Prague
1927

● Warsaw
1920, 1923,
1930, 1934

• Cracow

Vienna ●
1940

● Budapest
1922

● Belgrade
1934, 1939

● Bucharest
1934

Athens ●
1928

1920, 1921
London ●

● Paris
1920, 1921,
1931, 1934,
1938

• Berne

● 1929
Split

● Rome
1921, 1938

● Barcelona
1932

● Madrid
1932

● Porto

1944. German Propaganda Ministry declares that "if it were possible to checkmate the 300 secret Jewish kings who rule the world, the peoples of this earth would at last find their peace"

In about 1840 the Jews were said to have held a secret Parliament to discuss the Jewish domination of the world

● Principal editions of the "Protocols of Zion", with dates of first and other printings

In 1903 a Russian newspaper published what claimed to be a Jewish plan for world dominion. These "Protocols of Zion" became a focal point of anti-semitic beliefs and actions in the forty succeeding years

"Have we been struggling these tragic years to blow up and extirpate the secret organisation of German world domination only to find beneath it another, more dangerous because more secret? Have we, by straining every fibre of our national body, escaped a PAX GERMANICA only to fall into a PAX JUDAEICA".
THE TIMES (London) 1920

1934-1937. Court proceedings declare the "Protocols" to be "ridiculous nonsense" and "immoral"

● Other editions
New York 1920
Boston 1920
Chicago 1934
Brazil 1936

65

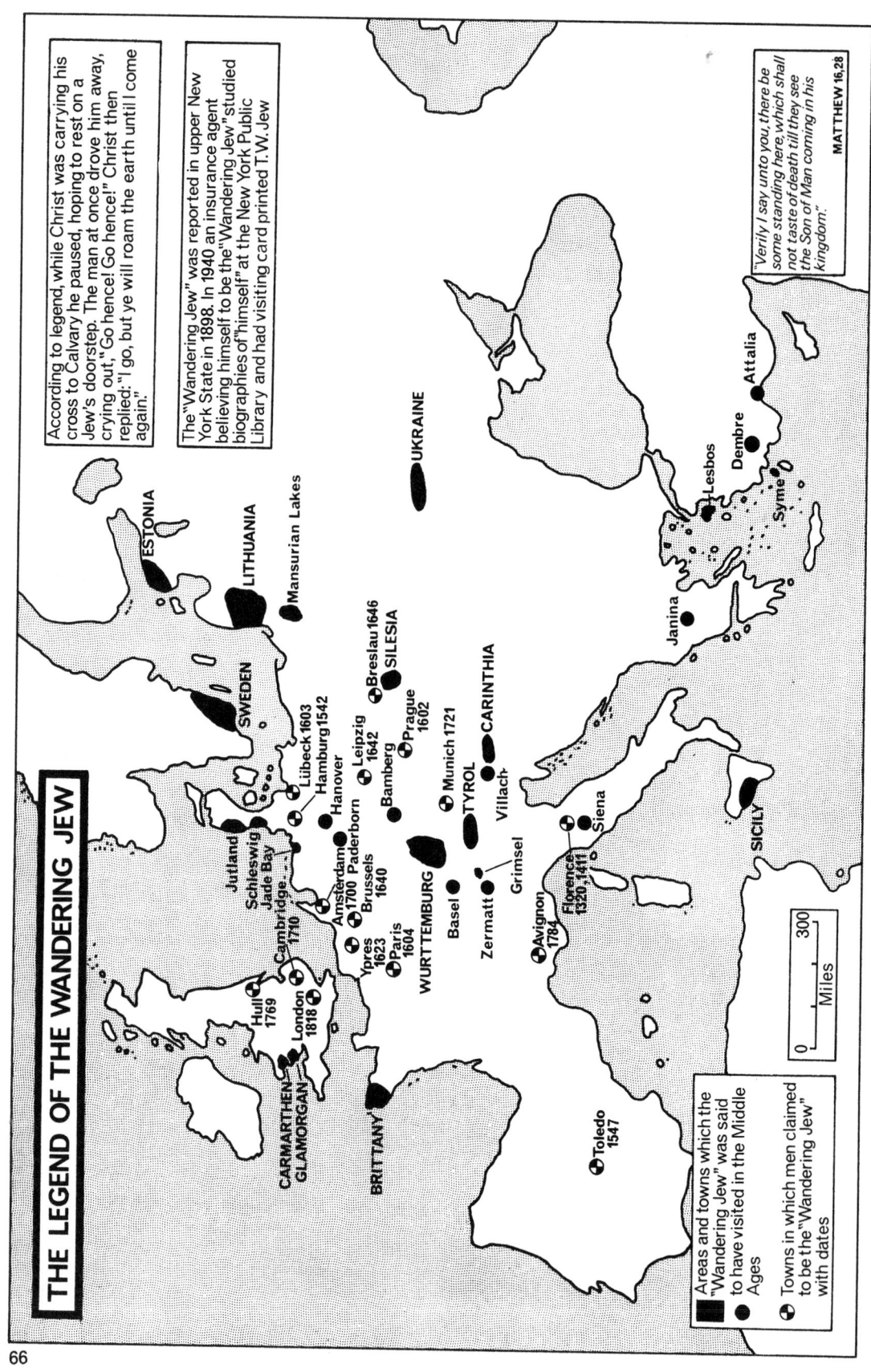

THE LEGEND OF THE WANDERING JEW

According to legend, while Christ was carrying his cross to Calvary he paused, hoping to rest on a Jew's doorstep. The man at once drove him away, crying out, "Go hence! Go hence!" Christ then replied: "I go, but ye will roam the earth untill come again."

The "Wandering Jew" was reported in upper New York State in 1898. In 1940 an insurance agent believing himself to be the "Wandering Jew" studied biographies of "himself" at the New York Public Library and had visiting card printed T.W. Jew.

"Verily I say unto you, there be some standing here, which shall not taste of death till they see the Son of Man coming in his kingdom."

MATTHEW 16,28

ESTONIA
LITHUANIA
Mansurian Lakes
SWEDEN
UKRAINE
Lübeck 1603
Hamburg 1542
Hanover
Leipzig 1642
Breslau 1646
SILESIA
Prague 1602
Bamberg
Munich 1721
Janina
Jutland
Schleswig
Jade Bay
Amsterdam
Paderborn 1700
Brussels 1640
WURTTEMBURG
Basel
TYROL
CARINTHIA
Villach
Grimsel
Siena
Lesbos
Dembre
Attalia
Syme
Cambridge 1710
Ypres 1623
Paris 1604
Zermatt
Avignon 1784
Florence 1320,7411
Hull 1769
London 1818
CARMARTHEN GLAMORGAN
BRITTANY
SICILY
Toledo 1547

0   300
Miles

Areas and towns which the "Wandering Jew" was said to have visited in the Middle Ages

Towns in which men claimed to be the "Wandering Jew" with dates

66

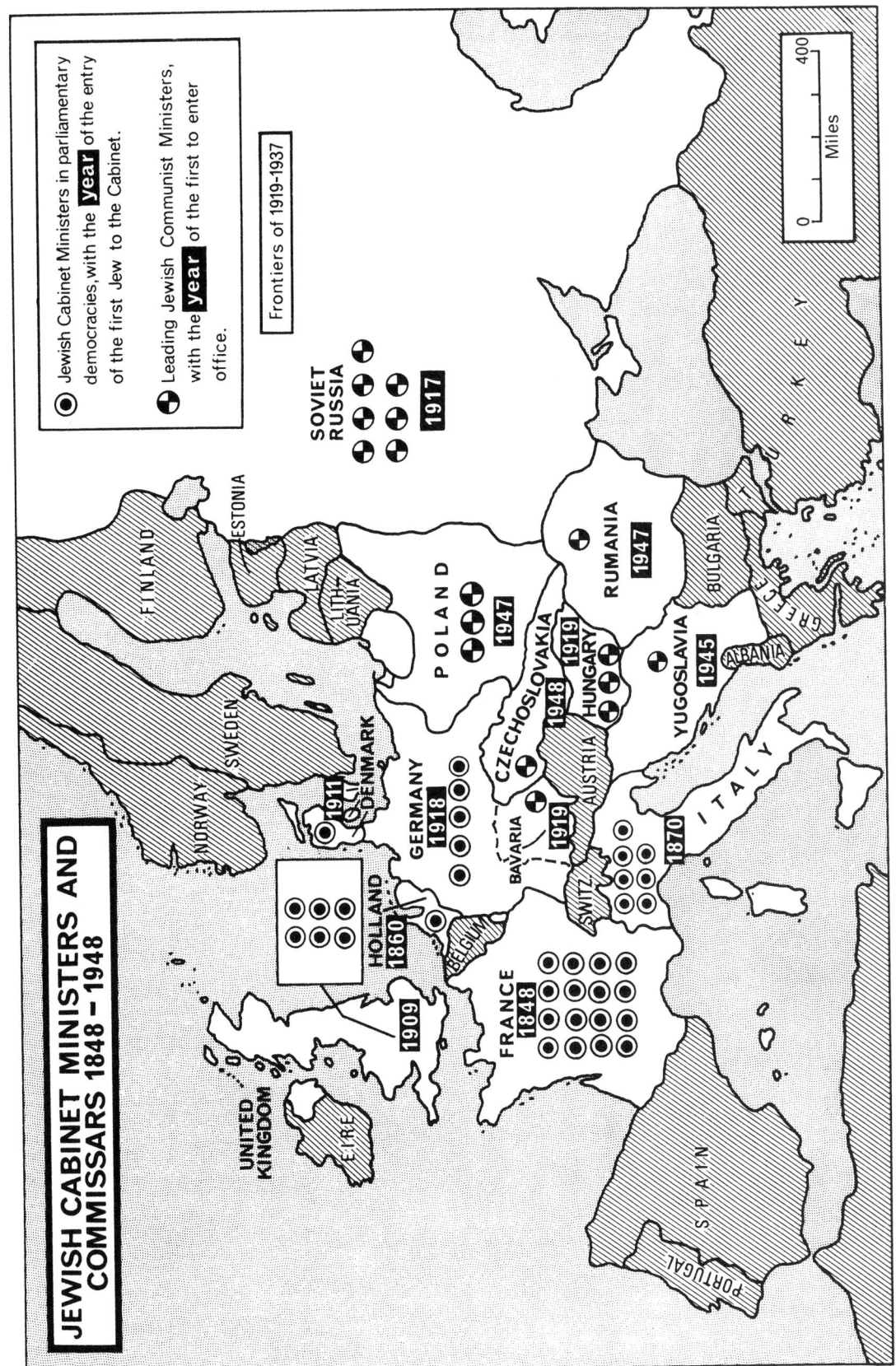

JEWISH CABINET MINISTERS AND COMMISSARS 1848 – 1948

Jewish Cabinet Ministers in parliamentary democracies, with the **year** of the entry of the first Jew to the Cabinet.

Leading Jewish Communist Ministers, with the **year** of the first to enter office.

Frontiers of 1919-1937

400

Miles

0

UNITED KINGDOM

EIRE

HOLLAND **1860**

1909

BELGIUM

FRANCE **1848**

GERMANY **1918**

1911

DENMARK

NORWAY

SWEDEN

FINLAND

ESTONIA

LATVIA

LITH-UANIA

POLAND **1947**

SOVIET RUSSIA **1917**

BAVARIA **1919**

SWITZ.

AUSTRIA

CZECHOSLOVAKIA **1948**

HUNGARY **1919**

ITALY **1870**

YUGOSLAVIA **1945**

RUMANIA **1947**

BULGARIA

ALBANIA

GREECE

TURKEY

SPAIN

PORTUGAL

67

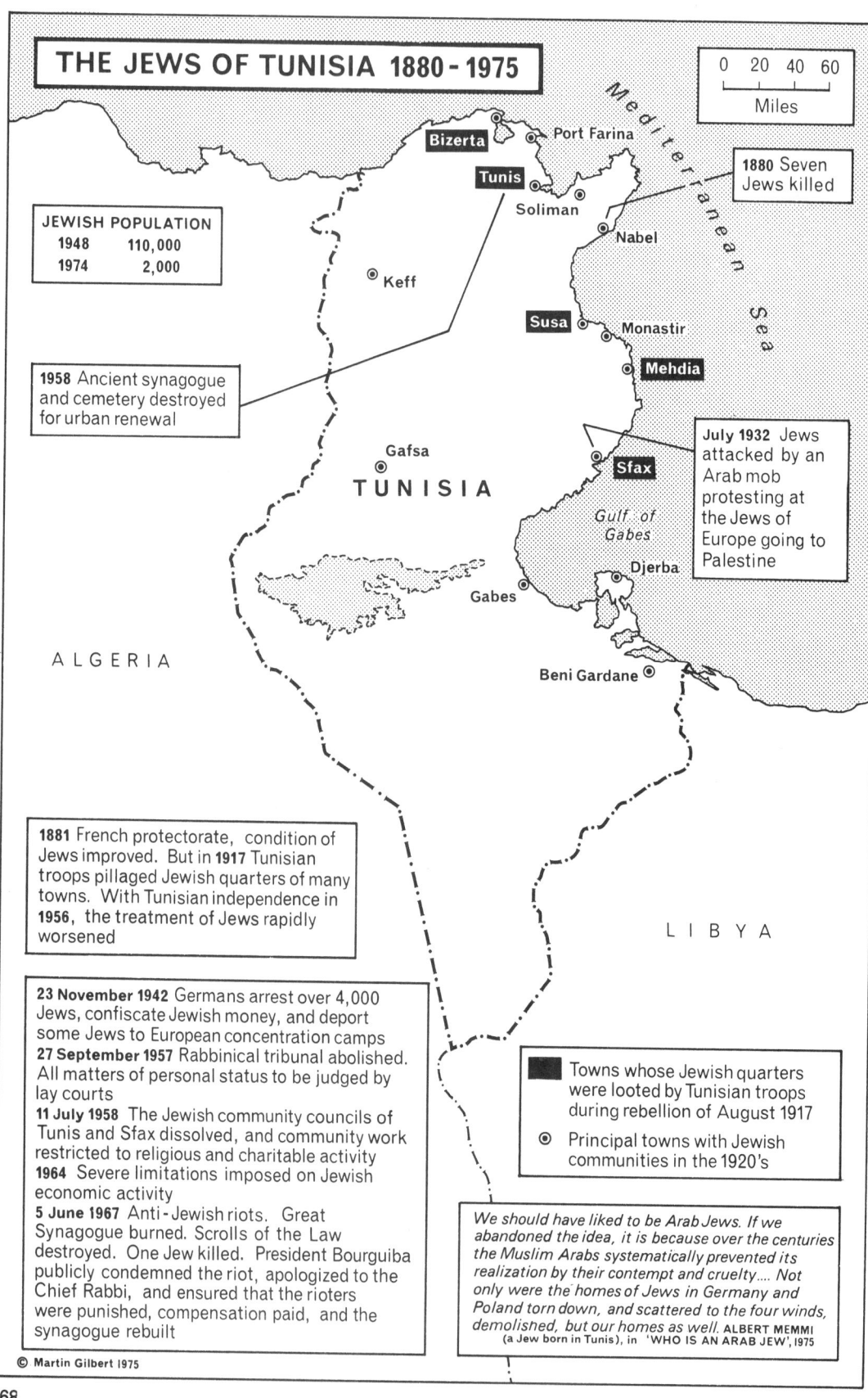

THE JEWS OF TUNISIA 1880-1975

0 20 40 60
Miles

Mediterranean Sea

Bizerta

Port Farina

1880 Seven Jews killed

Tunis

Soliman

Nabel

JEWISH POPULATION
1948   110,000
1974   2,000

Keff

Susa

Monastir

Mehdia

1958 Ancient synagogue and cemetery destroyed for urban renewal

Gafsa

TUNISIA

Sfax

July 1932 Jews attacked by an Arab mob protesting at the Jews of Europe going to Palestine

Gulf of Gabes

Djerba

Gabes

ALGERIA

Beni Gardane

LIBYA

1881 French protectorate, condition of Jews improved. But in **1917** Tunisian troops pillaged Jewish quarters of many towns. With Tunisian independence in **1956**, the treatment of Jews rapidly worsened

23 November 1942 Germans arrest over 4,000 Jews, confiscate Jewish money, and deport some Jews to European concentration camps
27 September 1957 Rabbinical tribunal abolished. All matters of personal status to be judged by lay courts
11 July 1958 The Jewish community councils of Tunis and Sfax dissolved, and community work restricted to religious and charitable activity
1964 Severe limitations imposed on Jewish economic activity
5 June 1967 Anti-Jewish riots. Great Synagogue burned. Scrolls of the Law destroyed. One Jew killed. President Bourguiba publicly condemned the riot, apologized to the Chief Rabbi, and ensured that the rioters were punished, compensation paid, and the synagogue rebuilt

■ Towns whose Jewish quarters were looted by Tunisian troops during rebellion of August 1917

⊙ Principal towns with Jewish communities in the 1920's

We should have liked to be Arab Jews. If we abandoned the idea, it is because over the centuries the Muslim Arabs systematically prevented its realization by their contempt and cruelty.... Not only were the homes of Jews in Germany and Poland torn down, and scattered to the four winds, demolished, but our homes as well. ALBERT MEMMI (a Jew born in Tunis), in 'WHO IS AN ARAB JEW', 1975

© **Martin Gilbert** 1975

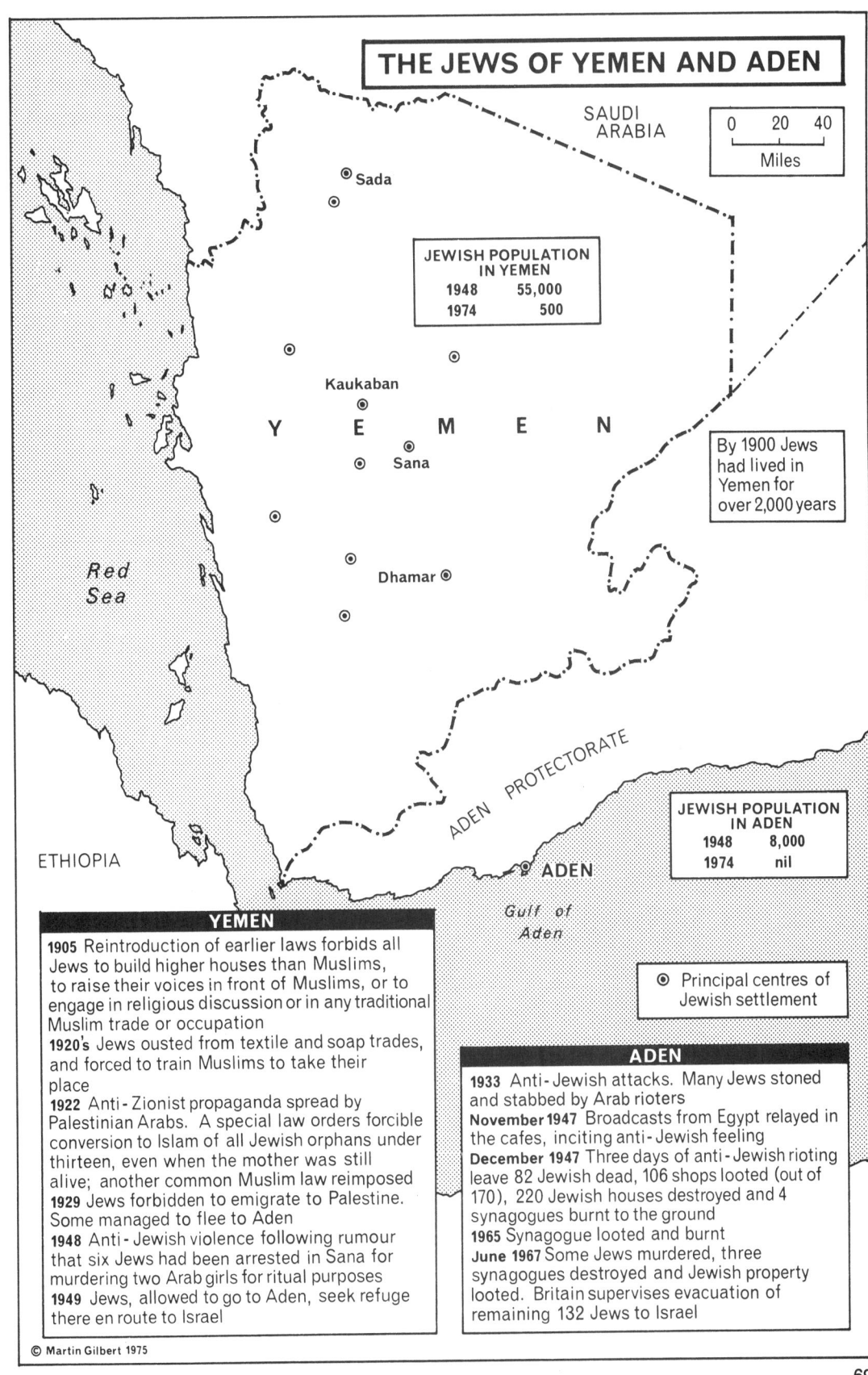

THE JEWS OF YEMEN AND ADEN

SAUDI ARABIA

0   20   40
Miles

⊙ Sada
⊙

JEWISH POPULATION IN YEMEN
1948   55,000
1974   500

⊙

⊙   ⊙

Kaukaban
⊙

Y   E   M   E   N

⊙   Sana

By 1900 Jews had lived in Yemen for over 2,000 years

⊙

⊙
Dhamar ⊙

⊙

Red Sea

ADEN PROTECTORATE

ETHIOPIA

⊙ ADEN

JEWISH POPULATION IN ADEN
1948   8,000
1974   nil

Gulf of Aden

⊙ Principal centres of Jewish settlement

YEMEN

1905 Reintroduction of earlier laws forbids all Jews to build higher houses than Muslims, to raise their voices in front of Muslims, or to engage in religious discussion or in any traditional Muslim trade or occupation
1920's Jews ousted from textile and soap trades, and forced to train Muslims to take their place
1922 Anti-Zionist propaganda spread by Palestinian Arabs. A special law orders forcible conversion to Islam of all Jewish orphans under thirteen, even when the mother was still alive; another common Muslim law reimposed
1929 Jews forbidden to emigrate to Palestine. Some managed to flee to Aden
1948 Anti-Jewish violence following rumour that six Jews had been arrested in Sana for murdering two Arab girls for ritual purposes
1949 Jews, allowed to go to Aden, seek refuge there en route to Israel

ADEN

1933 Anti-Jewish attacks. Many Jews stoned and stabbed by Arab rioters
November 1947 Broadcasts from Egypt relayed in the cafes, inciting anti-Jewish feeling
December 1947 Three days of anti-Jewish rioting leave 82 Jewish dead, 106 shops looted (out of 170), 220 Jewish houses destroyed and 4 synagogues burnt to the ground
1965 Synagogue looted and burnt
June 1967 Some Jews murdered, three synagogues destroyed and Jewish property looted. Britain supervises evacuation of remaining 132 Jews to Israel

© Martin Gilbert 1975

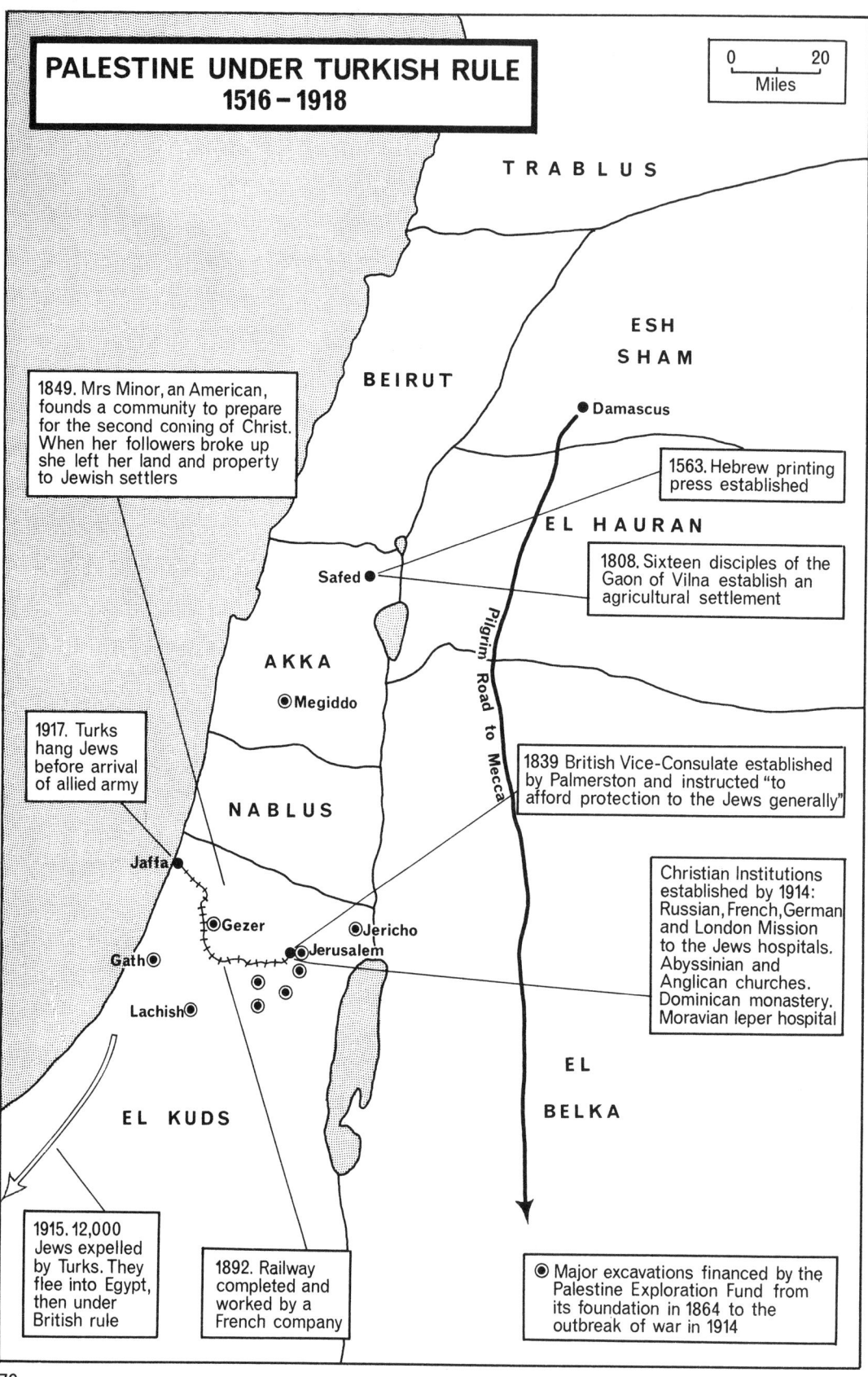

PALESTINE UNDER TURKISH RULE 1516 – 1918

0   20
Miles

TRABLUS

ESH SHAM

● Damascus

BEIRUT

1849. Mrs Minor, an American, founds a community to prepare for the second coming of Christ. When her followers broke up she left her land and property to Jewish settlers

1563. Hebrew printing press established

EL HAURAN

1808. Sixteen disciples of the Gaon of Vilna establish an agricultural settlement

Safed ●

AKKA

◉Megiddo

Pilgrim Road to Mecca

1917. Turks hang Jews before arrival of allied army

NABLUS

1839 British Vice-Consulate established by Palmerston and instructed "to afford protection to the Jews generally"

Jaffa ●

◉Gezer

◉Jericho
◉Jerusalem

Gath◉

Christian Institutions established by 1914: Russian, French, German and London Mission to the Jews hospitals. Abyssinian and Anglican churches. Dominican monastery. Moravian leper hospital

◉

◉ ◉

Lachish◉

◉

EL KUDS

EL BELKA

1915. 12,000 Jews expelled by Turks. They flee into Egypt, then under British rule

1892. Railway completed and worked by a French company

◉ Major excavations financed by the Palestine Exploration Fund from its foundation in 1864 to the outbreak of war in 1914

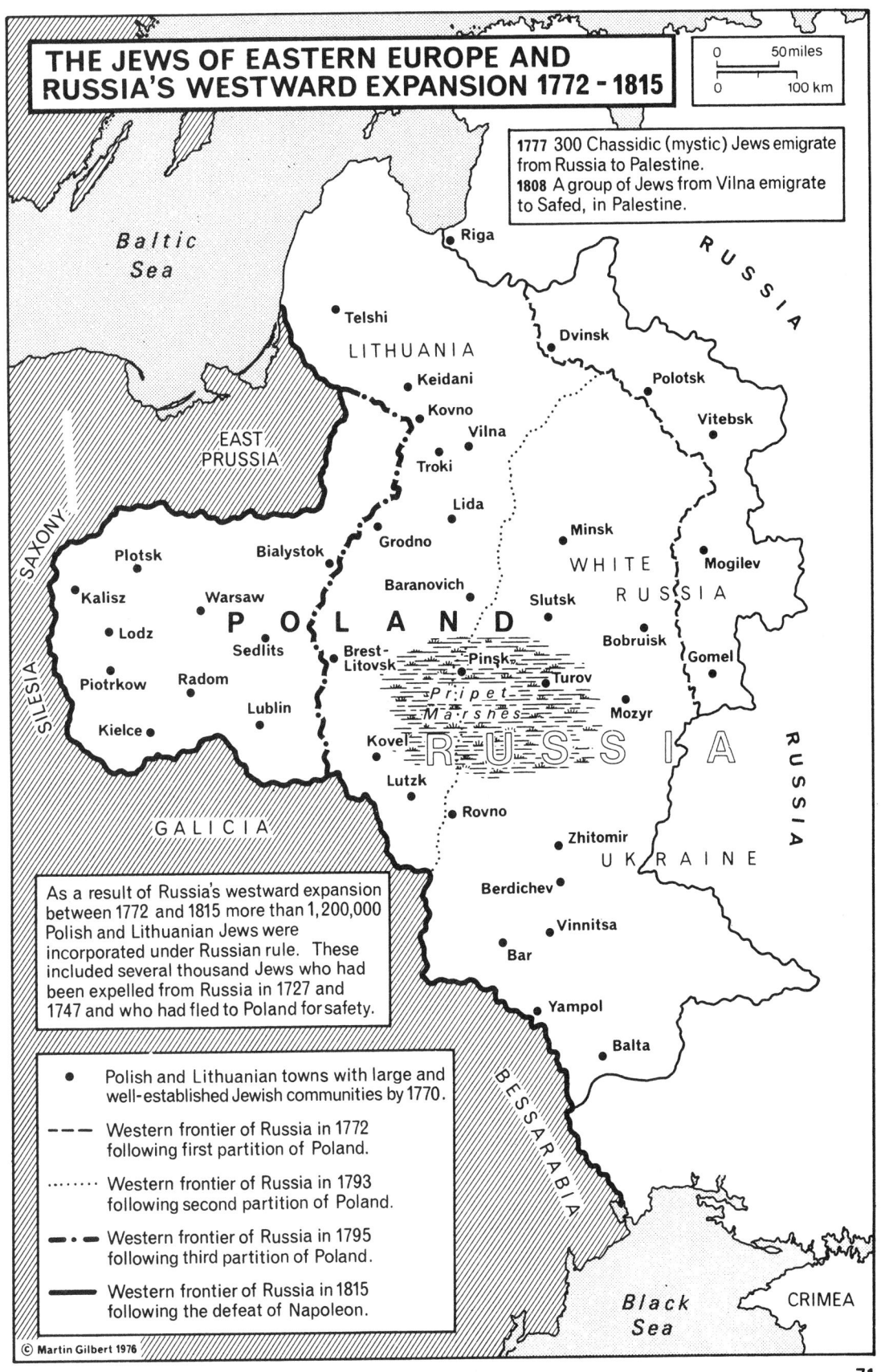

THE JEWS OF EASTERN EUROPE AND RUSSIA'S WESTWARD EXPANSION 1772 - 1815

0   50 miles
0   100 km

1777 300 Chassidic (mystic) Jews emigrate from Russia to Palestine.
1808 A group of Jews from Vilna emigrate to Safed, in Palestine.

Baltic Sea

RUSSIA

• Riga

• Telshi

LITHUANIA

• Dvinsk

• Polotsk

• Keidani

• Vitebsk

• Kovno

EAST PRUSSIA

• Vilna

• Troki

SAXONY

• Lida

• Minsk

• Grodno

• Plotsk

• Bialystok

WHITE RUSSIA

• Mogilev

• Kalisz

• Warsaw

P O L A N D

• Baranovich

• Slutsk

• Lodz

• Sedlits

• Brest-Litovsk

• Pinsk

• Bobruisk

• Gomel

SILESIA

• Piotrkow

• Radom

• Lublin

Pripet Marshes

• Turov

R U S S I A

• Mozyr

• Kielce

• Kovel

• Lutzk

GALICIA

As a result of Russia's westward expansion between 1772 and 1815 more than 1,200,000 Polish and Lithuanian Jews were incorporated under Russian rule. These included several thousand Jews who had been expelled from Russia in 1727 and 1747 and who had fled to Poland for safety.

•• Rovno

• Zhitomir

U K R A I N E

• Berdichev

• Vinnitsa

• Bar

RUSSIA

• Yampol

BESSARABIA

• Balta

• Polish and Lithuanian towns with large and well-established Jewish communities by 1770.

– – – Western frontier of Russia in 1772 following first partition of Poland.

.... Western frontier of Russia in 1793 following second partition of Poland.

–·– Western frontier of Russia in 1795 following third partition of Poland.

——— Western frontier of Russia in 1815 following the defeat of Napoleon.

Black Sea

CRIMEA

© Martin Gilbert 1976

71

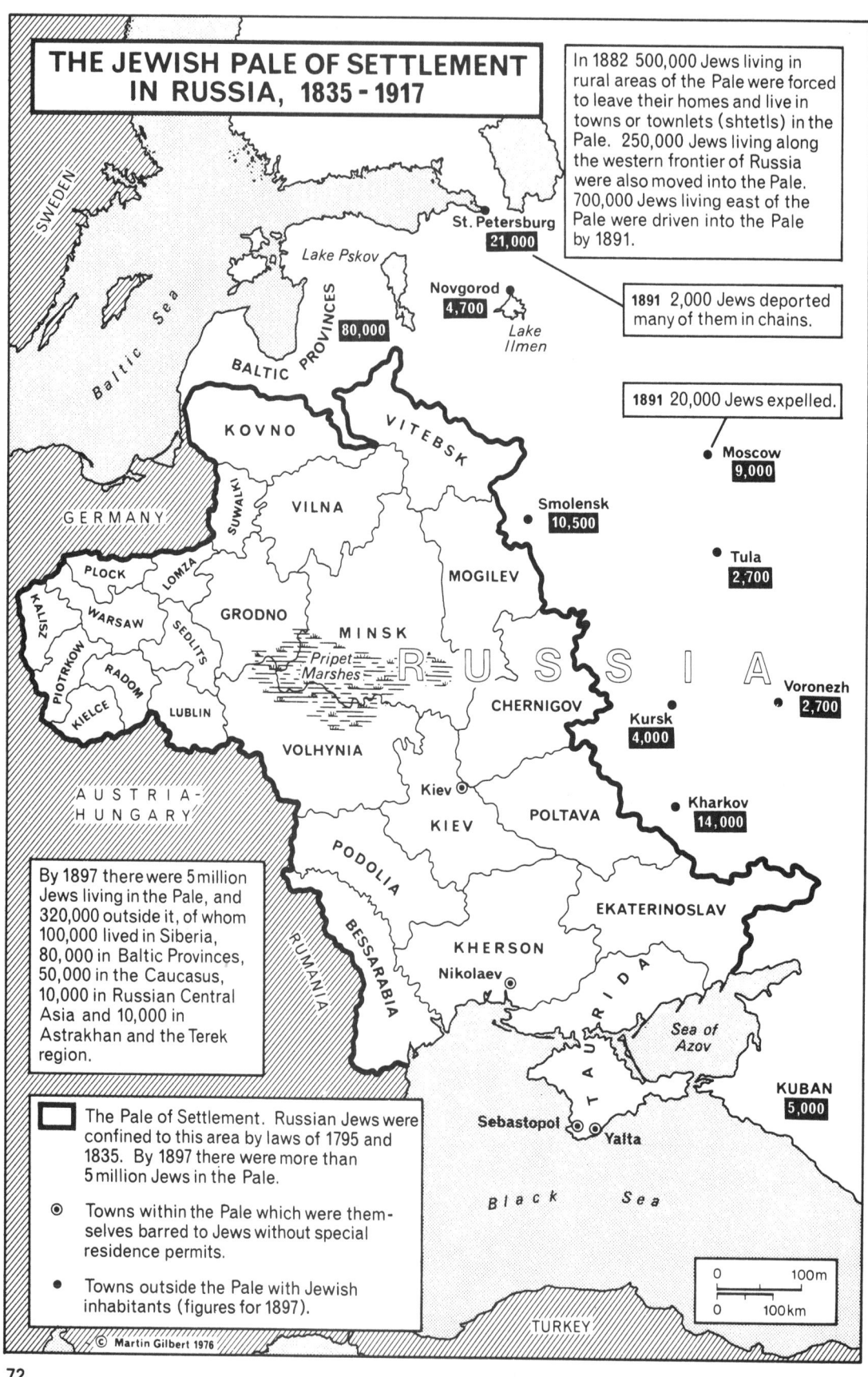

THE JEWISH PALE OF SETTLEMENT IN RUSSIA, 1835 - 1917

In 1882 500,000 Jews living in rural areas of the Pale were forced to leave their homes and live in towns or townlets (shtetls) in the Pale. 250,000 Jews living along the western frontier of Russia were also moved into the Pale. 700,000 Jews living east of the Pale were driven into the Pale by 1891.

1891 2,000 Jews deported many of them in chains.

1891 20,000 Jews expelled.

SWEDEN

Baltic Sea

GERMANY

St. Petersburg
21,000

Lake Pskov

Novgorod
4,700

Lake Ilmen

BALTIC PROVINCES
80,000

KOVNO

VITEBSK

SUWALKI

VILNA

Moscow
9,000

Smolensk
10,500

PLOCK

LOMZA

GRODNO

MOGILEV

Tula
2,700

KALISZ

WARSAW

SEDLITS

MINSK

Pripet Marshes

R U S S I A

Voronezh
2,700

PIOTRKOW

RADOM

LUBLIN

CHERNIGOV

Kursk
4,000

KIELCE

VOLHYNIA

Kiev

AUSTRIA-HUNGARY

PODOLIA

KIEV

POLTAVA

Kharkov
14,000

By 1897 there were 5 million Jews living in the Pale, and 320,000 outside it, of whom 100,000 lived in Siberia, 80,000 in Baltic Provinces, 50,000 in the Caucasus, 10,000 in Russian Central Asia and 10,000 in Astrakhan and the Terek region.

RUMANIA

BESSARABIA

EKATERINOSLAV

KHERSON

Nikolaev

T A U R I D A

Sea of Azov

Sebastopol

Yalta

KUBAN
5,000

☐ The Pale of Settlement. Russian Jews were confined to this area by laws of 1795 and 1835. By 1897 there were more than 5 million Jews in the Pale.

⊙ Towns within the Pale which were themselves barred to Jews without special residence permits.

● Towns outside the Pale with Jewish inhabitants (figures for 1897).

Black Sea

0 ——— 100m
0 ——— 100km

TURKEY

© Martin Gilbert 1976

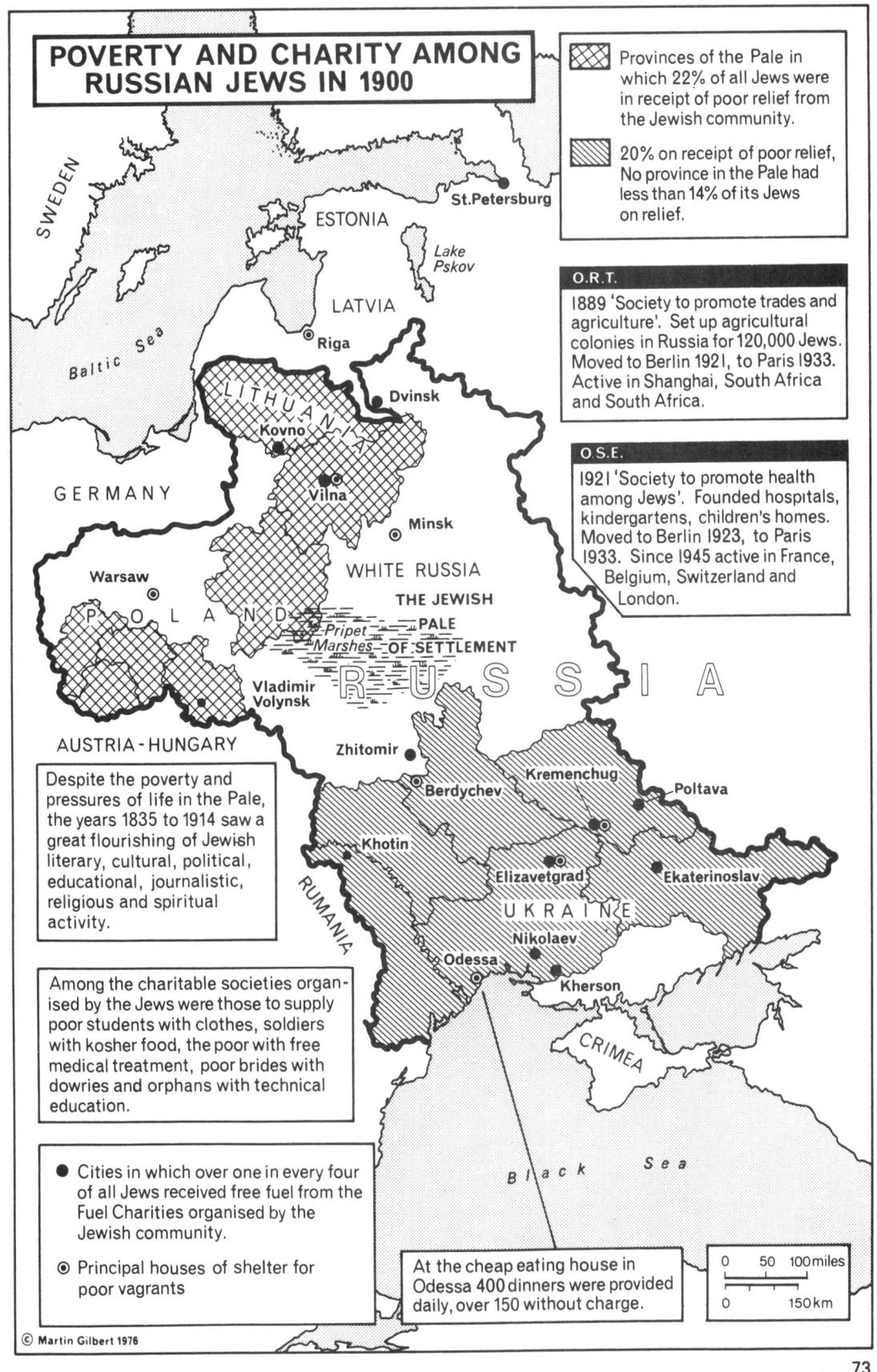

POVERTY AND CHARITY AMONG RUSSIAN JEWS IN 1900

Provinces of the Pale in which 22% of all Jews were in receipt of poor relief from the Jewish community.

20% on receipt of poor relief. No province in the Pale had less than 14% of its Jews on relief.

O.R.T.

1889 'Society to promote trades and agriculture'. Set up agricultural colonies in Russia for 120,000 Jews. Moved to Berlin 1921, to Paris 1933. Active in Shanghai, South Africa and South Africa.

O.S.E.

1921 'Society to promote health among Jews'. Founded hospitals, kindergartens, children's homes. Moved to Berlin 1923, to Paris 1933. Since 1945 active in France, Belgium, Switzerland and London.

SWEDEN

ESTONIA

St.Petersburg

Lake Pskov

LATVIA

Baltic Sea

Riga

Dvinsk

LITHUANIA

Kovno

GERMANY

Vilna

Minsk

WHITE RUSSIA

Warsaw

POLAND

THE JEWISH

PALE

Pripet Marshes

OF SETTLEMENT

R U S S I A

Vladimir Volynsk

AUSTRIA - HUNGARY

Zhitomir

Despite the poverty and pressures of life in the Pale, the years 1835 to 1914 saw a great flourishing of Jewish literary, cultural, political, educational, journalistic, religious and spiritual activity.

Berdychev

Kremenchug

Poltava

Khotin

Elizavetgrad

Ekaterinoslav

RUMANIA

U K R A I N E

Nikolaev

Among the charitable societies organised by the Jews were those to supply poor students with clothes, soldiers with kosher food, the poor with free medical treatment, poor brides with dowries and orphans with technical education.

Odessa

Kherson

CRIMEA

● Cities in which over one in every four of all Jews received free fuel from the Fuel Charities organised by the Jewish community.

◉ Principal houses of shelter for poor vagrants

Black Sea

At the cheap eating house in Odessa 400 dinners were provided daily, over 150 without charge.

| 0 | 50 | 100 miles |
| 0 | | 150 km |

© Martin Gilbert 1976

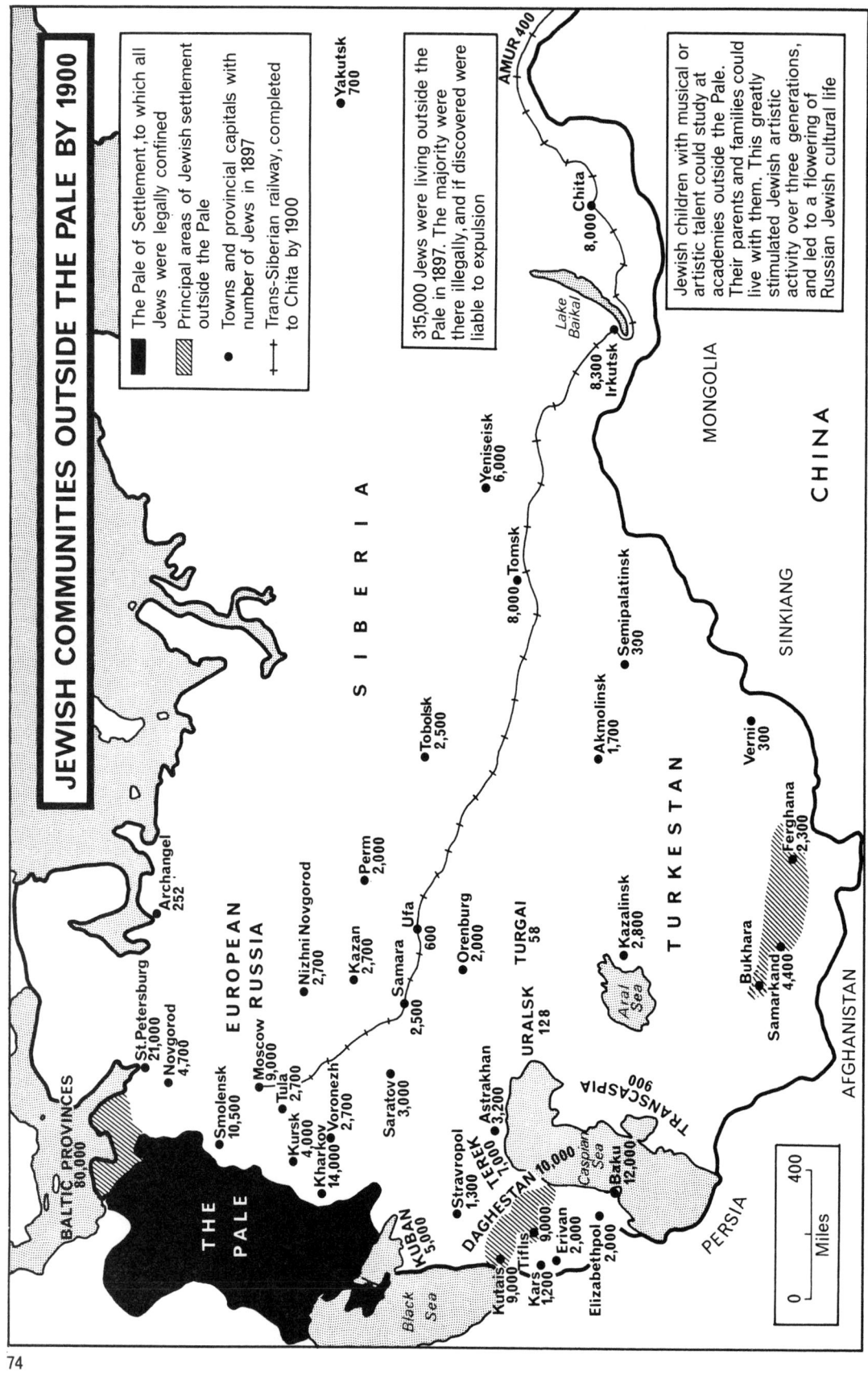

JEWISH COMMUNITIES OUTSIDE THE PALE BY 1900

■ The Pale of Settlement, to which all Jews were legally confined

▨ Principal areas of Jewish settlement outside the Pale

● Towns and provincial capitals with number of Jews in 1897

┼┼┼ Trans-Siberian railway, completed to Chita by 1900

315,000 Jews were living outside the Pale in 1897. The majority were there illegally, and if discovered were liable to expulsion

Jewish children with musical or artistic talent could study at academies outside the Pale. Their parents and families could live with them. This greatly stimulated Jewish artistic activity over three generations, and led to a flowering of Russian Jewish cultural life

AMUR 400

● Yakutsk 700

● Chita 8,000

Lake Baikal

● Irkutsk 8,300

MONGOLIA

CHINA

SIBERIA

● Yeniseisk 6,000

● Tomsk 8,000

● Semipalatinsk 300

SINKIANG

● Tobolsk 2,500

● Akmolinsk 1,700

● Verni 300

TURKESTAN

● Ferghana 2,300

EUROPEAN RUSSIA

● Archangel 252

● Perm 2,000

● Nizhni Novgorod 2,700

● Kazan 2,700

Samara ● Ufa 600

● 2,500

● Orenburg 2,000

TURGAI 58

Aral Sea

● Kazalinsk 2,800

● Bukhara

Samarkand ● 4,400

● St.Petersburg 21,000

● Novgorod 4,700

● Smolensk 10,500

● Moscow 9,000

● Kursk 4,000

Tula ● 2,700

● Kharkov 14,000

● Voronezh 2,700

Saratov ● 3,000

URALSK 128

TRANSCASPIA 900

AFGHANISTAN

BALTIC PROVINCES 80,000

THE PALE

● Stravropol 1,300

TEREK 7,000

Astrakhan ● 3,200

DAGHESTAN 10,000

Caspian Sea

● Baku 12,000

PERSIA

KUBAN 5,000

Kutais ● 9,000

Tiflis ● 9,000

● Erivan 2,000

● Kars 1,200

● Elizabethpol 2,000

Black Sea

0   400
└────────┘
    Miles

74

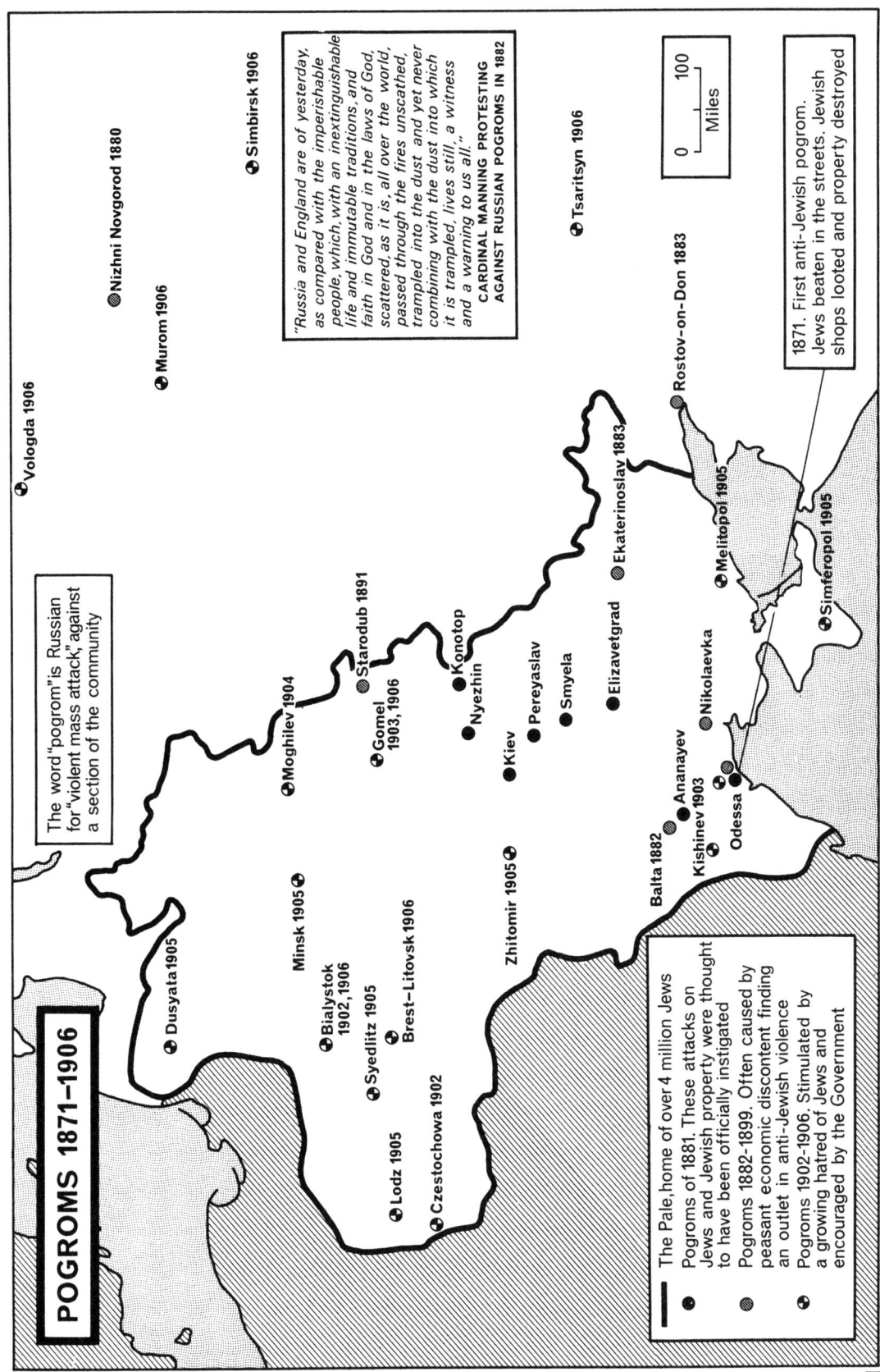

POGROMS 1871–1906

The word "pogrom" is Russian for "violent mass attack," against a section of the community

"Russia and England are of yesterday, as compared with the imperishable people, which, with an inextinguishable life and immutable traditions, and faith in God and in the laws of God, scattered, as it is, all over the world, passed through the fires unscathed, trampled into the dust and yet never combining with the dust into which it is trampled, lives still, a witness and a warning to us all."
CARDINAL MANNING PROTESTING AGAINST RUSSIAN POGROMS IN 1882

1871. First anti-Jewish pogrom. Jews beaten in the streets. Jewish shops looted and property destroyed

● Simbirsk 1906

◎ Nizhni Novgorod 1880

◎ Murom 1906

✣ Vologda 1906

✣ Tsaritsyn 1906

◉ Rostov-on-Don 1883

◉ Melitopol 1905

✣ Simferopol 1905

◉ Ekaterinoslav 1883

◉ Starodub 1891

◉ Konotop

✣ Moghilev 1904

✣ Gomel 1903, 1906

● Nyezhin

● Pereyaslav

● Smyela

● Kiev

◉ Elizavetgrad

● Ananayev

◉ Nikolaevka

● Kishinev 1903

◎ Odessa

● Balta 1882

Zhitomir 1905 ✣

Minsk 1905 ✣

✣ Dusyata 1905

✣ Bialystok 1902, 1906

✣ Syedlitz 1905

Brest–Litovsk 1906

✣ Lodz 1905

✣ Czestochowa 1902

Miles
0   100

The Pale, home of over 4 million Jews

● Pogroms of 1881. These attacks on Jews and Jewish property were thought to have been officially instigated

◎ Pogroms 1882-1899. Often caused by peasant economic discontent finding an outlet in anti-Jewish violence

✣ Pogroms 1902-1906. Stimulated by a growing hatred of Jews and encouraged by the Government

75

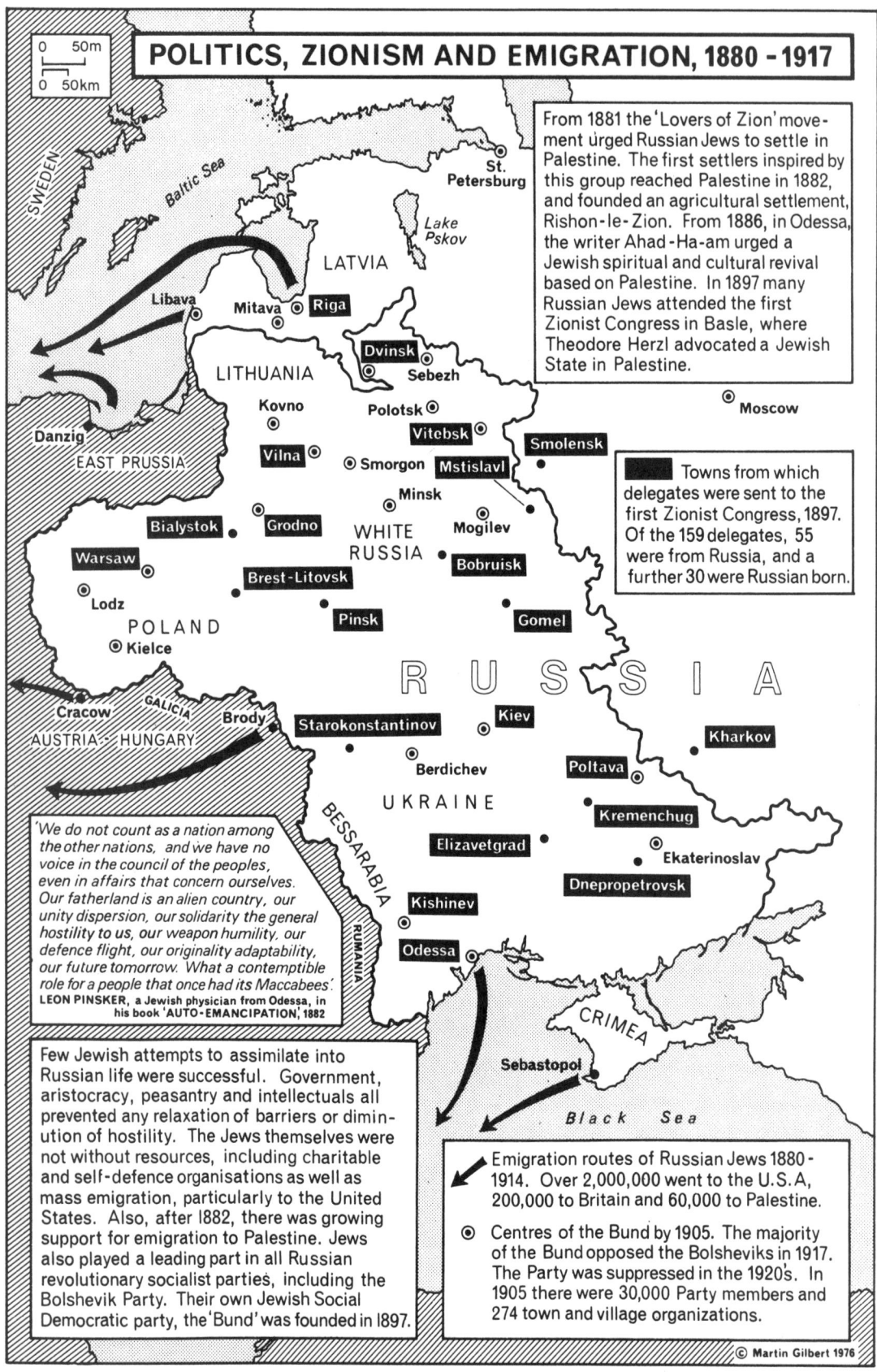

POLITICS, ZIONISM AND EMIGRATION, 1880 - 1917

0 50m
0 50km

From 1881 the 'Lovers of Zion' move-ment urged Russian Jews to settle in Palestine. The first settlers inspired by this group reached Palestine in 1882, and founded an agricultural settlement, Rishon-le-Zion. From 1886, in Odessa, the writer Ahad-Ha-am urged a Jewish spiritual and cultural revival based on Palestine. In 1897 many Russian Jews attended the first Zionist Congress in Basle, where Theodore Herzl advocated a Jewish State in Palestine.

Towns from which delegates were sent to the first Zionist Congress, 1897. Of the 159 delegates, 55 were from Russia, and a further 30 were Russian born.

SWEDEN

Baltic Sea

St. Petersburg

Lake Pskov

LATVIA

Libava
Mitava Riga
Dvinsk
Sebezh

LITHUANIA
Kovno
Polotsk
Vitebsk
Smolensk

Moscow

Danzig
EAST PRUSSIA
Vilna
Smorgon Mstislavl
Minsk

Bialystok Grodno
WHITE RUSSIA
Mogilev

Warsaw
Brest-Litovsk
Bobruisk

Lodz
POLAND
Pinsk
Gomel

Kielce

R U S S I A

Cracow
GALICIA Brody
AUSTRIA - HUNGARY

Starokonstantinov
Kiev
Kharkov

Berdichev
Poltava

UKRAINE
Kremenchug

BESSARABIA
Elizavetgrad
Ekaterinoslav

Dnepropetrovsk

RUMANIA
Kishinev

'We do not count as a nation among the other nations, and we have no voice in the council of the peoples, even in affairs that concern ourselves. Our fatherland is an alien country, our unity dispersion, our solidarity the general hostility to us, our weapon humility, our defence flight, our originality adaptability, our future tomorrow. What a contemptible role for a people that once had its Maccabees'.
LEON PINSKER, a Jewish physician from Odessa, in his book 'AUTO-EMANCIPATION', 1882

Odessa

CRIMEA

Sebastopol

Black Sea

Few Jewish attempts to assimilate into Russian life were successful. Government, aristocracy, peasantry and intellectuals all prevented any relaxation of barriers or dimin-ution of hostility. The Jews themselves were not without resources, including charitable and self-defence organisations as well as mass emigration, particularly to the United States. Also, after 1882, there was growing support for emigration to Palestine. Jews also played a leading part in all Russian revolutionary socialist parties, including the Bolshevik Party. Their own Jewish Social Democratic party, the 'Bund' was founded in 1897.

Emigration routes of Russian Jews 1880-1914. Over 2,000,000 went to the U.S.A, 200,000 to Britain and 60,000 to Palestine.

Centres of the Bund by 1905. The majority of the Bund opposed the Bolsheviks in 1917. The Party was suppressed in the 1920's. In 1905 there were 30,000 Party members and 274 town and village organizations.

© Martin Gilbert 1976

76

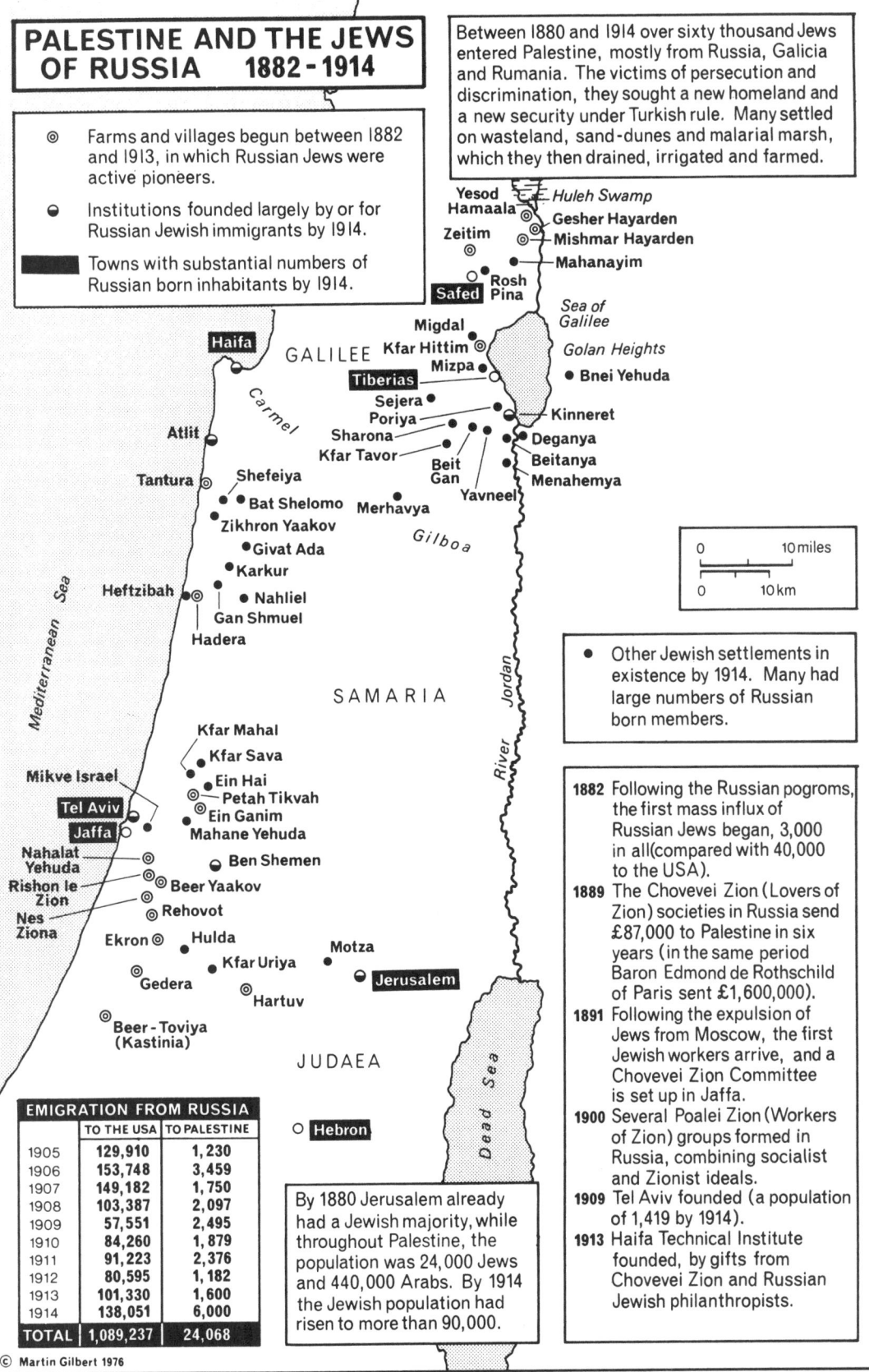

PALESTINE AND THE JEWS OF RUSSIA   1882-1914

Between 1880 and 1914 over sixty thousand Jews entered Palestine, mostly from Russia, Galicia and Rumania. The victims of persecution and discrimination, they sought a new homeland and a new security under Turkish rule. Many settled on wasteland, sand-dunes and malarial marsh, which they then drained, irrigated and farmed.

◎ Farms and villages begun between 1882 and 1913, in which Russian Jews were active pioneers.

◖ Institutions founded largely by or for Russian Jewish immigrants by 1914.

▮ Towns with substantial numbers of Russian born inhabitants by 1914.

Yesod Hamaala
Huleh Swamp
Gesher Hayarden
Zeitim
Mishmar Hayarden
Mahanayim
Rosh Pina
Safed
Sea of Galilee
Haifa
GALILEE
Migdal
Kfar Hittim
Mizpa
Golan Heights
Tiberias
Bnei Yehuda
Sejera
Carmel
Poriya
Kinneret
Sharona
Deganya
Kfar Tavor
Beitanya
Atlit
Beit Gan
Menahemya
Tantura
Shefeiya
Yavneel
Bat Shelomo
Merhavya
Zikhron Yaakov
Givat Ada
Karkur
Gilboa
Heftzibah
Nahliel
Gan Shmuel
Hadera

Mediterranean Sea

SAMARIA

River Jordan

| | 0 | 10 miles |
| 0 | 10 km | |

● Other Jewish settlements in existence by 1914. Many had large numbers of Russian born members.

Kfar Mahal
Kfar Sava
Mikve Israel
Ein Hai
Petah Tikvah
Tel Aviv
Ein Ganim
Jaffa
Mahane Yehuda
Nahalat Yehuda
Ben Shemen
Rishon le Zion
Beer Yaakov
Nes Ziona
Rehovot
Ekron
Hulda
Motza
Kfar Uriya
Jerusalem
Gedera
Hartuv
Beer-Toviya (Kastinia)
JUDAEA

Dead Sea

1882 Following the Russian pogroms, the first mass influx of Russian Jews began, 3,000 in all (compared with 40,000 to the USA).

1889 The Chovevei Zion (Lovers of Zion) societies in Russia send £87,000 to Palestine in six years (in the same period Baron Edmond de Rothschild of Paris sent £1,600,000).

1891 Following the expulsion of Jews from Moscow, the first Jewish workers arrive, and a Chovevei Zion Committee is set up in Jaffa.

1900 Several Poalei Zion (Workers of Zion) groups formed in Russia, combining socialist and Zionist ideals.

1909 Tel Aviv founded (a population of 1,419 by 1914).

1913 Haifa Technical Institute founded, by gifts from Chovevei Zion and Russian Jewish philanthropists.

EMIGRATION FROM RUSSIA		
	TO THE USA	TO PALESTINE
1905	129,910	1,230
1906	153,748	3,459
1907	149,182	1,750
1908	103,387	2,097
1909	57,551	2,495
1910	84,260	1,879
1911	91,223	2,376
1912	80,595	1,182
1913	101,330	1,600
1914	138,051	6,000
TOTAL	1,089,237	24,068

Hebron

By 1880 Jerusalem already had a Jewish majority, while throughout Palestine, the population was 24,000 Jews and 440,000 Arabs. By 1914 the Jewish population had risen to more than 90,000.

© Martin Gilbert 1976

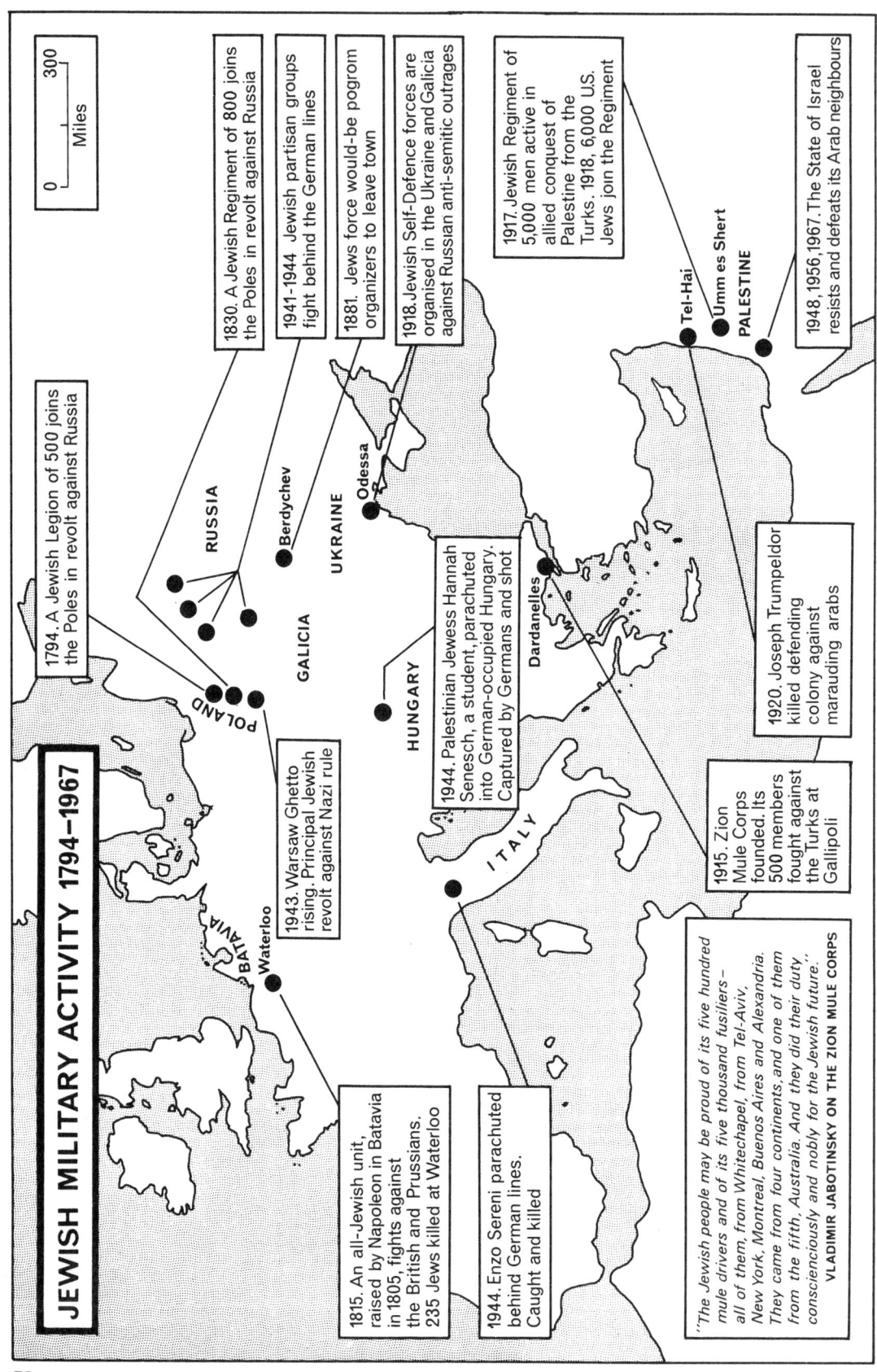

JEWISH MILITARY ACTIVITY 1794–1967

1794. A Jewish Legion of 500 joins the Poles in revolt against Russia

1830. A Jewish Regiment of 800 joins the Poles in revolt against Russia

1941-1944 Jewish partisan groups fight behind the German lines

1881. Jews force would-be pogrom organizers to leave town

1918. Jewish Self-Defence forces are organised in the Ukraine and Galicia against Russian anti-semitic outrages

1917. Jewish Regiment of 5,000 men active in allied conquest of Palestine from the Turks. 1918, 6,000 U.S. Jews join the Regiment

1948,1956,1967. The State of Israel resists and defeats its Arab neighbours

1943. Warsaw Ghetto rising. Principal Jewish revolt against Nazi rule

1944. Palestinian Jewess Hannah Senesch, a student, parachuted into German-occupied Hungary. Captured by Germans and shot

1920. Joseph Trumpeldor killed defending colony against marauding arabs

1815. An all-Jewish unit, raised by Napoleon in Batavia in 1805, fights against the British and Prussians. 235 Jews killed at Waterloo

1944. Enzo Sereni parachuted behind German lines. Caught and killed

1915. Zion Mule Corps founded. Its 500 members fought against the Turks at Gallipoli

RUSSIA

Berdychev

UKRAINE

Odessa

GALICIA

POLAND

HUNGARY

Dardanelles

Tel-Hai

Umm es Shert

PALESTINE

ITALY

Waterloo

BATAVIA

"The Jewish people may be proud of its five hundred mule drivers and of its five thousand fusiliers – all of them, from Whitechapel, from Tel-Aviv, New York, Montreal, Buenos Aires and Alexandria. They came from four continents, and one of them from the fifth, Australia. And they did their duty, conscienciously and nobly for the Jewish future." **VLADIMIR JABOTINSKY ON THE ZION MULE CORPS**

0   300

Miles

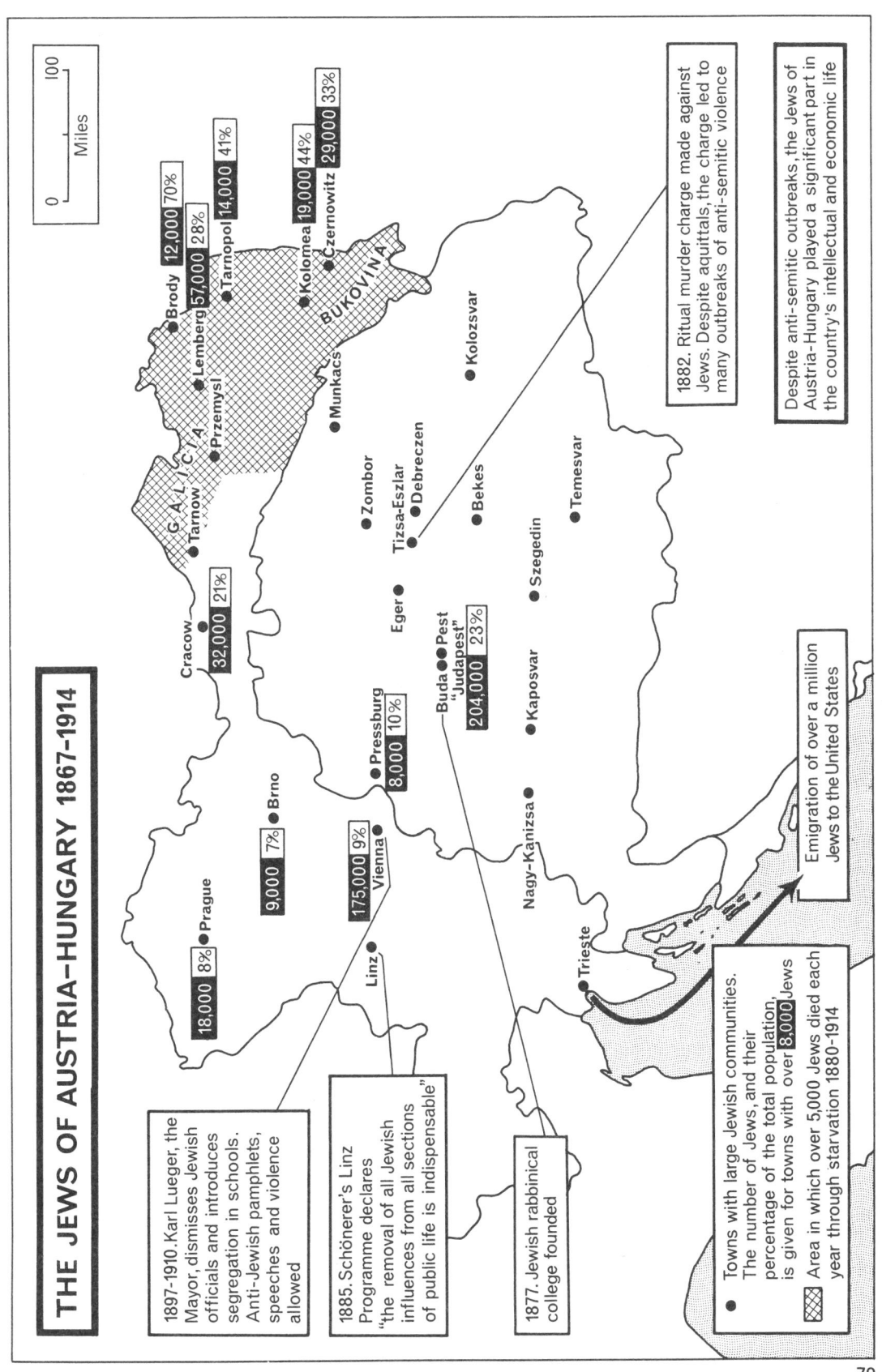

THE JEWS OF AUSTRIA–HUNGARY 1867–1914

1897-1910. Karl Lueger, the Mayor, dismisses Jewish officials and introduces segregation in schools. Anti-Jewish pamphlets, speeches and violence allowed

1885. Schönerer's Linz Programme declares "the removal of all Jewish influences from all sections of public life is indispensable"

1877. Jewish rabbinical college founded

1882. Ritual murder charge made against Jews. Despite aquittals, the charge led to many outbreaks of anti-semitic violence

Despite anti-semitic outbreaks, the Jews of Austria-Hungary played a significant part in the country's intellectual and economic life

Emigration of over a million Jews to the United States

- Towns with large Jewish communities. The number of Jews, and their percentage of the total population, is given for towns with over 8,000 Jews

▨ Area in which over 5,000 Jews died each year through starvation 1880-1914

18,000 8% ●Prague

9,000 7% ●Brno

175,000 9% ●Vienna

Linz ●

Pressburg ● 8,000 10%

32,000 21% Cracow ●

Tarnow ● G A L I C I A

Przemysl ●

Brody ● 12,000 70%

Lemberg 57,000 28%

Tarnopol 14,000 41%

Kolomea 19,000 44%

Czernowitz 29,000 33%

B U K O V I N A

Munkacs ●

Kolozsvar ●

Zombor ●

Eger ●

Tizsa-Eszlar ● Debreczen ●

Bekes ●

Temesvar ●

Szegedin ●

Kaposvar ●

Buda ●● Pest "Judapest" 204,000 23%

Nagy-Kanizsa ●

Trieste ●

Miles 0 100

79

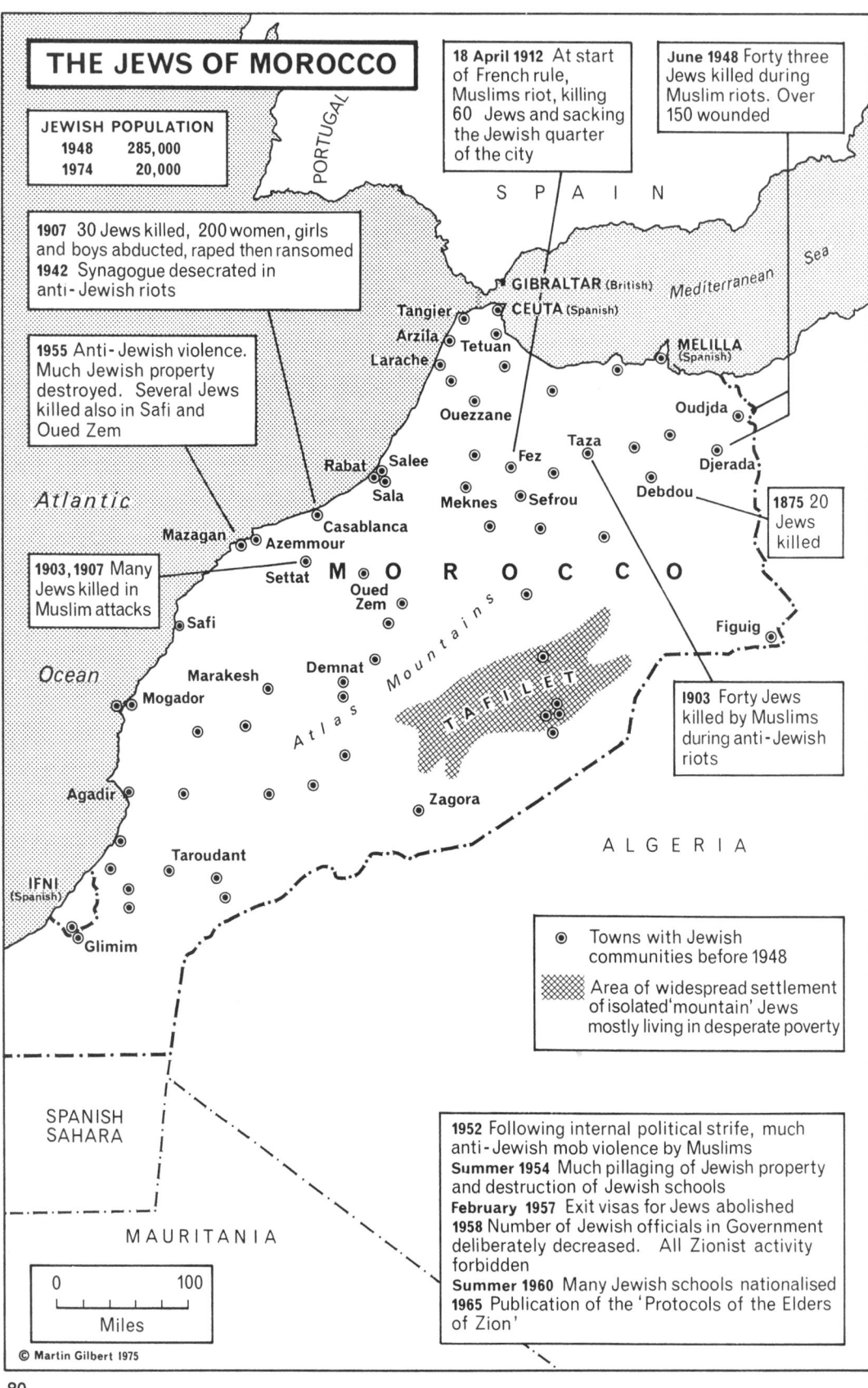

THE JEWS OF MOROCCO

JEWISH POPULATION
1948   285,000
1974   20,000

1907 30 Jews killed, 200 women, girls and boys abducted, raped then ransomed
1942 Synagogue desecrated in anti-Jewish riots

1955 Anti-Jewish violence. Much Jewish property destroyed. Several Jews killed also in Safi and Oued Zem

1903, 1907 Many Jews killed in Muslim attacks

18 April 1912 At start of French rule, Muslims riot, killing 60 Jews and sacking the Jewish quarter of the city

June 1948 Forty three Jews killed during Muslim riots. Over 150 wounded

PORTUGAL

S   P   A   I   N

Mediterranean   Sea

GIBRALTAR (British)
CEUTA (Spanish)
Tangier
Arzila   Tetuan
Larache

MELILLA (Spanish)

Oudjda

Atlantic

Rabat   Salee
Sala
Casablanca
Meknes   Sefrou
Mazagan   Azemmour
Settat   Oued
Zem

Fez   Taza

Debdou

Djerada

1875 20 Jews killed

M   O   R   O   C   C   O

Safi

Ocean

Marakesh
Demnat

Mogador

Atlas   *Mountains*

TAFILLET

Figuig

1903 Forty Jews killed by Muslims during anti-Jewish riots

Agadir

Taroudant

Zagora

A   L   G   E   R   I   A

IFNI (Spanish)

Glimim

⊙ Towns with Jewish communities before 1948

▨ Area of widespread settlement of isolated 'mountain' Jews mostly living in desperate poverty

SPANISH
SAHARA

1952 Following internal political strife, much anti-Jewish mob violence by Muslims
Summer 1954 Much pillaging of Jewish property and destruction of Jewish schools
February 1957 Exit visas for Jews abolished
1958 Number of Jewish officials in Government deliberately decreased. All Zionist activity forbidden
Summer 1960 Many Jewish schools nationalised
1965 Publication of the 'Protocols of the Elders of Zion'

MAURITANIA

0   100
Miles

© Martin Gilbert 1975

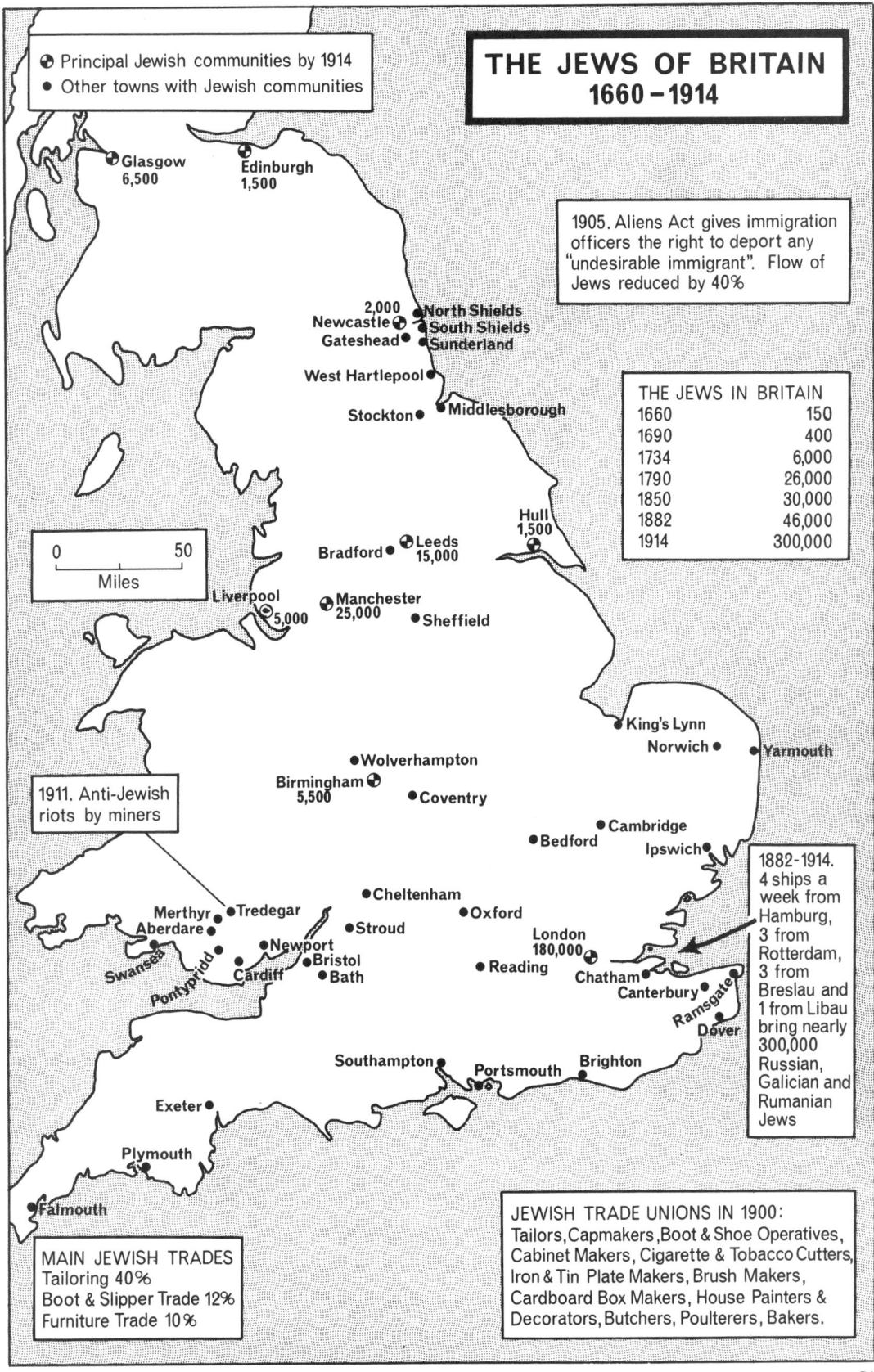

THE JEWS OF BRITAIN
1660–1914

Legend:
- ⊕ Principal Jewish communities by 1914
- ● Other towns with Jewish communities

1905. Aliens Act gives immigration officers the right to deport any "undesirable immigrant". Flow of Jews reduced by 40%

THE JEWS IN BRITAIN	
1660	150
1690	400
1734	6,000
1790	26,000
1850	30,000
1882	46,000
1914	300,000

1911. Anti-Jewish riots by miners

1882–1914. 4 ships a week from Hamburg, 3 from Rotterdam, 3 from Breslau and 1 from Libau bring nearly 300,000 Russian, Galician and Rumanian Jews

MAIN JEWISH TRADES
Tailoring 40%
Boot & Slipper Trade 12%
Furniture Trade 10%

JEWISH TRADE UNIONS IN 1900:
Tailors, Capmakers, Boot & Shoe Operatives, Cabinet Makers, Cigarette & Tobacco Cutters, Iron & Tin Plate Makers, Brush Makers, Cardboard Box Makers, House Painters & Decorators, Butchers, Poulterers, Bakers.

Map locations:
- Glasgow 6,500
- Edinburgh 1,500
- Newcastle 2,000
- North Shields
- South Shields
- Gateshead
- Sunderland
- West Hartlepool
- Stockton
- Middlesborough
- Hull 1,500
- Bradford
- Leeds 15,000
- Liverpool 5,000
- Manchester 25,000
- Sheffield
- King's Lynn
- Norwich
- Yarmouth
- Wolverhampton
- Birmingham 5,500
- Coventry
- Cambridge
- Bedford
- Ipswich
- Cheltenham
- Oxford
- Merthyr
- Tredegar
- Aberdare
- Stroud
- Newport
- London 180,000
- Bristol
- Cardiff
- Bath
- Reading
- Chatham
- Canterbury
- Ramsgate
- Dover
- Swansea
- Pontypridd
- Southampton
- Portsmouth
- Brighton
- Exeter
- Plymouth
- Falmouth

Scale: 0 — 50 Miles

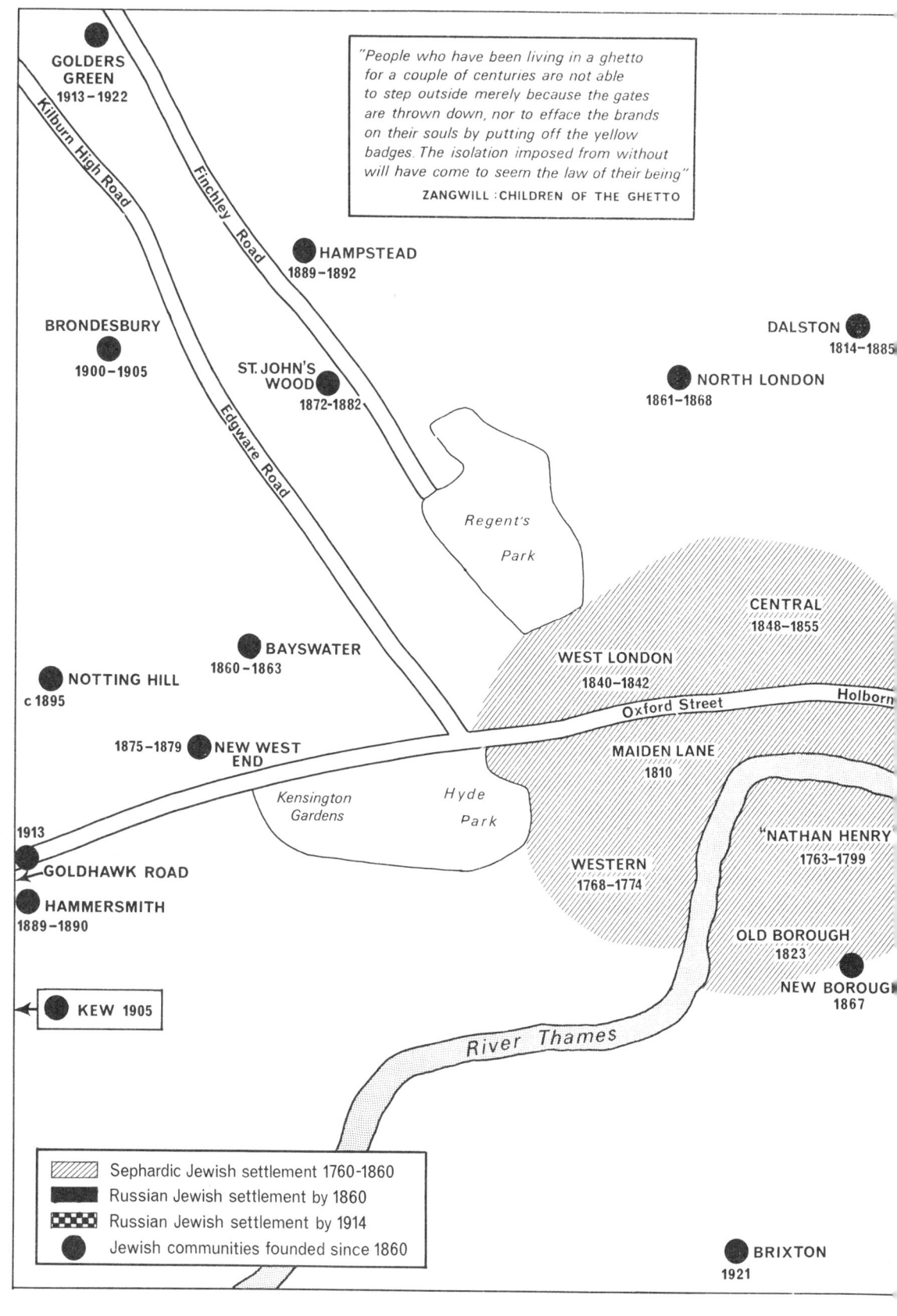

GOLDERS
GREEN
1913–1922

Kilburn High Road

Finchley Road

HAMPSTEAD
1889–1892

DALSTON
1814–1885

BRONDESBURY
1900–1905

ST. JOHN'S
WOOD
1872–1882

NORTH LONDON
1861–1868

Edgware Road

Regent's
Park

CENTRAL
1848–1855

BAYSWATER
1860–1863

WEST LONDON
1840–1842

NOTTING HILL
c 1895

Oxford Street

Holborn

1875–1879 NEW WEST
END

MAIDEN LANE
1810

Kensington
Gardens

Hyde
Park

"NATHAN HENRY
1763–1799

1913

GOLDHAWK ROAD

WESTERN
1768–1774

HAMMERSMITH
1889–1890

OLD BOROUGH
1823

NEW BOROUGH
1867

KEW 1905

River Thames

> "People who have been living in a ghetto
> for a couple of centuries are not able
> to step outside merely because the gates
> are thrown down, nor to efface the brands
> on their souls by putting off the yellow
> badges. The isolation imposed from without
> will have come to seem the law of their being"
>
> ZANGWILL : CHILDREN OF THE GHETTO

Sephardic Jewish settlement 1760–1860
Russian Jewish settlement by 1860
Russian Jewish settlement by 1914
Jewish communities founded since 1860

BRIXTON
1921

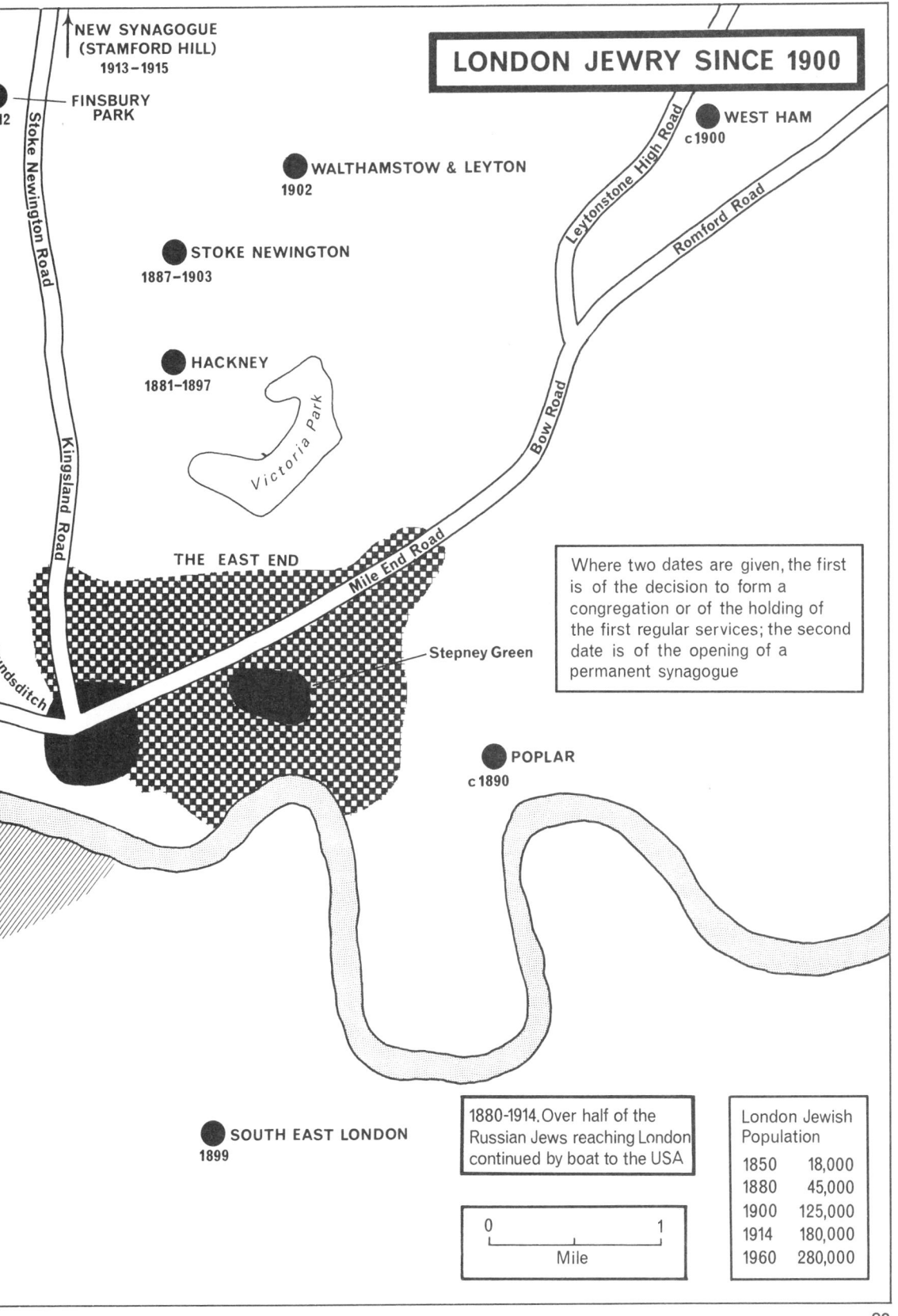

NEW SYNAGOGUE
(STAMFORD HILL)
1913–1915

FINSBURY PARK

12

Stoke Newington Road

LONDON JEWRY SINCE 1900

WEST HAM
c 1900

Leytonstone High Road

Romford Road

WALTHAMSTOW & LEYTON
1902

STOKE NEWINGTON
1887–1903

Kingsland Road

HACKNEY
1881–1897

Victoria Park

Bow Road

THE EAST END

Mile End Road

undsditch

Stepney Green

Where two dates are given, the first
is of the decision to form a
congregation or of the holding of
the first regular services; the second
date is of the opening of a
permanent synagogue

POPLAR
c 1890

SOUTH EAST LONDON
1899

1880-1914. Over half of the
Russian Jews reaching London
continued by boat to the USA

London Jewish
Population

1850	18,000
1880	45,000
1900	125,000
1914	180,000
1960	280,000

0   1
Mile

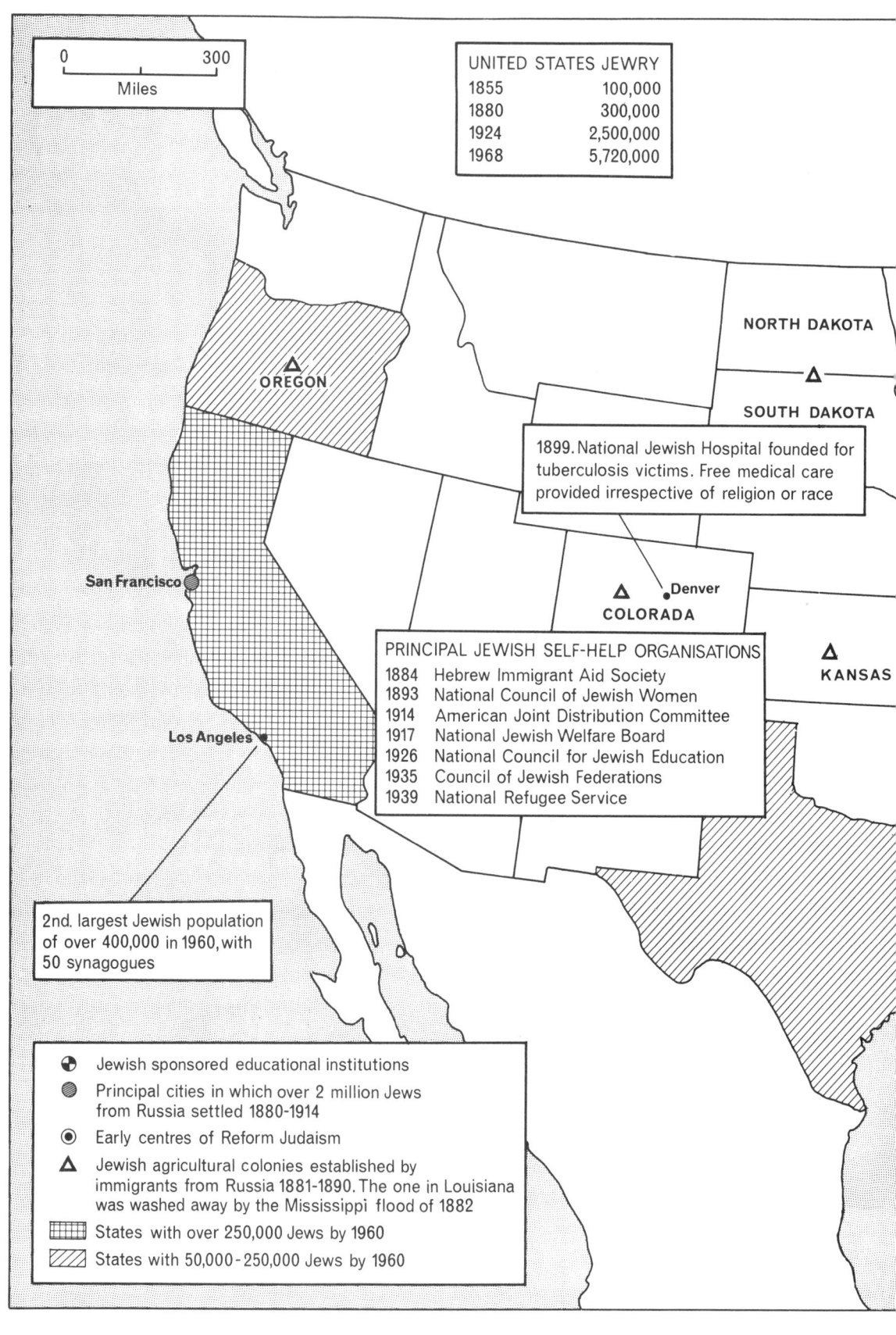

0	300

Miles

UNITED STATES JEWRY
1855   100,000
1880   300,000
1924   2,500,000
1968   5,720,000

NORTH DAKOTA

SOUTH DAKOTA

1899. National Jewish Hospital founded for
tuberculosis victims. Free medical care
provided irrespective of religion or race

OREGON

San Francisco

Los Angeles

●Denver
COLORADA

KANSAS

PRINCIPAL JEWISH SELF-HELP ORGANISATIONS
1884   Hebrew Immigrant Aid Society
1893   National Council of Jewish Women
1914   American Joint Distribution Committee
1917   National Jewish Welfare Board
1926   National Council for Jewish Education
1935   Council of Jewish Federations
1939   National Refugee Service

2nd. largest Jewish population
of over 400,000 in 1960, with
50 synagogues

☻   Jewish sponsored educational institutions

◍   Principal cities in which over 2 million Jews
    from Russia settled 1880-1914

◉   Early centres of Reform Judaism

△   Jewish agricultural colonies established by
    immigrants from Russia 1881-1890. The one in Louisiana
    was washed away by the Mississippi flood of 1882

▦   States with over 250,000 Jews by 1960

▨   States with 50,000-250,000 Jews by 1960

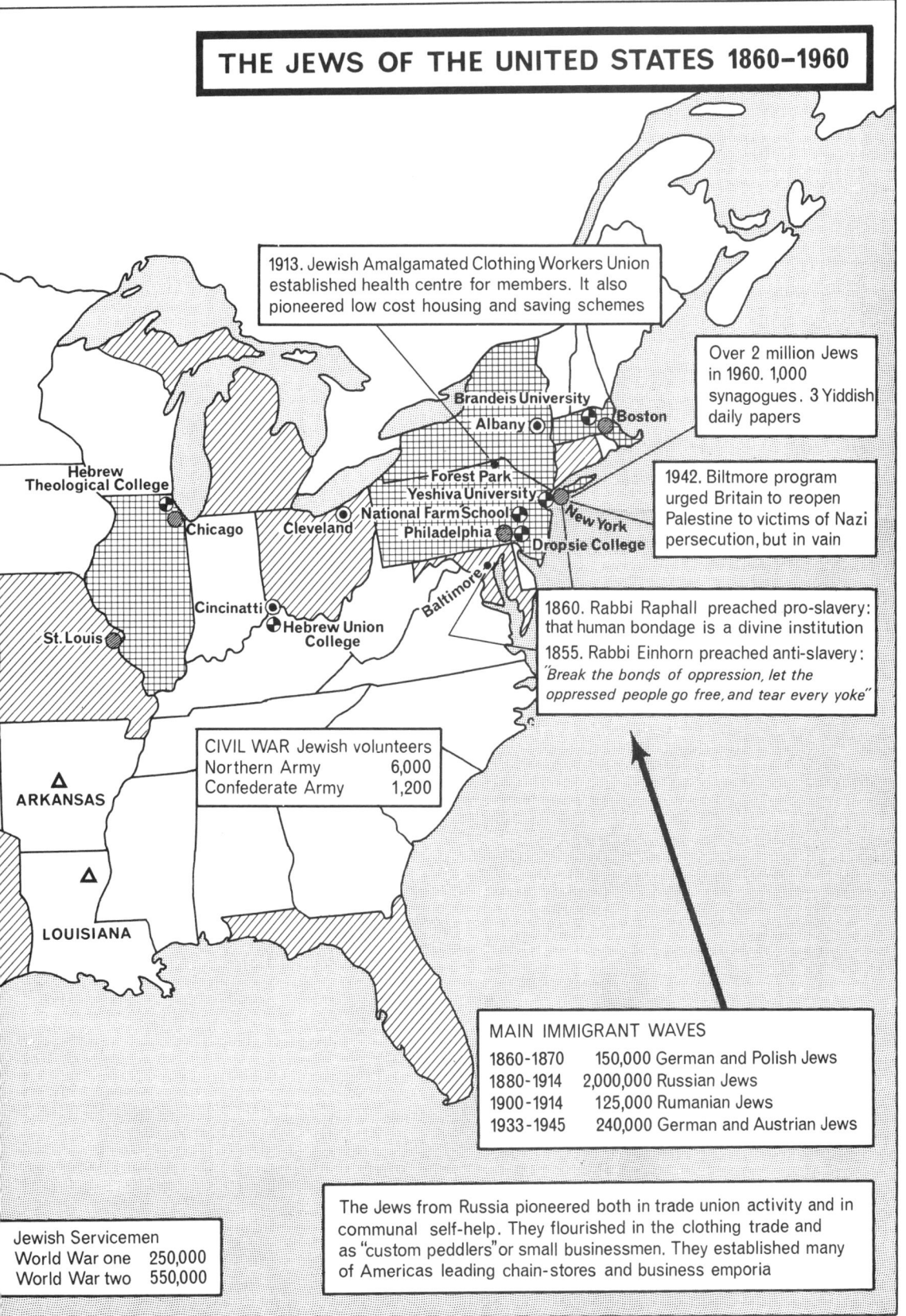

THE JEWS OF THE UNITED STATES 1860–1960

1913. Jewish Amalgamated Clothing Workers Union established health centre for members. It also pioneered low cost housing and saving schemes

Over 2 million Jews in 1960. 1,000 synagogues. 3 Yiddish daily papers

1942. Biltmore program urged Britain to reopen Palestine to victims of Nazi persecution, but in vain

1860. Rabbi Raphall preached pro-slavery: that human bondage is a divine institution

1855. Rabbi Einhorn preached anti-slavery: "Break the bonds of oppression, let the oppressed people go free, and tear every yoke"

Brandeis University
Albany
Boston
Hebrew Theological College
Forest Park
Yeshiva University
Chicago
Cleveland
National Farm School
Philadelphia
New York
Dropsie College
Cincinatti
Hebrew Union College
St. Louis
Baltimore

ARKANSAS

LOUISIANA

CIVIL WAR Jewish volunteers
Northern Army   6,000
Confederate Army   1,200

MAIN IMMIGRANT WAVES
1860-1870   150,000 German and Polish Jews
1880-1914   2,000,000 Russian Jews
1900-1914   125,000 Rumanian Jews
1933-1945   240,000 German and Austrian Jews

The Jews from Russia pioneered both in trade union activity and in communal self-help. They flourished in the clothing trade and as "custom peddlers" or small businessmen. They established many of Americas leading chain-stores and business emporia

Jewish Servicemen
World War one   250,000
World War two   550,000

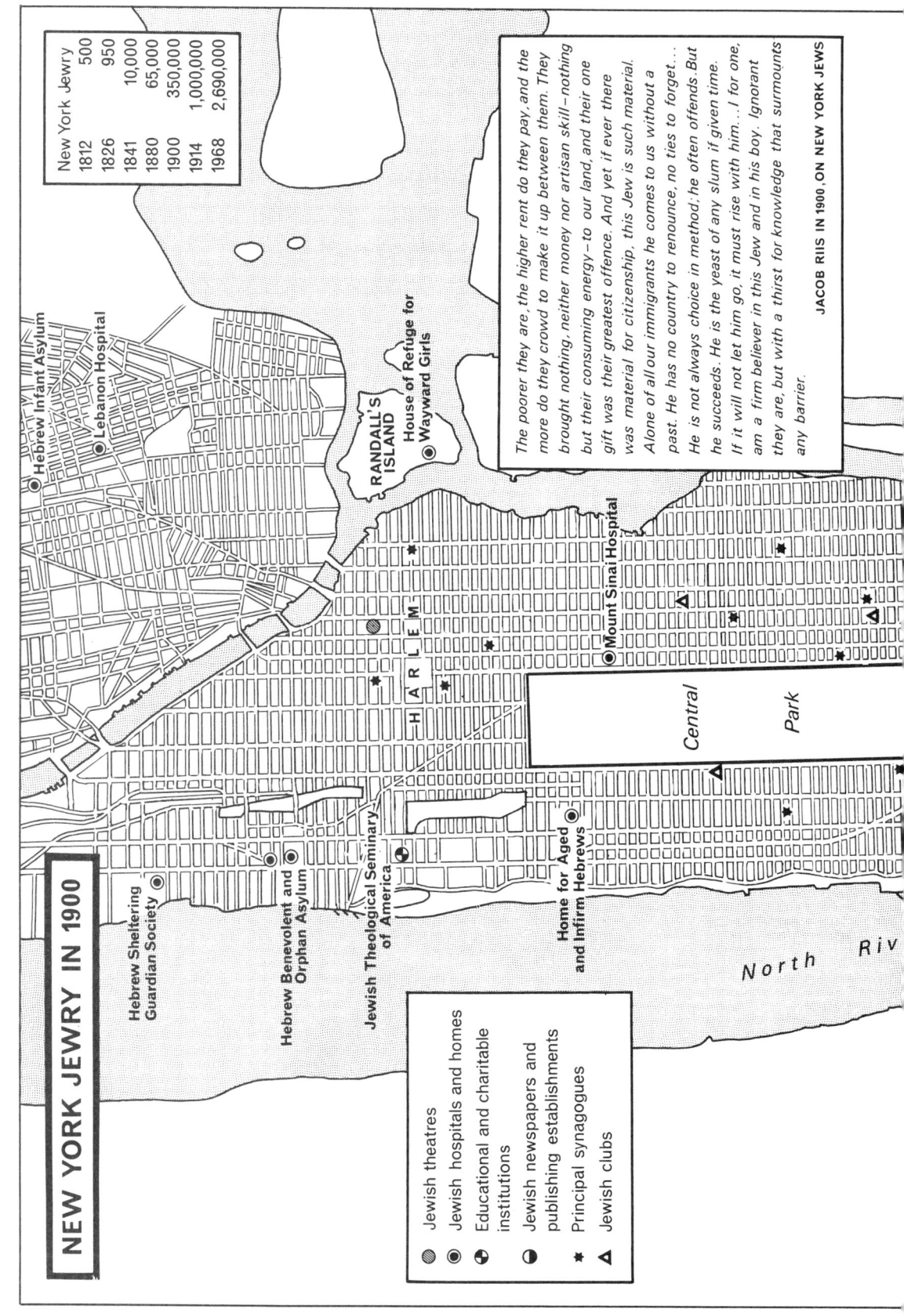

NEW YORK JEWRY IN 1900

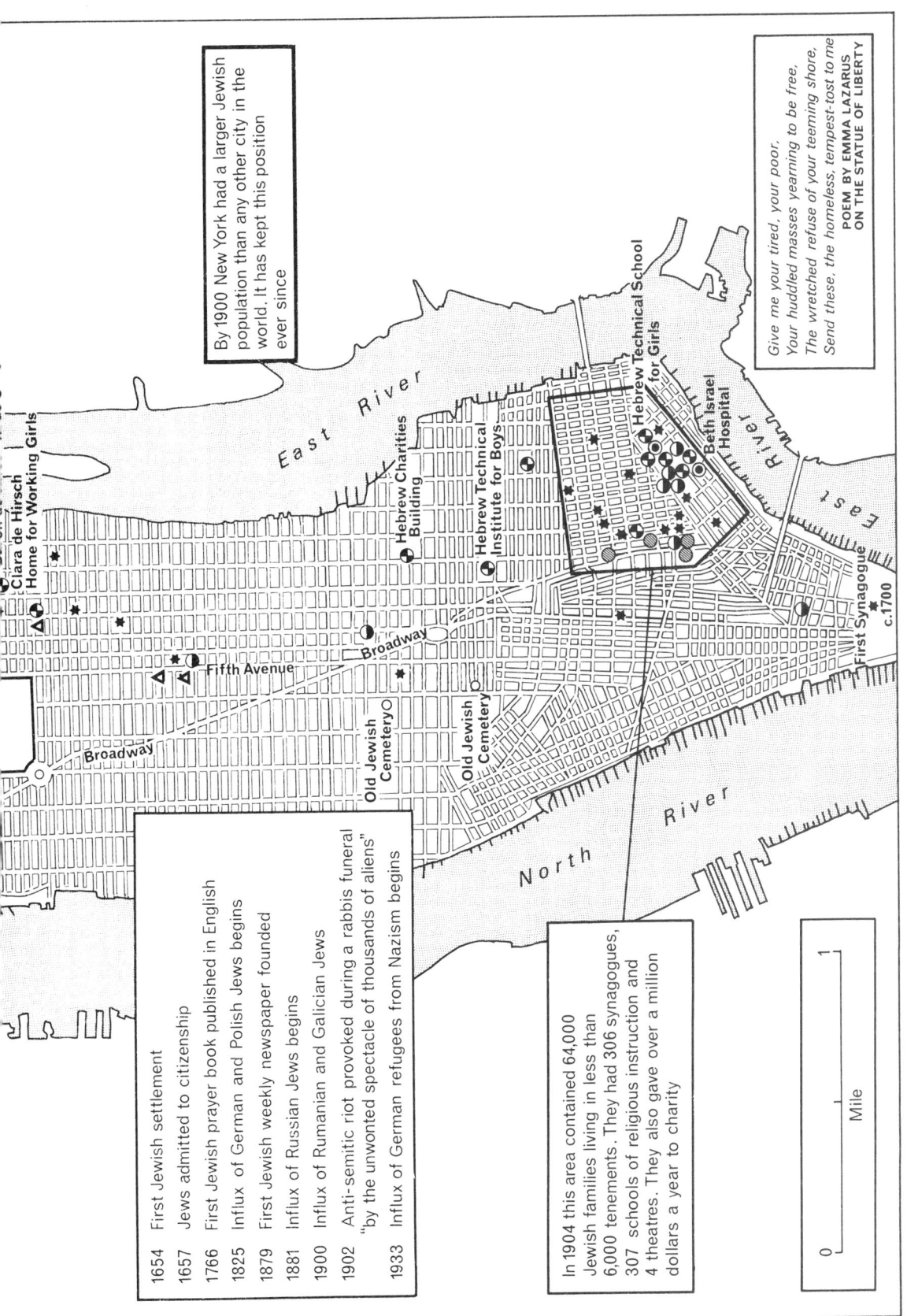

By 1900 New York had a larger Jewish population than any other city in the world. It has kept this position ever since

Clara de Hirsch
Home for Working Girls

East River

Hebrew Charities Building

Hebrew Technical Institute for Boys

Hebrew Technical School for Girls

Beth Israel Hospital

Fifth Avenue

Broadway

Broadway

Old Jewish Cemetery

Old Jewish Cemetery

First Synagogue c.1700

East River

North River

Give me your tired, your poor,
Your huddled masses yearning to be free,
The wretched refuse of your teeming shore,
Send these, the homeless, tempest-tost to me
**POEM BY EMMA LAZARUS
ON THE STATUE OF LIBERTY**

1654 First Jewish settlement

1657 Jews admitted to citizenship

1766 First Jewish prayer book published in English

1825 Influx of German and Polish Jews begins

1879 First Jewish weekly newspaper founded

1881 Influx of Russian Jews begins

1900 Influx of Rumanian and Galician Jews

1902 Anti-semitic riot provoked during a rabbis funeral "by the unwonted spectacle of thousands of aliens"

1933 Influx of German refugees from Nazism begins

In 1904 this area contained 64,000 Jewish families living in less than 6,000 tenements. They had 306 synagogues, 307 schools of religious instruction and 4 theatres. They also gave over a million dollars a year to charity

0   1
Mile

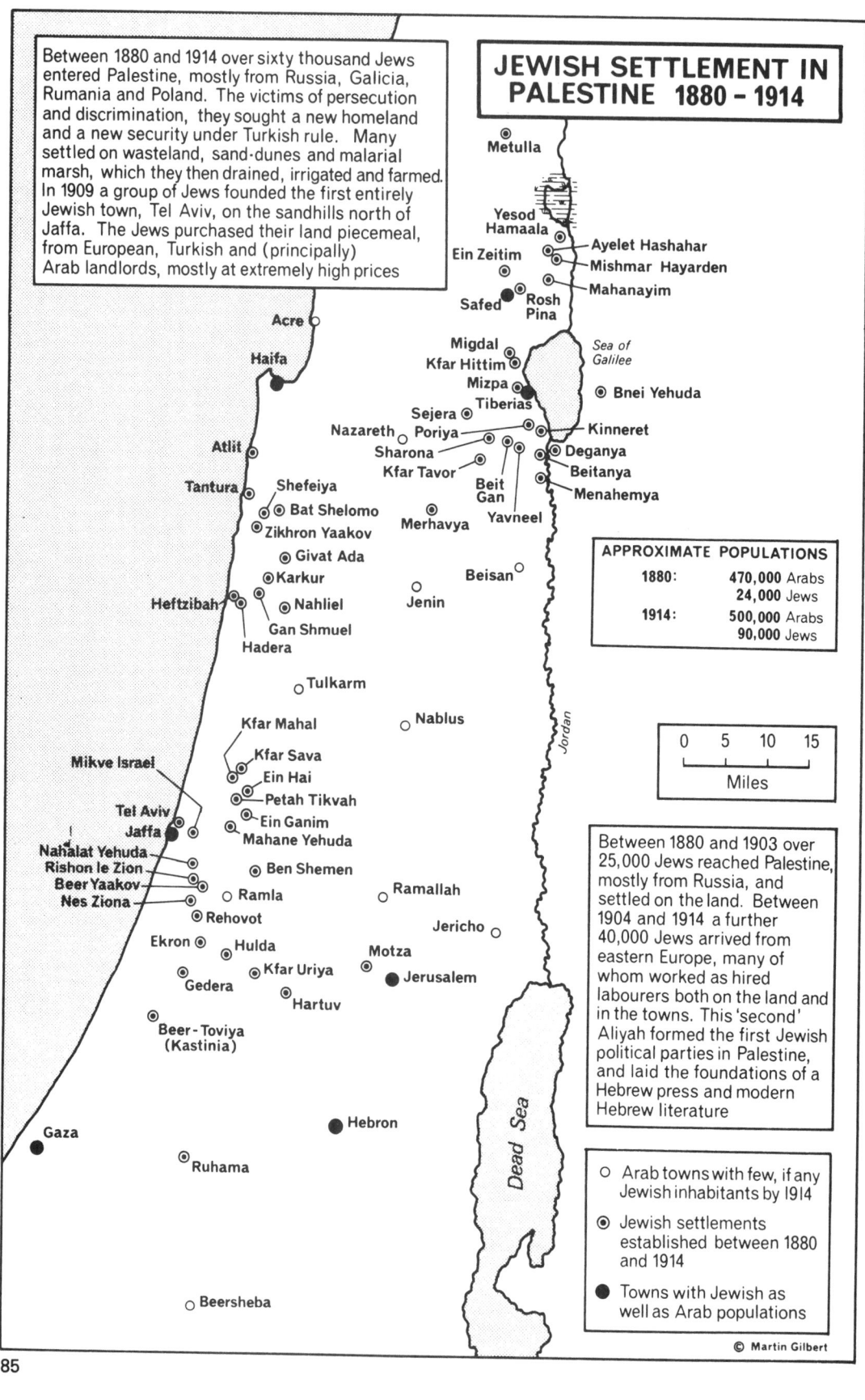

JEWISH SETTLEMENT IN PALESTINE 1880 – 1914

Between 1880 and 1914 over sixty thousand Jews entered Palestine, mostly from Russia, Galicia, Rumania and Poland. The victims of persecution and discrimination, they sought a new homeland and a new security under Turkish rule. Many settled on wasteland, sand-dunes and malarial marsh, which they then drained, irrigated and farmed. In 1909 a group of Jews founded the first entirely Jewish town, Tel Aviv, on the sandhills north of Jaffa. The Jews purchased their land piecemeal, from European, Turkish and (principally) Arab landlords, mostly at extremely high prices

Metulla

Yesod Hamaala

Ein Zeitim
Ayelet Hashahar
Mishmar Hayarden
Mahanayim

Safed
Rosh Pina

Acre

Haifa

Migdal
Kfar Hittim
Mizpa
Sea of Galilee
Tiberias
Bnei Yehuda

Sejera
Nazareth
Poriya
Kinneret
Sharona
Deganya
Kfar Tavor
Beitanya
Beit Gan
Menahemya
Yavneel

Atlit

Tantura
Shefeiya
Bat Shelomo
Merhavya
Zikhron Yaakov
Givat Ada
Beisan
Karkur
Jenin
Heftzibah
Nahliel
Gan Shmuel
Hadera

Tulkarm

Kfar Mahal
Nablus
Kfar Sava
Mikve Israel
Ein Hai
Tel Aviv
Petah Tikvah
Jaffa
Ein Ganim
Nahalat Yehuda
Mahane Yehuda
Rishon le Zion
Ben Shemen
Beer Yaakov
Ramallah
Nes Ziona
Ramla
Rehovot
Jericho
Ekron
Hulda
Motza
Kfar Uriya
Jerusalem
Gedera
Hartuv

Beer-Toviya
(Kastinia)

Dead Sea

Gaza
Hebron
Ruhama

Jordan

Beersheba

APPROXIMATE POPULATIONS

1880:	470,000 Arabs
	24,000 Jews
1914:	500,000 Arabs
	90,000 Jews

0 5 10 15
Miles

Between 1880 and 1903 over 25,000 Jews reached Palestine, mostly from Russia, and settled on the land. Between 1904 and 1914 a further 40,000 Jews arrived from eastern Europe, many of whom worked as hired labourers both on the land and in the towns. This 'second' Aliyah formed the first Jewish political parties in Palestine, and laid the foundations of a Hebrew press and modern Hebrew literature

○ Arab towns with few, if any Jewish inhabitants by 1914

◉ Jewish settlements established between 1880 and 1914

● Towns with Jewish as well as Arab populations

© Martin Gilbert

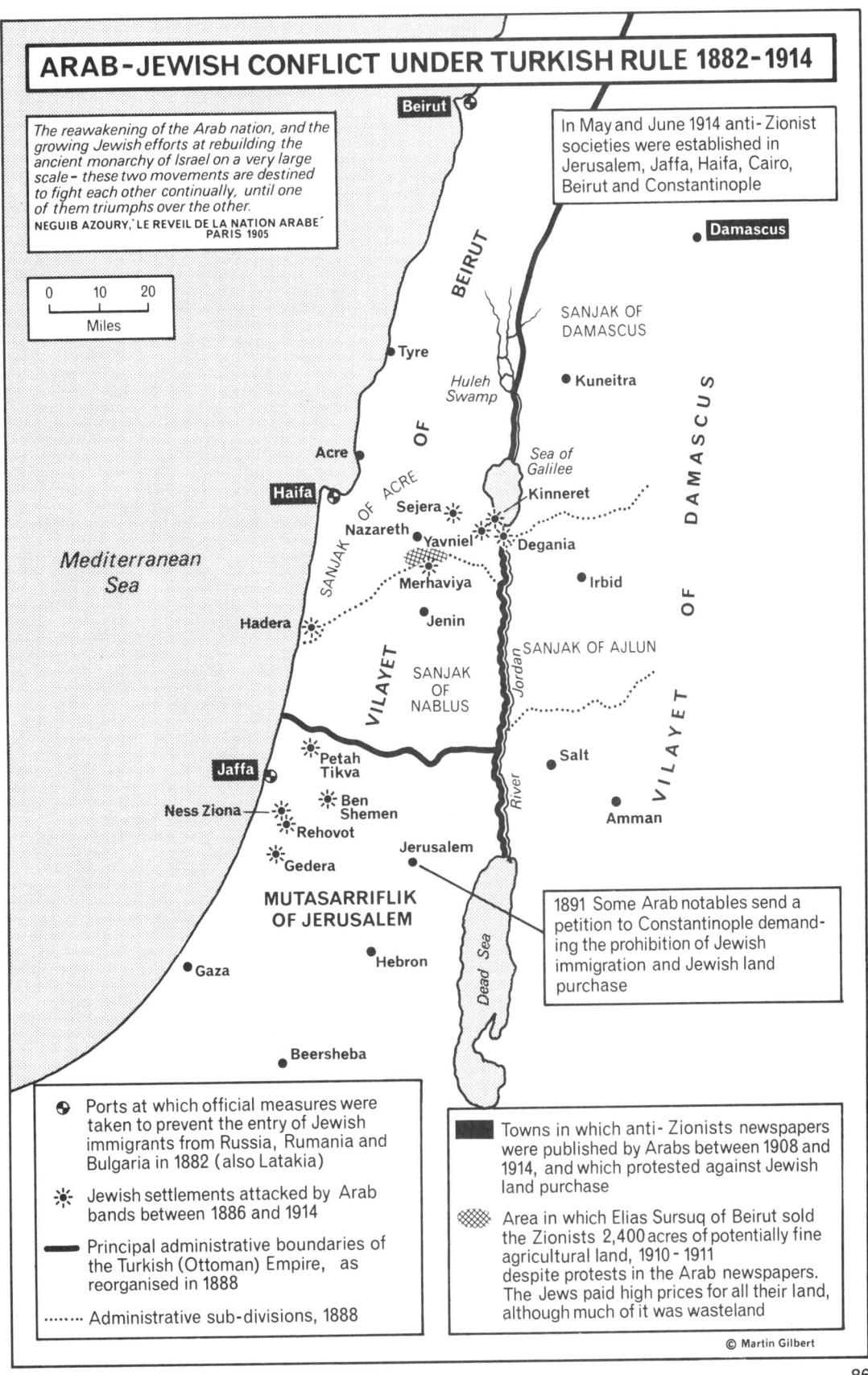

ARAB-JEWISH CONFLICT UNDER TURKISH RULE 1882-1914

The reawakening of the Arab nation, and the growing Jewish efforts at rebuilding the ancient monarchy of Israel on a very large scale – these two movements are destined to fight each other continually, until one of them triumphs over the other.
NEGUIB AZOURY,`LE REVEIL DE LA NATION ARABE´ PARIS 1905

In May and June 1914 anti-Zionist societies were established in Jerusalem, Jaffa, Haifa, Cairo, Beirut and Constantinople

0   10   20
Miles

Beirut

Damascus

VILAYET OF BEIRUT

SANJAK OF DAMASCUS

Tyre

Huleh Swamp

Kuneitra

VILAYET OF DAMASCUS

Acre

SANJAK OF ACRE

Sea of Galilee

Haifa

Sejera

Kinneret

Nazareth

Yavniel

Degania

Mediterranean Sea

Merhaviya

Irbid

Hadera

Jenin

SANJAK OF AJLUN

VILAYET

SANJAK OF NABLUS

Jordan River

Salt

VILAYET OF

Jaffa

Petah Tikva

Ness Ziona

Ben Shemen

Rehovot

Amman

Gedera

Jerusalem

MUTASARRIFLIK OF JERUSALEM

1891 Some Arab notables send a petition to Constantinople demanding the prohibition of Jewish immigration and Jewish land purchase

Gaza

Hebron

Dead Sea

Beersheba

⊕ Ports at which official measures were taken to prevent the entry of Jewish immigrants from Russia, Rumania and Bulgaria in 1882 (also Latakia)

☀ Jewish settlements attacked by Arab bands between 1886 and 1914

━ Principal administrative boundaries of the Turkish (Ottoman) Empire, as reorganised in 1888

······ Administrative sub-divisions, 1888

� Towns in which anti-Zionists newspapers were published by Arabs between 1908 and 1914, and which protested against Jewish land purchase

▨ Area in which Elias Sursuq of Beirut sold the Zionists 2,400 acres of potentially fine agricultural land, 1910 - 1911 despite protests in the Arab newspapers. The Jews paid high prices for all their land, although much of it was wasteland

© Martin Gilbert

86

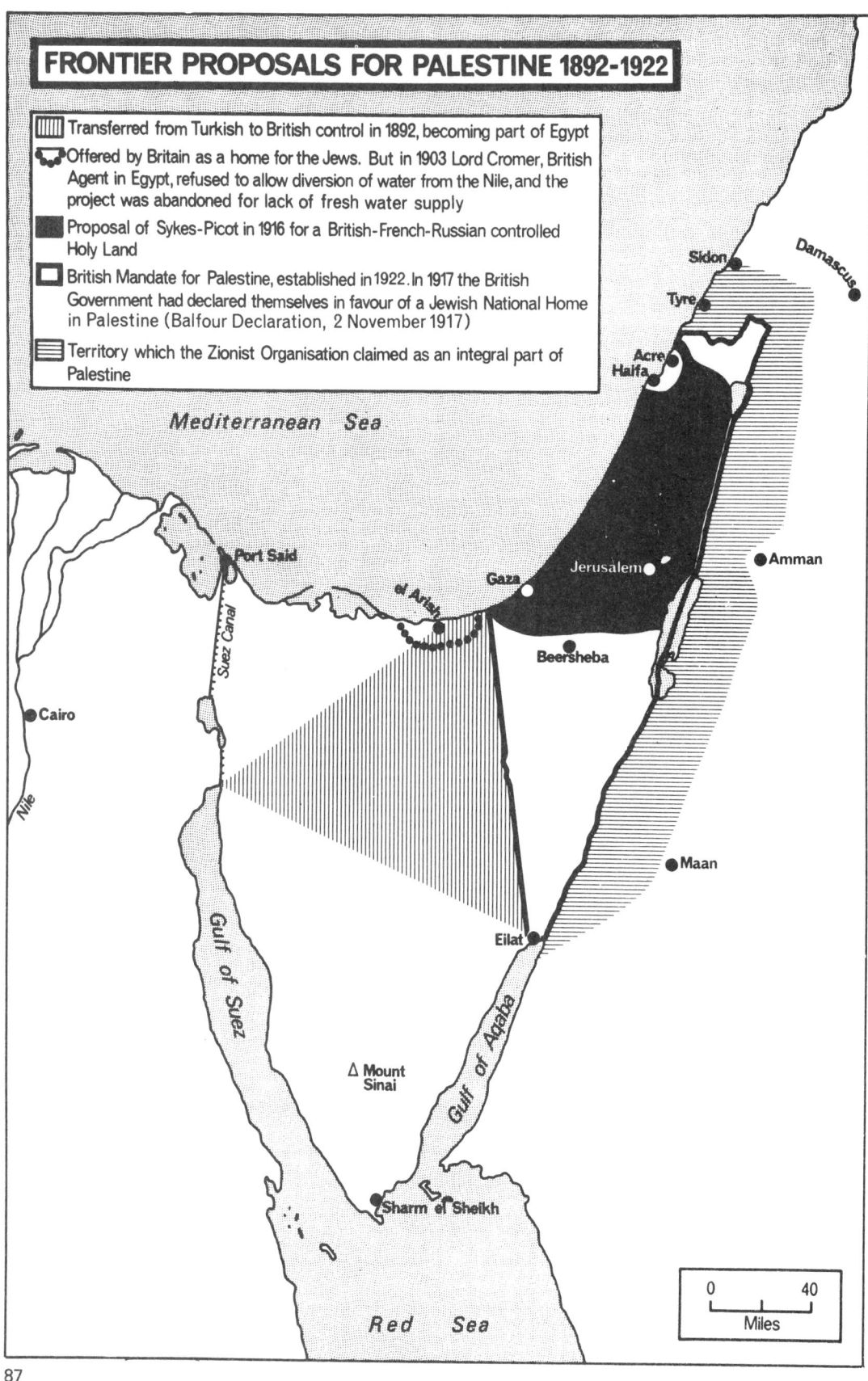

FRONTIER PROPOSALS FOR PALESTINE 1892-1922

Transferred from Turkish to British control in 1892, becoming part of Egypt

Offered by Britain as a home for the Jews. But in 1903 Lord Cromer, British Agent in Egypt, refused to allow diversion of water from the Nile, and the project was abandoned for lack of fresh water supply

Proposal of Sykes-Picot in 1916 for a British-French-Russian controlled Holy Land

British Mandate for Palestine, established in 1922. In 1917 the British Government had declared themselves in favour of a Jewish National Home in Palestine (Balfour Declaration, 2 November 1917)

Territory which the Zionist Organisation claimed as an integral part of Palestine

Mediterranean Sea

Damascus

Sidon

Tyre

Acre
Haifa

Port Said

el Arish

Gaza

Jerusalem

Amman

Beersheba

Suez Canal

Cairo

Nile

Maan

Gulf of Suez

△ Mount Sinai

Eilat

Gulf of Aqaba

Sharm el Sheikh

0   40
Miles

Red Sea

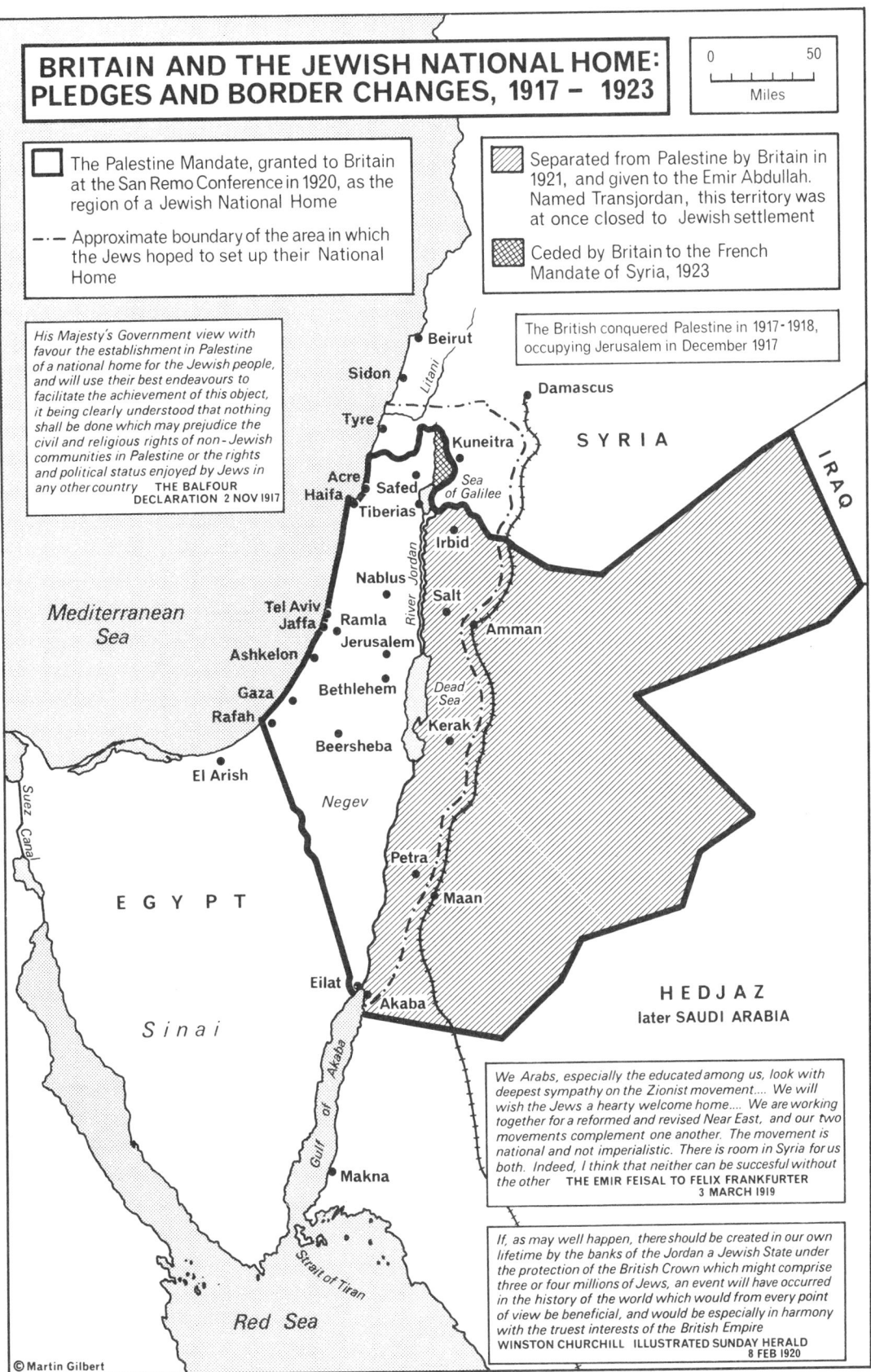

BRITAIN AND THE JEWISH NATIONAL HOME: PLEDGES AND BORDER CHANGES, 1917 – 1923

0   50
Miles

☐ The Palestine Mandate, granted to Britain at the San Remo Conference in 1920, as the region of a Jewish National Home

–·– Approximate boundary of the area in which the Jews hoped to set up their National Home

▨ Separated from Palestine by Britain in 1921, and given to the Emir Abdullah. Named Transjordan, this territory was at once closed to Jewish settlement

▨ Ceded by Britain to the French Mandate of Syria, 1923

His Majesty's Government view with favour the establishment in Palestine of a national home for the Jewish people, and will use their best endeavours to facilitate the achievement of this object, it being clearly understood that nothing shall be done which may prejudice the civil and religious rights of non-Jewish communities in Palestine or the rights and political status enjoyed by Jews in any other country **THE BALFOUR DECLARATION 2 NOV 1917**

The British conquered Palestine in 1917-1918, occupying Jerusalem in December 1917

Beirut

Sidon

Damascus

Tyre

Kuneitra   S Y R I A

Litani

Acre   Safed   *Sea of Galilee*

Haifa   Tiberias

Irbid

Mediterranean Sea

Nablus   Salt

Tel Aviv   *River Jordan*

Jaffa   Ramla   Amman

Jerusalem

Ashkelon

Gaza   Bethlehem   *Dead Sea*

Rafah   Kerak

Beersheba

El Arish

Negev

Suez Canal

E G Y P T   Petra

Maan

Eilat   H E D J A Z

Akaba   later SAUDI ARABIA

Sinai

Gulf of Akaba

We Arabs, especially the educated among us, look with deepest sympathy on the Zionist movement.... We will wish the Jews a hearty welcome home.... We are working together for a reformed and revised Near East, and our two movements complement one another. The movement is national and not imperialistic. There is room in Syria for us both. Indeed, I think that neither can be succesful without the other **THE EMIR FEISAL TO FELIX FRANKFURTER 3 MARCH 1919**

Makna

Strait of Tiran

Red Sea

If, as may well happen, there should be created in our own lifetime by the banks of the Jordan a Jewish State under the protection of the British Crown which might comprise three or four millions of Jews, an event will have occurred in the history of the world which would from every point of view be beneficial, and would be especially in harmony with the truest interests of the British Empire **WINSTON CHURCHILL ILLUSTRATED SUNDAY HERALD 8 FEB 1920**

© Martin Gilbert

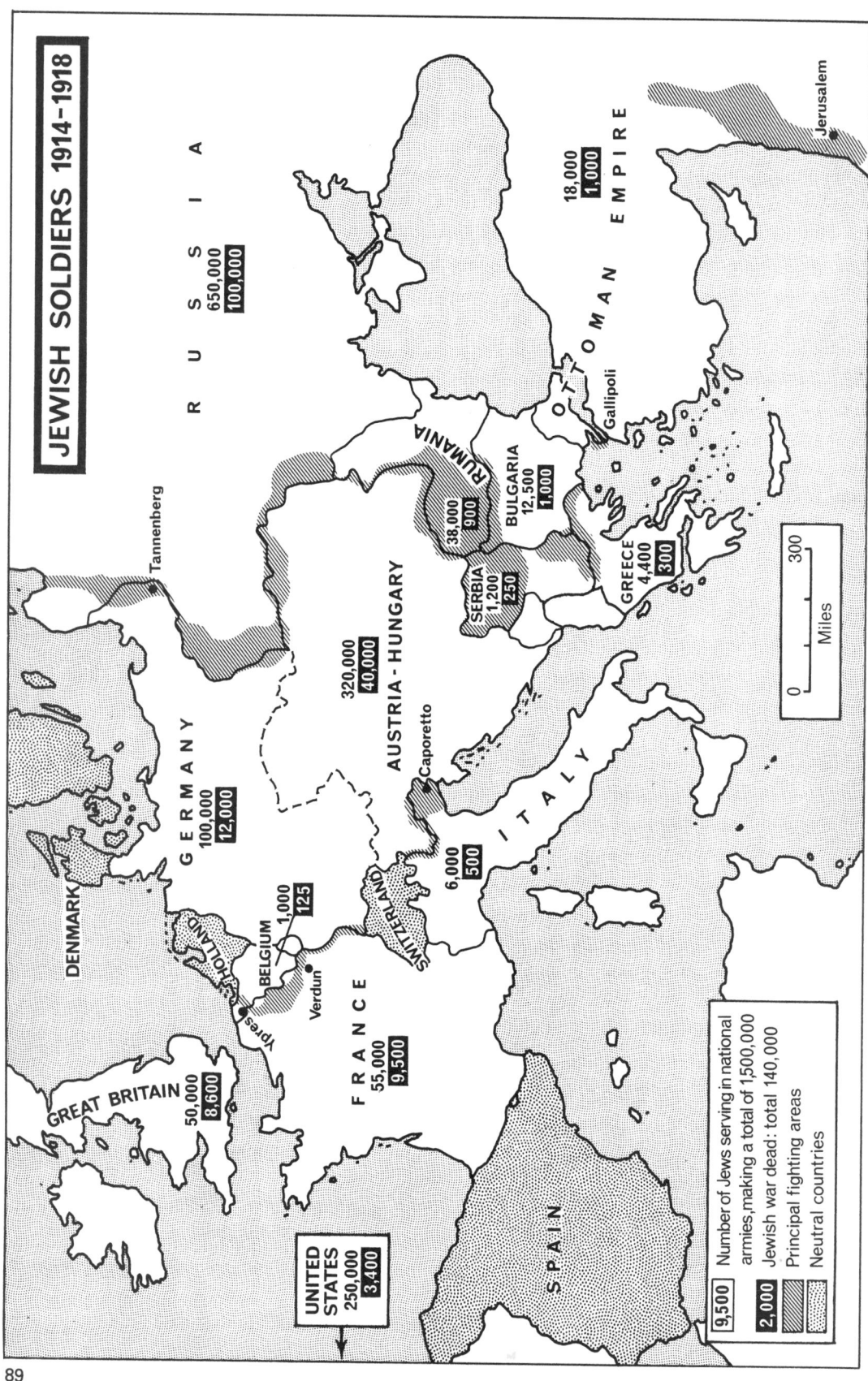

JEWISH SOLDIERS 1914–1918

RUSSIA
650,000
100,000

OTTOMAN EMPIRE
18,000
1,000

Jerusalem

Tannenberg

Gallipoli

RUMANIA
38,000
900

BULGARIA
12,500
1,000

SERBIA
1,200
250

GREECE
4,400
300

AUSTRIA-HUNGARY
320,000
40,000

Caporetto

GERMANY
100,000
12,000

ITALY
6,000
500

DENMARK

BELGIUM
1,000
125

POLAND

SWITZERLAND

Ypres

Verdun

FRANCE
55,000
9,500

GREAT BRITAIN
50,000
8,600

SPAIN

UNITED STATES
250,000
3,400

300
Miles
0

9,500 Number of Jews serving in national
armies, making a total of 1,500,000

2,000 Jewish war dead: total 140,000

Principal fighting areas

Neutral countries

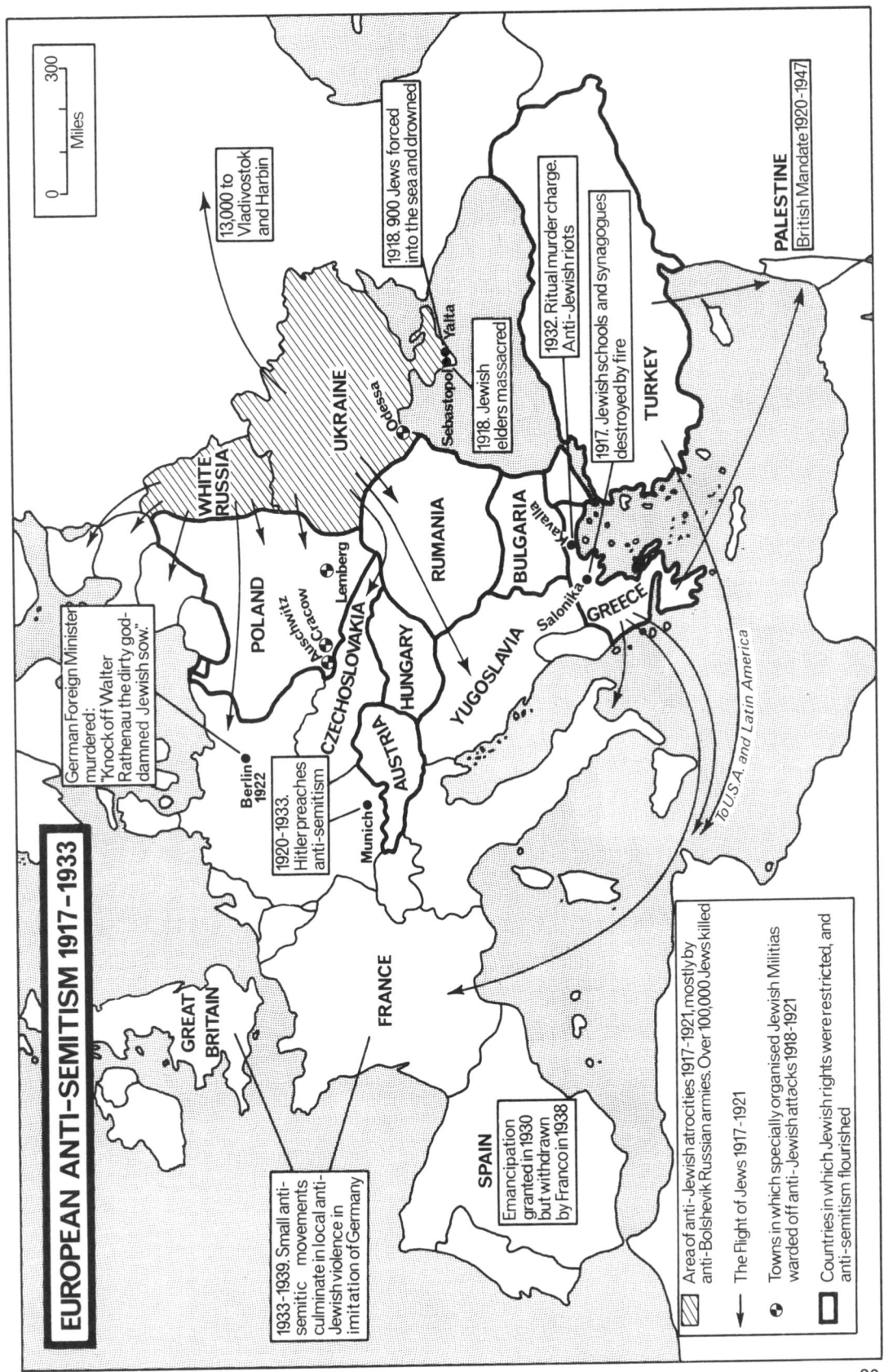

EUROPEAN ANTI-SEMITISM 1917-1933

300
Miles
0

13,000 to
Vladivostok
and Harbin

1918. 900 Jews forced
into the sea and drowned

1932. Ritual murder charge.
Anti-Jewish riots

PALESTINE
British Mandate 1920-1947

1918. Jewish
elders massacred

1917. Jewish schools and synagogues
destroyed by fire

WHITE
RUSSIA

UKRAINE

Odessa

Sebastopol Yalta

RUMANIA

TURKEY

BULGARIA

Lemberg

POLAND

Kavalla

German Foreign Minister
murdered:
"Knock off Walter
Rathenau the dirty god-
damned Jewish sow."

Cracow

Auschwitz

CZECHOSLOVAKIA

HUNGARY

YUGOSLAVIA

Salonika

GREECE

To U.S.A. and Latin America

Berlin
1922

AUSTRIA

1920-1933.
Hitler preaches
anti-semitism

Munich

GREAT
BRITAIN

FRANCE

1933-1939. Small anti-
semitic movements
culminate in local anti-
Jewish violence in
imitation of Germany

SPAIN

Emancipation
granted in 1930
but withdrawn
by Franco in 1938

Area of anti-Jewish atrocities 1917-1921, mostly by
anti-Bolshevik Russian armies. Over 100,000 Jews killed

The Flight of Jews 1917-1921

Towns in which specially organised Jewish Militias
warded off anti-Jewish attacks 1918-1921

Countries in which Jewish rights were restricted, and
anti-semitism flourished

90

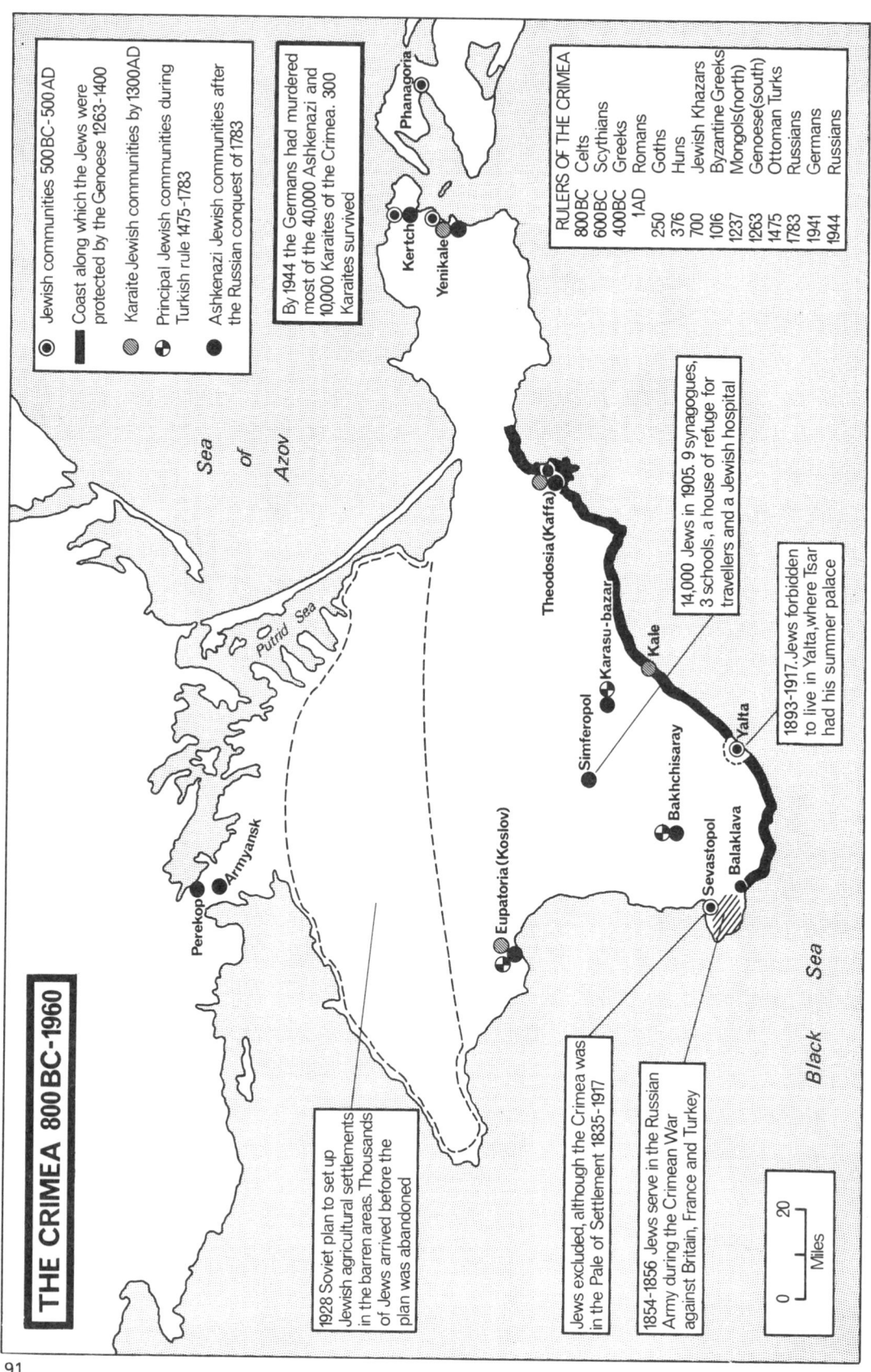

THE CRIMEA 800BC-1960

Jewish communities 500BC-500AD

Coast along which the Jews were protected by the Genoese 1263-1400

Karaite Jewish communities by 1300AD

Principal Jewish communities during Turkish rule 1475-1783

Ashkenazi Jewish communities after the Russian conquest of 1783

By 1944 the Germans had murdered most of the 40,000 Ashkenazi and 10,000 Karaites of the Crimea. 300 Karaites survived

RULERS OF THE CRIMEA

800BC	Celts
600BC	Scythians
400BC	Greeks
1AD	Romans
250	Goths
376	Huns
700	Jewish Khazars
1016	Byzantine Greeks
1237	Mongols(north)
1263	Genoese(south)
1475	Ottoman Turks
1783	Russians
1941	Germans
1944	Russians

Phanagoria

Kertch

Yenikale

Sea of Azov

Putrid Sea

Theodosia (Kaffa)

Karasu-bazar

Kale

Simferopol

Bakhchisaray

Yalta

14,000 Jews in 1905. 9 synagogues, 3 schools, a house of refuge for travellers and a Jewish hospital

1893-1917, Jews forbidden to live in Yalta, where Tsar had his summer palace

Armyansk

Perekop

Eupatoria (Koslov)

Sevastopol

Balaklava

1928 Soviet plan to set up Jewish agricultural settlements in the barren areas. Thousands of Jews arrived before the plan was abandoned

Jews excluded, although the Crimea was in the Pale of Settlement 1835-1917

1854-1856 Jews serve in the Russian Army during the Crimean War against Britain, France and Turkey

Black Sea

0 20
Miles

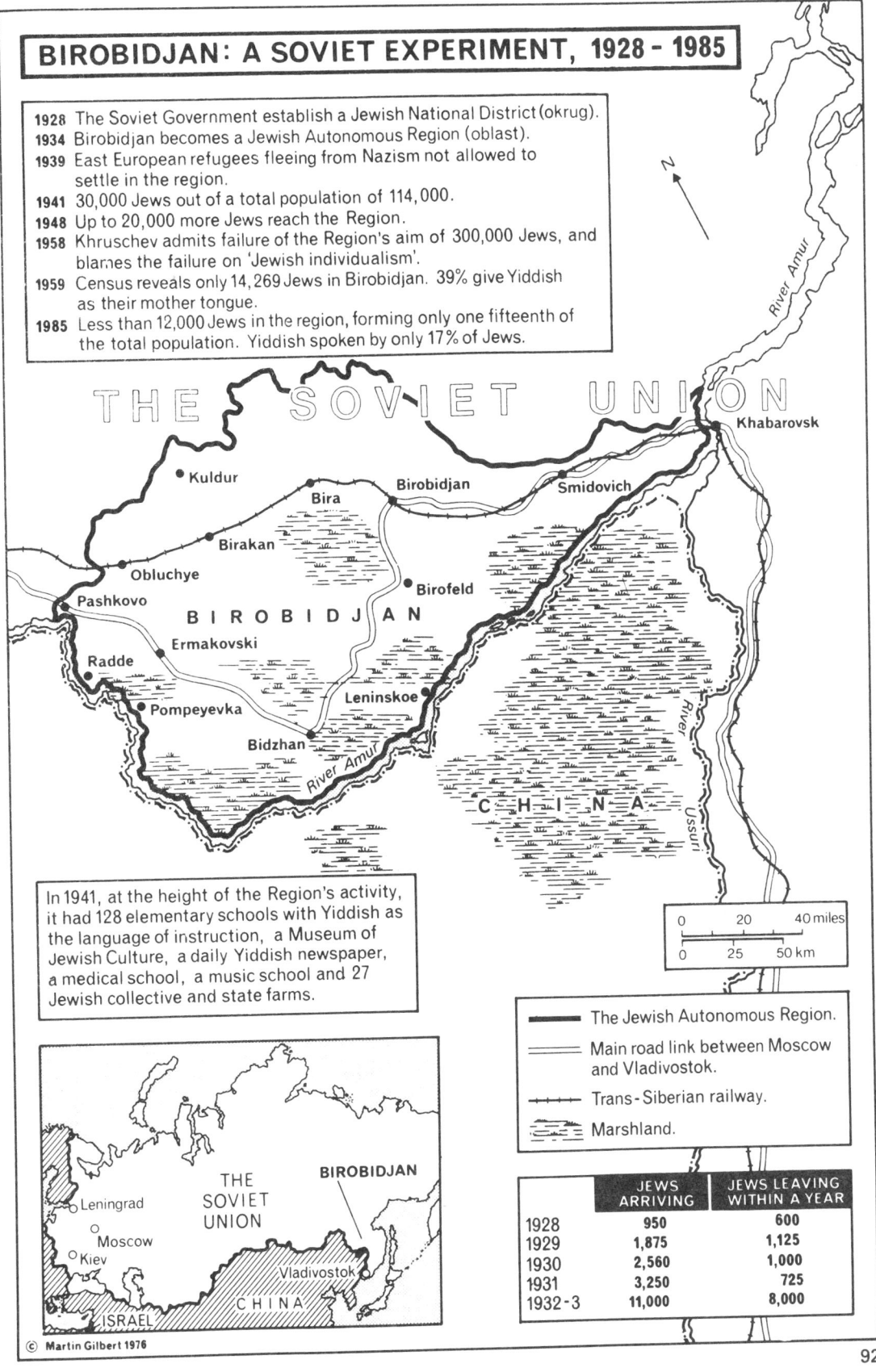

BIROBIDJAN: A SOVIET EXPERIMENT, 1928 - 1985

1928 The Soviet Government establish a Jewish National District (okrug).
1934 Birobidjan becomes a Jewish Autonomous Region (oblast).
1939 East European refugees fleeing from Nazism not allowed to settle in the region.
1941 30,000 Jews out of a total population of 114,000.
1948 Up to 20,000 more Jews reach the Region.
1958 Khruschev admits failure of the Region's aim of 300,000 Jews, and blames the failure on 'Jewish individualism'.
1959 Census reveals only 14,269 Jews in Birobidjan. 39% give Yiddish as their mother tongue.
1985 Less than 12,000 Jews in the region, forming only one fifteenth of the total population. Yiddish spoken by only 17% of Jews.

THE SOVIET UNION

Kuldur

Bira
Birobidjan
Smidovich
Khabarovsk

Birakan

Obluchye
Birofeld

Pashkovo

B I R O B I D J A N

Ermakovski

Radde

Leninskoe

Pompeyevka

Bidzhan

River Amur

River Amur

River Ussuri

C H I N A

In 1941, at the height of the Region's activity, it had 128 elementary schools with Yiddish as the language of instruction, a Museum of Jewish Culture, a daily Yiddish newspaper, a medical school, a music school and 27 Jewish collective and state farms.

0	20	40 miles
0	25	50 km

—— The Jewish Autonomous Region.

═══ Main road link between Moscow and Vladivostok.

+++ Trans-Siberian railway.

Marshland.

THE SOVIET UNION

BIROBIDJAN

Leningrad
Moscow
Kiev
Vladivostok
CHINA
ISRAEL

© Martin Gilbert 1976

	JEWS ARRIVING	JEWS LEAVING WITHIN A YEAR
1928	950	600
1929	1,875	1,125
1930	2,560	1,000
1931	3,250	725
1932-3	11,000	8,000

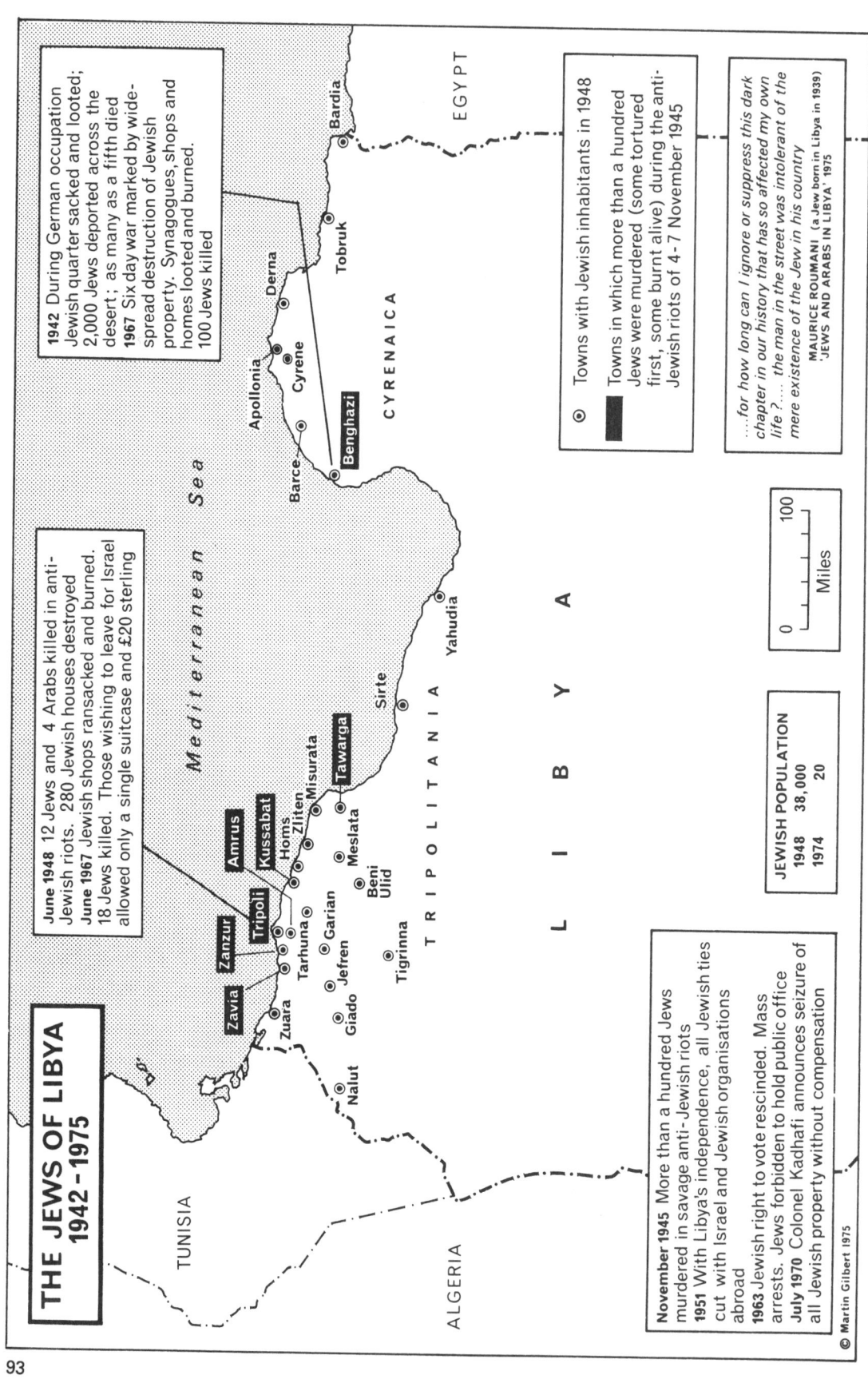

THE JEWS OF LIBYA 1942–1975

1942 During German occupation Jewish quarter sacked and looted; 2,000 Jews deported across the desert ; as many as a fifth died **1967** Six day war marked by widespread destruction of Jewish property. Synagogues, shops and homes looted and burned. 100 Jews killed

June 1948 12 Jews and 4 Arabs killed in anti-Jewish riots. 280 Jewish houses destroyed **June 1967** Jewish shops ransacked and burned. 18 Jews killed. Those wishing to leave for Israel allowed only a single suitcase and £20 sterling

November 1945 More than a hundred Jews murdered in savage anti-Jewish riots **1951** With Libya's independence, all Jewish ties cut with Israel and Jewish organisations abroad **1963** Jewish right to vote rescinded. Mass arrests. Jews forbidden to hold public office **July 1970** Colonel Kadhafi announces seizure of all Jewish property without compensation

◉ Towns with Jewish inhabitants in 1948

▰ Towns in which more than a hundred Jews were murdered (some tortured first, some burnt alive) during the anti-Jewish riots of 4-7 November 1945

....for how long can I ignore or suppress this dark chapter in our history that has so affected my own life ?.... the man in the street was intolerant of the mere existence of the Jew in his country
MAURICE ROUMANI (a Jew born in Libya in 1939) 'JEWS AND ARABS IN LIBYA' 1975

JEWISH POPULATION	
1948	38,000
1974	20

0 ⊢⊢⊢⊢⊢⊢⊢⊢ 100
Miles

EGYPT

Bardia

Tobruk

Derna

Apollonia

Cyrene

Barce

Benghazi

CYRENAICA

Mediterranean Sea

Yahudia

Sirte

Tawarga

Misurata

Zliten

Homs

Meslata

Beni Ulid

Kussabat

Amrus

Zanzur

Tripoli

Tarhuna

Garian

Jefren

Tigrinna

Zavia

Zuara

Giado

Nalut

T R I P O L I T A N I A

L I B Y A

TUNISIA

ALGERIA

© Martin Gilbert 1975

93

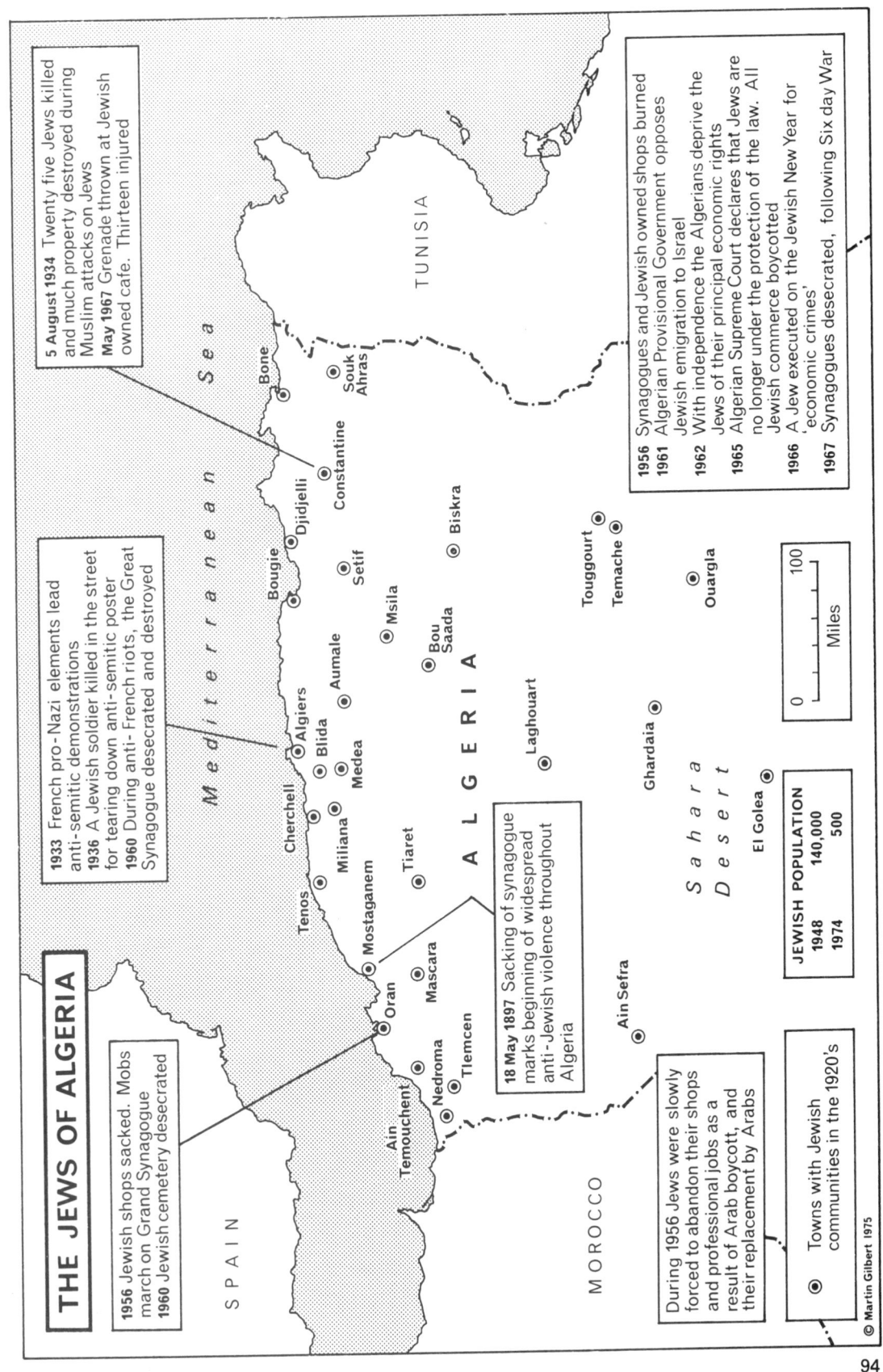

THE JEWS OF ALGERIA

1956 Jewish shops sacked. Mobs march on Grand Synagogue
1960 Jewish cemetery desecrated

5 August 1934 Twenty five Jews killed and much property destroyed during Muslim attacks on Jews
May 1967 Grenade thrown at Jewish owned cafe. Thirteen injured

1933 French pro-Nazi elements lead anti-semitic demonstrations
1936 A Jewish soldier killed in the street for tearing down anti-semitic poster
1960 During anti-French riots, the Great Synagogue desecrated and destroyed

1956 Synagogues and Jewish owned shops burned
1961 Algerian Provisional Government opposes Jewish emigration to Israel
1962 With independence the Algerians deprive the Jews of their principal economic rights
1965 Algerian Supreme Court declares that Jews are no longer under the protection of the law. All Jewish commerce boycotted
1966 A Jew executed on the Jewish New Year for 'economic crimes'
1967 Synagogues desecrated, following Six day War

18 May 1897 Sacking of synagogue marks beginning of widespread anti-Jewish violence throughout Algeria

During 1956 Jews were slowly forced to abandon their shops and professional jobs as a result of Arab boycott, and their replacement by Arabs

JEWISH POPULATION	
1948	140,000
1974	500

⊙   Towns with Jewish communities in the 1920's

S P A I N

Mediterranean Sea

T U N I S I A

M O R O C C O

S a h a r a   D e s e r t

A L G E R I A

Bone
Souk Ahras
Constantine
Djidjelli
Bougie
Setif
Biskra
Msila
Bou Saada
Aumale
Medea
Blida
Algiers
Cherchell
Miliana
Tiaret
Tenos
Mostaganem
Mascara
Oran
Tlemcen
Nedroma
Ain Temouchent
Ain Sefra
Laghouart
Ghardaia
El Golea
Ouargla
Touggourt
Temache

0   100
|——————|
Miles

© Martin Gilbert 1975

94

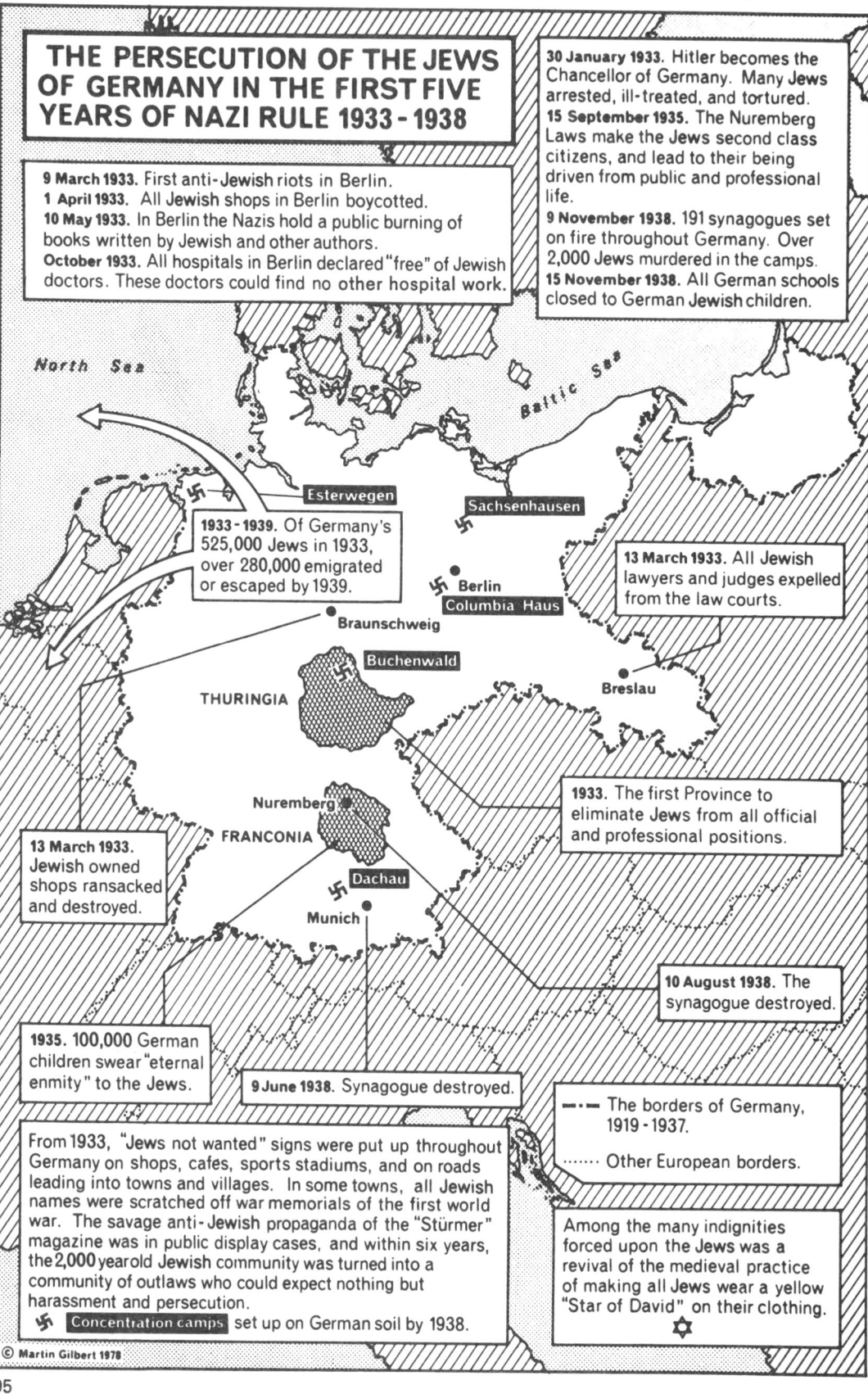

THE PERSECUTION OF THE JEWS OF GERMANY IN THE FIRST FIVE YEARS OF NAZI RULE 1933-1938

30 January 1933. Hitler becomes the Chancellor of Germany. Many Jews arrested, ill-treated, and tortured.
15 September 1935. The Nuremberg Laws make the Jews second class citizens, and lead to their being driven from public and professional life.
9 November 1938. 191 synagogues set on fire throughout Germany. Over 2,000 Jews murdered in the camps.
15 November 1938. All German schools closed to German Jewish children.

9 March 1933. First anti-Jewish riots in Berlin.
1 April 1933. All Jewish shops in Berlin boycotted.
10 May 1933. In Berlin the Nazis hold a public burning of books written by Jewish and other authors.
October 1933. All hospitals in Berlin declared "free" of Jewish doctors. These doctors could find no other hospital work.

North Sea

Baltic Sea

Esterwegen

Sachsenhausen

1933-1939. Of Germany's 525,000 Jews in 1933, over 280,000 emigrated or escaped by 1939.

● Berlin
Columbia Haus

13 March 1933. All Jewish lawyers and judges expelled from the law courts.

● Braunschweig

Buchenwald

THURINGIA

● Breslau

Nuremberg ●
FRANCONIA

1933. The first Province to eliminate Jews from all official and professional positions.

13 March 1933. Jewish owned shops ransacked and destroyed.

Dachau

● Munich

10 August 1938. The synagogue destroyed.

1935. 100,000 German children swear "eternal enmity" to the Jews.

9 June 1938. Synagogue destroyed.

—·— The borders of Germany, 1919-1937.

······· Other European borders.

From 1933, "Jews not wanted" signs were put up throughout Germany on shops, cafes, sports stadiums, and on roads leading into towns and villages. In some towns, all Jewish names were scratched off war memorials of the first world war. The savage anti-Jewish propaganda of the "Stürmer" magazine was in public display cases, and within six years, the 2,000 year old Jewish community was turned into a community of outlaws who could expect nothing but harassment and persecution.

Concentration camps set up on German soil by 1938.

Among the many indignities forced upon the Jews was a revival of the medieval practice of making all Jews wear a yellow "Star of David" on their clothing.
✡

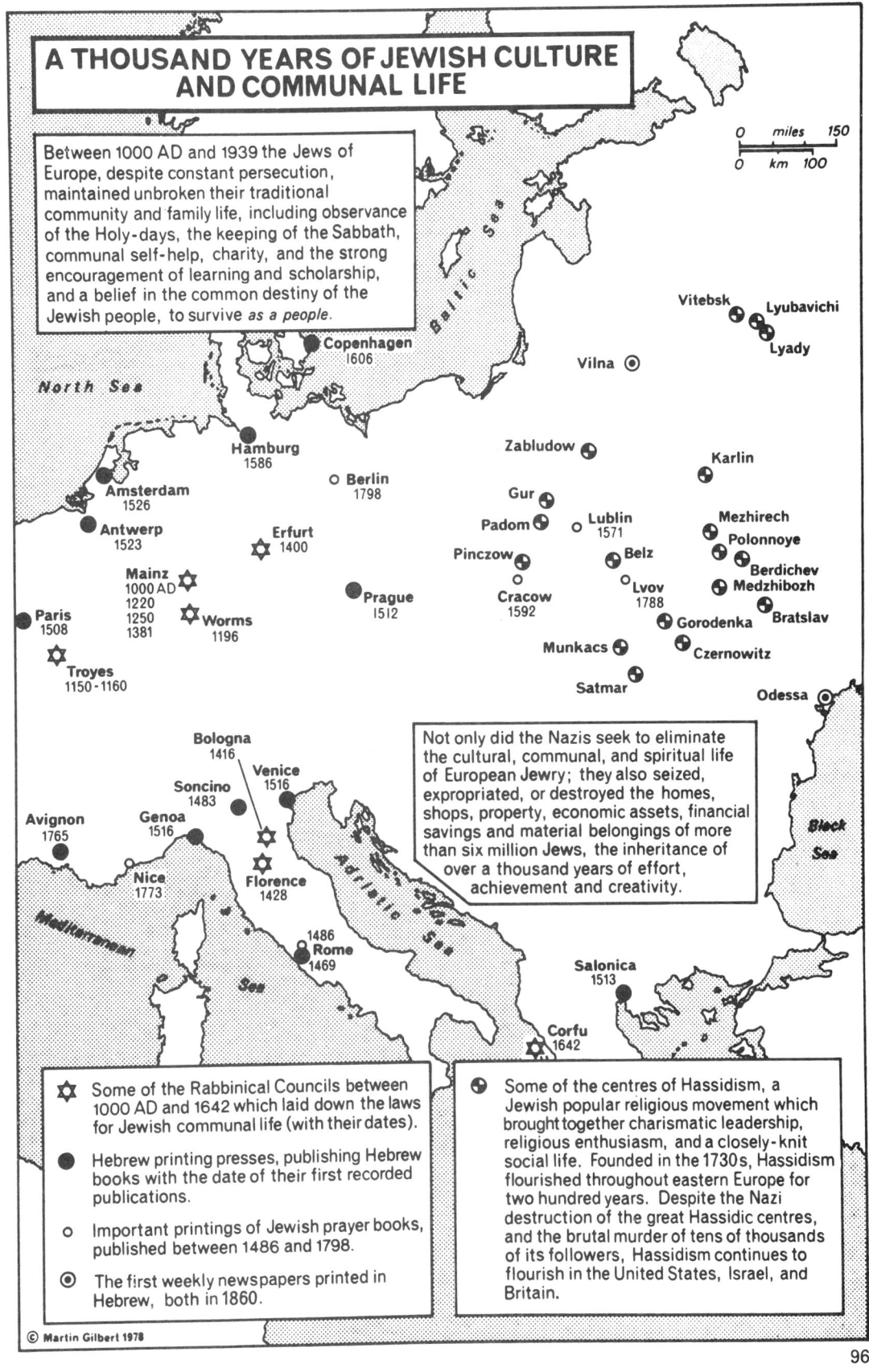

A THOUSAND YEARS OF JEWISH CULTURE AND COMMUNAL LIFE

Between 1000 AD and 1939 the Jews of Europe, despite constant persecution, maintained unbroken their traditional community and family life, including observance of the Holy-days, the keeping of the Sabbath, communal self-help, charity, and the strong encouragement of learning and scholarship, and a belief in the common destiny of the Jewish people, to survive *as a people*.

Not only did the Nazis seek to eliminate the cultural, communal, and spiritual life of European Jewry; they also seized, expropriated, or destroyed the homes, shops, property, economic assets, financial savings and material belongings of more than six million Jews, the inheritance of over a thousand years of effort, achievement and creativity.

North Sea
Baltic Sea
Mediterranean Sea
Adriatic Sea
Black Sea

miles 150
km 100

Vitebsk
Lyubavichi
Lyady
Vilna
Copenhagen 1606
Zabludow
Karlin
Hamburg 1586
Berlin 1798
Gur
Mezhirech
Amsterdam 1526
Padom
Lublin 1571
Polonnoye
Antwerp 1523
Erfurt 1400
Pinczow
Belz
Berdichev
Mainz 1000 AD 1220 1250 1381
Prague 1512
Cracow 1592
Lvov 1788
Medzhibozh
Paris 1508
Worms 1196
Gorodenka
Bratslav
Troyes 1150-1160
Munkacs
Czernowitz
Satmar
Odessa

Bologna 1416
Soncino 1483
Venice 1516
Avignon 1765
Genoa 1516
Nice 1773
Florence 1428
1486 Rome 1469
Salonica 1513
Corfu 1642

✡ Some of the Rabbinical Councils between 1000 AD and 1642 which laid down the laws for Jewish communal life (with their dates).

● Hebrew printing presses, publishing Hebrew books with the date of their first recorded publications.

○ Important printings of Jewish prayer books, published between 1486 and 1798.

◉ The first weekly newspapers printed in Hebrew, both in 1860.

✠ Some of the centres of Hassidism, a Jewish popular religious movement which brought together charismatic leadership, religious enthusiasm, and a closely-knit social life. Founded in the 1730s, Hassidism flourished throughout eastern Europe for two hundred years. Despite the Nazi destruction of the great Hassidic centres, and the brutal murder of tens of thousands of its followers, Hassidism continues to flourish in the United States, Israel, and Britain.

© Martin Gilbert 1978

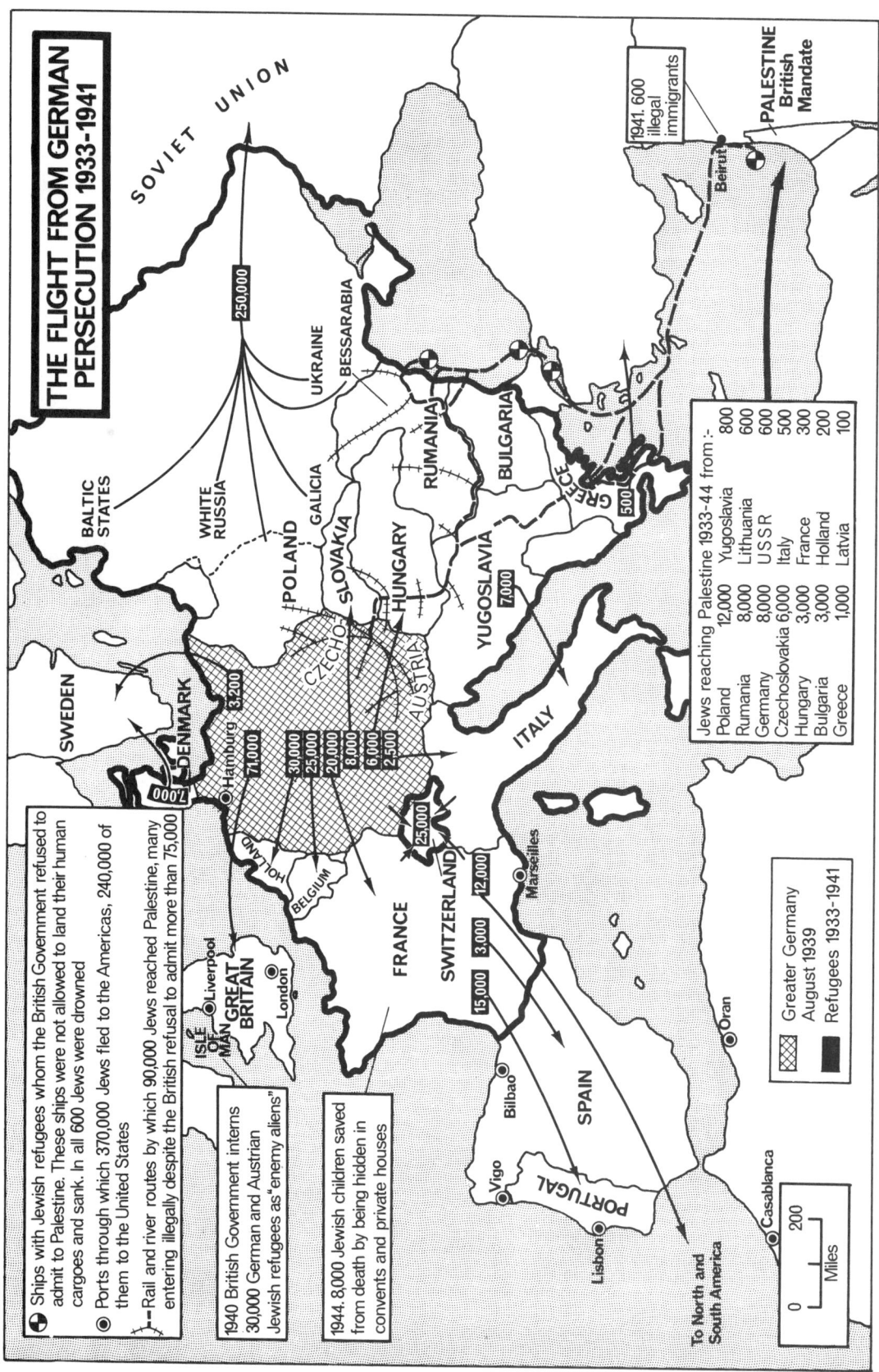

THE FLIGHT FROM GERMAN PERSECUTION 1933-1941

SOVIET UNION

250,000

BALTIC STATES

WHITE RUSSIA

UKRAINE

BESSARABIA

POLAND

GALICIA

SLOVAKIA

RUMANIA

HUNGARY

BULGARIA

YUGOSLAVIA

GREECE

500

7,000

SWEDEN

DENMARK

7,000

Hamburg 3,200

CZECHO

AUSTRIA

ITALY

71,000
30,000
25,000
20,000
8,000
6,000
2,500

HOLLAND

BELGIUM

25,000

FRANCE

SWITZERLAND

12,000

3,000

15,000

Marseilles

ISLE OF MAN

Liverpool

GREAT BRITAIN

London

SPAIN

Bilbao

Vigo

PORTUGAL

Lisbon

Oran

Casablanca

PALESTINE
British Mandate

1941. 600 illegal immigrants

Beirut

Jews reaching Palestine 1933-44 from:-

Poland	12,000	Yugoslavia	800
Rumania	8,000	Lithuania	600
Germany	8,000	USSR	600
Czechoslovakia	6,000	Italy	500
Hungary	3,000	France	300
Bulgaria	3,000	Holland	200
Greece	1,000	Latvia	100

Greater Germany
August 1939

Refugees 1933-1941

Ships with Jewish refugees whom the British Government refused to admit to Palestine. These ships were not allowed to land their human cargoes and sank. In all 600 Jews were drowned

Ports through which 370,000 Jews fled to the Americas, 240,000 of them to the United States

Rail and river routes by which 90,000 Jews reached Palestine, many entering illegally despite the British refusal to admit more than 75,000

1940 British Government interns 30,000 German and Austrian Jewish refugees as "enemy aliens"

1944. 8,000 Jewish children saved from death by being hidden in convents and private houses

To North and South America

0   200
Miles

THE CONCENTRATION CAMPS

Between 1939 and 1945, six million unarmed and innocent Jewish civilians - men, women, children and babies- were murdered in Nazi-controlled Europe, as part of a deliberate policy to destroy all traces of Jewish life and culture. As many as two million of these were killed in their own towns and villages, some confined in ghettoes where death by slow starvation was a deliberate Nazi policy, others taken to be shot at mass-murder sites near where they lived. The remaining four million Jews were forced from their homes and taken by train to distant concentration camps, where they were murdered by being worked to death, starved to death, beaten to death, shot, or gassed.

Vaivara

Klooga
ESTONIA

LATVIA

LITHUANIA

North Sea

USSR

Stutthof

Neuengamme

Ravensbrück

Chelmno

Treblinka

Bergen-Belsen

Sachsenhausen

POLAND

Sobibor

Mittelbau Dora

Gross Rosen

Auschwitz

Maidanek

Buchenwald

GERMANY

Belzec

Flossenberg

Plaszow

Natzweiler

CZECHOSLOVAKIA

FRANCE

Dachau

Mauthausen

AUSTRIA

HUNGARY

RUMANIA

Gospič

Jasenovac

YUGOSLAVIA

Sajmište

Among the hundreds of thousands of *non*-Jews sent by the Nazis to concentration camps were anti-Nazis, Jehovah's Witnesses, homosexuals, the mentally ill, and the chronically sick. In addition, more than 250,000 Gypsies were murdered, in a Nazi attempt to eliminate Gypsies as well as Jews from the map of Europe.

ITALY

Adriatic Sea

Auschwitz concentration camp in which more than 2 *million* people were murdered between 1941 and 1944, including Jews, Gypsies, and Soviet prisoners-of-war.

Camps set up solely for the murder of Jews.

Other camps in which Jews and non-Jews were put to forced labour, starved, tortured, and murdered in conditions of the worst imaginable cruelty. Most of these camps had "satellite" labour camps nearby.

In many of the camps shown here so-called "medical" experiments were carried out, without anaesthetics, solely to satisfy the curiosity and sadism of the doctors. Hundreds of otherwise healthy "patients" were tortured and murdered during these experiments.

0 — 100 miles

0 — 100 km

© Martin Gilbert 1978

98

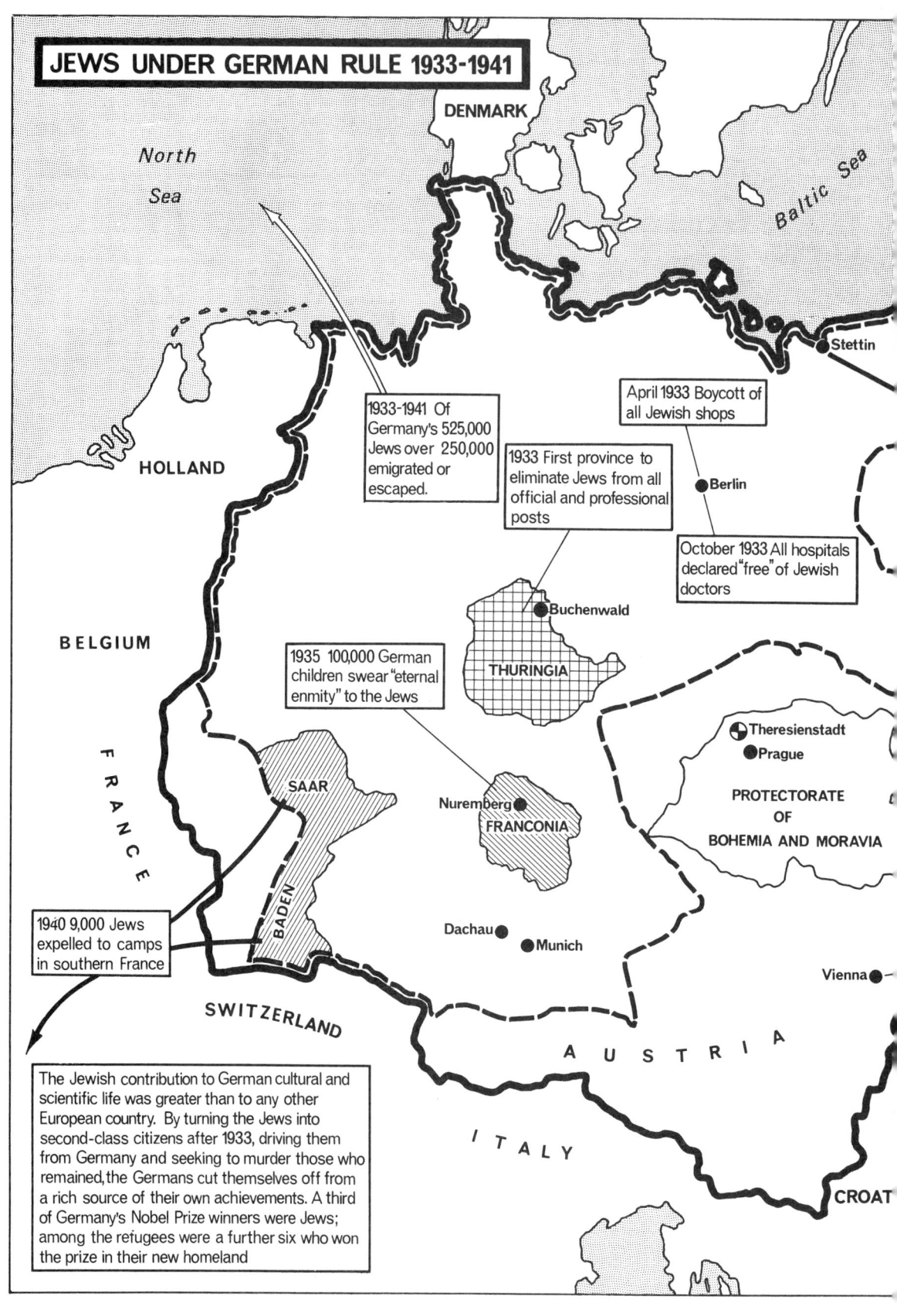

JEWS UNDER GERMAN RULE 1933-1941

DENMARK

North
Sea

Baltic Sea

Stettin

1933-1941 Of
Germany's 525,000
Jews over 250,000
emigrated or
escaped.

April 1933 Boycott of
all Jewish shops

1933 First province to
eliminate Jews from all
official and professional
posts

Berlin

October 1933 All hospitals
declared "free" of Jewish
doctors

HOLLAND

BELGIUM

Buchenwald

1935 100,000 German
children swear "eternal
enmity" to the Jews

THURINGIA

Theresienstadt
Prague

PROTECTORATE
OF
BOHEMIA AND MORAVIA

F
R
A
N
C
E

SAAR

Nuremberg
FRANCONIA

B
A
D
E
N

1940 9,000 Jews
expelled to camps
in southern France

Dachau
Munich

Vienna

SWITZERLAND

A U S T R I A

The Jewish contribution to German cultural and
scientific life was greater than to any other
European country. By turning the Jews into
second-class citizens after 1933, driving them
from Germany and seeking to murder those who
remained, the Germans cut themselves off from
a rich source of their own achievements. A third
of Germany's Nobel Prize winners were Jews;
among the refugees were a further six who won
the prize in their new homeland

I T A L Y

CROAT

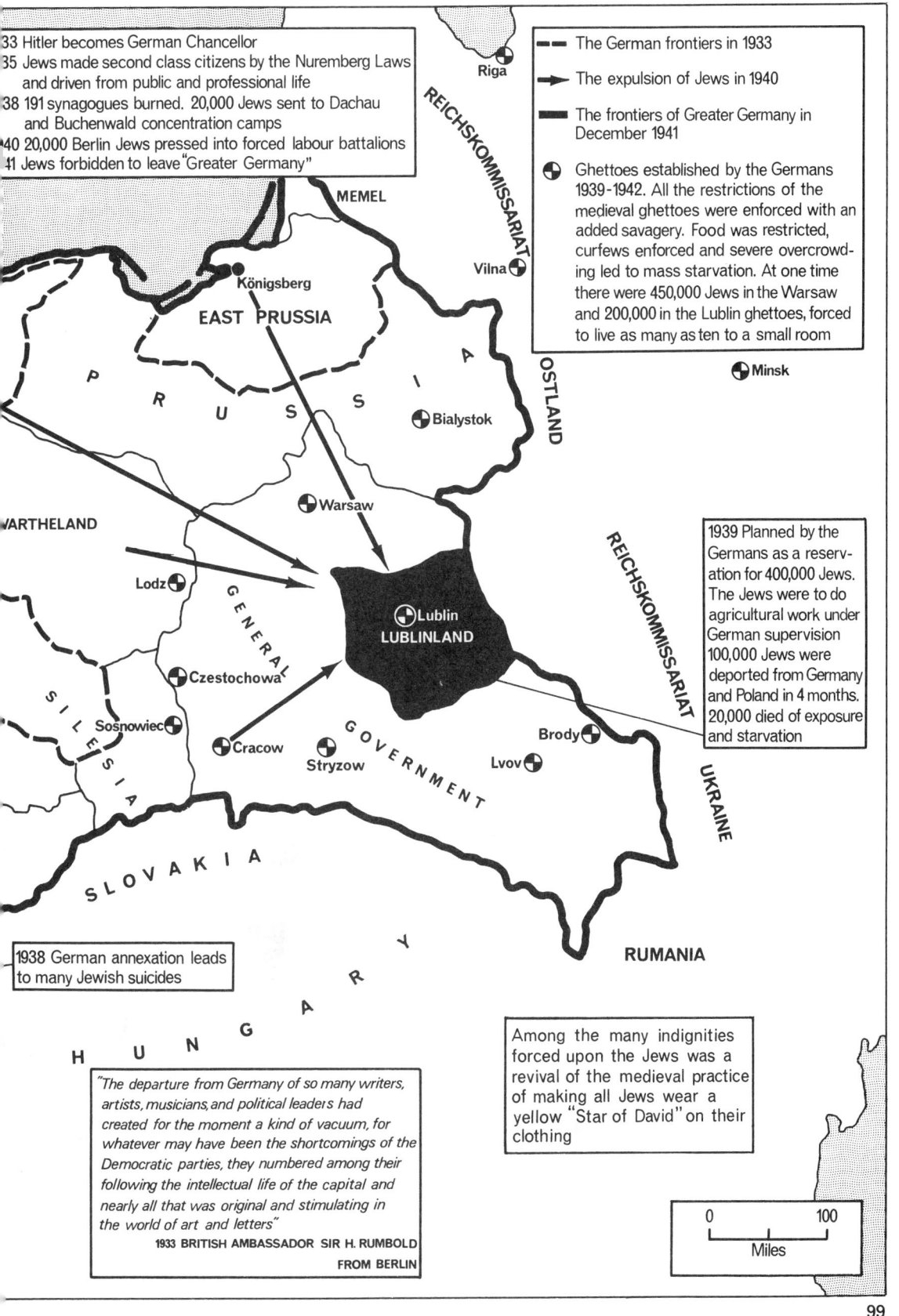

33 Hitler becomes German Chancellor

35 Jews made second class citizens by the Nuremberg Laws
   and driven from public and professional life

38 191 synagogues burned. 20,000 Jews sent to Dachau
   and Buchenwald concentration camps

40 20,000 Berlin Jews pressed into forced labour battalions

41 Jews forbidden to leave "Greater Germany"

- - - The German frontiers in 1933

→ The expulsion of Jews in 1940

▬▬ The frontiers of Greater Germany in
December 1941

⊕ Ghettoes established by the Germans
1939-1942. All the restrictions of the
medieval ghettoes were enforced with an
added savagery. Food was restricted,
curfews enforced and severe overcrowd-
ing led to mass starvation. At one time
there were 450,000 Jews in the Warsaw
and 200,000 in the Lublin ghettoes, forced
to live as many as ten to a small room

Riga

REICHSKOMMISSARIAT

MEMEL

OSTLAND

Vilna ⊕

Königsberg

EAST PRUSSIA

P R U S S I A

⊕ Bialystok

⊕ Minsk

⊕ Warsaw

WARTHELAND

REICHSKOMMISSARIAT

Lodz ⊕

G E N E R A L

⊕ Lublin
LUBLINLAND

1939 Planned by the
Germans as a reserv-
ation for 400,000 Jews.
The Jews were to do
agricultural work under
German supervision
100,000 Jews were
deported from Germany
and Poland in 4 months.
20,000 died of exposure
and starvation

S I L E S I A

⊕ Czestochowa

⊕ Sosnowiec

G O V E R N M E N T

Brody ⊕

⊕ Cracow
⊕ Stryzow

Lvov ⊕

UKRAINE

S L O V A K I A

RUMANIA

1938 German annexation leads
to many Jewish suicides

H U N G A R Y

Among the many indignities
forced upon the Jews was a
revival of the medieval practice
of making all Jews wear a
yellow "Star of David" on their
clothing

"The departure from Germany of so many writers,
artists, musicians, and political leaders had
created for the moment a kind of vacuum, for
whatever may have been the shortcomings of the
Democratic parties, they numbered among their
following the intellectual life of the capital and
nearly all that was original and stimulating in
the world of art and letters"
1933 BRITISH AMBASSADOR SIR H. RUMBOLD
FROM BERLIN

0   100
Miles

THE SEARCH FOR SAFETY 1933-1945

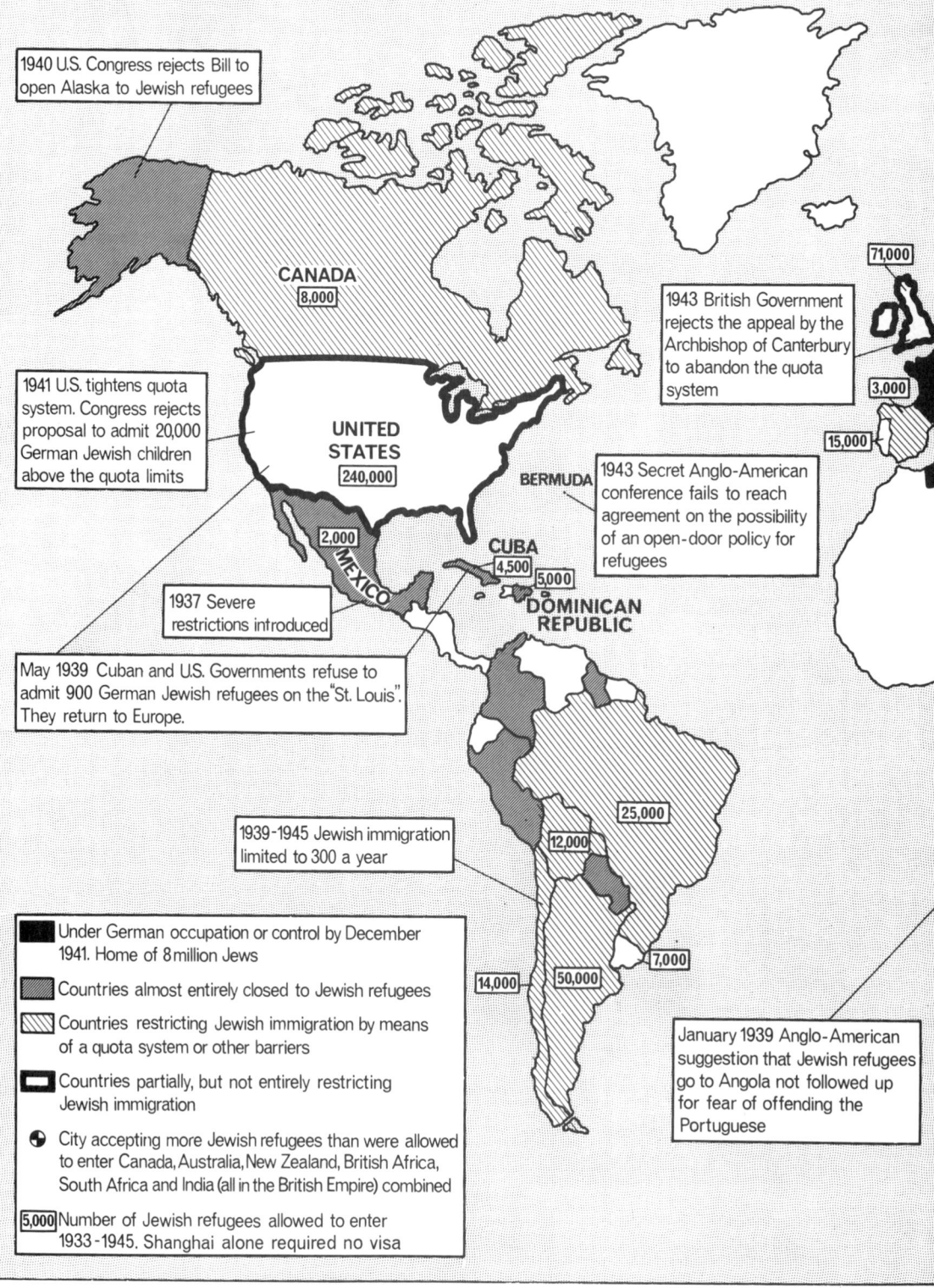

1940 U.S. Congress rejects Bill to open Alaska to Jewish refugees

1941 U.S. tightens quota system. Congress rejects proposal to admit 20,000 German Jewish children above the quota limits

1937 Severe restrictions introduced

May 1939 Cuban and U.S. Governments refuse to admit 900 German Jewish refugees on the "St. Louis". They return to Europe.

1939-1945 Jewish immigration limited to 300 a year

1943 British Government rejects the appeal by the Archbishop of Canterbury to abandon the quota system

1943 Secret Anglo-American conference fails to reach agreement on the possibility of an open-door policy for refugees

January 1939 Anglo-American suggestion that Jewish refugees go to Angola not followed up for fear of offending the Portuguese

CANADA
8,000

UNITED STATES
240,000

BERMUDA

MEXICO
2,000

CUBA
4,500

5,000
DOMINICAN REPUBLIC

71,000

3,000

15,000

25,000

12,000

14,000

50,000

7,000

■ Under German occupation or control by December 1941. Home of 8 million Jews

▨ Countries almost entirely closed to Jewish refugees

▨ Countries restricting Jewish immigration by means of a quota system or other barriers

▭ Countries partially, but not entirely restricting Jewish immigration

✪ City accepting more Jewish refugees than were allowed to enter Canada, Australia, New Zealand, British Africa, South Africa and India (all in the British Empire) combined

5,000 Number of Jewish refugees allowed to enter 1933-1945. Shanghai alone required no visa

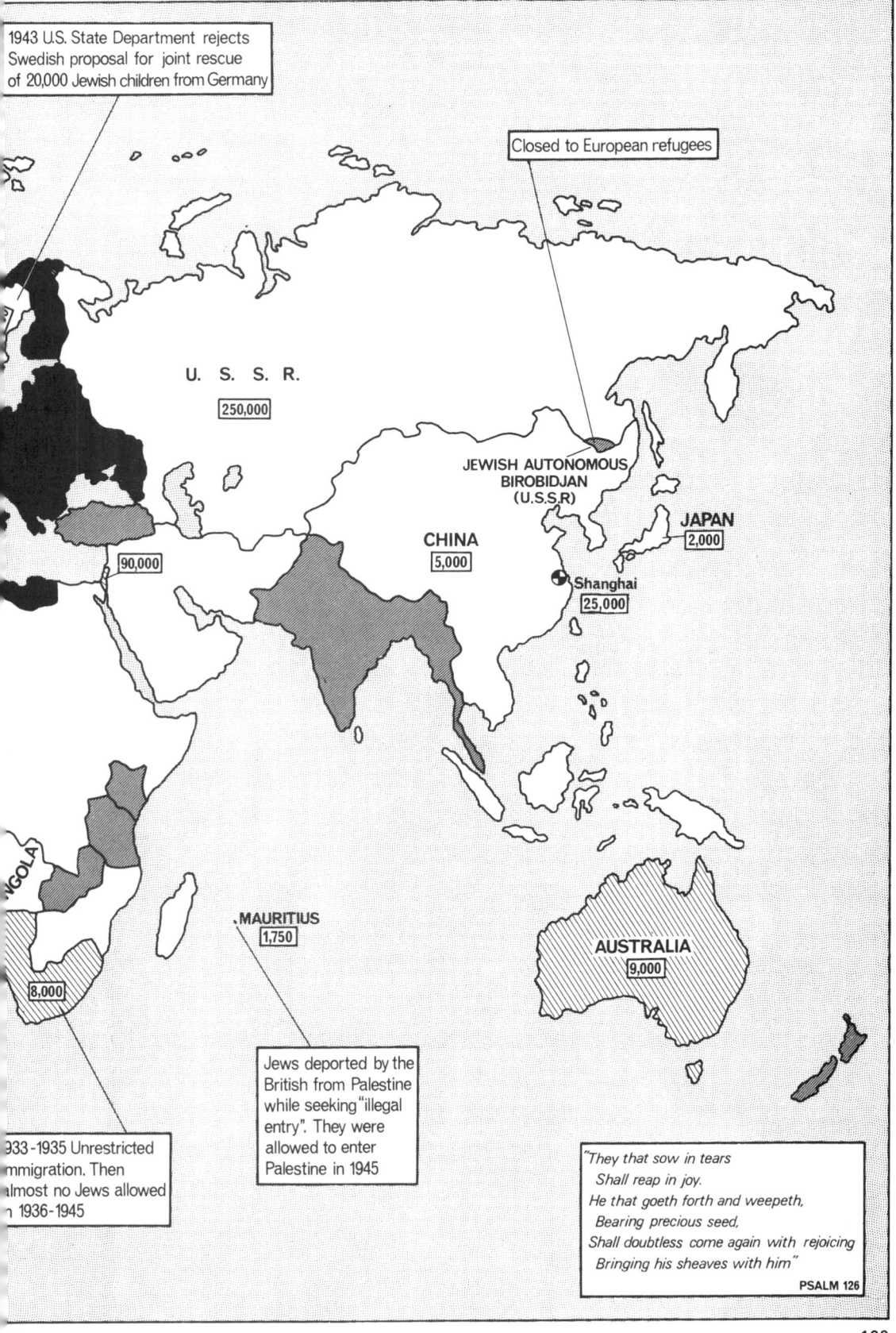

1943 U.S. State Department rejects Swedish proposal for joint rescue of 20,000 Jewish children from Germany

Closed to European refugees

U. S. S. R.
250,000

JEWISH AUTONOMOUS BIROBIDJAN (U.S.S.R)

JAPAN
2,000

CHINA
5,000

Shanghai
25,000

90,000

NGOLA

8,000

.MAURITIUS
1,750

AUSTRALIA
9,000

Jews deported by the British from Palestine while seeking "illegal entry". They were allowed to enter Palestine in 1945

933-1935 Unrestricted mmigration. Then almost no Jews allowed n 1936-1945

"They that sow in tears
Shall reap in joy.
He that goeth forth and weepeth,
Bearing precious seed,
Shall doubtless come again with rejoicing
Bringing his sheaves with him"
PSALM 126

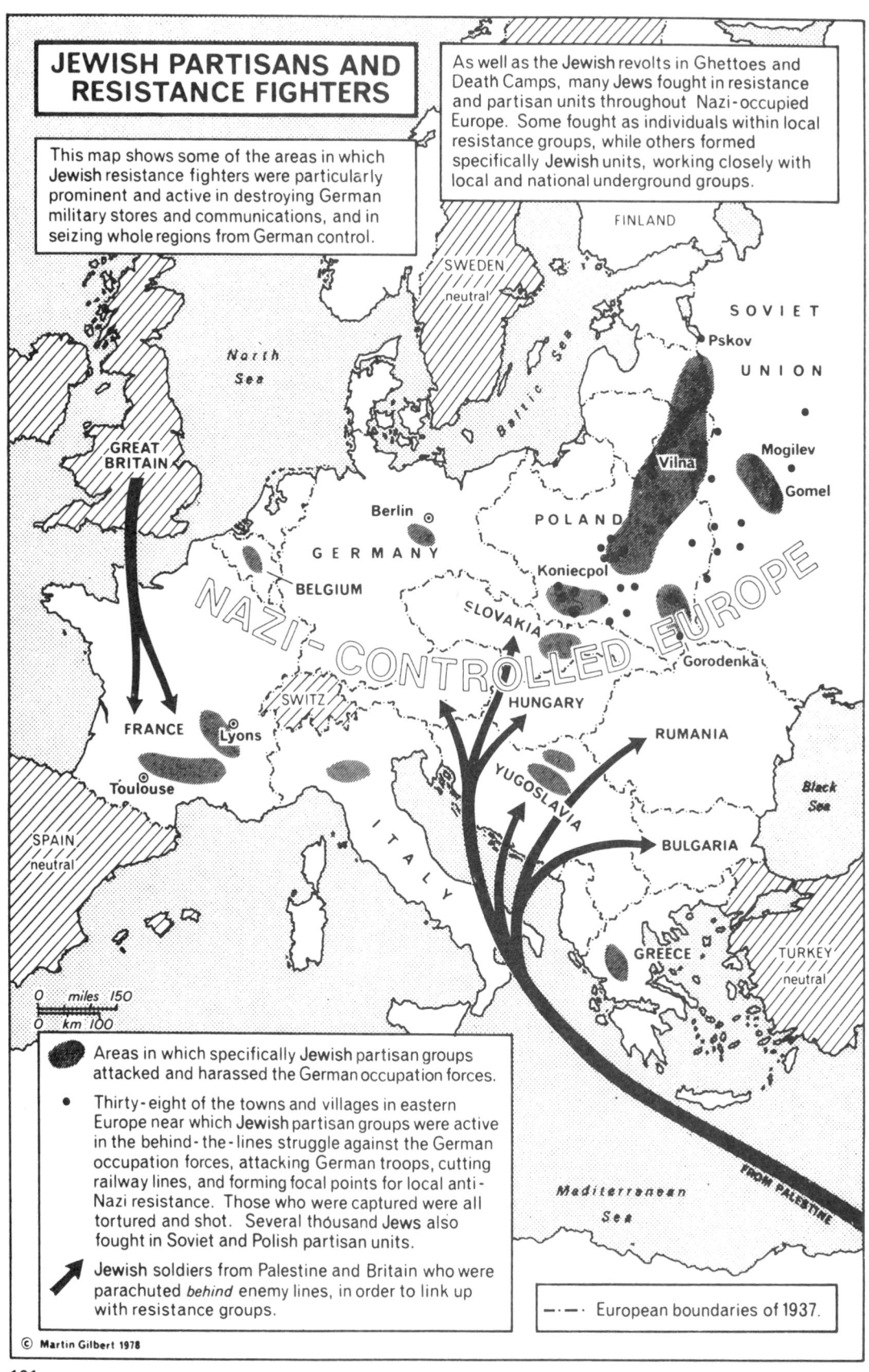

JEWISH PARTISANS AND RESISTANCE FIGHTERS

As well as the Jewish revolts in Ghettoes and Death Camps, many Jews fought in resistance and partisan units throughout Nazi-occupied Europe. Some fought as individuals within local resistance groups, while others formed specifically Jewish units, working closely with local and national underground groups.

This map shows some of the areas in which Jewish resistance fighters were particularly prominent and active in destroying German military stores and communications, and in seizing whole regions from German control.

FINLAND

SWEDEN
neutral

North
Sea

Baltic Sea

S O V I E T

Pskov

U N I O N

Mogilev

GREAT
BRITAIN

Vilna

Gomel

Berlin ⊙

P O L A N D

G E R M A N Y

BELGIUM

Koniecpol

NAZI-CONTROLLED EUROPE

SLOVAKIA

Gorodenka

SWITZ

HUNGARY

RUMANIA

FRANCE
Lyons ⊙

Black
Sea

Toulouse ⊙

YUGOSLAVIA

I T A L Y

BULGARIA

SPAIN
neutral

GREECE

TURKEY
neutral

0   miles 150
0   km 100

FROM PALESTINE

Mediterranean
Sea

Areas in which specifically Jewish partisan groups attacked and harassed the German occupation forces.

• Thirty-eight of the towns and villages in eastern Europe near which Jewish partisan groups were active in the behind-the-lines struggle against the German occupation forces, attacking German troops, cutting railway lines, and forming focal points for local anti-Nazi resistance. Those who were captured were all tortured and shot. Several thousand Jews also fought in Soviet and Polish partisan units.

Jewish soldiers from Palestine and Britain who were parachuted *behind* enemy lines, in order to link up with resistance groups.

—·—· European boundaries of 1937.

© Martin Gilbert 1978

JEWISH REVOLTS 1942-1945

Despite the overwhelming military strength of the German forces, many Jews, while weakened by hunger and terrorised by Nazi brutality, nevertheless rose in revolt against their fate, not only in many of the Ghettoes in which they were forcibly confined, but even in the concentration camps themselves, snatching from the very gates of death the slender possibility of survival.

✡ Ghettoes in which Jews rose up in revolt against the Germans, with dates. Many of those who revolted were able to escape to the woods, and to join Jewish, Polish or Soviet partisan groups.

卐 Death camps in which the Jews revolted, with date of the revolt. In almost every instance, those who revolted were later caught and murdered.

This map shows twenty of the Ghettoes and five of the death camps in which Jews joined together and sought, often almost unarmed, to strike back at their tormentors. These twenty-five uprisings are among the most noble and courageous episodes not only of Jewish, but of world history.

PONARY
19 MAY 1944

Vilna
1 SEPTEMBER 1943

River Neimen

0 miles 50
0 km 80

Mir
9 AUGUST 1942

Nieswiesz
22 JULY 1942

Bialystok
16 AUGUST 1943

Kuldichvo
25 MARCH 1943

Kletsk
21 JULY 1943

River Vistula

TREBLINKA
2 AUGUST 1943

Lakhva
3 SEPTEMBER 1942

Warsaw
19 APRIL 1943

Minsk Mazowiecki
10 JANUARY 1943

CHELMNO
17 JANUARY 1945

Krushin
17 DECEMBER 1942

SOBIBOR
14 OCTOBER 1943

River Bug

Chenstochov
25 OCTOBER 1943

Lublin
3 NOVEMBER 1943

Lutsk
12 OCTOBER 1942

Bedzin
3 AUGUST 1943

Tuchin
3 SEPTEMBER 1942

River Vistula

Tarnow
1 SEPTEMBER 1943

Brody
17 MAY 1943

AUSCHWITZ
7 OCTOBER 1944

Kremenetz
9 SEPTEMBER 1942

Lvov
1 JUNE 1943

River

Dniester

Stryj
28 APRIL 1943

C Z E C H O S L O V A K I A

HUNGARY

© Martin Gilbert 1978

102

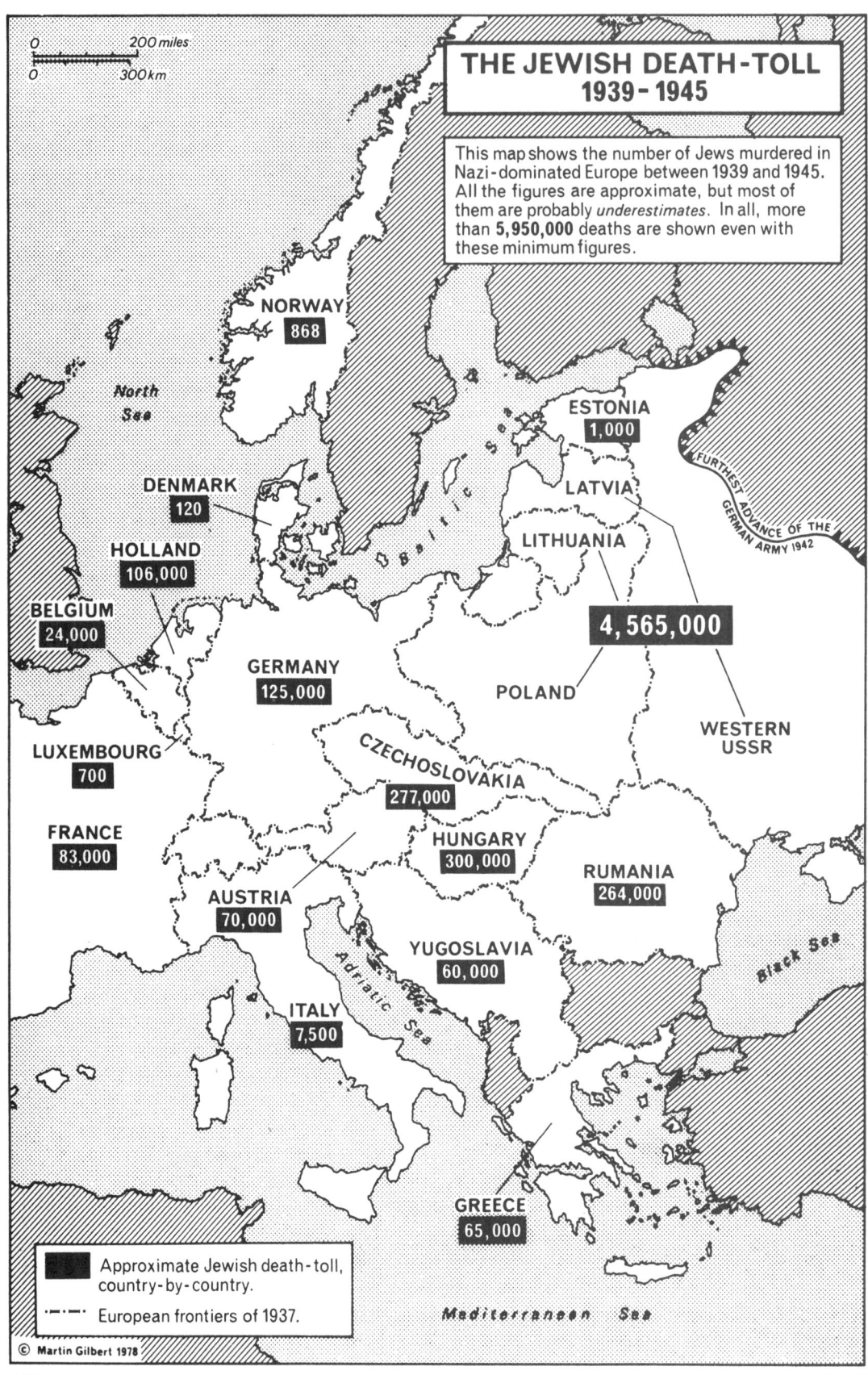

THE JEWISH DEATH-TOLL
1939-1945

This map shows the number of Jews murdered in Nazi-dominated Europe between 1939 and 1945. All the figures are approximate, but most of them are probably *underestimates*. In all, more than **5,950,000** deaths are shown even with these minimum figures.

0 — 200 miles
0 — 300 km

North Sea

NORWAY 868

ESTONIA 1,000

FURTHEST ADVANCE OF THE GERMAN ARMY 1942

DENMARK 120

LATVIA

HOLLAND 106,000

LITHUANIA

BELGIUM 24,000

4,565,000

GERMANY 125,000

POLAND

WESTERN USSR

LUXEMBOURG 700

CZECHOSLOVAKIA 277,000

FRANCE 83,000

HUNGARY 300,000

RUMANIA 264,000

AUSTRIA 70,000

YUGOSLAVIA 60,000

Adriatic Sea

Black Sea

ITALY 7,500

GREECE 65,000

Approximate Jewish death-toll, country-by-country.

— · — · — European frontiers of 1937.

© Martin Gilbert 1978

Mediterranean Sea

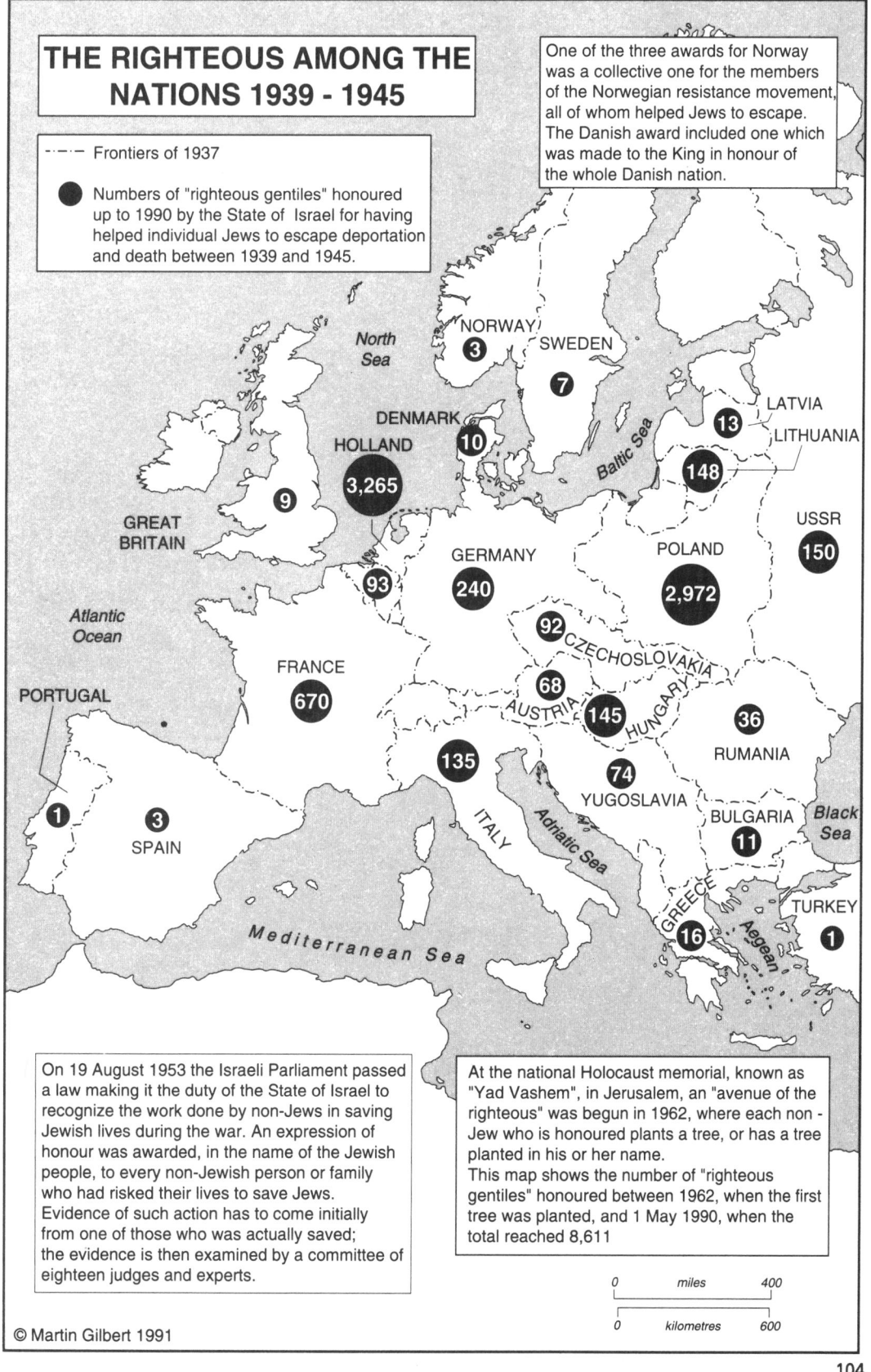

THE RIGHTEOUS AMONG THE NATIONS 1939 - 1945

One of the three awards for Norway was a collective one for the members of the Norwegian resistance movement, all of whom helped Jews to escape. The Danish award included one which was made to the King in honour of the whole Danish nation.

--- Frontiers of 1937

● Numbers of "righteous gentiles" honoured up to 1990 by the State of Israel for having helped individual Jews to escape deportation and death between 1939 and 1945.

North Sea

NORWAY **3**

SWEDEN **7**

LATVIA **13**

LITHUANIA

DENMARK

HOLLAND **10**

3,265

Baltic Sea

USSR **150**

GREAT BRITAIN **9**

GERMANY **240**

POLAND **2,972**

Atlantic Ocean

93

92

CZECHOSLOVAKIA

68

AUSTRIA

HUNGARY

145

36

RUMANIA

FRANCE **670**

135

74

YUGOSLAVIA

BULGARIA **11**

Black Sea

PORTUGAL **1**

3 SPAIN

ITALY

Adriatic Sea

GREECE **16**

Aegean

TURKEY **1**

Mediterranean Sea

On 19 August 1953 the Israeli Parliament passed a law making it the duty of the State of Israel to recognize the work done by non-Jews in saving Jewish lives during the war. An expression of honour was awarded, in the name of the Jewish people, to every non-Jewish person or family who had risked their lives to save Jews. Evidence of such action has to come initially from one of those who was actually saved; the evidence is then examined by a committee of eighteen judges and experts.

At the national Holocaust memorial, known as "Yad Vashem", in Jerusalem, an "avenue of the righteous" was begun in 1962, where each non-Jew who is honoured plants a tree, or has a tree planted in his or her name.
This map shows the number of "righteous gentiles" honoured between 1962, when the first tree was planted, and 1 May 1990, when the total reached 8,611

| 0 | miles | 400 |
| 0 | kilometres | 600 |

© Martin Gilbert 1991

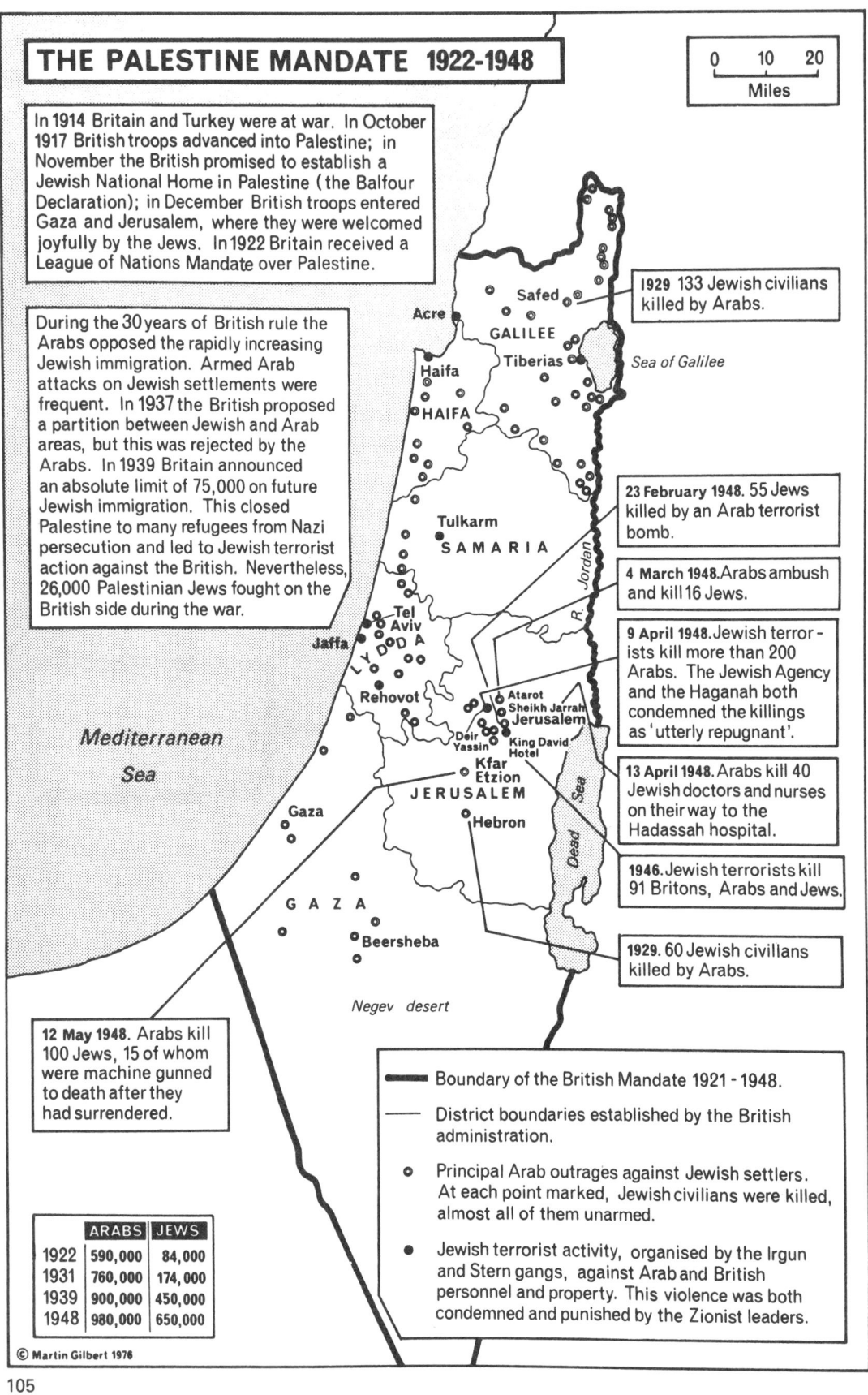

THE PALESTINE MANDATE 1922-1948

0   10   20
Miles

In 1914 Britain and Turkey were at war. In October 1917 British troops advanced into Palestine; in November the British promised to establish a Jewish National Home in Palestine (the Balfour Declaration); in December British troops entered Gaza and Jerusalem, where they were welcomed joyfully by the Jews. In 1922 Britain received a League of Nations Mandate over Palestine.

During the 30 years of British rule the Arabs opposed the rapidly increasing Jewish immigration. Armed Arab attacks on Jewish settlements were frequent. In 1937 the British proposed a partition between Jewish and Arab areas, but this was rejected by the Arabs. In 1939 Britain announced an absolute limit of 75,000 on future Jewish immigration. This closed Palestine to many refugees from Nazi persecution and led to Jewish terrorist action against the British. Nevertheless, 26,000 Palestinian Jews fought on the British side during the war.

1929 133 Jewish civilians killed by Arabs.

23 February 1948. 55 Jews killed by an Arab terrorist bomb.

4 March 1948. Arabs ambush and kill 16 Jews.

9 April 1948. Jewish terror- ists kill more than 200 Arabs. The Jewish Agency and the Haganah both condemned the killings as 'utterly repugnant'.

13 April 1948. Arabs kill 40 Jewish doctors and nurses on their way to the Hadassah hospital.

1946. Jewish terrorists kill 91 Britons, Arabs and Jews.

1929. 60 Jewish civilians killed by Arabs.

12 May 1948. Arabs kill 100 Jews, 15 of whom were machine gunned to death after they had surrendered.

Acre
Safed
GALILEE
Tiberias
Sea of Galilee
Haifa
HAIFA
Tulkarm
S A M A R I A
R. Jordan
Tel Aviv
Jaffa
L Y D D A
Rehovot
Atarot
Sheikh Jarrah
Jerusalem
Deir Yassin
King David Hotel
Kfar Etzion
J E R U S A L E M
Gaza
Hebron
Mediterranean Sea
Dead Sea
G A Z A
Beersheba
Negev desert

▬▬ Boundary of the British Mandate 1921 - 1948.

─── District boundaries established by the British administration.

⊙ Principal Arab outrages against Jewish settlers. At each point marked, Jewish civilians were killed, almost all of them unarmed.

● Jewish terrorist activity, organised by the Irgun and Stern gangs, against Arab and British personnel and property. This violence was both condemned and punished by the Zionist leaders.

	ARABS	JEWS
1922	590,000	84,000
1931	760,000	174,000
1939	900,000	450,000
1948	980,000	650,000

© Martin Gilbert 1976

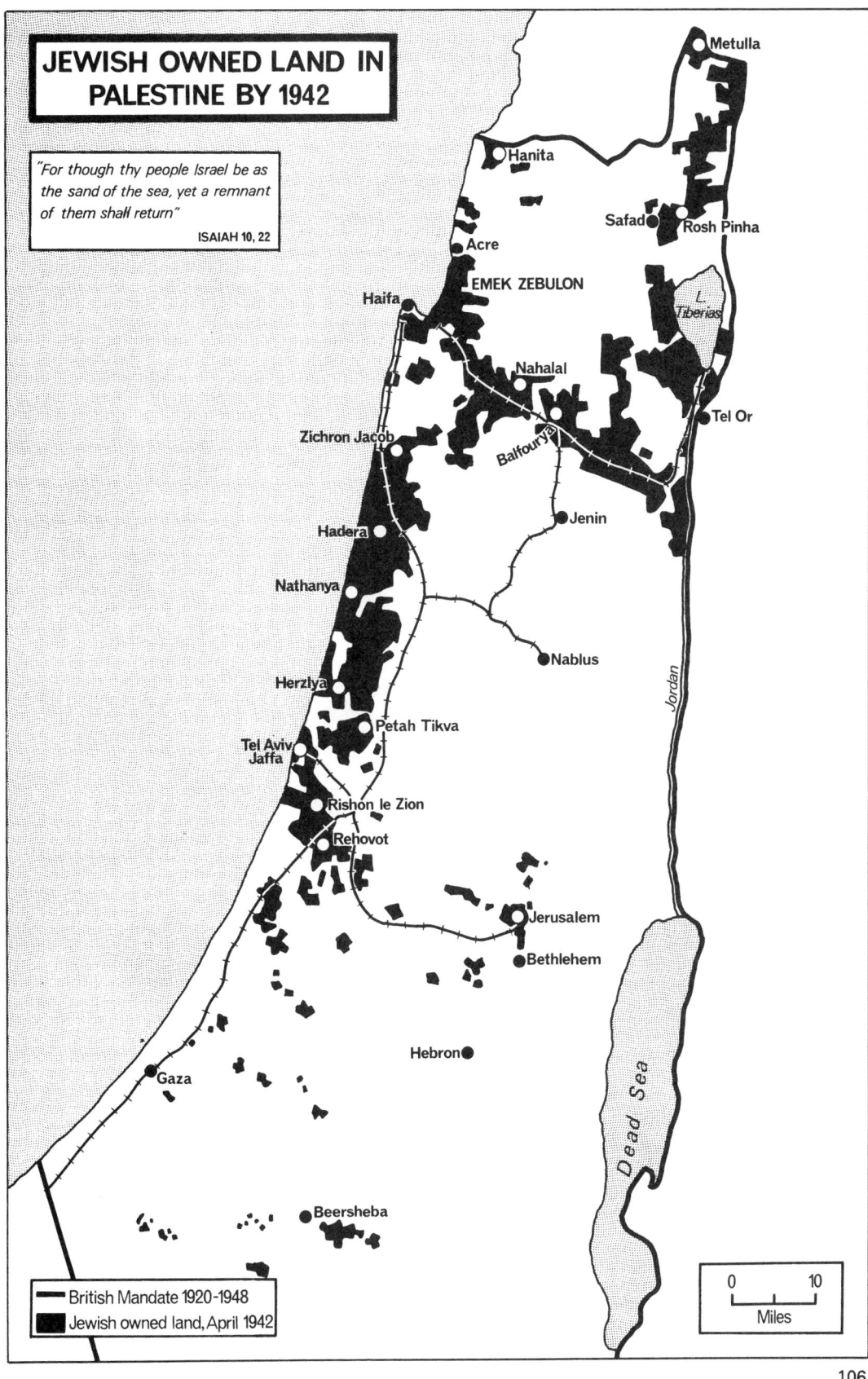

JEWISH OWNED LAND IN PALESTINE BY 1942

"For though thy people Israel be as the sand of the sea, yet a remnant of them shall return"

ISAIAH 10, 22

Metulla

Hanita

Safad

Rosh Pinha

Acre

EMEK ZEBULON

L. Tiberias

Haifa

Nahalal

Zichron Jacob

Balfourya

Tel Or

Jenin

Hadera

Nathanya

Nablus

Herzlya

Petah Tikva

Tel Aviv
Jaffa

Rishon le Zion

Rehovot

Jerusalem

Bethlehem

Jordan

Hebron

Gaza

Dead Sea

Beersheba

— British Mandate 1920-1948

■ Jewish owned land, April 1942

0   10

Miles

OTHER ZIONS 1652-1946

11 1884 First colony of Russian Jews, established by London Mansion House Committee. By 1902 several thousand Jews had settled in Saskatchewan

10 1880-1902 Russian and Rumanian Jews look to Cyprus as a Jewish national home. Several hundred Jews bought land

5 1819 Proposal for a Jewish colony along the upper Mississippi and Missouri rivers

4 c.1730 Hermann Moritz of Saxony argues in favour of a Jewish State in South America with himself as King

7 1825 Mordecai Noah establishes Jewish "State" of Ararat on Grand Island near Niagara Falls. Some Jews settled here in 1826

2 1654 British ruled (1650-1657) seen as a possible haven for the Jews of Europe

1 1652 Dutch West India Company establishes Jewish colony

3 1659 French West India Company supports plans for a Jewish colony

15 1904 A thousand Jews establish a colony in Brazil

13 1903 British Government offers El Arish to the Jews, but the British Agent in Egypt refuses to allow the colony to use water from the Nile for irrigation

12 1892 Baron de Hirsch sets up Jewish Colonization Association aimed at settling 3,000,000 Jews from Russia in Argentina. Only 45,000 settlers by 1914, after which numbers fell

14 1903 British offer Guas Ngishu plateau of Kenya to the Jews, but this was rejected in 1905 by Zionists, who demanded Palestine, then under Turkish rule

CANADA

UNITED STATES

Curaçao

Surinam Cayenne

BRAZIL
Recife

ARGENTINE

"O that I had wings like a dove!
For then I would fly away and be at rest"
PSALM 55

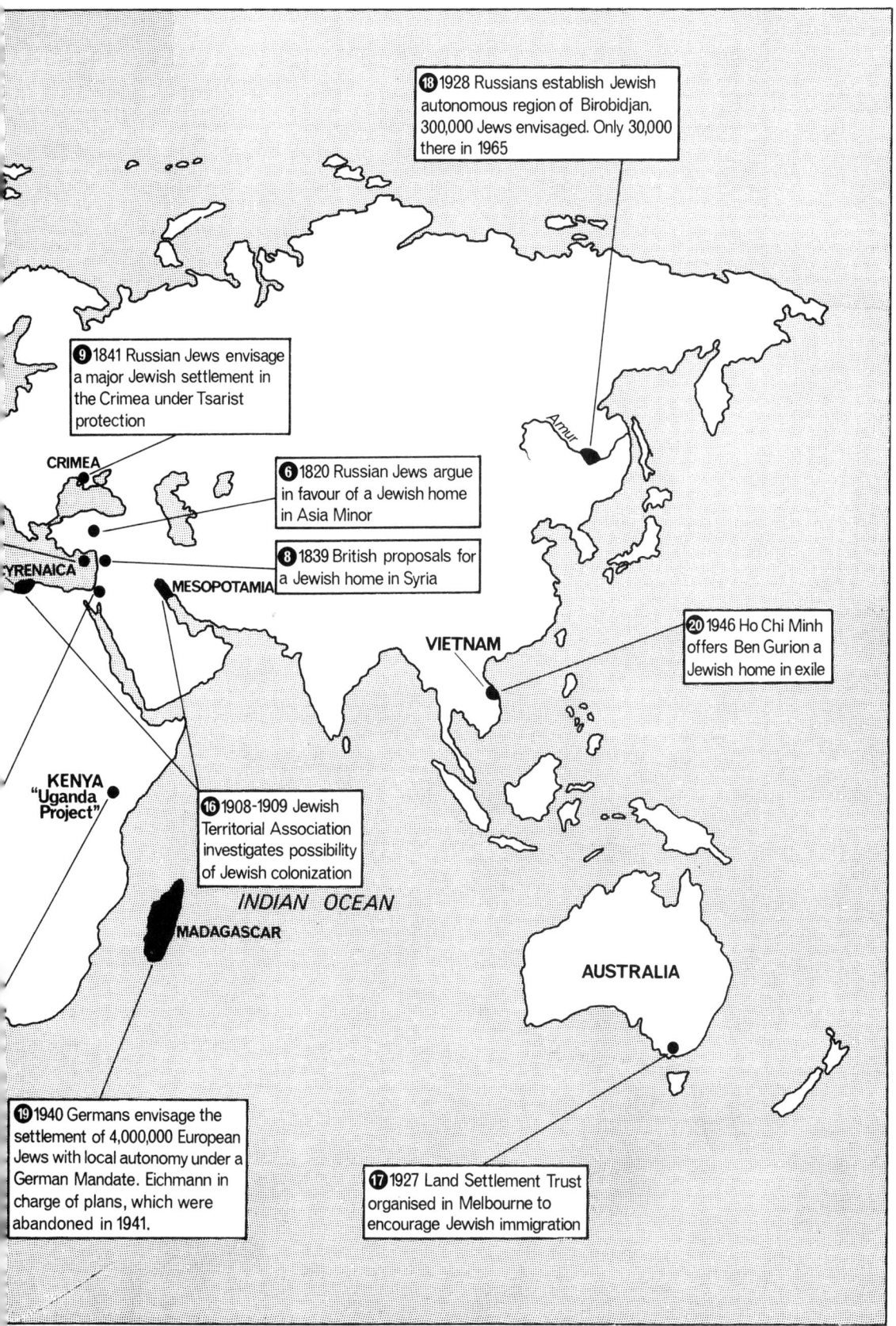

18 1928 Russians establish Jewish autonomous region of Birobidjan. 300,000 Jews envisaged. Only 30,000 there in 1965

9 1841 Russian Jews envisage a major Jewish settlement in the Crimea under Tsarist protection

CRIMEA

6 1820 Russian Jews argue in favour of a Jewish home in Asia Minor

8 1839 British proposals for a Jewish home in Syria

CYRENAICA

MESOPOTAMIA

Amur

VIETNAM

20 1946 Ho Chi Minh offers Ben Gurion a Jewish home in exile

KENYA "Uganda Project"

16 1908-1909 Jewish Territorial Association investigates possibility of Jewish colonization

INDIAN OCEAN

MADAGASCAR

AUSTRALIA

19 1940 Germans envisage the settlement of 4,000,000 European Jews with local autonomy under a German Mandate. Eichmann in charge of plans, which were abandoned in 1941.

17 1927 Land Settlement Trust organised in Melbourne to encourage Jewish immigration

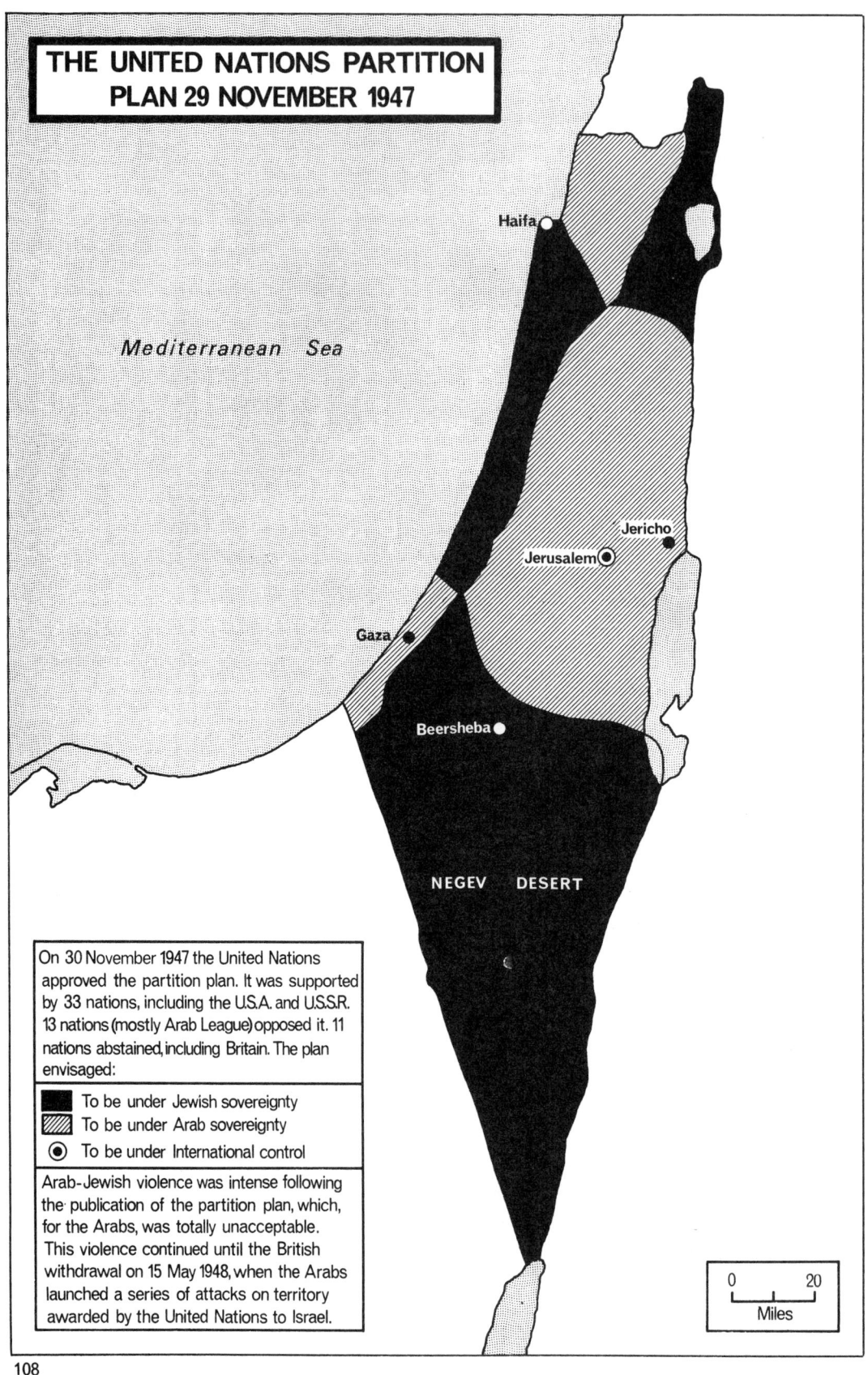

THE UNITED NATIONS PARTITION PLAN 29 NOVEMBER 1947

Mediterranean Sea

Haifa

Jericho

Jerusalem

Gaza

Beersheba

NEGEV DESERT

On 30 November 1947 the United Nations
approved the partition plan. It was supported
by 33 nations, including the U.S.A. and U.S.S.R.
13 nations (mostly Arab League) opposed it. 11
nations abstained, including Britain. The plan
envisaged:

- To be under Jewish sovereignty
- To be under Arab sovereignty
- To be under International control

Arab-Jewish violence was intense following
the publication of the partition plan, which,
for the Arabs, was totally unacceptable.
This violence continued until the British
withdrawal on 15 May 1948, when the Arabs
launched a series of attacks on territory
awarded by the United Nations to Israel.

0   20
Miles

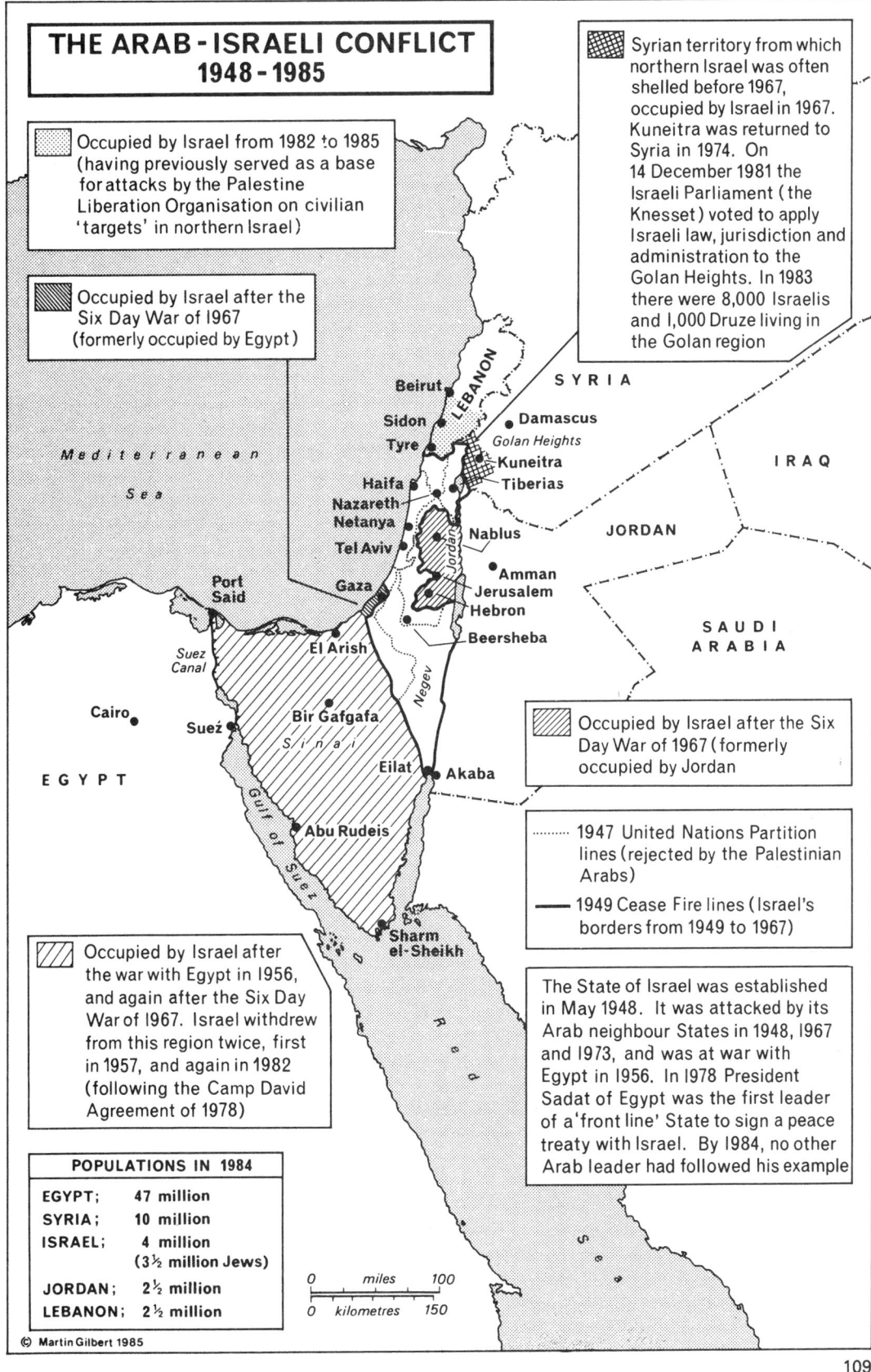

THE ARAB-ISRAELI CONFLICT
1948-1985

Occupied by Israel from 1982 to 1985 (having previously served as a base for attacks by the Palestine Liberation Organisation on civilian 'targets' in northern Israel)

Occupied by Israel after the Six Day War of 1967 (formerly occupied by Egypt)

Syrian territory from which northern Israel was often shelled before 1967, occupied by Israel in 1967. Kuneitra was returned to Syria in 1974. On 14 December 1981 the Israeli Parliament (the Knesset) voted to apply Israeli law, jurisdiction and administration to the Golan Heights. In 1983 there were 8,000 Israelis and 1,000 Druze living in the Golan region

Occupied by Israel after the Six Day War of 1967 (formerly occupied by Jordan

.... 1947 United Nations Partition lines (rejected by the Palestinian Arabs)

———— 1949 Cease Fire lines (Israel's borders from 1949 to 1967)

Occupied by Israel after the war with Egypt in 1956, and again after the Six Day War of 1967. Israel withdrew from this region twice, first in 1957, and again in 1982 (following the Camp David Agreement of 1978)

The State of Israel was established in May 1948. It was attacked by its Arab neighbour States in 1948, 1967 and 1973, and was at war with Egypt in 1956. In 1978 President Sadat of Egypt was the first leader of a 'front line' State to sign a peace treaty with Israel. By 1984, no other Arab leader had followed his example

POPULATIONS IN 1984	
EGYPT;	47 million
SYRIA;	10 million
ISRAEL;	4 million
	(3½ million Jews)
JORDAN;	2½ million
LEBANON;	2½ million

Mediterranean Sea

Beirut
Sidon
Tyre
Haifa
Nazareth
Netanya
Tel Aviv
Gaza
Port Said
El Arish
Suez Canal
Cairo
Suez
Bir Gafgafa
Sinai
Eilat
Akaba
EGYPT
Gulf of Suez
Abu Rudeis
Sharm el-Sheikh
Red Sea

LEBANON
SYRIA
Damascus
Golan Heights
Kuneitra
Tiberias
Nablus
Jordan
Amman
Jerusalem
Hebron
Beersheba
Negev
JORDAN
IRAQ
SAUDI ARABIA

| 0 | miles | 100 |
| 0 | kilometres | 150 |

© Martin Gilbert 1985

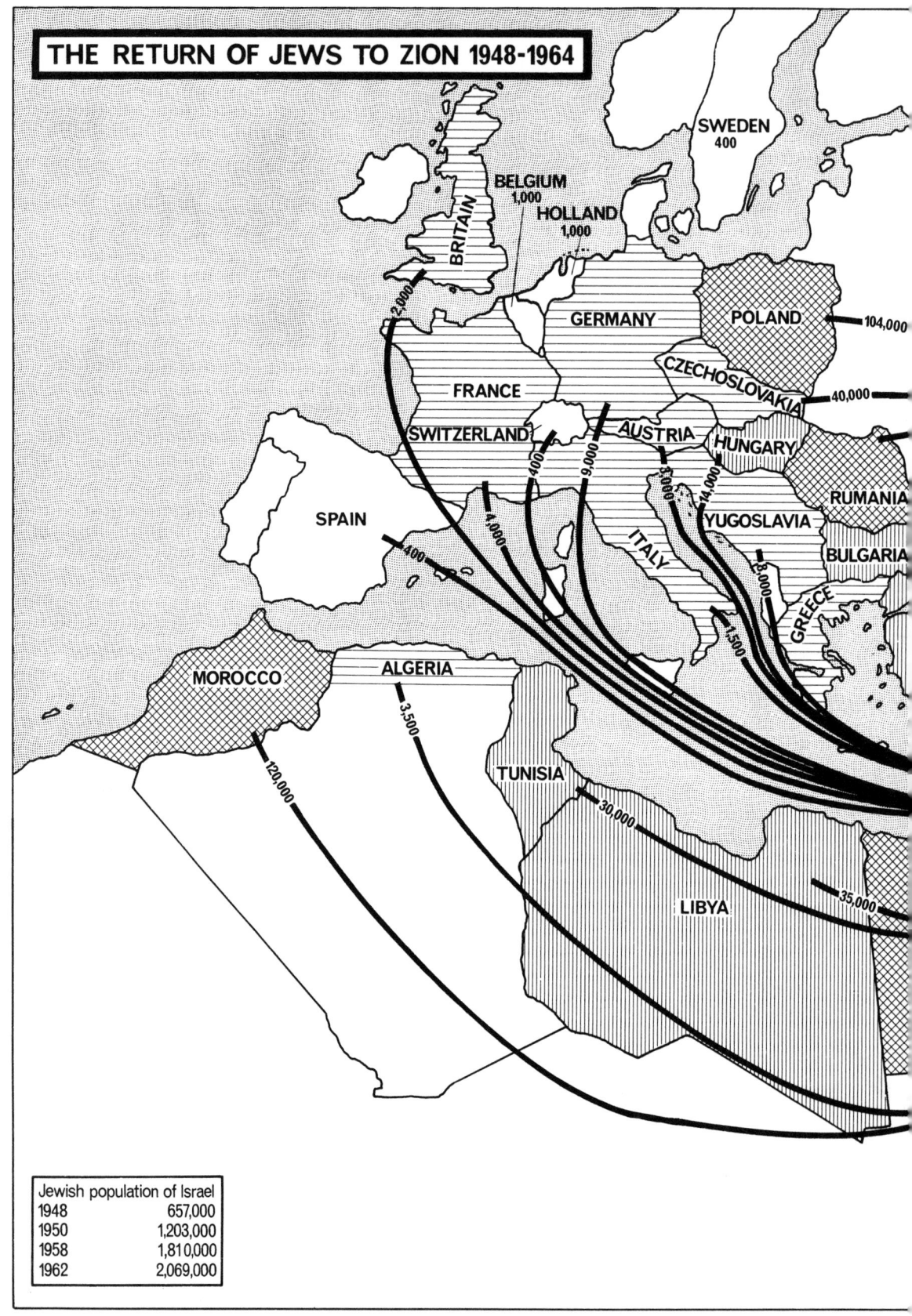

THE RETURN OF JEWS TO ZION 1948–1964

SWEDEN
400

BRITAIN

BELGIUM
1,000

HOLLAND
1,000

GERMANY

POLAND
104,000

CZECHOSLOVAKIA
40,000

FRANCE

SWITZERLAND

AUSTRIA

HUNGARY

RUMANIA

SPAIN

ITALY

YUGOSLAVIA

BULGARIA

GREECE

MOROCCO

ALGERIA

TUNISIA

LIBYA

2,000

400

9,000

44,000

5,000

8,000

4,500

4,000

400

3,500

120,000

30,000

35,000

Jewish population of Israel	
1948	657,000
1950	1,203,000
1958	1,810,000
1962	2,069,000

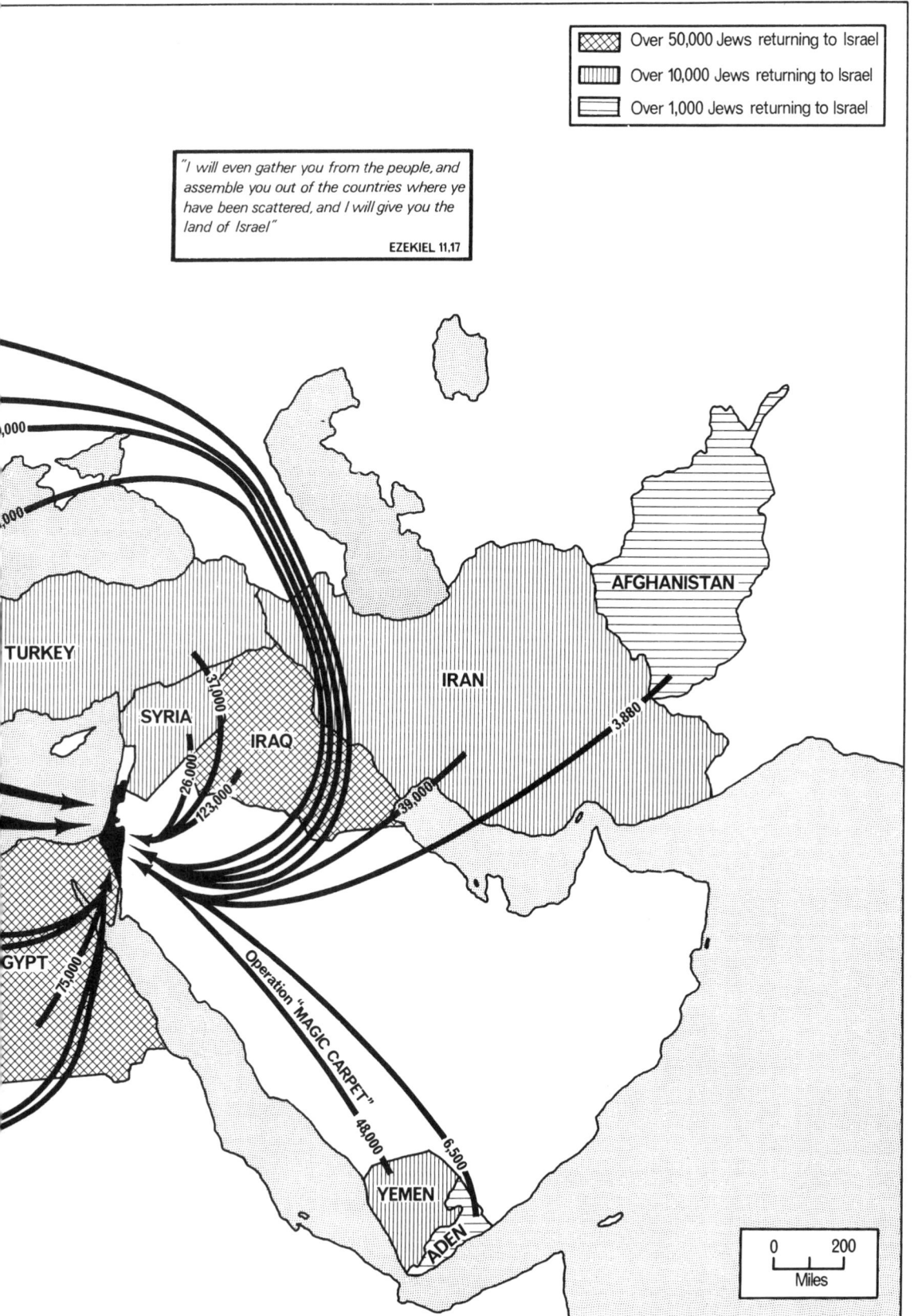

Over 50,000 Jews returning to Israel

Over 10,000 Jews returning to Israel

Over 1,000 Jews returning to Israel

"I will even gather you from the people, and
assemble you out of the countries where ye
have been scattered, and I will give you the
land of Israel"

EZEKIEL 11,17

TURKEY

SYRIA

IRAQ

IRAN

AFGHANISTAN

31,000

26,000

123,000

39,000

3,880

GYPT

75,000

Operation "MAGIC CARPET"

48,000

6,500

YEMEN

ADEN

0   200
Miles

110

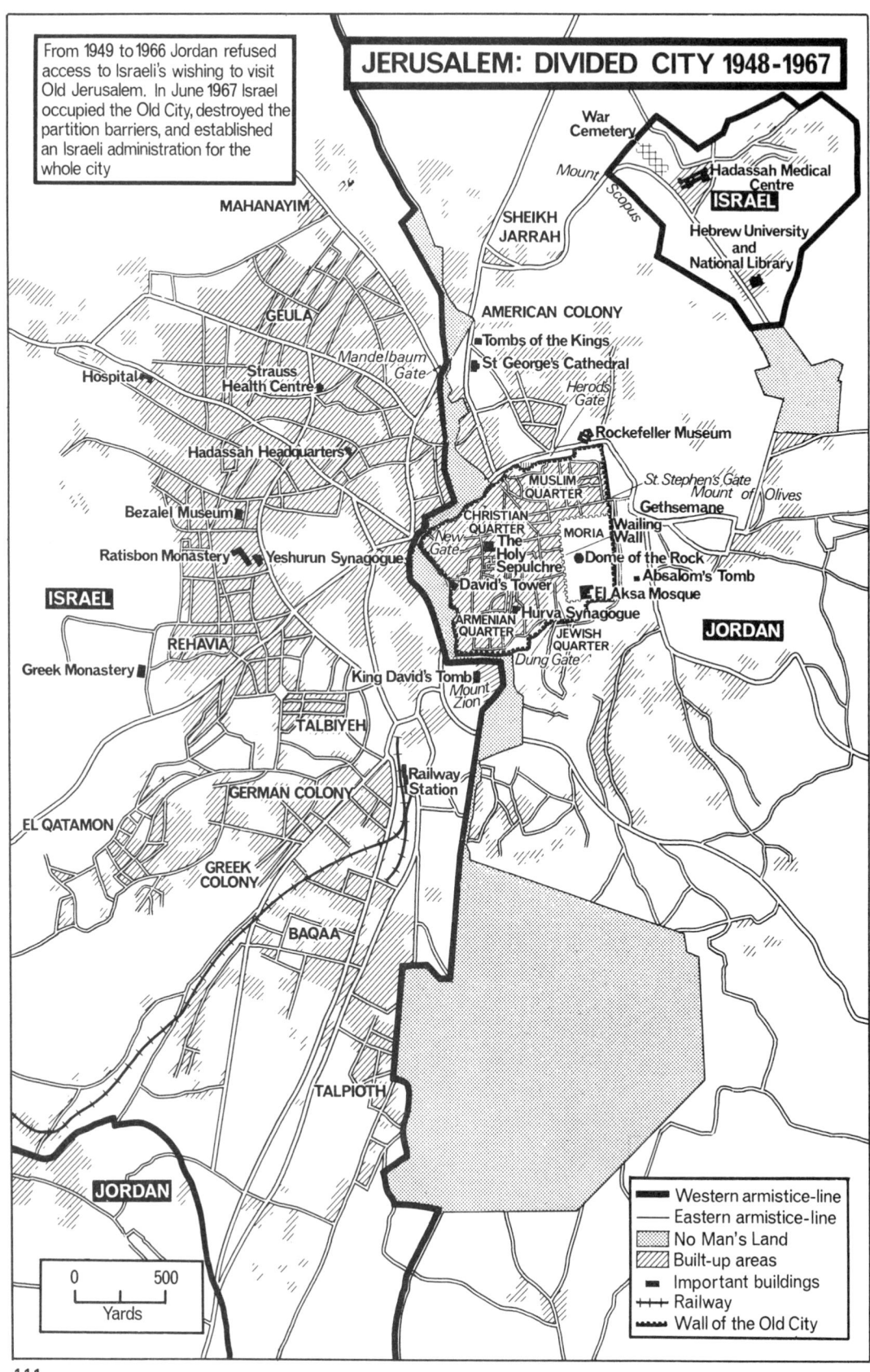

JERUSALEM: DIVIDED CITY 1948-1967

From 1949 to 1966 Jordan refused access to Israeli's wishing to visit Old Jerusalem. In June 1967 Israel occupied the Old City, destroyed the partition barriers, and established an Israeli administration for the whole city

War Cemetery

Mount *Scopus*

Hadassah Medical Centre

ISRAEL

Hebrew University and National Library

MAHANAYIM

SHEIKH JARRAH

GEULA

AMERICAN COLONY

Tombs of the Kings

St George's Cathedral

Herods Gate

Strauss Health Centre

Mandelbaum Gate

Hospital

Rockefeller Museum

Hadassah Headquarters

MUSLIM QUARTER

St. Stephen's Gate

Mount of Olives

Gethsemane

Bezalel Museum

CHRISTIAN QUARTER

New Gate

MORIA

Wailing Wall

Ratisbon Monastery

Yeshurun Synagogue

The Holy Sepulchre

Dome of the Rock

Absalom's Tomb

ISRAEL

David's Tower

El Aksa Mosque

REHAVIA

Hurva Synagogue

Greek Monastery

ARMENIAN QUARTER

JEWISH QUARTER

JORDAN

Dung Gate

King David's Tomb

Mount Zion

TALBIYEH

Railway Station

GERMAN COLONY

EL QATAMON

GREEK COLONY

BAQAA

TALPIOTH

JORDAN

0   500

Yards

Western armistice-line
Eastern armistice-line
No Man's Land
Built-up areas
Important buildings
Railway
Wall of the Old City

111

ANTI-JEWISH TRIALS AND EXECUTIONS 1961-1963

On 25 February 1963 the Western press - and three days later the Soviet press - published a letter from the British philosopher Bertrand Russell to Nikita Khruschev, protesting against the death sentence for economic crimes. On 6 April 1963, after Khruschev had denounced Russell's letter as a 'vicious slander' against the Soviet Union, Russell wrote again, describing the economic charges and the sentences as 'gravely disturbing'.

Between July 1961 and March 1963, in the Soviet Union, at least 110 death sentences were imposed for 'economic crimes'. Of these 110, at least 68 were Jews. The 'economic crimes' of which they were accused included 'currency speculation', 'embezzlement of foodstuffs', 'counterfeiting of coins', 'plundering of public property', 'speculation in footwear', 'speculation in fruit', and 'embezzlement of curtain material'. All 68 Jews were sentenced to death by shooting, most of them specifically 'without right of appeal', followed by the confiscation of their property by the State.

Ural Mountains

SIBERIA

Sverdlovsk **two**

Lake Balkhash

Leningrad **five**

Volga

THE

Baltic Sea

Moscow **eight**

Kaunas **one**

Vilna **four**

Minsk **six**

SOVIET

Ural

UNION

Frunze **four**

Dzhambul **one**

Pripet Marshes

Saratov **one**

Aral Sea

Tashkent **one**

Khmelnitsky **two**

Kharkov **six**

Ivana-Frankovsk **two**

Lvov **one**

Kiev **two**

Vashkovitz **one**

Dnepropetrovsk **three**

Odessa **three**

Caspian Sea

Nikolaevo **one**

Chernovtsy **six**

Piatigorsk **one**

Caucasus

Tiflis **one**

Baku **one**

Kishinev **five**

Black Sea

Kutais **one**

Mediterranean Sea

ISRAEL

| 0 | 200 miles |
| 0 | 400 km |

● Towns in which Jews were tried, and then shot for 'economic crimes', 1961 - 1963, with the number shot in each town shown in black:

In the Ukraine, where 2% of the population were Jews, Jews accounted for 83% of those sentenced to death. Thus, of twelve people tried for the same 'economic crime' in Kharkov in January 1963, all six Jewish defendants were sentenced to death, while all the six non-Jewish defendants received prison sentences.

© Martin Gilbert 1976

THE JEWS OF IRAQ IN THE TWENTIETH CENTURY

0 ___ 50
Miles

1935 Jews removed from Government Service. Many Jews forbidden to travel to Palestine
1936 Ten Jews killed by Arab riots in Baghdad and Basra. Teaching of Hebrew prohibited
1947 No Jewish children accepted in Government schools
August 1948 Zionism declared a crime (with Nazism, Communism, Atheism and Anarchism) Many Jews imprisoned, some hanged
10 March 1950 Official decree confiscates all property of Jews leaving for Israel, and appoints a special custodian to sell it by public auction. All emigrants' bank accounts seized by the State
25 February 1958 Abolition of Jewish Community Status. All community property, including schools and hospitals, transferred to Government

3 March 1968 Law No 10 forbids Jews to receive more than 100 Iraqi dinars per month for sale of immovable property (in 1948 the Jewish community had been made to pay 250,000 dinars towards the Iraqi war effort against Israel, and towards the Palestinian Arab refugees)
1969 Nine Jews hanged for 'Zionist' activities in January; 2 hanged for 'spying for Israel and the CIA' in August; 2 killed in September; 4 killed in November
October 1972 Many Jews arrested. 16 disappear without trace. More than 20 murdered
April 1973 A family of 5 Jews murdered in their home

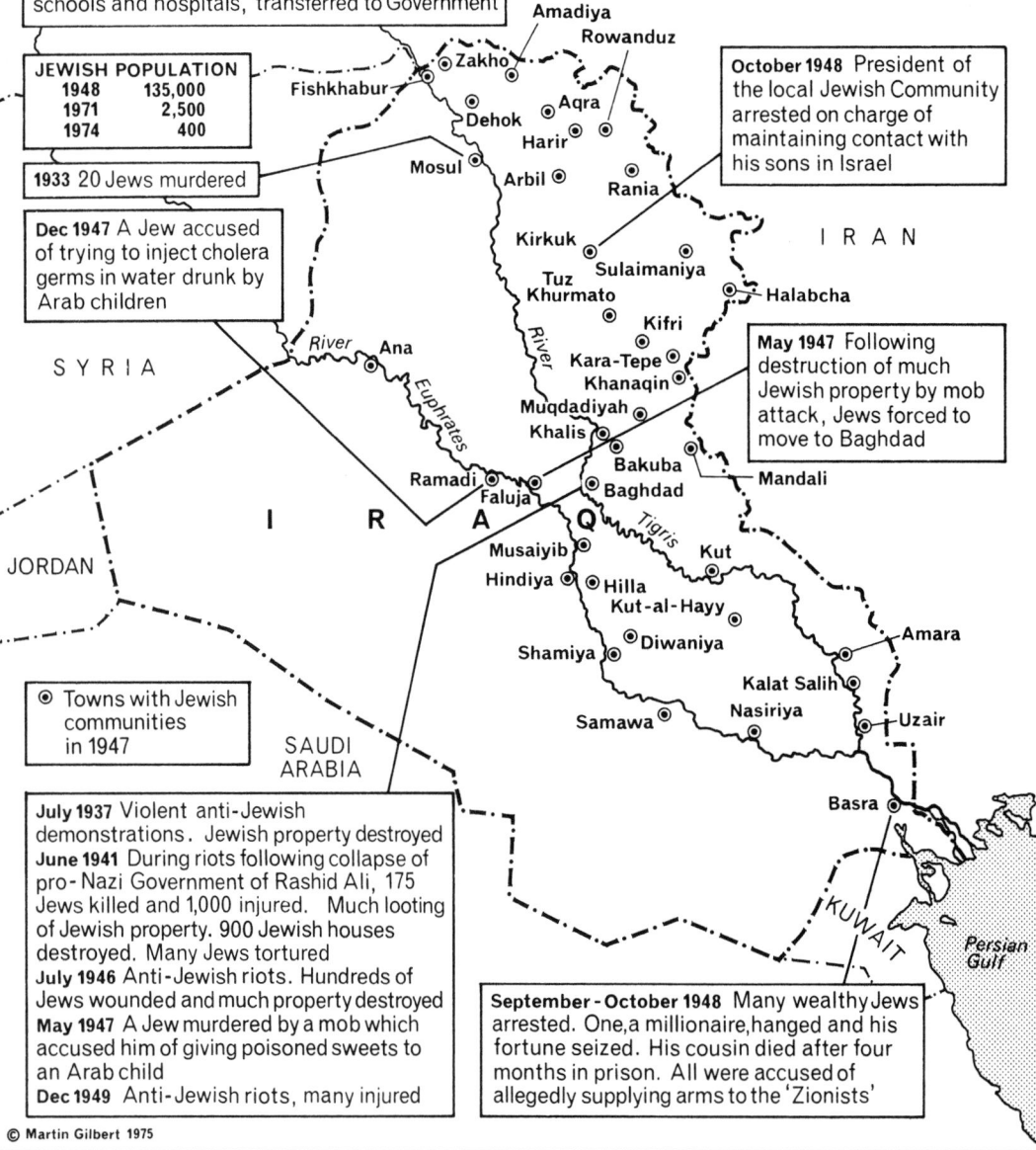

JEWISH POPULATION	
1948	135,000
1971	2,500
1974	400

1933 20 Jews murdered

Dec 1947 A Jew accused of trying to inject cholera germs in water drunk by Arab children

October 1948 President of the local Jewish Community arrested on charge of maintaining contact with his sons in Israel

May 1947 Following destruction of much Jewish property by mob attack, Jews forced to move to Baghdad

⊙ Towns with Jewish communities in 1947

July 1937 Violent anti-Jewish demonstrations. Jewish property destroyed
June 1941 During riots following collapse of pro-Nazi Government of Rashid Ali, 175 Jews killed and 1,000 injured. Much looting of Jewish property. 900 Jewish houses destroyed. Many Jews tortured
July 1946 Anti-Jewish riots. Hundreds of Jews wounded and much property destroyed
May 1947 A Jew murdered by a mob which accused him of giving poisoned sweets to an Arab child
Dec 1949 Anti-Jewish riots, many injured

September-October 1948 Many wealthy Jews arrested. One, a millionaire, hanged and his fortune seized. His cousin died after four months in prison. All were accused of allegedly supplying arms to the 'Zionists'

© Martin Gilbert 1975

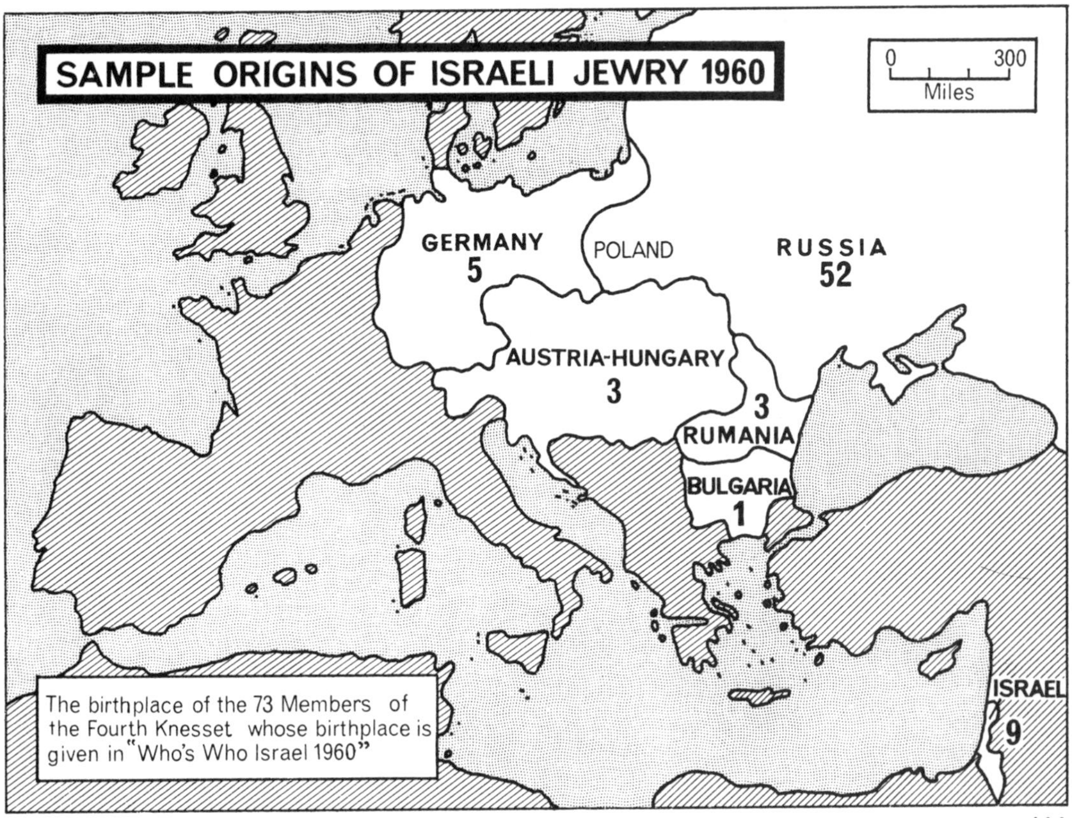

SAMPLE ORIGINS OF ISRAELI JEWRY 1960

0 — 300
Miles

GERMANY
5

POLAND

RUSSIA
52

AUSTRIA-HUNGARY
3

3
RUMANIA

BULGARIA
1

ISRAEL
9

The birthplace of the 73 Members of
the Fourth Knesset whose birthplace is
given in "Who's Who Israel 1960"

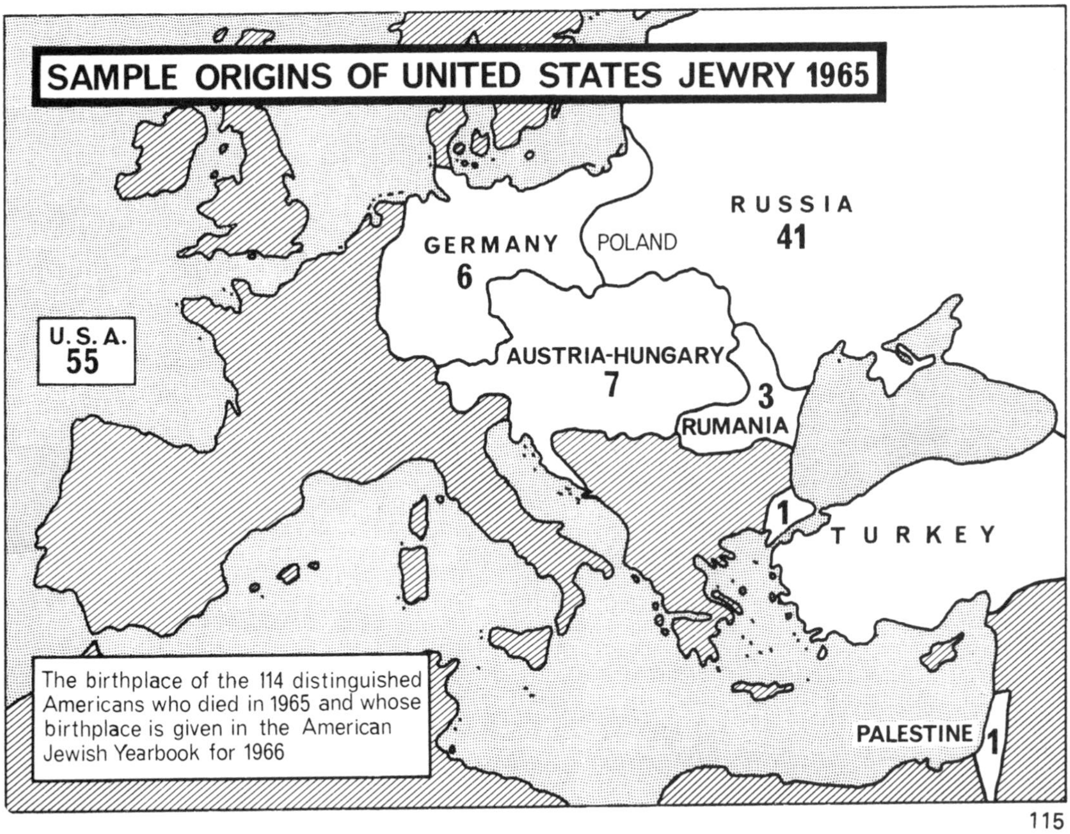

114

SAMPLE ORIGINS OF UNITED STATES JEWRY 1965

GERMANY
6

POLAND

RUSSIA
41

U.S.A.
55

AUSTRIA-HUNGARY
7

3
RUMANIA

1

T U R K E Y

The birthplace of the 114 distinguished
Americans who died in 1965 and whose
birthplace is given in the American
Jewish Yearbook for 1966

PALESTINE 1

115

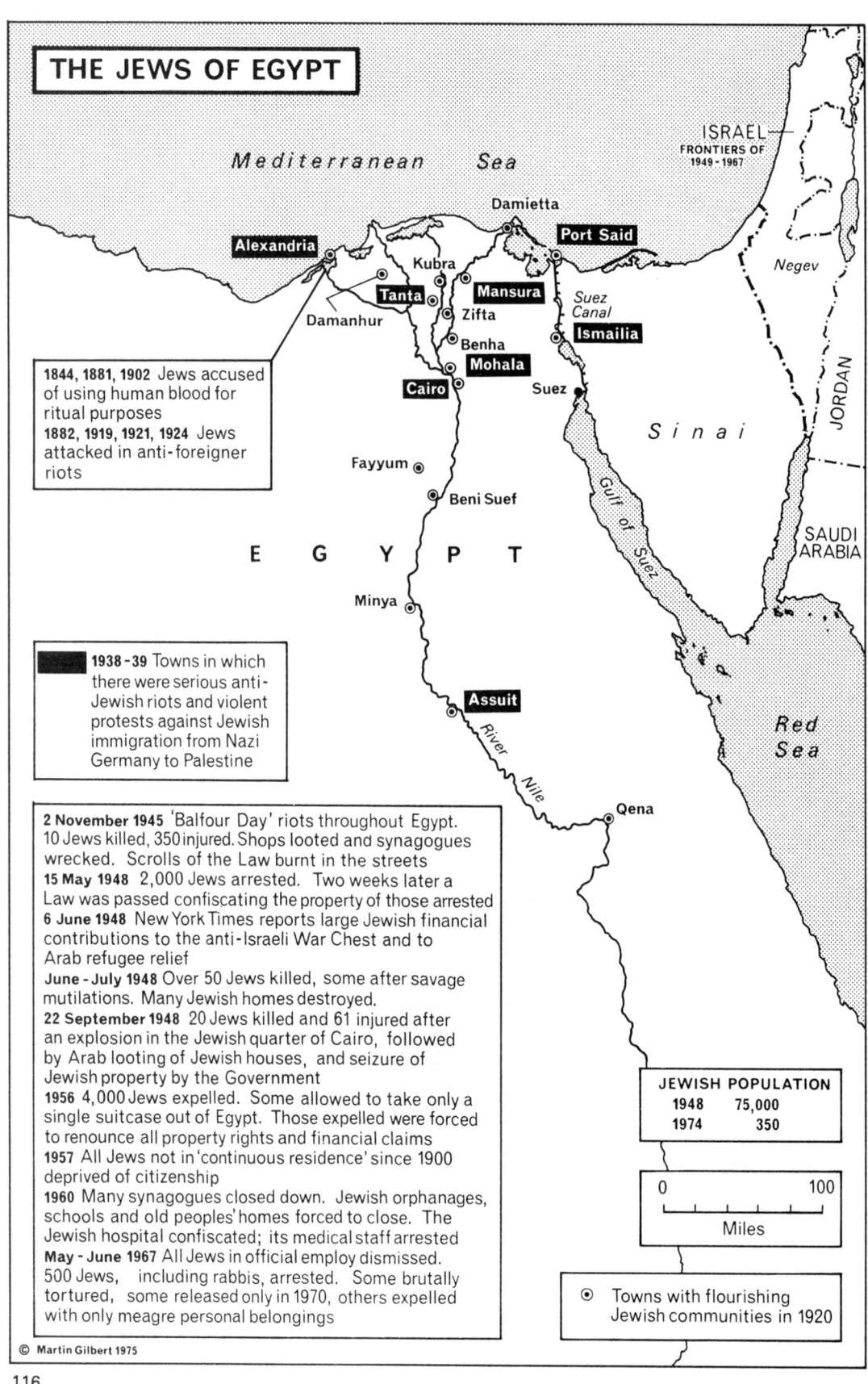

THE JEWS OF EGYPT

Mediterranean Sea

ISRAEL
FRONTIERS OF
1949-1967

Damietta

Alexandria

Kubra

Port Said

Negev

Tanta

Mansura

Zifta

Suez Canal

Damanhur

Benha

Ismailia

Mohala

Cairo

Suez

JORDAN

S i n a i

1844, 1881, 1902 Jews accused of using human blood for ritual purposes
1882, 1919, 1921, 1924 Jews attacked in anti-foreigner riots

Fayyum

Beni Suef

SAUDI
ARABIA

E   G   Y   P   T

Minya

1938-39 Towns in which there were serious anti-Jewish riots and violent protests against Jewish immigration from Nazi Germany to Palestine

Gulf of Suez

Assuit

Red Sea

River Nile

Qena

2 November 1945 'Balfour Day' riots throughout Egypt. 10 Jews killed, 350 injured. Shops looted and synagogues wrecked. Scrolls of the Law burnt in the streets
15 May 1948 2,000 Jews arrested. Two weeks later a Law was passed confiscating the property of those arrested
6 June 1948 New York Times reports large Jewish financial contributions to the anti-Israeli War Chest and to Arab refugee relief
June - July 1948 Over 50 Jews killed, some after savage mutilations. Many Jewish homes destroyed.
22 September 1948 20 Jews killed and 61 injured after an explosion in the Jewish quarter of Cairo, followed by Arab looting of Jewish houses, and seizure of Jewish property by the Government
1956 4,000 Jews expelled. Some allowed to take only a single suitcase out of Egypt. Those expelled were forced to renounce all property rights and financial claims
1957 All Jews not in 'continuous residence' since 1900 deprived of citizenship
1960 Many synagogues closed down. Jewish orphanages, schools and old peoples' homes forced to close. The Jewish hospital confiscated; its medical staff arrested
May - June 1967 All Jews in official employ dismissed. 500 Jews, including rabbis, arrested. Some brutally tortured, some released only in 1970, others expelled with only meagre personal belongings

JEWISH POPULATION
| 1948 | 75,000 |
| 1974 | 350 |

0   100
Miles

⊙ Towns with flourishing Jewish communities in 1920

© Martin Gilbert 1975

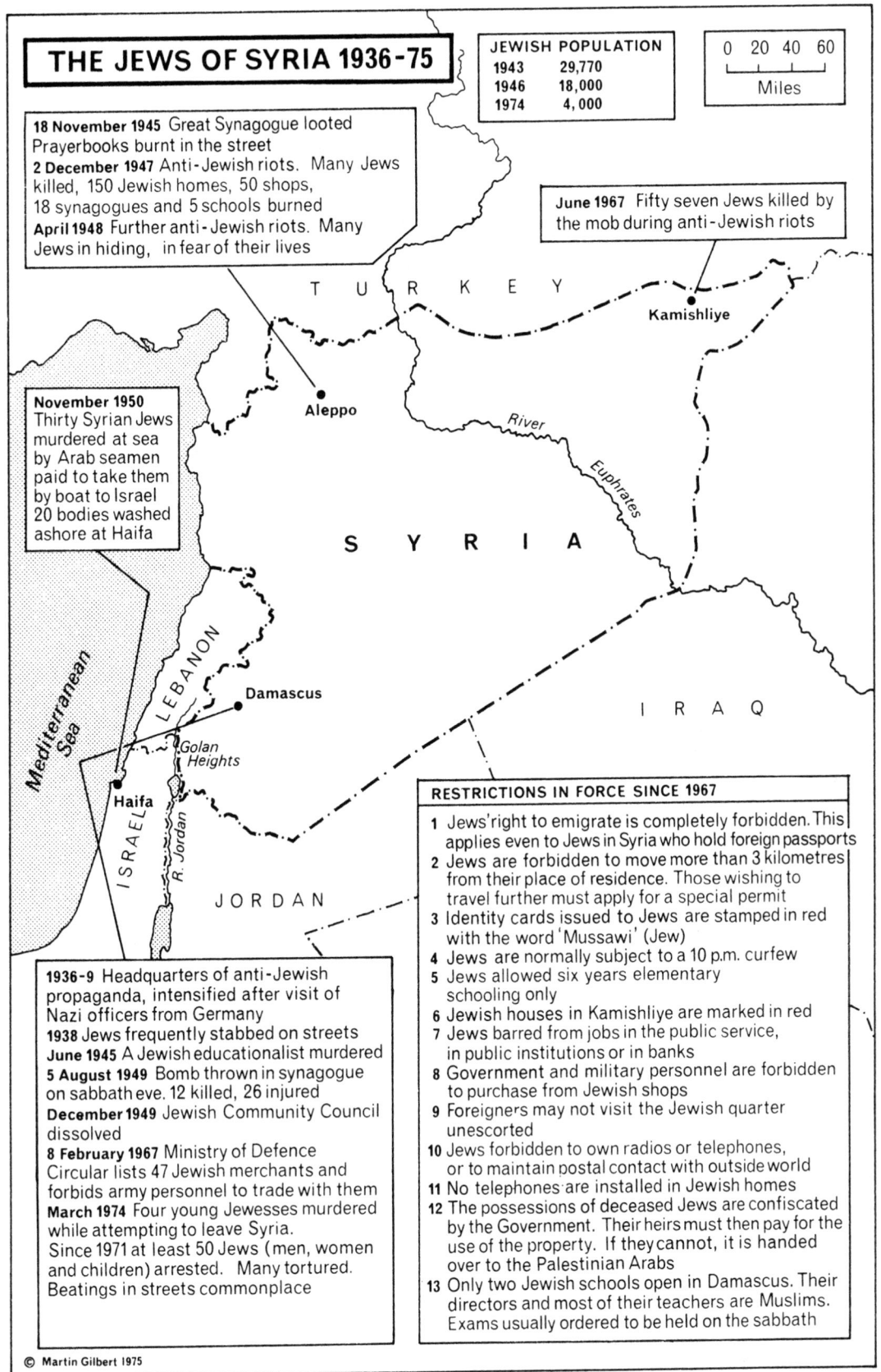

THE JEWS OF SYRIA 1936-75

JEWISH POPULATION
1943   29,770
1946   18,000
1974   4,000

0   20   40   60
Miles

18 November 1945 Great Synagogue looted Prayerbooks burnt in the street
2 December 1947 Anti-Jewish riots. Many Jews killed, 150 Jewish homes, 50 shops, 18 synagogues and 5 schools burned
April 1948 Further anti-Jewish riots. Many Jews in hiding, in fear of their lives

June 1967 Fifty seven Jews killed by the mob during anti-Jewish riots

T U R K E Y

Kamishliye

November 1950
Thirty Syrian Jews murdered at sea by Arab seamen paid to take them by boat to Israel 20 bodies washed ashore at Haifa

Aleppo

River

Euphrates

S Y R I A

Mediterranean Sea

L E B A N O N

Damascus

Golan Heights

I R A Q

Haifa

I S R A E L

R. Jordan

J O R D A N

1936-9 Headquarters of anti-Jewish propaganda, intensified after visit of Nazi officers from Germany
1938 Jews frequently stabbed on streets
June 1945 A Jewish educationalist murdered
5 August 1949 Bomb thrown in synagogue on sabbath eve. 12 killed, 26 injured
December 1949 Jewish Community Council dissolved
8 February 1967 Ministry of Defence Circular lists 47 Jewish merchants and forbids army personnel to trade with them
March 1974 Four young Jewesses murdered while attempting to leave Syria.
Since 1971 at least 50 Jews (men, women and children) arrested. Many tortured. Beatings in streets commonplace

RESTRICTIONS IN FORCE SINCE 1967
1   Jews' right to emigrate is completely forbidden. This applies even to Jews in Syria who hold foreign passports
2   Jews are forbidden to move more than 3 kilometres from their place of residence. Those wishing to travel further must apply for a special permit
3   Identity cards issued to Jews are stamped in red with the word 'Mussawi' (Jew)
4   Jews are normally subject to a 10 p.m. curfew
5   Jews allowed six years elementary schooling only
6   Jewish houses in Kamishliye are marked in red
7   Jews barred from jobs in the public service, in public institutions or in banks
8   Government and military personnel are forbidden to purchase from Jewish shops
9   Foreigners may not visit the Jewish quarter unescorted
10 Jews forbidden to own radios or telephones, or to maintain postal contact with outside world
11 No telephones are installed in Jewish homes
12 The possessions of deceased Jews are confiscated by the Government. Their heirs must then pay for the use of the property. If they cannot, it is handed over to the Palestinian Arabs
13 Only two Jewish schools open in Damascus. Their directors and most of their teachers are Muslims. Exams usually ordered to be held on the sabbath

© Martin Gilbert 1975

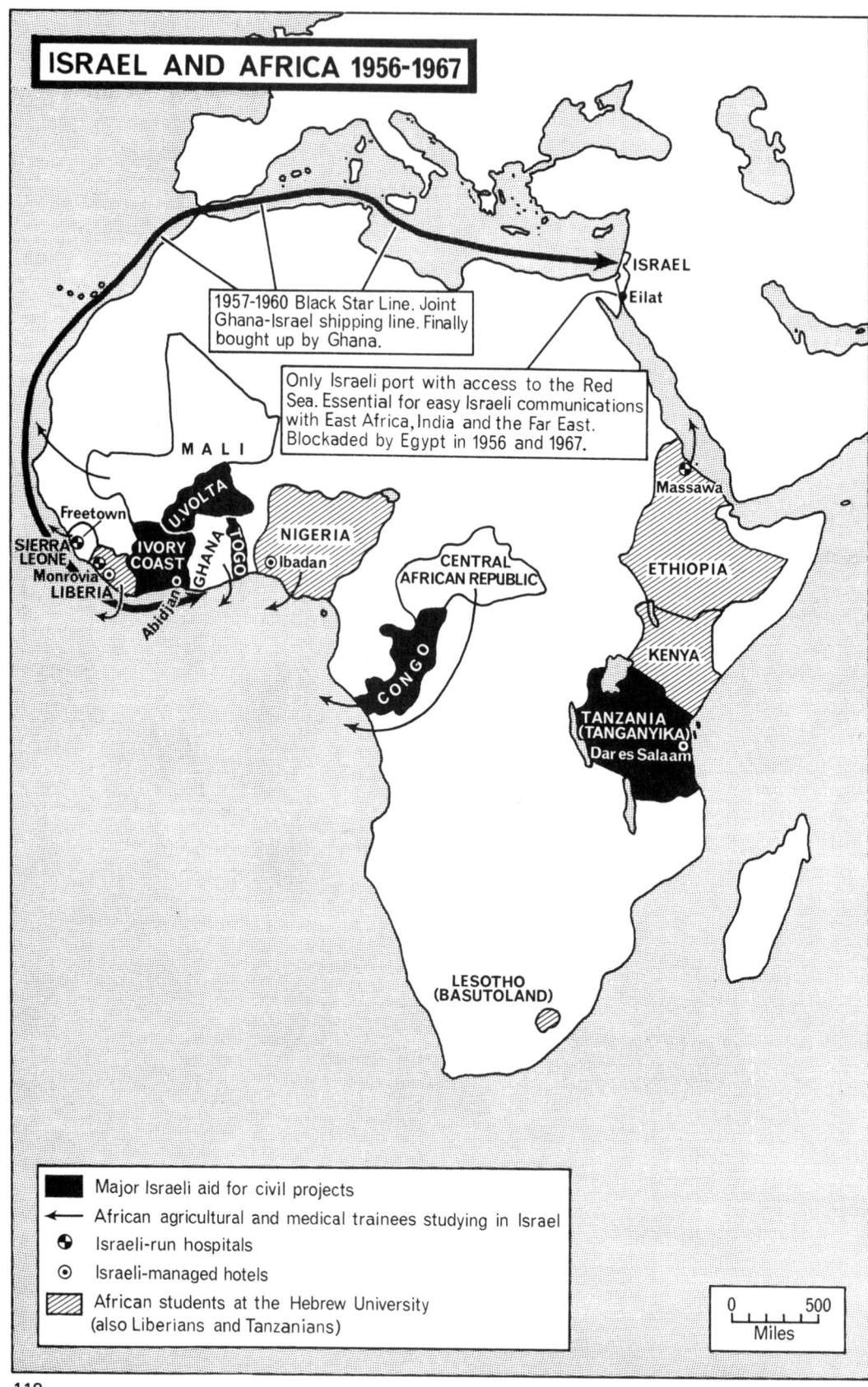

ISRAEL AND AFRICA 1956-1967

1957-1960 Black Star Line. Joint Ghana-Israel shipping line. Finally bought up by Ghana.

Only Israeli port with access to the Red Sea. Essential for easy Israeli communications with East Africa, India and the Far East. Blockaded by Egypt in 1956 and 1967.

ISRAEL

Eilat

Massawa

MALI

U.VOLTA

Freetown

SIERRA LEONE

IVORY COAST

GHANA

TOGO

Monrovia
LIBERIA

Abidjan

NIGERIA

Ibadan

CENTRAL AFRICAN REPUBLIC

CONGO

ETHIOPIA

KENYA

TANZANIA (TANGANYIKA)

Dar es Salaam

LESOTHO (BASUTOLAND)

■ Major Israeli aid for civil projects

← African agricultural and medical trainees studying in Israel

◐ Israeli-run hospitals

◉ Israeli-managed hotels

▨ African students at the Hebrew University (also Liberians and Tanzanians)

0   500
Miles

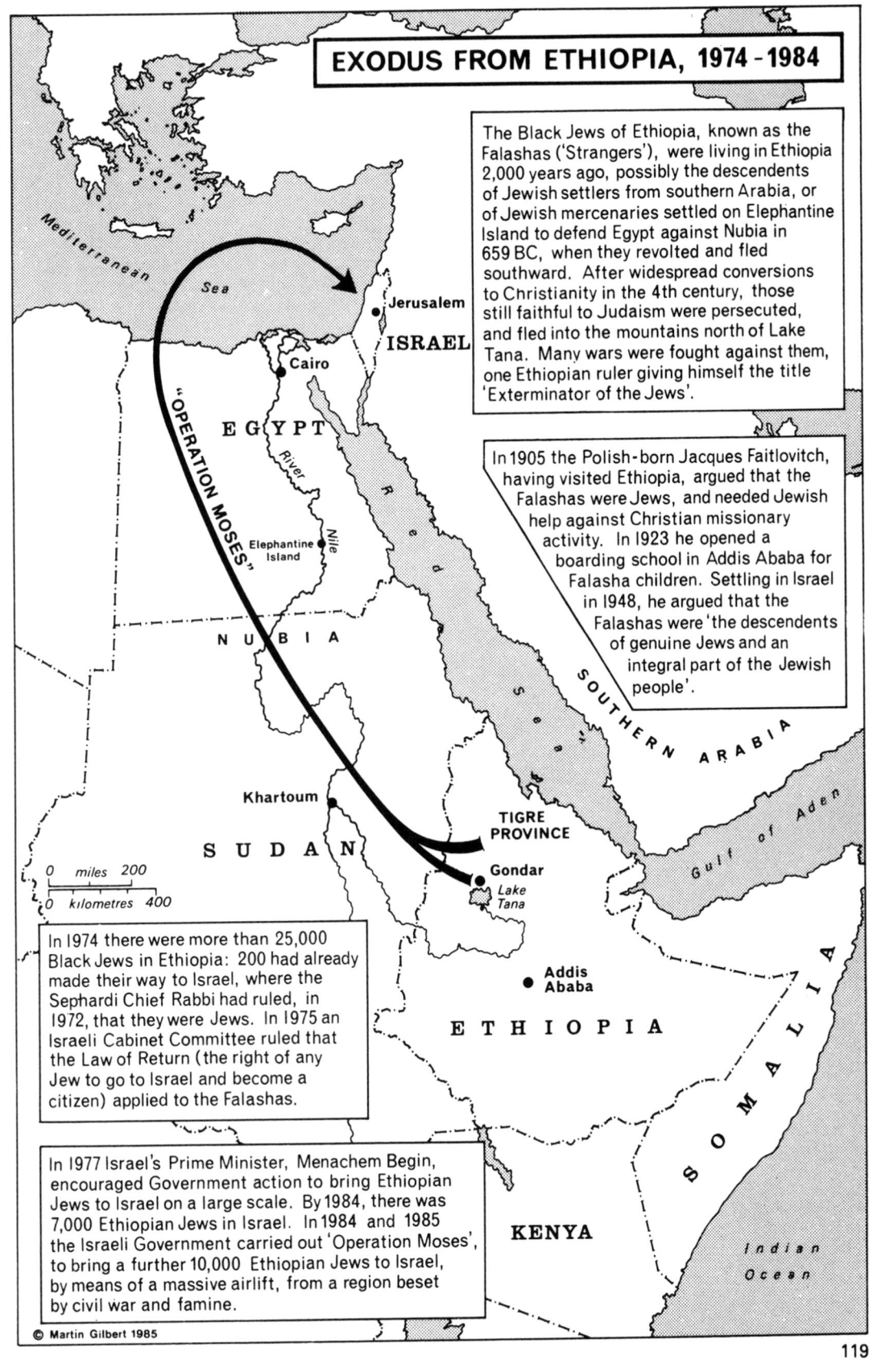

EXODUS FROM ETHIOPIA, 1974 - 1984

The Black Jews of Ethiopia, known as the Falashas ('Strangers'), were living in Ethiopia 2,000 years ago, possibly the descendents of Jewish settlers from southern Arabia, or of Jewish mercenaries settled on Elephantine Island to defend Egypt against Nubia in 659 BC, when they revolted and fled southward. After widespread conversions to Christianity in the 4th century, those still faithful to Judaism were persecuted, and fled into the mountains north of Lake Tana. Many wars were fought against them, one Ethiopian ruler giving himself the title 'Exterminator of the Jews'.

In 1905 the Polish-born Jacques Faitlovitch, having visited Ethiopia, argued that the Falashas were Jews, and needed Jewish help against Christian missionary activity. In 1923 he opened a boarding school in Addis Ababa for Falasha children. Settling in Israel in 1948, he argued that the Falashas were 'the descendents of genuine Jews and an integral part of the Jewish people'.

In 1974 there were more than 25,000 Black Jews in Ethiopia: 200 had already made their way to Israel, where the Sephardi Chief Rabbi had ruled, in 1972, that they were Jews. In 1975 an Israeli Cabinet Committee ruled that the Law of Return (the right of any Jew to go to Israel and become a citizen) applied to the Falashas.

In 1977 Israel's Prime Minister, Menachem Begin, encouraged Government action to bring Ethiopian Jews to Israel on a large scale. By 1984, there was 7,000 Ethiopian Jews in Israel. In 1984 and 1985 the Israeli Government carried out 'Operation Moses', to bring a further 10,000 Ethiopian Jews to Israel, by means of a massive airlift, from a region beset by civil war and famine.

© Martin Gilbert 1985

PRISONERS OF ZION
1968-1985

Between 1968 and 1985 more than 200 Soviet Jews who had applied to emigrate to Israel were imprisoned by the Soviet authorities, most in conditions of great hardship. Many of those imprisoned were subjected to extreme brutalities, near-starvation, and solitary confinement in sub-zero temperatures. These 'Prisoners of Zion' were among an estimated 10,000 political and religious prisoners held in prisons and labour camps throughout the Soviet Union. After persistent international protest, more than half of the 200 were allowed to leave Russia for Israel. Others, however, were being arrested at the same time, tried, and imprisoned in their place. A small number of Jews were also sent to psychiatric institutions after they had applied to emigrate. In 1988 following Gorbachev's rise to power, all Jewish prisoners were released and allowed to emigrate: most of them went to Israel.

SWEDEN

FINLAND

Baltic Sea

Kirov

Perm

Sverdlovsk

Leningrad

In June 1970 many Leningrad Jews were arrested for protesting publicly against the Soviet Government's refusal to let them emigrate to Israel. In December 1970 a group of young Jews, mostly from Riga, were sentenced to death or long imprisonment for planning to seize a Soviet plane in order to fly abroad, and eventually to reach Israel. After Western protests, the two death sentences were commuted to imprisonment.

Riga

Kalinin

Vladimir

Kazan

Chernyakhovsk

Vilnius

Moscow

Riazan

SOVIET UNION

River Don

Mordovian prison camp region

Lvov

Kiev

Kharkov

Valuki

Vinnitsa

UKRAINE

Kalmyskaya prison camp region

Aral Sea

Kamenets - Podolsk

Dneprodzerzhinsk

Chernovtsy

Kishinev

Bendery

Kherson

Rostov - on - Don

Odessa

Caucasus

Caspian Sea

Black Sea

Derbent

Tbilisi

Rustavi

⊙ Home towns of those Soviet Jews who sought visas to emigrate to Israel and were subsequetly arrested, tried and imprisoned.

■ Principal prison camps and prison camp regions to which they were sent.

0   miles   200

0   kilometres   300

© Martin Gilbert 1991

• Jerusalem

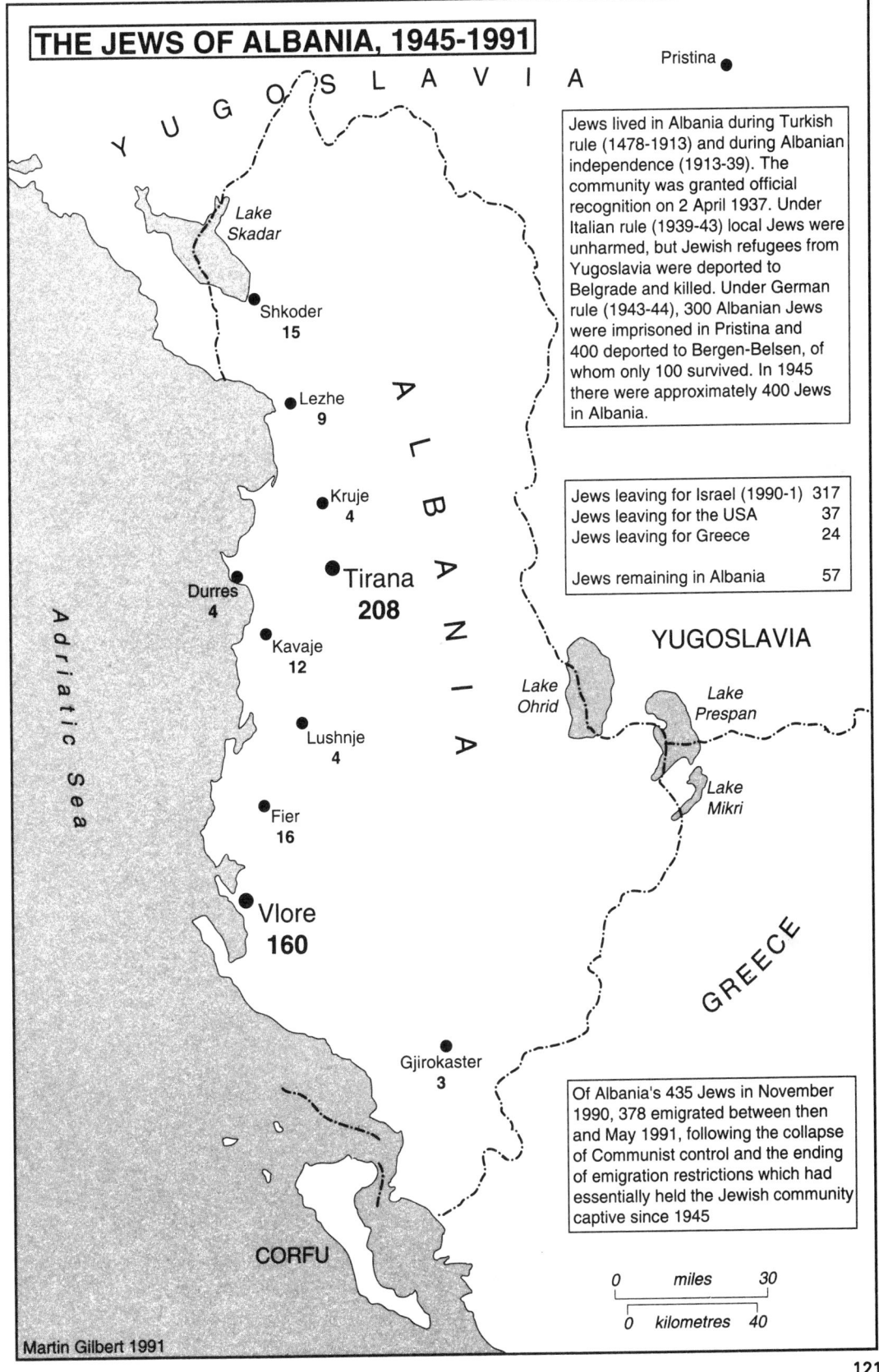

THE JEWS OF ALBANIA, 1945-1991

Pristina

Jews lived in Albania during Turkish rule (1478-1913) and during Albanian independence (1913-39). The community was granted official recognition on 2 April 1937. Under Italian rule (1939-43) local Jews were unharmed, but Jewish refugees from Yugoslavia were deported to Belgrade and killed. Under German rule (1943-44), 300 Albanian Jews were imprisoned in Pristina and 400 deported to Bergen-Belsen, of whom only 100 survived. In 1945 there were approximately 400 Jews in Albania.

Jews leaving for Israel (1990-1)	317
Jews leaving for the USA	37
Jews leaving for Greece	24
Jews remaining in Albania	57

Of Albania's 435 Jews in November 1990, 378 emigrated between then and May 1991, following the collapse of Communist control and the ending of emigration restrictions which had essentially held the Jewish community captive since 1945

YUGOSLAVIA

Lake Skadar

Shkoder
15

Lezhe
9

ALBANIA

Kruje
4

Tirana
208

Durres
4

Kavaje
12

Lushnje
4

Fier
16

Vlore
160

Adriatic Sea

Lake Ohrid

YUGOSLAVIA

Lake Prespan

Lake Mikri

GREECE

Gjirokaster
3

CORFU

0	miles	30

0	kilometres	40

Martin Gilbert 1991

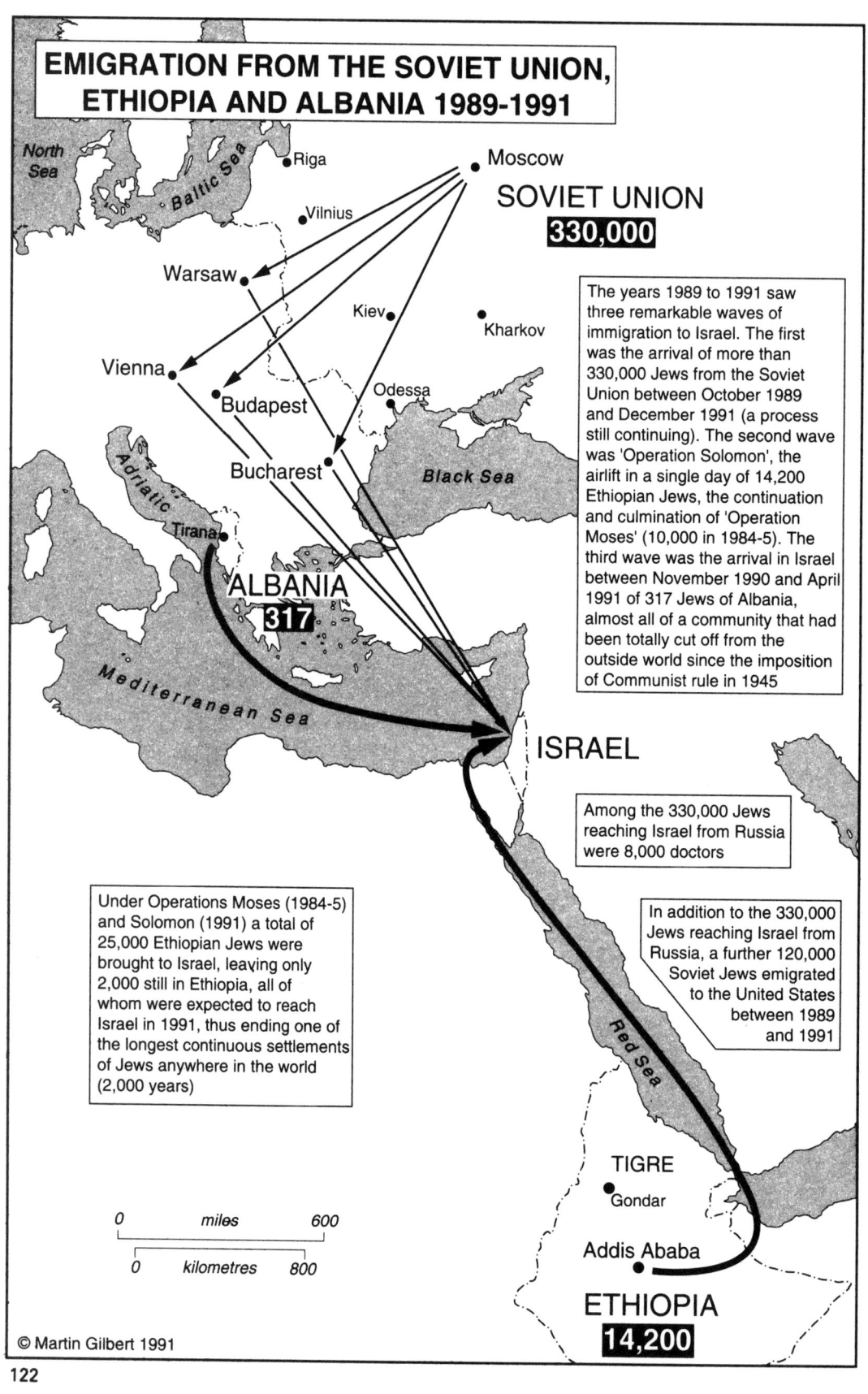

EMIGRATION FROM THE SOVIET UNION, ETHIOPIA AND ALBANIA 1989-1991

North Sea

Baltic Sea

Riga

Moscow

SOVIET UNION
330,000

Vilnius

Warsaw

Kiev

Kharkov

Vienna

Budapest

Odessa

Bucharest

Black Sea

Adriatic

Tirana

ALBANIA
317

Mediterranean Sea

The years 1989 to 1991 saw three remarkable waves of immigration to Israel. The first was the arrival of more than 330,000 Jews from the Soviet Union between October 1989 and December 1991 (a process still continuing). The second wave was 'Operation Solomon', the airlift in a single day of 14,200 Ethiopian Jews, the continuation and culmination of 'Operation Moses' (10,000 in 1984-5). The third wave was the arrival in Israel between November 1990 and April 1991 of 317 Jews of Albania, almost all of a community that had been totally cut off from the outside world since the imposition of Communist rule in 1945

ISRAEL

Among the 330,000 Jews reaching Israel from Russia were 8,000 doctors

Under Operations Moses (1984-5) and Solomon (1991) a total of 25,000 Ethiopian Jews were brought to Israel, leaving only 2,000 still in Ethiopia, all of whom were expected to reach Israel in 1991, thus ending one of the longest continuous settlements of Jews anywhere in the world (2,000 years)

In addition to the 330,000 Jews reaching Israel from Russia, a further 120,000 Soviet Jews emigrated to the United States between 1989 and 1991

Red Sea

TIGRE

Gondar

Addis Ababa

ETHIOPIA
14,200

| 0 | miles | 600 |
| 0 | kilometres | 800 |

© Martin Gilbert 1991

THE JEWISH WORLD IN 1991

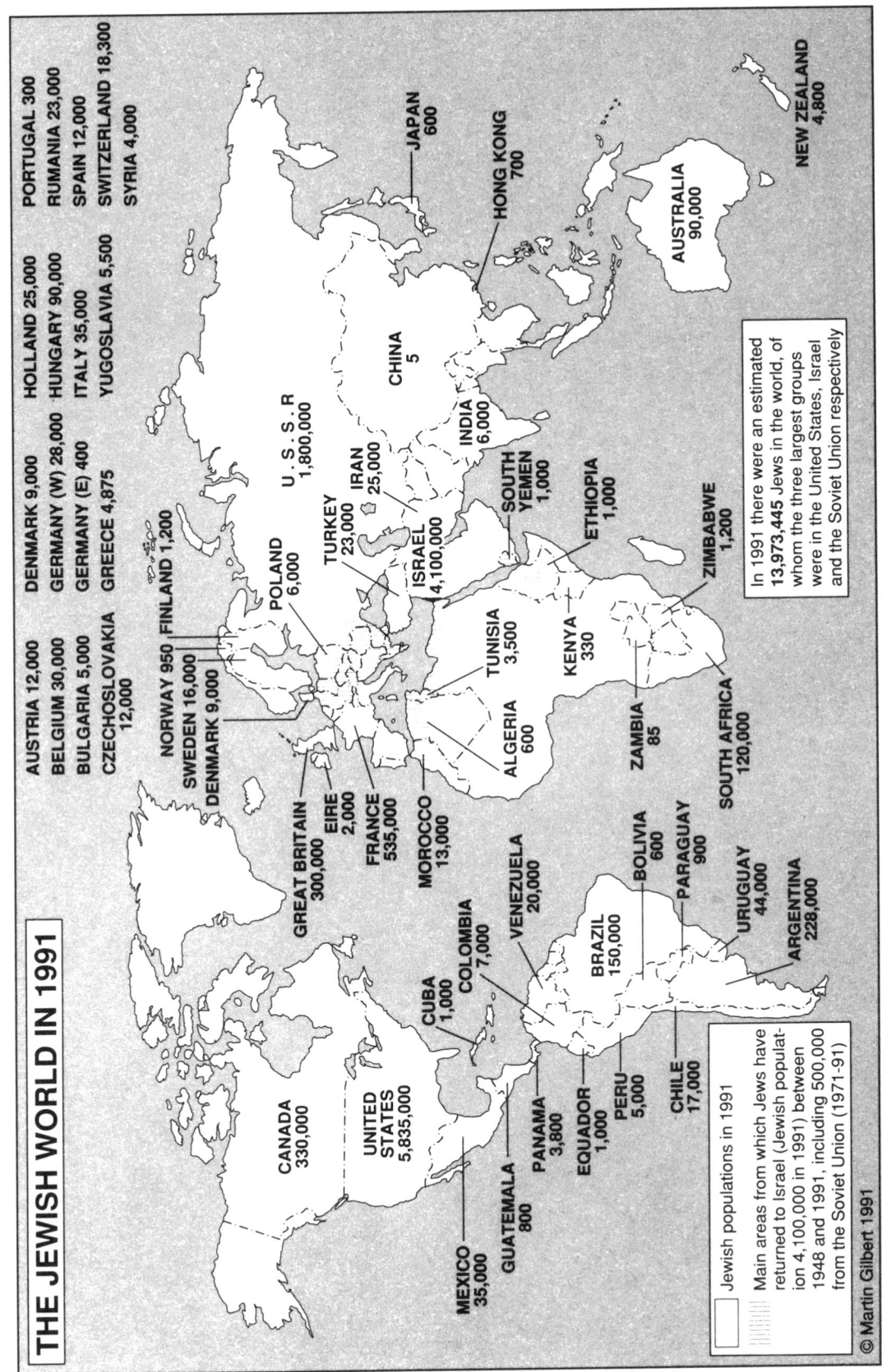

PORTUGAL 300
RUMANIA 23,000
SPAIN 12,000
SWITZERLAND 18,300
SYRIA 4,000

HOLLAND 25,000
HUNGARY 90,000
ITALY 35,000
YUGOSLAVIA 5,500

DENMARK 9,000
GERMANY (W) 28,000
GERMANY (E) 400
GREECE 4,875

AUSTRIA 12,000
BELGIUM 30,000
BULGARIA 5,000
CZECHOSLOVAKIA 12,000

NORWAY 950 FINLAND 1,200
SWEDEN 16,000
DENMARK 9,000

JAPAN 600

HONG KONG 700

AUSTRALIA 90,000

NEW ZEALAND 4,800

CHINA 5

INDIA 6,000

U.S.S.R 1,800,000

IRAN 25,000

TURKEY 23,000

ISRAEL 4,100,000

SOUTH YEMEN 1,000

ETHIOPIA 1,000

ZIMBABWE 1,200

TUNISIA 3,500

KENYA 330

ALGERIA 600

ZAMBIA 85

SOUTH AFRICA 120,000

POLAND 6,000

GREAT BRITAIN 300,000
EIRE 2,000
FRANCE 535,000
MOROCCO 13,000

VENEZUELA 20,000

BOLIVIA 600
PARAGUAY 900

URUGUAY 44,000
ARGENTINA 228,000

BRAZIL 150,000

CUBA 1,000
COLOMBIA 7,000

PANAMA 3,800
EQUADOR 1,000
PERU 5,000
CHILE 17,000

GUATEMALA 800

MEXICO 35,000

CANADA 330,000

UNITED STATES 5,835,000

In 1991 there were an estimated 13,973,445 Jews in the world, of whom the three largest groups were in the United States, Israel and the Soviet Union respectively

Jewish populations in 1991

Main areas from which Jews have returned to Israel (Jewish population 4,100,000 in 1991) between 1948 and 1991, including 500,000 from the Soviet Union (1971-91)

© Martin Gilbert 1991

123

Bibliography

The following bibliography is strictly selective. It consists of some eighty books which I myself have found useful while gathering material for the maps.

In addition to the books listed below, I have made frequent use of a number of general reference works, of which the most valuable were:

Isodore Singer (Managing Editor), *The Jewish Encyclopaedia*, 12 vols., New York, 1901–1906, the most comprehensive of all encyclopaedias on Jewish affairs.

Y. L. Katzenelson (Editor), *Yevreyskaya Entsiklopediya*, 16 vols., St. Petersburg, 1906–1913. An essential source for all problems of Russian Jewry.

Encyclopaedia Judaica, 16 vols. (Jerusalem, 1972). The most recent complete multi-volume encyclopaedia of Jewish history.

Cecil Roth (Editor-in-Chief), *The Standard Jewish Encyclopaedia*, one volume (New York, 1962). The fullest single-volume work of reference.

Israeli Department of Surveys and the Bialik Institute, *Atlas of Israel* (Jerusalem, 1956), contains an excellent bibliography of over a thousand cartographic sources relating to Israel.

General works on Jewish History

Nathan Ausubel, *Pictorial History of the Jewish People* (New York, 1954)

Salo W. Baron, *A Social and Religious History of the Jews* (New York, 1952–1960)

Edwyn R. Bevan and Charles Singer (editors), *The Legacy of Israel* (Oxford, 1927)

Max I. Dimont, *Jews, God and History* (New York, 1962)

Max L. Margolis and A. Marx, *A History of the Jewish People* (Philadelphia, 1964)

James William Parkes, *A History of the Jewish People* (London, 1962)

Cecil Roth, *A Short History of the Jewish People* (London, 1959)

Cecil Roth, *Personalities and Events in Jewish History* (Philadelphia, 1961)

Biblical and Classical Periods

W. F. Albright, *New Horizons in Biblical Research* (London, 1966)

M. Avi-Yonah, *Map of Roman Palestine* (Oxford, 1940)

Daniel-Rops, *Israel and the Ancient World* (Paris, 1943; London, 1949)

Luc Grollenberg, *Atlas de la Bible* (London, 1956)

James Hastings, *Dictionary of the Bible* (London, 1963)

Jean Juster, *Les Juifs dans l'empire romain* (Paris, 1914)

Harry J. Leon, *The Jews of Ancient Rome* (Philadelphia, 1960)

Benjamin Maisler, *Historical Atlas of Palestine* (Jerusalem, 1942)

W. O. E. Osterley, *The Jews and Judaism During the Greek Period* (London, 1941)

John William Parkes, *Jesus, Paul and the Jews* (London, 1936)

George Adam Smith, *Historical Geography of the Holy Land* (London, 1894)

John Stirling, *An Atlas of the Life of Christ* (London, 1954)

John Stirling, *An Atlas Illustrating the Acts of the Apostles and the Epistles* (London, 1954)

Yigael Yadin, *Masada* (London, 1965)

Yigael Yadin, *Bar-Kokhba* (London, 1971)

Medieval Period

Marcus Nathan Adler, *The Itinery of Benjamin of Tudela* (London, 1907)

George K. Anderson, *The Legend of the Wandering Jew* (Providence, 1965)

Salo Baron, *The Jewish Community; Its History and Structure* (Philadelphia, 1942)

Herbert Ivan Bloom, *The Economic Activities of the Jews of Amsterdam* (Williamsport, 1937)

Claude Reignier Conder, *The Latin Kingdom of Jerusalem 1099–1291* (London, 1897)

D. M. Dunlop, *The History of the Jewish Khazars* (Princeton, 1954)

Louis Finkelstein, *Jewish Self-Government in the Middle Ages* (New York, 1924)

Walter Joseph Fischel, *Jews in the Economic and Political Life of Medieval Islam* (London, 1937)

Solomon Grayzel, *The Church and the Jews in the Thirteenth Century* (New York, 1966)

Julius H. Greenstone, *The Messianic Idea in Jewish History* (Philadelphia, 1906)

Henry Kamen, *The Spanish Inquisition* (London, 1965)

Robert S. Lopez and Irving W. Raymond (eds.), *Medieval Trade in the Mediterranean World* (New York, 1955)

Leon Nemoy, *Karaite Anthology* (New Haven, 1952)

Abraham A. Neuman, *The Jews in Spain* (Philadelphia, 1944)

James William Parkes, *The Conflict of the Church and the Synagogue* (London, 1934)

David Philipson, *Old European Jewries* (Harrisburg, 1894)

L. Rabinowitz, *Jewish Merchant Adventurers* (London, 1948)

Cecil Roth, *The History of the Jews of Italy* (Philadelphia, 1946)

Cecil Roth, *A History of the Marranos* (Philadelphia, 1942)

Cecil Roth, *A History of the Jews in England* (Oxford, 1941)

Cecil Roth, *The Jews of Medieval Oxford* (Oxford, 1951)

Steven Runciman, *A History of the Crusades* (Cambridge, 1951)

Abba Hillel Silver, *A History of Messianic Speculation in Israel* (New York, 1927)

Joshua Starr, *Jews in the Byzantine Empire 641–1204* (Athens, 1939)

Joshua Starr, *Romania, the Jews of the Levant After the Fourth Crusade* (Paris, 1949)

William Charles White, *Chinese Jews* (Toronto, 1942)

Louis Wirth, *The Ghetto* (Chicago, 1928)

Modern Period

Reuben Ainsztein, *Jewish Resistance in Nazi-Occupied Eastern Europe* (London, 1974)

Karl Baedeker, *Austria-Hungary* (Leipzig, 1905)

Salo Baron, *The Russian Jew Under Tsars and Soviets* (New York, 1964)

Norman Bentwich, *They Found Refuge* (London, 1956)

Randolph S. Churchill and Winston S. Churchill, *The Six Day War* (London, 1967)

Israel Cohen, *A Short History of Zionism* (London, 1951)

Israel Cohen, *Contemporary Jewry* (London, 1950)

Israel Cohen, *Vilna* (Philadelphia, 1943)

Israel Cohen, *My Mission to Poland 1918–1919* (London, 1951)

Norman Cohn, *Warrant for Genocide* (London, 1967)

Moshe Dayan, *Diary of the Sinai Campaign* (London, 1966)

S. M. Dubnow, *History of the Jews in Russia and Poland* (Philadelphia, 1916–20)

Abba Eban, *Voice of Israel* (London, 1958)

Lloyd P. Gartner, *The Jewish Immigrant in England 1870–1914* (London, 1960)

Martin Gilbert, *The Jews of Arab Lands: Their History in Maps* (London, 1975)

Martin Gilbert, *The Jews of Russia and the Soviet Union: Their History in Maps* (London, 1976)

Louis Greenberg, *The Jews in Russia: The Struggle for Emancipation* (New Haven 1944 and 1951)

Philip Guedalla, *Napoleon and Palestine* (London, 1925)

Vladimir Jabotinsky, *The Story of the Jewish Legion* (New York, 1954)

Leo Jung (ed.), *Jewish Leaders 1750–1940* (Jerusalem, 1964)

Roderick Kedward, *The Dreyfus Affair* (London, 1964)

Mordechai E. Kreinin, *Israel and Africa* (New York, 1964)

Harry S. Linfield, *Statistics of Jews 1931* (New York, 1931)

Vivian David Lipman, *Social History of the Jews in England 1850–1950* (London, 1954)

Macmillan (publishers), *Atlas of the Arab World and the Middle East* (London, 1960)

Raphael Mahler, *A History of Modern Jewry 1780–1815* (London, 1971)

Arthur D. Morse, *While Six Million Died* (London, 1968)

Alfred Nossig, *Materialen Zur statistik der Judischen Stammes* (Vienna, 1897)

Edgar O'Ballance, *The Arab-Israeli War 1948* (London, 1956)

F. J. Pietri, *Napoléon et les Israélites* (Paris, 1965)

James William Parkes, *Arabs and Jews in the Middle East: a Tragedy of Errors* (London, 1967)

J. H. Patterson, *With the Judaeans in the Palestine Campaign* (London, 1922)

Leon Poliakov, *Harvest of Hate* (New York, 1954)

Malcolm J. Proudfoot, *European Refugees 1939–52* (London, 1957)

Peter George J. Pulzer, *The Rise of Political Anti-Semitism in Germany and Austria* (New York, 1964)

Gerald Reitlinger, *The Final Solution* (London, 1953)

Emmanuel Ringelblum, *Polish-Jewish Relations during the Second World War* (Jerusalem, 1974)

Adolf Rudnicki, *Ascent to Heaven* (London, 1951)

Harry Sacher, *Zionist Portraits* (London, 1959)

Joseph B. Schechtman, *On Wings of Eagles* (New York, 1961)

A. J. Sherman, *Island Refuge* (London, 1974)

Yuri Suhl (ed.), *They Fought Back* (London, 1968)

Christopher Sykes, *Cross Roads to Israel* (London, 1965)

M. U. Schappes, *A Documentary History of the Jews in the United States 1654–1875* (New York, 1950)

Leonard Stein, *The Balfour Declaration* (London, 1966)

Arieh Tartakower and Kurt R. Grossman, *The Jewish Refugee* (New York, 1944)

Chaim Weizmann, *Trial and Error* (London, 1952)

Israel Zangwill, *Children of the Ghetto* (London, 1892)